Contents

Introduction

Naomi Moller, Andreas Vossler, David W. Jones and David Kaposi

Contents

Introduction to understanding mental health and counselling

The Earth and a birds-eye street view. Both are factually accurate but distance changes how things are seen and understood.

Welcome to *Understanding mental health and counselling*. We hope you will enjoy reading this book and come to understand more about the key debates in mental health and counselling and the core approaches taken to working with mental health problems.

This opening chapter introduces the core aims of *Understanding mental health and counselling*, the three themes that are interwoven through the chapters, and the structure of the book. There is also a section on the terms used to describe people with mental health difficulties.

Core aims of this book

Existing resources on the broad topic of mental health often explore how it is currently, and has historically been, understood and how this understanding has impacted the evolution of mental health care, policy and law. Many such resources largely ignore what this might mean in practice for how to work ethically and effectively with a person who is in mental distress. Equally, many books about counselling theory and practice engage seriously with building knowledge around the topics necessary for ethical and effective practice, yet they pay scant consideration to broader understandings of mental health and ill-health and how these have shaped the field of counselling and psychotherapy.

The result of a failure to consider mental health and counselling holistically is, in the worst cases, that counselling theory is taught as if it were a cult, where criticality is discouraged and fervent support encouraged, while mental health is taught in a way that creates disdain for anyone trying to engage with a system so demonstrably flawed.

This book aims to do something both ambitious and radical: to create a resource that allows readers to consider the field of mental health from the practical to the conceptual and from the individual to society. The hope is to offer a perspective that combines a strong commitment to criticality (asking: But how do you know that?) with an acknowledgement that therapeutic practice often involves a deliberate stance of 'not-knowing' (Bion, 1967) in order to foster deep and empathic listening to the client. The stance is that it is important to hold on to two opposing ways of understanding. On the one hand, mental health is an area that is shifting and highly complex, full of seriously troubling experiences and practices and plagued by a lack of knowledge and arguments about the 'right' kind of knowledge. On the other hand, it is an area in which decisions must be made and actions taken, often quickly.

A word on terminology

Before going any further, it is important to say something about the terminology used in this book to refer to people with mental health concerns. Words are important because they shape how people are perceived and understood, and how they experience themselves. There are lots of words – slang, medical and everyday words – that have been used to describe people with mental health problems.

> ### Pause for reflection
>
> Briefly consider a few words that are used to describe people experiencing mental health problems. Then consider how you might think or feel about a person who was described by each word.

Language can perpetuate stigma and thus there is a commitment in this book to trying to use non-discriminatory language (alongside the recognition that there is debate about which terms are/are not discriminatory). For example, we avoid any language that suggests that a particular difficulty defines the person – such as 'depressive'. We also discuss the considerable and important debate about the use of medical language for mental health difficulties. The Time to Change campaign, which was set up to reduce the discrimination faced by people with mental health problems, provides guidelines on appropriate and inappropriate terminology (e.g. Time to Change, 2020). In line with this, we will be using the following terms in this book:

- person with mental health problems or difficulties

- service user

- client.

These terms all have slightly different meanings; for example, 'client' tends to mean someone who is having counselling, whereas 'service user' is often used to describe someone who has a broader engagement with mental health services. All these terms will therefore be used, depending on the topic being discussed.

As an additional point, it is worth saying something here about how we are using the terms 'counselling' and 'psychotherapy'. The distinction/overlap between these terms is hotly debated in some areas. In practice, the difference often (but not always) has something to do with the types of training people have. Psychotherapists typically undertake longer postgraduate training, while counsellors complete shorter, undergraduate/diploma training. For the sake of convenience we have decided to use both terms interchangeably. So when you read about 'counselling' and 'counsellors' this generally also includes 'psychotherapy' and 'psychotherapists' (and vice versa), unless stated otherwise.

Book themes

The aims of the book outlined above are reflected in the three principles that have informed the content:

- *Service-user and client voices*: Acknowledging that service users and clients are the most important people to consider, and that they may have been harmed by mental health and counselling services, a key focus of the book is on the critical importance of listening to the perceptions, understandings and experiences of mental health service users and counselling and psychotherapy clients.

- *Diverse experiences*: Understandings of mental health and assumptions about 'best' treatments have historically often disadvantaged, ignored or excluded minority groups. A second key theme of this book is thus around how diversity (e.g. in terms of ethnicity, sexuality and gender) impacts the understandings, expression and 'treatment' of mental health difficulties.

- *Research/methodology*: A key concern of the book is how 'knowledge' about mental health and counselling is established. The book critically examines the strengths and weaknesses of underlying research approaches/paradigms and the limitations and caveats around the knowledge they produce.

Book structure

Understanding mental health and counselling is organised into five parts.

Part 1   Understanding mental health: the emergence of the talking cure

This part introduces the fundamental debates about the contested nature of mental 'illness' and the institutions that have developed to provide 'treatment'.

- Chapter 1 outlines the historical development of psychiatry and psychological treatments.

- Chapter 2 introduces the service-user movement and outlines the concerted efforts of the people who have engaged with mental health systems to change them for the better.

- Chapter 3 examines the evolution of psychological treatments and 'talking cures'.

- Chapter 4 focuses on the debates about systems of classification and diagnosis.

Part 2   Presenting problems

This part focuses on the issues that cause people to seek therapy.

- Chapter 5 focuses on depression and anxiety.

- Chapter 6 considers how trauma and crisis are understood and worked with.

- Chapter 7 examines how our relationships influence our mental health and vice versa.

- Chapter 8 presents an overview of formulation, presented as an alternative to diagnosis, and provides a prelude to models of counselling, which are covered in Part 3.

Part 3   Models of working

This part introduces some of the main approaches used in counselling and psychotherapy.

- Chapter 9 introduces psychodynamic approaches.

- Chapter 10 focuses on cognitive behavioural therapy approaches.

- Chapter 11 introduces humanistic approaches.

- Chapter 12 considers pluralistic/integrative approaches.

Part 4   Counselling in practice

This part examines issues central to how counselling and psychotherapy are practised and how mental health problems are treated in different practice settings.

- Chapter 13 focuses on the therapeutic relationship in counselling and psychotherapy.

- Chapter 14 introduces counselling approaches that go 'beyond' the individual.

- Chapter 15 examines the rapidly developing field of technology-based counselling.

- Chapter 16 explores professional and ethical concerns in practice.

Part 5   Contemporary issues: mental health and society

In this part, the focus returns to social understandings of mental health and how social, political and economic forces inform contemporary practice.

- Chapter 17 examines how mental health and counselling research agendas and practices are often shaped by external forces.

- Chapter 18 considers the important links between ideas about mental disorder and criminal justice.

- Chapter 19 explores whether it can be helpful to think about mental health difficulties as societal versus individual problems.

- Chapter 20 reviews the debates about the idea that we now live in a 'therapeutic culture'.

The book ends with a conclusion drawing together these themes.

Activities, reflections, readings and images

We have included activities and 'pause for reflections' in each chapter. One aim of this is to help you reflect on your own understanding and opinion about the topics covered in the chapters. Another aim is to help you connect the material to your own experiences. Additionally, reflection – the ability to think about your thinking (and feelings) – is a key skill for counsellors, and so it is apposite to practise reflection in a book where the focus is mental health and counselling. We have also included suggestions for further readings at the end of each chapter.

Finally, we hope that you will enjoy the artwork in this book. The cover image was created by Fatma Durmush, an artist represented by the Bethlem Gallery. This gallery is based within the grounds of the Bethlem Royal Hospital, which supports artists who are current or former patients of the South London and Maudsley NHS Foundation Trust. Lucy Owen, the Interim Director of the gallery, explains: 'Our mission is to make an equitable space for our artists, leading change within arts, health and society.' Artist Fatma Durmush offers some personal background: 'I started painting when I was 37 years old. I wanted to bring colour into my world. I became ill and received art therapy but then went on to study painting and printmaking at the University of East London at undergraduate and masters level. At University I received encouragement and support and most of the students there were adults. Now I paint at home with passion.'

The images within this book were created by Open University students. Andreas Vossler, co-editor of this book, organised this crowdsourcing initiative. As he explains: 'We were overwhelmed by how many students submitted images for us to consider including in the book, with many submitting numerous photographs, paintings and drawings. It was difficult to select an image for each chapter, but we think they are amazing and we really hope you enjoy them.'

– Naomi, Andreas, David and David

References

Bion, W.R. (1967) 'Notes on memory and desire', in Langs, R. (ed.) *Classics in psychoanalytic technique*. New York, US and Oxford, UK: Jason Aronson, Inc., pp. 259–260.

Time to Change (2020) *Mind your language!* Available at: https://www.time-to-change.org.uk/media-centre/responsible-reporting/mind-your-language (Accessed date: 21 April 2020).

Part 1

Understanding mental health: the emergence of the talking cure

Chapter 1

The birth of psychiatry: questions of power, control and care

David W. Jones

Contents

Introduction

'Breathe' by Joanna Crane

Questions about 'mental health' and 'mental illness' loom large amid many media discussions about the health and well-being of the population and society. Those individuals understood as suffering from some form of mental distress or unhappiness might be offered, or may seek, help from a variety of sources, including psychologists, psychiatrists, mental health nurses, social workers, counsellors and psychotherapists. All these professionals might become involved in the provision of care or treatment. They might be employed within state-run hospitals or clinics, or they might provide private treatment for those willing and able to pay. This chapter will suggest that our awareness of the contemporary scene of mental health and illness can be aided by understanding where its ideas and practices have come from.

This chapter presents a history of 'psychiatry', with the word used as shorthand for the development of a set of ideas and practices that deal with what came to be defined as 'mental illness'. While the emergence of psychiatry was largely led by those who saw themselves as working within a medical specialism, many other interest groups and forces have shaped the development of the various institutions and practices surrounding the world of mental illness. Since any history limited to a single chapter can only tell part of the story, the focus here is on how that history needs to be understood as shaped by contradictory forces: power and control versus care and concern.

Indeed, it can reasonably be claimed that there are two contrasting versions of the history of psychiatry. The first might be called 'the progressive view' of the development of a dedicated field of practice that specialised in the treatment of 'mental' illness. It recognised areas of human suffering and misery that could be amenable to cure or alleviation if the right treatments were discovered and made available. The second, more critical view, is the **anti-psychiatry** perspective, which suggests that the profession of psychiatry and the surrounding notions of mental illness and health developed as important tools of a culture that has sought to marginalise and control those individuals whose behaviour deviates from the norm and might pose a threat to the social order.

The focus here is on the emergence of psychiatry within Great Britain, but it should be noted that its early development was embedded in European endeavours, with North American practices becoming important later on. It is certainly the case that psychiatry, now global in its reach, was very much a western enterprise. It is also important to be aware that, as this chapter deals with historical matters, it draws on language (e.g. 'lunacy' and 'mad') that would be considered offensive if used in the present day. These terms are preserved here, since there is uncertainty about how accurately they could be translated into modern language. Nowadays the term 'mad' tends to be equated with something like **psychosis**, where a person loses touch with reality, whereas in the past it has been used more generally to refer to states of mental turmoil.

Anti-psychiatry
A term used to describe a broad coalition of people and ideas who have opposed the theories and practices of psychiatry.

Psychosis
A psychiatric term that refers to an individual's state of mind that is 'out of touch' with reality. The individual has no understanding that they are in this state. Typical symptoms include hallucinations (hearing, smelling or seeing things that are not there) and delusions (believing something to be true that others deem impossible).

This chapter aims to:

- demonstrate how the field of psychiatry has been shaped through its development as a medical speciality, but also by the emergence of a psychological outlook that theorised a 'mind' that could become disordered and, therefore, could be subject to psychological treatment
- show that wider issues of social policy and criminal justice have also left their mark on the field of psychiatry
- highlight the considerable public debate surrounding the field, and the influence of popular opinion
- explore the increasing scope of psychiatry, which now covers all areas of life (from cradle to grave) and an ever-growing array of disorders.

1 'Madness' before psychiatry

Psychiatry
The specialist branch
of medicine concerned
with the treatment of
mental illness.

While the recognisable profession of **psychiatry** only emerged in the
nineteenth century, 'madness', as Porter (2002, p. 10) suggests, 'may be
as old as mankind'; follies, fools, madness, grief and despair are staples
of Shakespeare's plays (performed for the first time roughly between
1590 and 1610), for example. By the time that popular ideas and
everyday concerns were being written down and printed (a process
only just beginning in the seventeenth century), there was apparent
interest in what we would now view as 'mental illness'.

Often mentioned as a milestone on the path to the establishment of a
systematic literature was Robert Burton's (1638) *The anatomy of
melancholy*, first published in England in 1621. The word 'melancholy'
here appears not to specifically mean 'sadness' in the modern sense,
but rather conveys some general malaise or mental distress. It is a
sprawling compendium of seventeenth-century knowledge and
philosophy and an attempt to grapple with the causes of human
happiness and unhappiness. It was to be a hundred years later that
books more recognisable as medical texts on mental illness began to
emerge. Notable was *The English malady* written by George Cheyne in
1733, or as its subtitle further explained, 'a Treatise of nervous diseases
of all kinds; as spleen, vapours, lowness of spirits, hypochondriacal,
and hysterical distempers, etc.'. Cheyne (1733, p. i) notes the
observation of an English malady that came from 'foreigners and all
our neighbours on the continent', and acknowledges its accuracy,
suggesting as many as one-third of the population were so afflicted. He
proposed that among the causes were 'the moisture of our air, the
variableness of our weather' as well as modern social conditions
including 'the richness and heaviness of our food', the 'wealth and
abundance of the inhabitants', the sedentary lifestyles of the better off,
and the difficulties of 'living in great, populous, and consequently
unhealthy towns' (Cheyne, 1733, pp. i–ii).

It is difficult to know how well Cheyne's proposed eclectic jumble of
causes and cures (including the importance of diet, exercise, greed,
consumerism and state-of-the-art knowledge of physiology and the
workings of the nerves) was received at the time. Most people could
not read, let alone afford to buy a book (Stone, 1969), so Cheyne's
ideas would have been seen by a tiny minority of the population on
which he was commenting. In this respect, MacDonald's (1981) analysis

of the notes made by the seventeenth-century English medic Richard Napier perhaps give us a rare insight into the maladies suffered by ordinary people who sought help, and the available treatments before there were any recognisable specialist mental health professionals. While we might take some care not to simply translate Napier's categories (listed in the table below) into modern equivalents, the list that MacDonald creates does certainly *look* remarkably familiar (see Table 1.1).

Table 1.1 List of symptoms from Napier's notebooks

Most common	Less common, might be recognised today as serious	Less common and not so translatable
Troubled in mind	Suicidal	Tempted (to commit sin)
Melancholy	Mad	Laughs
Mopishness	Raging	Stubborn
Light-headed	Too little talk	Religious preoccupation
Simply sad	Too much talk	Screams
Took grief	Furious	
Fearful	Lunatic	
All religious symptoms	All infanticidal symptoms	

(Source: based on MacDonald, 1981, Table 4.1, p. 117)

The most common varieties of unhappiness seem to be versions of anxiety and fear, or of sadness: grief, melancholy and mopishness. MacDonald (1981) suggests that patients overwhelmed with feelings of sadness and lethargy and who were drawn from the peasant classes were likely to be labelled as 'mopish' by Napier, while those from the wealthier echelons with similar complaints were likely to be viewed as 'melancholic' (with its associations to delicacy and thoughtfulness). Contemporary questions about social class and diagnosis are taken up in other parts of this book, particularly Chapter 19.

MacDonald also analysed Napier's thinking around the causes of such maladies. He found that they could be divided into three categories:

- *supernatural* referred to astrological concerns

- *divine and diabolic* referred to the actions of God and the Devil

- *natural* referred to 'ordinary' adaptive responses and included grief, disappointments in love, physical problems, too much study or the balance of the 'humours'.

In terms of treatments, Napier was eclectic in his therapeutic outlook. Various interventions were aimed at the body, including those intended to restore the balance between the four bodily humours, or fluids (an idea that stems from an ancient understanding of good health). Thus, there were recommendations for purges: emetics and laxatives, as well as various forms of bloodletting (such as the application of leeches). Medicines, such as opiates (for lunacy and madness), were prescribed alongside astrological guidance and advice on diet, rest and exercise. MacDonald emphasises the holistic approach and the continuity with apparent everyday concerns, but mourns the fact that Napier was one of the last of his kind. There were already powerful forces gathering that would no longer construe mental unhappiness in such holistic terms. MacDonald suggests that the main driver for this change was the growing culture that venerated science and rationality and thus nurtured the medical speciality of psychiatry.

The following century, which witnessed the stirrings of this specialism was, in MacDonald's words, 'a disaster for the insane' as they became subject to crueller treatments and 'confined to madhouses and asylums' (MacDonald, 1981, p. 230). In making this claim, MacDonald, like many critics of the emergence of psychiatry, gestures towards the significance of Michel Foucault's work on the history of psychiatry. Foucault is perhaps the most influential critic of psychiatry, so it is worth dwelling on the crux of his argument, which can be summarised by this often quoted passage from the preface of his 1967 book *Madness and civilisation: a history of insanity in the age of reason*:

In the serene world of mental illness, modern man no longer communicates with the madman... As for a common language, there is no such thing; or rather, there is no such thing any longer; the constitution of madness as mental illness, at the end of the eighteenth century, affords the evidence of a broken dialogue, posits the separation as already effected, and thrusts into oblivion all those stammered, imperfect words without fixed syntax in which the exchange between madness and reason was made. The language of psychiatry, which is a monologue of reason about madness, has been established only on the basis of such a silence.

(Foucault, 1967, p. xii)

Foucault suggests that, before the 'age of reason', madness was a part of all of us and our communities. The modern era of reason, often called 'the enlightenment', was marked by great scientific endeavours that led to the Industrial Revolution, which demanded rational thought and behaviour from people. Any previous ways of thinking that were deemed irrational, illogical or erratic were no longer acceptable. To Foucault, psychiatry was an important mechanism for enforcing such norms. It invented a language that talked about insanity as if it were an object that was separate from one's self. Those judged to be 'insane' were banished from normality, so efforts could be made to separate, confine and treat 'them'. This perspective also applies to even the most benign-looking initiatives, such as 'moral treatment' (discussed below) and the various 'talking cures' (described in Chapter 3) that followed.

2   The birth of psychiatry as the medical specialism of the mind

Accounts of the history of psychiatry tend to place the origins of recognisable forms of a specialist profession at the very beginning of the nineteenth century (Porter, 2002; Scull, 1979a), with the formal establishment of professional associations and journals occurring in the 1840s. Before this there were 'mad-doctors' who ministered to the insane and confined them in 'madhouses', while occupying 'a niche slightly above a witch doctor in the public imagination' (Boime, 1991, p. 79).

The transformation was energised by two innovations that involved the identification of 'the mind' of the patient as itself a significant field of enquiry and treatment. Firstly, there was the emergence of moral treatment, a landmark that initiated the practice of systematic 'psychological' treatment. While on the one hand this was arguably a significant precursor to many different forms of psychological treatment that were to follow, it was also a key argument that justified the large-scale building of asylums across many parts of Europe and North America in the nineteenth century (Scull, 1979a). The asylums came to dominate the landscape of mental illness for well over a century and in many ways we still live in their shadow (Rogers and Pilgrim, 2014). Secondly, there was the development of a set of ideas that construed some instances of serious criminality (particularly involving violence) as symptoms of mental disorder. This claim of expertise in criminal and legal matters was fundamental to the aspiration for professional status and recognition (Goldstein, 1987). Both innovations were underpinned by the relatively novel idea of a psychological domain – a world of the mind – which could be explored and treated by those with sufficient expertise (Jones, 2017a).

Examination of these ideas illustrates how the development of psychiatry needs to be understood as a product of various and often contradictory forces. Alongside the intention to find ways of alleviating distress were the more entrepreneurial pressures of those who wanted to build professional status and earn a living. There were also the anxieties of governments conscious of the threat posed by those who did not conform to social norms.

2.1   The asylum movement and moral treatment

Activity 1.1: Experiences of asylums

Allow about 10 minutes

What thoughts and feelings come to you when you hear the word 'asylum'? Are they largely positive or negative? Can you identify what images give rise to these positive or negative feelings?

Spend some time trying to tease out why you feel the way you do.

Discussion

While the word 'asylum' – with its literal meaning of protection and safety – ought to have positive associations, for many the word will have negative meanings. Perhaps the negative associations are connected to the old asylums. As you have read, although the asylums were perhaps built with the intention of providing rest and safety, they became overcrowded, neglected and gloomy places. Perhaps our feelings are also influenced by the stigma that surrounds mental illness.

It might be interesting to reflect on whether this chapter changes your view of asylums.

The idea of confinement for those deemed insane was not new. Small-scale, private asylums operated by entrepreneurs who offered a paid service to take in and 'care' for the insane had proliferated through the eighteenth century. By the nineteenth century these institutions were being encouraged by a government which had a long-standing interest in controlling those whose deviant behaviour might threaten the social order. Since at least the sixteenth century, the government and local parishes had discouraged vagrancy and begging through a series of legislative initiatives called 'poor laws' (Brundage, 2002). The means of discouragement were frankly often cruel, with punishments such as whipping and branding dealt to those found vagrant.

As the perceived scale of the problem posed by the workless and destitute grew, a network of workhouses was built to provide minimal sustenance and accommodation to those too poor to support themselves. They also aimed to 'train' people in the values of labour and routine amid harsh environments that discouraged dependency.

Whatever our moral judgement of the philosophy, too many people were simply unable to respond to the regime, and the workhouses filled with people who were old, ill or had disabilities. The next move was to differentiate 'the poor' so that particular kinds of shelter might be offered to those who were unable to benefit from the workhouse regime. A significant milestone came with Section 20 of the *Vagrancy Act 1744*, which charged local magistrates with responsibility for paupers and so-called **pauper lunatics** in their district (Bynum, 1974).

Pauper lunatic
A term used in the eighteenth and nineteenth centuries to identify individuals who required local authority support due to poverty and who were also recognised to be suffering from insanity.

The identification of the 'pauper lunatic' as someone who required local authority support encouraged the expansion of private madhouses as they became a convenient means for local parishes to discharge their duty. These were controversial institutions, growing up as unregulated places of confinement with unclear rules about who could be confined against their will. In the early decades of the eighteenth century, the writer and journalist Daniel Defoe (author of *Moll Flanders* and *Robinson Crusoe*) noted the proliferation and wondered 'how many ladies and gentlewomen' were being locked away (Defoe, 1729, p. 23). He suggested that these private madhouses needed to be 'suppress'd, or at least subject to daily examination' (Defoe, 1729, p. 23). He reserved particular ire for a 'vile practice' that he suspected was common among wealthy men of 'sending their wives to mad-houses at every whim or dislike', allowing them to be 'undisturb'd in their debaucheries' (Defoe, 1729, p. 31). This claim was to be picked up in the twentieth century by a number of feminist critics of the psychiatric system. Chesler (1972) and Showalter (1985) argued that the institution of psychiatry and the various treatments that emerged through the nineteenth and into the twentieth centuries were profoundly patriarchal and were meant to pathologise and control women. The idea that the categories of insanity were aimed at women, and that asylums were correspondingly full of women, has been beguiling (Ussher, 1991).

Detailed analysis of asylum records, medical texts and cultural images suggests, however, that this was too simple a picture. As Busfield summarises, the idea that madness in the nineteenth century became 'a distinctly female malady' was certainly mistaken – it would be better to understand that 'assumptions of gender' were embedded within the multiplying 'diversification of medical categories of madness' (Busfield, 1994, p. 276).

Pause for reflection

Do you think there are differences in the way that men and women are portrayed as suffering from mental health problems?

Nevertheless, distaste grew about conditions in the private madhouses, and in the anxiety that 'anyone' might find themselves confined within them. This led the British Parliament to pass the *Madhouses Act 1774* that brought the unregulated private asylums under supervisory control through systems of licencing and inspection. It was into this space of regulation and care that the new profession was to emerge. The emergence of a specialism in 'insanity' from within the ranks of the various forms of so-called medical men (Jones, 1972) meant that commonplace treatments aimed to work on the bodies of sufferers. It has been argued that some of the treatments for insanity that looked particularly barbaric – involving the use of restraint or even beatings – were not wilfully cruel, but rather reflected the widespread belief that those who were without reason were in fact like animals and so had to be trained to behave (Scull, 1979b).

By the beginning of the nineteenth century some of the physical treatments were becoming quite elaborate. Benjamin Rush, who ran the Pennsylvania Asylum, designed the 'tranquilliser chair' which held the body still while allowing cold water to be applied to the head and warm water to the feet – acting 'as a sedative to the tongue and temper as well as the blood vessels' (Rush, cited in Scull, 1981, p. 34).

Figure 1.1 Benjamin Rush and his tranquilliser chair

Moral treatment
A form of treatment for insanity that supposed that a cure could be achieved through placing a patient in calm, restful and attractive surroundings, treating them with respect and encouraging good behaviour. It was a key argument for the construction of asylums in the nineteenth century.

Despite the continuing interest in physical treatment, in the decades leading up to the establishment of the profession of psychiatry there was a significant move towards a more psychological orientation. A very important innovation was that of **moral treatment** – the idea that a cure would follow from the provision of a calm environment away from the stresses of modern urban living, where staff treat the afflicted with dignity, kindness and respect. Significant innovations occurred at the York Retreat in England, led by the Tukes (a wealthy Quaker family who were not medics), and by the noted medic Philipe Pinel in France. Samuel Tuke (1813) emphasised the psychological nature of insanity and its treatment: 'If we adopt the opinion, that the disease originates in the mind, applications made immediately to it are obviously the most natural; and the most likely to be attended with success' (Tuke, 1813, p. 84). Tuke gave credit to the work of Pinel, who had claimed that patients undergoing moral treatment were 'treated with affability, soothed by consolation and sympathy' and thus put on a road to 'rapid convalescence' (Pinel, 1806, p. 67).

The rationale of this psychological form of treatment helped provide the new profession with a respectable identity. It construed insanity as identifiable and curable, which justified the construction of asylums. Eventually, this led to the *Lunacy Act 1845* and *County Asylums Act 1845*, which required all local authorities to provide an asylum.

Figure 1.2 shows what an early asylum would have looked like. This asylum was opened in 1851, designed in the Gothic style by the renowned architect William Fulljames who also designed churches, commercial buildings and a country house in Gloucestershire. It was originally built to accommodate 210 patients as a joint county asylum (Herefordshire, Monmouthshire, Brecon and Radnor), but at its peak had well over 1000 inmates.

Figure 1.2 A contemporary drawing of Joint Counties Lunatic Asylum, which was built following the *Lunacy Act 1845* and *County Asylums Act 1845*. It is quite typical in style: the country-house appearance was considered as important as the confinement that it provided.

These asylums were built under architectural assumptions that were very different from those of prisons and workhouses. They were designed to mimic grand houses and were placed within often large and pleasant grounds in order to create an atmosphere of calm and peace, thought crucial for cure (Edginton, 1997). In some important respects, their rapid success was their undoing. Scull (1979a) traces the increase in the numbers of so-called pauper lunatics (as a reasonable measure of the population of the asylums) and finds the numbers leapt from 16,821 in 1844 (representing a rate of 10.21 for every 10,000 of population) to 77,257 in 1890 (26.27 for every 10,000). This trend continued into the twentieth century. At their peak, in 1954, there were over 140,000 patients (in England) in psychiatric hospitals.

The substantial increase in the numbers of asylum inmates undoubtedly helped establish the idea that the psychiatric institutions were a necessary component of a modern society, but it also undermined the possibilities of moral treatment, as the new asylums quickly became overcrowded, underfunded and understaffed. They began to fully deserve the condemnation aimed at them through a new series of scandals about the poor conditions, even in the new asylums (Scull, 1996). Thus, eventually there was a turning away from the asylums through the second half of the twentieth century. Nevertheless, the asylums provided an institutional base for the emerging profession of psychiatry, while the claims for expertise in the criminal justice system were to raise its public profile.

Methodology: The connection between research and understanding history

Critics of psychiatry (such as Foucault) have often focused on the history of the profession. This might be for a number of reasons, including an interest in making links to past practices that can often appear barbaric. It might also be because an understanding of where our ideas and practices have come from can help us question our current assumptions.

The disciplines of psychology and psychiatry have been accused of being ahistorical – they do not take account of their own history and the circumstances that have created their own assumptions.

As this chapter suggests, however, there can be important differences between ways of understanding past events. Studies of history cannot use experiments as they are used in natural sciences, medicine and psychology. One might therefore pose the question: How do we decide which version of the past is the most accurate? Indeed, why might history (and one's understanding of it) be important to understanding psychiatry and psychology?

2.2 Moral insanity and criminological expertise

The earliest signs of the formal recognition of categories of 'insanity' come from processes of legal justice. For as long as we have written records, we know that systems of justice have recognised that those who were deemed to be suffering from insanity ought to be treated with some leniency (Walker, 1968). While the principle was recognised across time, there has been a long debate about how insanity might be reliably detected. The claim of expertise in this territory became an important facet of the case for recognition of the profession of psychiatry. Some of these developments are described in Chapter 18. For the purposes of this chapter we observe a series of initiatives in Germany, France, Britain and the US that aimed to define disorders of the mind that might be associated with criminality (Jones, 2016). Particular claims were made about 'monomanias', 'partial insanity' and **moral insanity**. These all emerged from the idea that the mind could be understood as an object of exploration, and that it was possible to identify particular aspects of the mind that might be disordered in a way that could lead to criminality and violence.

Despite some success in the courts, these ideas were considered too radical when debated in the public arena, fuelled by the relatively new phenomenon of a widespread and popular press. The newly formed profession of psychiatry moved away from these more nuanced psychological ideas and back towards their medical and physiological roots (Jones, 2017b). By the 1860s an unfortunate alliance was made between the new profession's need to profess expertise in the field of criminality and ideas about the significance of hereditary. The latter were given a new respectability thanks to Charles Darwin's *On the origin of species* (published in 1859). What emerged was a rather eugenical turn as assumptions were made about the heritability of criminality among an apparent underclass. These played out in programmes of confinement and sterilisation, most notably in the US (Rembis, 2011), leading up to their catastrophic use by the Nazi regime in the middle of the twentieth century (Breggin, 1993).

One important consequence of the medical profession's shift away from the psychological realm was that the ground of psychological enquiry became available to other professions for developing theories and treatments of the mind. As Chapter 3 will explore, it was initially psychoanalytic ideas, instigating the 'talking cures', that opened a new domain of psychological methods of investigation and treatment. To an

Moral insanity
A term used in the nineteenth century to refer to a supposed psychological disorder that was associated with antisocial and criminal behaviour.

Medical model
The idea that physical and mental difficulties experienced by an individual can be understood in terms of an identifiable disorder existing within that individual.

extent a split was established between the medical specialism of psychiatry – which has tended to maintain a strong allegiance to the **medical model** – and those who have sought the further exploration of 'psychological' treatments. The boundaries are porous, however; while the roots of psychiatry are firmly embedded in the world of physiology, the profession has also been significantly shaped by the belief in a 'mind' that is amenable to treatment (Jones, 2017a). At the same time, the assumptions of the medical model – that there is an illness located within the body (including the mind) of the individual – are quite widely accepted within the world of mental health, including in many models of counselling.

3 The fall of asylums and the move to community care

Whatever the motivations of those who planned and built the asylums across many countries in Europe and North America, there can be no doubting their popularity, as their populations greatly outgrew the intended numbers. The hopes of providing peace, rest and pleasant interaction with purposeful staff were dashed by overcrowding and understaffing. Asylums largely came to deserve their characterisation as dismal prisons, or warehouses for those who were unable to look after themselves or who were rejected by their families and communities (Scull, 1996). This all lent support to those who pointed to the coercive and controlling nature of the psychiatric enterprise itself. Just as the more subtle and psychological model of moral insanity failed to survive amid the storm of a hostile press, moral treatment also failed within the wholly underfunded new asylums. This failure pushed psychiatry back to a more despondent understanding of mental disorder, one based on assumptions of inherited weakness (Scull, 1996).

Asylum populations began to fall in the middle of the twentieth century, peaking in England in 1954 and falling rapidly after that (Tooth and Brooke, 1961). The reasons for this fall have been contested (Rogers and Pilgrim, 2014). Some have argued that the development of drug therapies (particularly the phenothiazines) allowed more people to live without confinement (e.g. Gelder, Mayou and Cowen, 2001). Others suggest that the development of the welfare state in the post-war period allowed families and communities to care for dependent people at home (Rogers and Pilgrim, 2014).

There was also a series of critiques of psychiatry that gained momentum from the 1950s through to the 1960s. In addition to Foucault's view of the significant role played by psychiatry in enforcing particular ways of being (as discussed in Section 1), some psychiatrists drew attention to meaning that might be found within apparent ravings of those judged to be ill (e.g. Laing, 1965). Others drew attention to the negative impact of the asylum environment itself (e.g. Goffman, 1961), and the potentially harmful effect of receiving such a stigmatised label (Scheff, 1966). Some questioned the logical impossibility of the idea that the mind could be regarded as suffering from a disease (Szasz, 1970). The critiques of psychiatry were also taking place within the profession itself as the effectiveness of the asylums was questioned (Brown and Wing, 1962).

Whatever the reason, by the 1980s the decline of the asylum population meant that the upkeep of these old-fashioned, and expensive-to-maintain buildings was a drain on resources. The government of the day therefore accelerated the closure of the asylums with its overt policy of 'community care' (Audit Commission, 1986). This policy promoted a shift of resources across a range of health and social care services, away from long-term institutional care and towards the support of people in their homes and communities. In some respects, this was nothing revolutionary; as will be described in Chapter 4, the post-war period witnessed an expansion of the diagnostic categories of mental disorder, which meant that mental illness was viewed as something prevalent across wider social groups. Thus, efforts were made to make services available to more people. While this book will discuss a number of initiatives in detail, an important dimension of all of them was the rise of child guidance clinics (Stewart, 2012). These may be the most remarkable sign of a government belief in the significance of mental health to the overall good of society. Monitoring children and treating poor mental health was considered to be an overall social good. These developments can be viewed through the different lenses of the contested perspectives – either as progressive developments that provided support for a greater range of difficulties, or as sinister means of control and manipulation. A significant move was attempted by the introduction of the *Mental Health Act 1959* (in England and Wales). It sought to fully incorporate psychiatric services within the newly emerged National Health Service and the associated arms of an enhanced welfare state.

Conclusion

This chapter has provided a brief introduction to the complex topic of the history of psychiatry. Such a brief survey can only point out some important features of this contested terrain on which the buildings of the asylums loom large. Contrasting perspectives present different understandings of the development of the asylums, fuelled as they were by the idea of moral treatment. Was the development of moral treatment, as Foucault and Scull suggest, an oppressive tactic of a society that was desperately anxious to enforce particular standards of behaviour, and to physically confine those who threatened the social order? Or was this a far more humane response to distress and dependency? In favour of the more cynical view are the links that can be made between poor law legislation and the development of workhouses (and then prisons). Indeed, despite the nobler aspirations, the asylums did become the gloomy warehouses of misery that have haunted the imagination of the world of mental health.

Public and media responses to mental health problems have formed a very significant force that shaped psychiatry. Arguably, there is no other area of medicine and perhaps social policy that has been so much debated and fought out in the public sphere. It would only be fair to conclude that psychiatry has been shaped by anxieties about the threat to social order potentially posed by people who were viewed as different – something that could be 'remedied' by their confinement and treatment in order to 'normalise' their behaviour.

Alternatively, it can be claimed that the idea of moral treatment suggested a kinder regime that was reflected in the architecture of the asylums, which was profoundly different from that of the prisons and workhouses. By the middle of the nineteenth century, the asylums were being built in the fashion of fine country houses with often extensive and pleasant grounds. Likewise, medics who were searching for new diagnostic categories to explain serious offending were doing so with the immediate motivation of saving the accused from execution, which they would inevitably face if they were judged to be 'sane' (and therefore guilty).

Whichever version is 'truer', it is certainly the case that the legacy of the asylums was to be considerable. The mass construction of asylums dominated the context for mental illness until the last decades of the twentieth century – with subsequent community care polices being an overt reaction to the asylum tradition. In addition, moral treatment can also be regarded as a forerunner of the talking cures.

The birth of psychiatry was also significantly linked to the identification of 'the mind' as a site of exploration and treatment. Debate is unresolved as to the substance of that mind. With its roots in medicine, it may be no surprise that the medical specialism of psychiatry often falls back on the idea that the processes of the mind are simply determined by those of the body. However, as Chapter 3 will demonstrate, some strands in the world of mental health have strongly maintained that the mind is a psychological domain that can be understood and treated by psychological methods.

Porter (2004) pointed out that the voices of those most affected by the history of psychiatry have not been well heard. Chapter 2 will address this important issue.

Further reading

- This text provides an overview of the complete history of 'madness'. Chapter 6 specifically looks at the rise of psychiatry: Porter, R. (2002) *Madness: a brief history*. Oxford: Oxford University Press.

- The following text offers more on the early roots of psychiatry as a branch of medicine and a psychological science:

  Jones, D.W. (2017) 'Moral insanity and psychological disorder: the hybrid roots of psychiatry', *History of Psychiatry*, 28(3), pp. 263–279.

- Here, Porter gives a voice to some of those treated as mad throughout history:

  Porter, R. (1987) *A social history of madness: stories of the insane*. London: Weidenfeld & Nicolson.

References

Audit Commission (1986) *Making a reality of aommunity care*. London: Audit Commission for Local Authorities in England and Wales, HMSO.

Boime, A. (1991) 'Portraying monomaniacs to service the alienist's monomania: Géricault and Georget', *Oxford Art Journal*, 14(1), pp. 79–91.

Breggin, P.R. (1993) 'Psychiatry's role in the holocaust', *International Journal of Risk and Safety in Medicine*, 4(2), pp. 133–148.

Brown, G.W. and Wing. J.K. (1962) 'A comparative clinical and social survey of three mental hospitals', *The Sociological Review: Monograph*, 5, pp. 145–171.

Brundage, A. (2002) *The English Poor Laws 1700–1930*. Basingstoke: Palgrave.

Burton, R. (1638) *The anatomy of melancholia: what it is with all kinds of causes, symptoms, prognostics and several cures of it. In three maine partitions with their several sections, members, and subsections. Philosophically, medicinally, historically, opened and cut up*. Oxford: Henry Cripps.

Busfield, J. (1994) 'The female malady? Men, women and madness in nineteenth century Britain', *Sociology*, 28(1), pp. 259–277.

Bynum, W.F. (1974) 'Rationales for therapy in British psychiatry: 1780–1835', *Medical History*, 18(4). pp. 317–344.

Chesler, P. (1972) *Women and madness*. New York: Avon Books.

Cheyne, G. (1733) *The English malady*. London: G. Strahan.

Defoe, D. (1729) *Augusta Triumphans: or, the way to make London the most flourishing city in the universe*. 2nd edn. London: Andrew Moreton.

Edginton, B. (1997) 'Moral architecture: the influence of the York Retreat on asylum design', *Health & Place*, 3(2), pp. 91–99.

Foucault, M. (1967) *Madness and civilization: a history of insanity in the age of reason*. Translated from the French by R. Howard. London: Tavistock Publications.

Gelder, M., Mayou, R. and Cowen, P. (2001) *Shorter Oxford textbook of psychiatry*. Oxford: Oxford University Press.

Goffman, E. (1961) *Asylums*. Harmondsworth: Penguin.

Goldstein, J. (1987) *Console and classify: the French psychiatric profession in the nineteenth century*. Cambridge: Cambridge University Press.

Jones, D.W. (2016) *Disordered personalities and crime: an analysis of the history of moral insanity*. Abingdon: Routledge.

Jones, D.W. (2017a) 'Moral insanity and psychological disorder: the hybrid roots of psychiatry', *History of Psychiatry*, 28(3), pp. 263–279.

Jones, D.W. (2017b) 'Psychopathy and the media', *Oxford Research Encyclopedia: Criminology and Criminal Justice*. New York: Oxford University Press.

Jones, K. (1972) *A history of the mental health services*. London: Routledge and Kegan Paul.

Laing, R.D. (1965) *The divided self*. Harmondsworth: Penguin.

MacDonald, M. (1981) *Mystical bedlam: madness, anxiety, and healing in seventeenth-century England*. Cambridge: Cambridge University Press.

Pinel, P. (1806) *A Treatise on insanity: in which are contained the principles of a new and more practical nosology of maniacal disorders than has yet been offered to the public*. Translated from the French by D.D. Davis. London: Caddell and Davies.

Porter, R. (2002) *Madness: a brief history*. Oxford: Oxford University Press.

Porter, R. (2004) *Madmen: a social history of madhouses, mad-doctors and lunatics*. Stroud: Tempus Publishing.

Rembis, M.A. (2011) *Defining deviance: sex, science, and delinquent girls, 1890–1960*. Urbana, Illinois: University of Illinois Press.

Rogers, A. and Pilgrim, D. (2014) *A sociology of health and mental illness*. 5th edn. Maidenhead: Open University Press/Mcgraw Hill.

Scheff, T. (1966) *Being mentally ill: a sociological theory*. London: Weidenfeld & Nicolson.

Scull, A. (1979a) *Museums of madness: the social organization of insanity in nineteenth-century England*. London: Allen Lane.

Scull, A. (1979b) 'Moral treatment reconsidered: some sociological comments on an episode in the history of British psychiatry', *Psychological Medicine*, 9(3), pp. 421–428.

Scull, A. (1996) 'Asylums: utopias and realities', in Tomlinson, D. and Carrier, J. (eds.) *Asylum in the community* . London: Routledge, pp 7–17.

Scull, A. (ed.) (1981) *Madhouses, mad-doctors and madmen: the social history of psychiatry in the Victorian era*. Philadelphia: University of Pennsylvania Press.

Showalter, E. (1985) *The female malady: women, madness and English culture 1830–1980*. London: Virago.

Stewart, J. (2012) '"The dangerous age of childhood": child guidance and the "normal" child in Great Britain, 1920–1950', *Paedagogica Historica*, 47, pp. 785–803.

Stone, L. (1969) 'Literacy and education in England 1640–1900', *Past and Present*, 42, pp. 69–139.

Szasz, T. (1970) *The manufacture of madness: a comparative study of the inquisition and the mental health movement*. New York: Harper and Row.

Tooth, G.C. and Brooke, E.M. (1961) 'Trends in the mental health population and their effect on future planning', *Lancet*, 1, pp. 710–713.

Tuke, S. (1813) *A description of the York Retreat*. Philadelphia: Isaac Peirce.

Ussher, J. (1991) *Women's madness: misogyny or mental illness?*. London: Harverster Wheatsheaf.

Walker, N. (1968) *Crime and insanity in England. Volume 1: The historical perspective*. Edinburgh: Edinburgh University Press.

Chapter 2

The service-user movement

Jo Lomani

Contents

Introduction

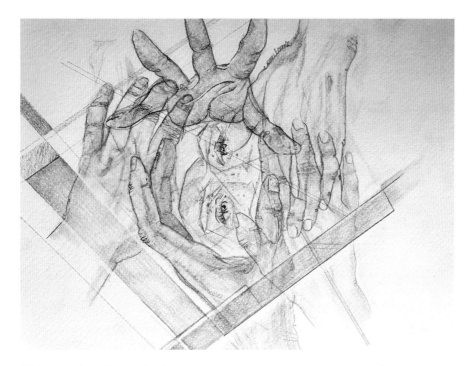

'Held back' by Rosie Cook

> There's really no such thing as the 'voiceless'. There are only the
> deliberately silenced, or the preferably unheard.

(Roy, 2004)

This chapter introduces the significance of the service-user movement
in the field of mental health. It begins by considering the term 'service
user' and moves on to exploring some of the history of the service-
user/survivor movement. The chapter then looks at issues in mental
health survivor activism, including an examination of some of the
ethical dilemmas and pitfalls. The second part of the chapter will take a
close look at service-user involvement and coproduction in mental
health research.

As this chapter progresses, it will become clear that the phrase
'service-user movement' is a misnomer. This is because mental health
patients have diverse perspectives, experiences and identities. We call
ourselves many different things: patients, peers, service users, clients,
survivors, consumers, people with lived experience, experts by

experience, people with a psychosocial disability, and some of us self-identify as 'mad'. These terms can reflect some very different and contested perspectives (Christmas and Sweeney, 2016). The chapter will use a number of these expressions, but for the sake of consistency it will tend to use 'service user' as a shorthand for a diverse range of terms.

If you aspire to work in the field of mental health, it is crucial that you recognise the immense power you will have over your clients. If you become a therapist, you will decide how long the sessions are; you will say when time is up; you will write notes about your client. You may discuss and interpret your client with a supervisor. Those of you who end up working within the formal mental health system may have even more power over service users, perhaps making decisions about the liberty and treatment of patients (as discussed further in Chapter 18).

Why is power so important? Because it is the abuse of power that provided the foundational context in which the survivor movement flourished. It was called the survivor movement because many patients have had to survive something terrible – something connected to power (or more specifically, to a lack of power). Historically, mental health patients have been silenced. The truth about their experiences of barbaric treatments and psychiatric interventions was kept locked behind the closed doors of early asylums. Yet even in those oppressive and restrictive contexts, patients found creative ways for their narratives to be heard. In her book *Agnes's jacket*, psychologist Gail Hornstein offered useful insights into these narratives:

> Despite every attempt to silence them, hundreds of other patients have managed to get their stories out, at least in disguised form. Today, in a vibrant underground network of "psychiatric survivor groups" all over the world, patients work together to unravel the mysteries of madness and help one another recover.
>
> (Hornstein, 2017)

This chapter aims to:

- summarise some of the key historical changes that have occurred within the service-user movement

- explore current issues and debates in the service-user movement, such as the impact of government policies and digital technologies

- outline the requirement of patient participation and involvement in mental health policy construction, and the inconsistent ways in which it is applied in practice

- explore the challenges faced by service-user researchers, such as the dynamics that exist between them and traditional researchers.

1 The development of the service-user movement

Most of us struggle with our mental health at some point in our lives. Most people's journeys to find support contain a mix of helpful and unhelpful experiences. Some people may see a mental health worker for a brief time, while others remain in services for many years. The service-user movement is a rather nebulous term. What exactly does it mean? Why has there been, and why does there continue to be, such prolific activism around mental health?

Service-user movement
A term used to describe the broad coalition of groups and individuals who speak out, individually and collectively, for their own rights and to draw attention to the difficulties experienced by those who have cause to use or receive mental health services.

In order to answer these questions, it is important to explore the oppressive context within which the **service-user movement** emerged. As you read in Chapter 1, conditions in the early asylums were often brutal. Asylum practices, even in relatively modern times, have included the use of chemical castration, prolonged seclusion and psychosurgery (Harrington, 2019). It was the brutality of historical psychiatry that forced patients into collective action and resistance. Years later they were joined by prominent, radical psychiatrists who were dissatisfied with conventional psychiatry. They began what is now referred to as the 'anti-psychiatry movement', which gained popularity in the 1960s. Academics and psychiatrists such as Ronald Laing, Thomas Szasz and Erving Goffman publicly challenged and undermined the legitimacy of psychiatry. More specifically, they highlighted the subjective nature of psychiatric diagnosis. These challenges were validating for patient activists, who themselves were trying to challenge damaging psychiatric narratives and win the right for people to maintain their own beliefs about their mental health experiences.

Missing from the works of these prominent anti-psychiatrists, however, is a record of the influence that their patients had on them – none of their writings or lectures were coproduced with service users (Section 3.1 looks at coproduction). Thus it is not the patient activists' names that are associated with the radical changes that took place during and after the formation of the anti-psychiatry movement. This is a significant point because a continuing aim of the survivor movement is to have its own independent voice.

The service-user movement is not one unified group of activists. It is a collective name for a multitude of groups and individuals who have, over the years, tried to improve care and treatment towards those who have become too distressed or overwhelmed to function. Service users have fought for the right to receive humane treatment, to access adequate housing and welfare provisions, to expect reasonable workplace adjustments and sometimes simply to remain free from psychiatric detainment. Wallcraft *et al.* offer the following definition of the movement:

> The 'service user/survivor movement' is a term used to describe the existence of numerous individuals who speak out for their own rights and those of others, and local groups and national organisations set up to provide mutual support or to promote the rights of current and former mental health service users to have a voice.
>
> (Wallcraft *et al.*, 2003, p. 11)

The right to one's own voice is important. Some describe themselves as 'mad activists' as an assertion of a positive identity; that is, they have chosen to use the word 'mad' rather than being subjected to a label imposed on them by psychiatric professionals.

Beginning in the 1980s, under Ronald Reagan (then president) in the US and Margaret Thatcher (then prime minister) in the UK, the ideals of 'self-management' in mental healthcare were promoted while, simultaneously, funds for mental health services were cut. Community-based mental health teams were established in the UK to save money and to prevent long-term institutionalisation, so patients were more likely to be managed at home. The service-user movement gained increasing popularity during this time, partly because (generally speaking) patients were no longer locked away indefinitely in asylums. Service-users' opinions began to differ in regard to whether mental health services should be reformed from the inside or abolished entirely (see Information box 2.1). Television and the media began to reveal the realities of mental health patient experiences. In 1983 the first television programme entirely edited by psychiatric survivors was broadcast in the UK. Hay's (1986) documentary *We're Not Mad…We're Angry!* enabled survivors to share their harrowing experiences and criticisms of the psychiatric system with a larger audience than ever before.

Information box 2.1: Reformation versus abolition

Service-user activist groups responded to the psychiatric reforms of the 1980s with conflicting agendas. Some groups aligned themselves with the reforms – they believed that they could improve the existing mental health services by working within and alongside them. Other groups retained their abolitionist stance (i.e. where the aim is to get rid of psychiatry). Some groups formed alliances with prominent anti-psychiatry professionals. Different group agendas had an influence on how patients referred to themselves. For example, patients who wanted to work within the system in order to pursue psychiatric reform began to identify as 'consumers' or 'service users', while those who promoted psychiatric abolition were more likely to define themselves as 'survivors' to reflect the violent nature of their psychiatric experiences and the harm inflicted on them.

The service-user movement has always struggled with the tension between those who wish to improve existing mental health services and those who wish to dismantle these services in order to create something better. In truth, most of us probably identify somewhere between these positions.

1.1   Improving services or assimilating threat?

Assimilation and co-option
These terms refer to a process whereby service-user groups become incorporated within professional organisations and their oppositional voice can therefore be neutralised.

History suggests that **assimilation and co-option** happen when a social justice movement becomes popular enough to present a threat to established power structures. Thus, some survivors avoid too much cooperation with formal services:

> Once a social justice movement becomes co-opted, it has in turn been immobilized as it is swept up into becoming a part or extension of the larger group or system(s) it initially sought to dismantle and transform. Both co-option and oppression are insidious and sneaky processes: the path to co-option is often paved with the very best of intentions and the oppressed are often at first unaware of their own oppression.

(Feldman, 2018)

Despite these anxieties, several features of service-user activism have been professionalised and are now integrated within the mental health system (Voronka, 2019). 'Peer support', for example, originated within the survivor movement – people have always found ways to support one another within mental health institutions, so it became an integral part of early activism. Due to the grassroots and context-dependent nature of peer support, there is no single definition, though there are common themes:

> Peer support occurs between people who share similar life experiences and as a result can provide each other with reciprocal support, advice, empathy, validation and sense of belonging and community which professionals and/or others who have not endured the same difficult situations may not be able to.
>
> (Murphy and Higgins, 2018, p. 441)

Grassroots peer support can subvert the power dynamics within the mental health system by providing support mechanisms for patients who are defined by the users themselves. Nowadays, mental health peer support exists in many forms, such as one-to-one (Gillard and Holley, 2014), group (Castelein et al., 2008), and online, which is becoming increasingly popular (Barak et al., 2008). Since 2009, various forms of peer support have been formalised within the UK mental health system (Munn-Giddings et al., 2009). The introduction of the peer support worker role within statutory services has generated employment for thousands of people who have experienced mental health problems and used services. However, the lack of agreed definitions of peer support has opened the term up to be co-opted into ways of working that re-enact the problematic power differentials that it originally began to counteract (Faulkner, 2013). A clear tension exists between formalised peer support and 'grassroots' peer support, with the former predominantly focusing on service-provider outcomes (e.g. standardised depression scores) rather than service-user led priorities (e.g. support for accessing benefits or stable housing).

In addition to problems of assimilation, there are many structural and attitudinal barriers that peer support workers must endure once they are employed. Overt discrimination and microaggressions from other, non-service-user staff are common (Sinclair, 2018), and I am aware from my own experience and observations that there is no career progression.

Despite the problems associated with formalised peer support roles, many service users really value the opportunity to use their **lived experience** in a paid, professional capacity (Basset *et al.*, 2010).

Lived experience
The value given to those who have experience of difficulties or mental health services and the expert knowledge this gives them.

2   The service-user movement today

Activity 2.1 below provides the opportunity to evaluate your own ideas about what being a service user means, before going on to explore the current context of the service-user movement.

Activity 2.1: Who is a service user?

Allow about 10–15 minutes

What do you think of when you imagine a mental health service user? Based on your own ideas and on your reading of the chapter so far, try to answer the following questions concerning who should be allowed to identify as a service user.

1   Can people who have used mental health services and are now trained mental health professionals be considered service users? Which services must people have used in order to qualify for service-user status?

2   If someone has stopped using mental health services, can they still identify as a service user?

3   Are there any differences between a service user who has been sectioned and a service user who has undergone counselling?

4   How distressed does someone have to be to be able to say they have 'lived experience'? Should they have to declare this experience?

5   Should carers or family members who have supported loved ones with their mental health problems have as much say in the future development of mental health services as those who have directly used these services?

Discussion

These questions represent some of the fierce debates currently taking place in the service-user movement. There are no easy answers to them. To demonstrate the complexity of these debates, consider the following case:

I once attended a meeting that brought together therapists and service users. During the meeting I challenged a senior psychologist by pointing out that, if the meeting was intended for service users, then the language ought to be jargon free. The practitioner explained that, as part of his training, he had been required to undergo private therapy for several years. He therefore identified as a service user and used the language he felt most comfortable with.

These kinds of scenarios raise questions about who is given the 'service user' label. Should it be reserved for those who have gone through the mental health system in some way due to suffering, or can someone be considered a service user when they have not sought those services purely out of need? What ultimately makes someone a service user?

Many people are drawn to work within helping professions as a result of their own various experiences of mental health problems. Like many people, I work in the mental health sector because I want to use my lived experience of mental health services to bring about positive change. The introduction of lived-experience roles within the western mental health system has, for the first time in history, created a degree of transparency around the dual identity of service provider and service user. While many people consider this to be a step in the right direction with regards to breaking down an unhelpful 'them versus us' narrative, there are many service users who are wary of this. Although normalising the experience of mental health difficulties in this way may break down stigma associated with the label of being 'mentally ill', there is a downside. Those of us who have endured the more abusive aspects of the mental health system can have our experiences somewhat erased. We are lumped together under a single identity, making service-user activism more difficult.

The service-user movement today is vast – thriving in some areas, struggling in others. The many groups and individuals that make up the movement are positioned somewhere on a very diverse continuum of belief about how to effect change. Some groups are fully integrated and funded by organisations within the mental health system. At the opposite end, there are groups who seek to operate not only outside of the mental health system but outside of capitalist structures altogether.

In recent years, many service users have refocused efforts to tackle socio-political oppression. A fellow service user recently said to me that we used to fight against oppressive treatment in the mental health system but nowadays we are far more likely to die from neglect than from bad treatment. This idea sums up the stark reality that many people with mental health problems now face. It is obvious to state that, in order to identify as a service user, services need to exist. In response to the fiscal crisis in 2008, the UK Conservative and Liberal Democrat coalition government implemented crushing austerity policies that disproportionately impacted people with mental health problems. UK National Health Service (NHS) mental health trusts have suffered budget cuts of eight per cent per year since 2011 (Griffiths, 2019). In the past ten years, almost a third of mental health beds have disappeared, along with 6800 mental health nurses (Griffiths, 2019).

Financial support for many people with mental health problems was withdrawn after they were assessed using stringent criteria designed to shift people away from disability benefits. Many service users were thrown into financial despair. A report found that disability assessments led to an additional 590 suicides, 279,000 extra cases of self-reported mental health problems and an additional 725,000 prescriptions for antidepressants between 2010 and 2013 (Barr *et al.*, 2016).

Austerity and the resulting neglect of mental health services generated new unities and divisions within the service-user movement. For example, those of us who had previously rejected psychiatric diagnoses as unscientific and invalid were suddenly required to prove our mental health impairments by emphasising our diagnoses. Those of us who had focused our activism on improving or dismantling psychiatry were suddenly propelled to join other disability activists in fighting against governmental and economic persecution because we were fighting the same battles.

This chapter has explored how the service-user movement began in opposition to the visibly oppressive treatment of patients within a medico-psychiatric system. Stories of harm by psychiatric survivors centre on diagnosis, forced treatment, electroconvulsive therapy, detainment, coercion and restraint, drug treatment, chronic neglect and other overt abuses of power. However, there are many other disciplines operating within the current western mental health system, each capable of causing harm to service users. Multidisciplinary teams often include psychotherapists, psychologists, counsellors, occupational therapists, social workers and other support staff.

It is important to note that patients can also be harmed by various interventions including psychological and psychotherapeutic ones (Jarrett, 2008). In my experience as a service user, the psychologist who wrote an incorrect and non-collaborative formulation of my problems was as harmful as the psychiatric nurse who forcibly injected and traumatised me as a non-consenting patient.

Furthermore, allied mental health professionals, such as psychologists, therapists and counsellors, may hold problematic beliefs that negatively impact on mental health service users. For example, Bartlett, Smith and King (2009) conducted a survey of over 1300 mental health professionals and found that more than 200 had offered some form of LGBTQ+ conversion therapy (an oppressive practice whereby a mental health professional believes that sexual orientation or gender identity is something that can be 'cured' and attempts to provide therapy toward meeting that aim). In fact, there remains a widespread (incorrect) belief among healthcare staff that identifying as LGBTQ+ is a mental disorder (Stonewall, 2015).

2.1   The service-user movement in the digital age

Before digital media, the service-user movement maintained momentum by producing user-created printed materials, such as magazines, newsletters and books. An example of this was a Canadian survivor-led magazine called *Phoenix Rising* founded in 1980 (activist artwork from the magazine is shown in Figure 2.1). *Asylum* magazine was established in the UK in 1986 and is still active at the time of writing in 2020. With the rise of digital media, service users can now interact with fellow survivors at the click of a button. This has led to an explosion of new writings and campaigns. The different approaches taken by a diverse range of survivor groups are now instantly visible and most groups are open for anyone to engage with.

Figure 2.1 An example of activist art, by Rudy Loewe

More recently, the rise of mental health 'zines' as a counter-culture to academia/published knowledge has enabled more radical sections of society to express their views on issues around mental health. They are often a form of DIY press that includes politically motivated cartoons and articles. Zines have enabled a modern form of peer support by exposing the lesser-known realities of many oppressed survivors (Bedei, 2016).

3   Nothing about us without us: research practice and the service-user movement

'Nothing about us without us' is a phrase that originated within the disability rights movement. The phrase grew in popularity after it was used in an influential book by James Charlton (Charlton, 2000). The service-user movement has always drawn on the exceptional activism and thinking initiated by disability campaigners. Although many of us with mental health difficulties do not identify with a disability, we recognise the benefits of using a human rights-based approach in our activism. The phrase 'nothing about us without us' has been used by mental health survivors to highlight that many decisions and discussions happened about 'us', without any consultation or attempt at collaboration. In 2017, National Survivor User Network (NSUN) members created a manifesto that intended to 'pressure mental health services to make the principal of "nothing about us without us" a reality at all levels, through meaningful involvement in decisions about our own individual care and genuine co-production to develop services' (NSUN, 2017, p. 3).

Arguably, obtaining the right to share our experiences and opinions with policymakers, researchers and service providers has been one of the greatest achievements of the service-user movement. Service-user involvement is now, at a policy level, required throughout all mental health service developments and research. Most mental health research will not receive funding unless researchers provide a clear strategy for mental health patient engagement. However, despite this policy requirement, collaboration is 'patchy and slow and often concentrated at the lowest levels of involvement' (Ocloo and Matthews, 2016). The patient involvement that does happen has brought with it an array of difficulties and criticisms, to which this chapter now turns.

3.1   Coproduction and patient participation and involvement

Figure 2.2 Another example of activist art, by Rachel Rowan Olive

Formal structures to enable **coproduction** within healthcare settings began around 1996. The National Institute for Health Research established a government-funded patient participation and involvement group aptly named INVOLVE (INVOLVE, 2012). **Patient participation and involvement** (PPI) in mental health settings began informally. Service providers would, for example, garner the opinions of patients about a new service parameter or some aspect of their care. PPI has now developed into a formal policy requirement (Department of Health, 2005).

The involvement and consultation of service users in mental health service environments has brought an array of difficulties. Despite the requirement to involve service users, there is no standardised way of doing this. Thus, the various services and organisations have very different ways of implementing their PPI requirements. In recognition of this, the National Survivor User Network developed the *4Pi*

Coproduction
A deliberative process that requires service-user members and 'professionals' to be involved on an equal footing throughout every stage of the design and delivery of research.

Patient participation and involvement
Usually refers to a process in which patients (service users) are consulted about some aspect(s) of a predetermined research process.

National Involvement Standards report, which offers best practice guidelines around PPI (Faulkner *et al.*, 2015).

Moreover, PPI and consultation are troubled by cultural differences and power differentials between professionals and service users. These differences can make involvement in PPI groups quite challenging. Non-service-user mental health leaders, commissioners and researchers have their own professionalised cultures and norms around acceptable ways to act, speak and share opinions (Kortteisto, Laitila and Pitkänen, 2018). Sometimes these are directly in contrast to the ways that service users express themselves. Misunderstandings are common, and what service users say during involvement meetings can be dismissed if said in the 'wrong way' or if it does not align with a predetermined agenda (e.g. Church, 1996).

Methodology: Selecting participants for PPI

Another issue in PPI concerns the selection of group members. Those with the power to select participants for PPI will have their own prejudices and biases. This can lead to the exclusion of important perspectives, as Ocloo and Matthews explain: 'PPI often involves a narrow group of individuals, with the handpicking of just one or two "appropriate" or "acquiescent" patient representatives to be involved in committees or projects. Patient representatives are less commonly drawn from black and minority ethnic groups and are often middle class' (Ocloo and Matthews, 2016, p. 629).

The rise of psychiatry, psychology and psychotherapy is correlated with the wealth of a country (Kalathil, 2011), so the service-user movement has tended to be more prevalent in the global West. This is problematic because it has led to overwhelmingly Eurocentric, white narratives within PPI and service-user research, while black, Asian and minority ethnic (BAME) service users are already disproportionately marginalised within mental health settings (Kalathil, 2008; Kalathil, 2011).

The requirement to involve service users in mental health service delivery, research and design has brought with it a large degree of tokenism and a culture of tokenistic involvement. Only a superficial effort is made to represent service users, and only to show that rules or expectations are being met, rather than because it is right or fair (Beresford, 2013). Tokenistic service-user involvement has led many service users to experience 'consultation fatigue' (Beresford, 2003, p. 102). Tokenism in service-user involvement is demeaning, silencing and ultimately counterproductive. It can be extremely re-traumatising for those who take part (Rose, 2018, p. 158). Thus, the perspectives and experiences gathered through such selection will not always reflect the range of views among service users. This will cast doubt on the capacity of the research to generalise any research findings.

3.2   Service user-led research: a voice of our own?

Being a service-user researcher is challenging. Many such researchers, like myself, favour experiential knowledge and novel 'mad epistemologies'. Note that 'mad studies' and 'mad knowledge' are terms used to describe a key feature of the service-user movement. 'Mad pride' began as a way to reclaim the stigmatising identity of being labelled as a 'mad person'. This eventually branched out into academia and has since developed into a discipline of its own. Service-user researchers tend to value lived experience over traditional academic research values such as positivism, objectivity and neutrality. This poses a threat to mainstream academia and inevitably disrupts the status quo within these settings. Due to our experiences, service-user researchers may be the first to call out oppressive and exclusionary practices, enabling the critique of dominant discourses in traditional mental health research settings (Harding, 1991). From my own experience, traditional researchers can become defensive and, in turn, service-user researchers can be labelled as 'problematic' or 'subversive'.

In addition to navigating complex workplace dynamics, there are many values that service-user researchers bring into research settings that are not easily reconcilable with elitist, hierarchical, non-democratic institutions such as universities. From experience, it is evident that some service users prioritise what is best for the movement, in which case an 'activist' identity overrides a 'research' identity. This is in direct contrast to the competitive and individualistic culture fostered and perpetuated by mainstream academia. As a fellow service-user researcher wondered, how can there be any solidarity among us when it matters so much whose name is first on the next research paper? By its very nature, the research context can undermine solidarity and collective identity. Some service-user researchers (e.g. Nicki, 2016) have managed to avoid these dynamics by examining and publishing purely autobiographical accounts of their own experiences of 'madness' and systemic oppression.

Pause for reflection

Do you think people with lived experience should always be included in mental health research? If you have your own experiences of mental distress, how might you draw on these while doing your own research in this area?

People with mental health difficulties are frequently vocationally disadvantaged by the lack of adjustments and understanding within the workplace (Shaw Trust, 2018). As a person who experiences distress consistent with post-traumatic stress disorder, it is more acceptable for me to say that I require time off work for a physical health problem rather than because I have experienced repeated nightmares and flashbacks for the past two weeks and have reached a point of mental exhaustion. Despite the protections offered under the *Equality Act 2010*, people with mental health problems remain heavily stigmatised in the workplace (Walton, 2003; Sainsbury Centre for Mental Health, 2007). Many service-user researchers, like myself, work part-time or on temporary contracts. We are excluded from more stable opportunities due to stigma and the episodic nature of mental distress. Additionally, there is currently no formal career progression for a 'service-user researcher'.

Despite the issues surrounding service-user research, the idea that 'mad' people could work in mental health academic contexts would have been unthinkable 30 years ago. This progress is to be celebrated. We have begun to reclaim mental health knowledge production.

We still, however, have a long way to go as Sarah Carr, a well-known service-user researcher, explains:

> 20 years later, does PPI merely serve to give a tokenistic competitive edge to nonuser-led academic studies, with patients and service users basically being positioned as factory hands in the psy industrial research complex? Are we marketable commodities? If so where does this leave service user and survivor researchers in academia, who want to be principal investigators, create new knowledge, have clear critical standpoints and may be grounded as activists in the service user and survivor movement? Does PPI as it is now constituted in England mean we shall always be the bridesmaid, but never the bride?
>
> (Carr, 2019, p. 1143)

Conclusion

The service-user movement encompasses a variety of individuals who have an array of experiences and identities. Although the movement began as a way of collectively resisting oppressive psychiatric practices, it has since evolved into something much broader. This includes the legitimisation of survivor knowledge as a distinctive epistemology, not merely in opposition to dominant discourses of psychiatry but as a unique discipline.

You may have lived experience of mental health difficulties yourself. Learning how to use these in a therapeutic context can be of enormous value. Taking time to understand your own distress is an essential part of becoming a skilled helper. As this chapter maintains, it is only by speaking out about our mental distress that we can begin to break down some of the social stigma attached to mental health issues.

It is important to understand the contexts and struggles endured by many people who have been through the mental health system. It is important that practitioners engage with service-users'/survivors' experiences, including by taking an active interest in current mental health activism. This improves practitioners' skills, making them more attuned to their clients' needs and, ultimately, more effective in their work.

Further reading

- The following text is an excellent resource for anyone wishing to go into the helping professions. It contains chapters written by both survivors and non-survivors, which all critically explore the role of mainstream psychiatry in mental healthcare:

  Watson, J. (ed.) (2019) *Drop the disorder! Challenging the culture of psychiatric diagnosis.* Monmouth: PCCS Books.

- This book provides a good summary of some of the issues around using lived experience in research and of being a service-user researcher:

  Sweeney, A., Beresford, P., Faulkner, A., Nettle, M. and Rose, D. (eds.) (2009) *This is survivor research.* Monmouth: PCCS Books.

- Romme *et al.* have produced a collection of first-person accounts of recovery from mental distress associated with hearing voices. It provides an interesting alternative perspective on schizophrenia:

  Romme, M., Escher, S., Dillon, J., Corstens, D. and Morris, M. (2009) *Living with voices: 50 stories of recovery.* Ross-on-Wye: PCCS Books.

References

Barak, A., Hen, L., Boniel-Nissim, M., and Shapira, N.A. (2008) 'A comprehensive review and a meta-analysis of the effectiveness of internet-based psychotherapeutic interventions'. *Journal of Technology in Human services*, 26(2–4), pp. 109–160.

Barr B., Taylor-Robinson, D., Stuckler, D., Loopstra, R., Reeves, A. and Whitehead, M. (2016) "First, do no harm': are disability assessments associated with adverse trends in mental health? A longitudinal ecological study', *Journal of Epidemiol Community Health*, 70(4), pp. 339–345.

Bartlett, A., Smith, G. and King, M. (2009) 'The response of mental health professionals to clients seeking help to change or redirect same-sex sexual orientation', *BMC Psychiatry*, 9(1), p. 11.

Basset, T., Faulkner, A., Repper, J. and Stamou, E. (2010) *Lived experience leading the way: peer support in mental health*. London: Together for Mental Wellbeing. Available at: https://www.together-uk.org/mental-health-resources/research (Accessed: 5 February 2020).

Bedei, C. (2016) *The mental health zines filling the gap that therapy doesn't*. Available at: https://www.dazeddigital.com/artsandculture/article/32004/1/the-mental-health-zines-filling-the-gap-that-therapy-doesn-t (Accessed: 20 January 2020).

Beresford, P. (2003) *It's our lives: a short theory of knowledge, distance and experience*. London: Citizen Press in association with Shaping Our Lives. Available at: https://shapingourlives.org.uk/wp-content/uploads/2015/03/ItsOurLives.pdf (Accessed: 5 February 2020).

Beresford, P. (2013) *Beyond the usual suspects, towards inclusive user involvement*. London: Shaping Our Lives.

Carr, S. (2019) "I am not your nutter': a personal reflection on commodification and comradeship in service user and survivor research', *Disability & Society*, 34(7–8), pp. 1140–1153. doi:10.1080/09687599.2019.1608424.

Castelein, S., Bruggeman, R., Van Busschbach, J.T., Van Der Gaag, M., Stant, A.D., Knegtering, H. and Wiersma, D. (2008) 'The effectiveness of peer support groups in psychosis: a randomized controlled trial', *Acta Psychiatrica Scandinavica*, 118(1), pp. 64–72. doi:10.1111/j.1600-0447.2008.01216.x.

Charlton, J.I. (2000) *Nothing about us without us: disability oppression and empowerment*. Berkeley and Los Angeles: University of California Press.

Christmas, D. and Sweeney, A. (2016) 'Service user, patient, survivor or client…has the time come to return to 'patient'?', *British Journal of Psychiatry*, 209(1), pp. 9–13. doi:10.1192/bjp.bp.115.167221.

Church, K. (1996) 'Beyond "bad manners": the power relations of "consumer participation" in Ontario's community mental health system', *Canadian Journal of Community Mental Health*, 15(2), pp. 27–44.

Department of Health (2005) *Department of Health Departmental Report 2005*. Cm 6254. London: TSO.

Faulkner, A. (2013) *Mental health peer support in England: piecing together the jigsaw*. London: Mind.

Faulkner, A., Yiannoullou, S., Kalathil, J., Crepaz-Keay, D., Singer, F., James, N. and Kallevik, J. (2015) *4PI National Involvement Standards*. London: National Survivor User Network (NSUN).

Feldman, B.M. (2018) 'The co-option and oppression of a social justice movement: professionalized peer support services', *Medium*. Available at: https://medium.com/@feldman.brooke.m/the-co-option-and-oppression-of-a-social-justice-movement-professionalized-peer-support-services-2b857903c150 (Accessed: 9 August 2019).

Gillard, S. and Holley, J. (2014) 'Peer workers in mental health services: literature overview', *Advances in Psychiatric Treatment*, 20(4), pp. 286–292.

Griffiths, T. (2019) *Austerity and NHS cuts: wrecking our mental health*. Available at: https://keepournhspublic.com/austerity-wrecking-mental-health/ (Accessed: 6 February 2020).

Harding, S. (1991) *Whose science? Whose knowledge? Thinking from women's lives*. New York: Cornell University Press.

Harrington, A. (2019) *Mind fixers: psychiatry's troubled search for the biology of mental illness*. New York: W.W. Norton.

Hornstein, G.A. (2017) *Agnes's jacket: a psychologist's search for the meanings of madness. Revised and updated with a new epilogue by the author*. New York: Routledge.

INVOLVE, National Institute for Health Research (2012) *Briefing notes for researchers: public involvement in NHS, public health and social care research*. UK: INVOLVE Eastleigh. Available at: https://www.invo.org.uk/wp-content/uploads/2014/11/9938_INVOLVE_Briefing_Notes_WEB.pdf (Accessed: 5 February 2020).

Jarrett, C. (2008) 'When therapy causes harm', *The Psychologist*, 21, pp. 10–12. Available at: https://thepsychologist.bps.org.uk/volume-21/edition-1/when-therapy-causes-harm (Accessed: 27 August 2019).

Kalathil, J. (2008) *Dancing to our own tunes: reassessing black and minority ethnic mental health service user involvement*. London: National Survivor User Network in collaboration with Catch-a-Fiya. (Accessed: 5 October 2019).

Kalathil, J. (2011) *Dancing to our own tunes: reassessing black and minority ethnic service user involvement, Reprint of the 2008 Report with a review of work to take the recommendations forward*. London: The Afiya Trust and National Survivor User Network (NSUN). Available at: https://www.academia.edu/3297509/

Dancing_to_our_own_tunes_Reassessing_black_and_minority_ethnic_mental_health_service_user_involvement (Accessed: 5 February 2020).

Kortteisto, T., Laitila, M. and Pitkänen, A. (2018) 'Attitudes of mental health professionals towards service user involvement', *Scandinavian Journal of Caring Sciences*, 32(2), pp. 681–689.

We're Not Mad…We're Angry! (1986) Directed by J. Hay. [Feature film]. United Kingdom: Multiple Image.

Munn-Giddings, C., Boyce, M., Smith, L. and Campbell, S. (2009) 'The innovative role of user-led organisations', *A Life in the Day*, 13(3), pp. 14–20.

Murphy, R. and Higgins, A. (2018) 'The complex terrain of peer support in mental health: what does it all mean?', *Journal of Psychiatric and Mental Health Nursing*, 25(7), pp. 441–448. doi:10.1111/jpm.12474.

National Survivor User Network (NSUN) (2017) *Members' manifesto 2017: our voice, our vision, our values*. Available at: https://www.nsun.org.uk/Handlers/Download.ashx?IDMF=f59be826-edaf-42b9-8294-725e56fc9b74 (Accessed: 12 August 2019).

Nicki, A. (2016) 'Borderline personality disorder, discrimination, and survivors of chronic childhood trauma', *IJFAB: International Journal of Feminist Approaches to Bioethics*, 9(1), pp. 218–245. doi:10.3138/ijfab.9.1.218.

Ocloo, J. and Matthews, R. (2016) 'From tokenism to empowerment: progressing patient and public involvement in healthcare improvement', *BMJ Quality and Safety*, 25(8), pp. 626–632. doi:10.1136/bmjqs-2015-004839.

Rose, N. (2018) *Our psychiatric future*. Chichester: John Wiley & Sons.

Roy, A. (2004) 'Arundhati Roy: the 2004 Sydney Peace Prize lecture', *Real Voice*, 8 November. Available at: https://realvoice.blogspot.com/2004/11/arundhati-roy-2004-sydney-peace-prize.html (Accessed: 20 July 2017).

Sinclair, A. (2018) 'Help yourself to our staff kitchen: a peer worker's reflections on microaggressions', *The Journal of Mental Health Training, Education and Practice*, 13(3), pp. 167–172. Available at: https://www.emerald.com/insight/content/doi/10.1108/JMHTEP-06-2017-0042/full/html. doi:10.1108/JMHTEP-06-2017-0042 (Accessed: 26 February 2020).

Sainsbury Centre for Mental Health (2007) *Mental Health at work: developing the business case*. Available at: http://www.impact.ie/wp-content/uploads/2015/07/Mental-Health-at-Work.pdf (Accessed: 23 November 2015).

Shaw Trust (2018) *Mental health at work: still the last taboo*. Bristol: Shaw Trust Policy Institute.

Stonewall (2015) *Unhealthy attitudes: the treatment of LGBT people within health and social care services*. London: Stonewall.

Voronka, J. (2019) 'Storytelling beyond the psychiatric gaze', *Canadian Journal of Disability Studies*, 8(4), pp. 8–30. Available at: https://cjds.uwaterloo.ca/index.php/cjds/article/view/522. (Accessed: 6 February 2020).

Wallcraft, J., Rose, D., Reid, J.J.A. and Sweeney, A. (2003) *On our own terms: users and survivors of mental health services working together for support and change*. London: The Sainsbury Centre for Mental Health.

Walton, L. (2003) 'Exploration of the attitudes of employees towards the provision of counselling within a profit-making organisation', *Counselling Psychotherapy Research*, 3(1), pp. 65–71.

Chapter 3

The history of the talking cure

Sarah Marks

Contents

Introduction

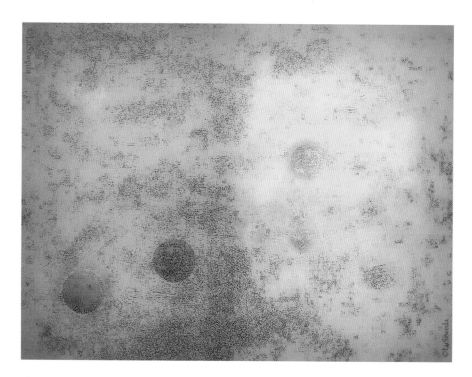

'Silence is enough' by Lu Szweda

Few today would challenge the argument that therapy should be made available to people experiencing mental health difficulties. Since the mid-twentieth century, therapeutic concepts and practices have become a common motif in everyday culture, from newspaper advice columns to prime-time television. But the idea that mental distress can be ameliorated through talking with a trained professional is a remarkably modern one. As a term, 'psychotherapy' has existed since the 1870s, but its original usage had a wider range of meanings than it does today, including an understanding that both mental and physical ailments could be cured by hypnosis and the suggestive power of an authoritative therapist figure (Carroy, 2000; Chaney, 2017; Shamdasani, 2005; Shamdasani, 2017).

As Chapter 1 explained, the suggestion that the mind could be cured without physical treatment (or religious intervention) only emerged in earnest towards the end of the eighteenth century, with the birth of moral treatment. Freud's invention of psychoanalysis further shifted the meaning of psychotherapy, through its unique focus on interpreting the patient's free associations, dream content and reminiscences of childhood, as well as how the patient behaved and felt towards the analyst. In contrast with histories of psychiatry, the volume of publications specifically on the history of psychotherapy is generally smaller and has tended to focus on the development of psychoanalysis at the expense of other approaches. This chapter will examine the impact of psychoanalysis on the development of psychotherapy, but it will also look more broadly at competing ideas which emerged later in the twentieth century, and which remain influential today.

Specifically, this chapter will map the development of three of the dominant approaches to psychotherapy:

- psychoanalysis and psychodynamic psychotherapies

- cognitive and behavioural therapies

- Rogerian counselling and the humanistic tradition.

The chapter will argue that historical research suggests we need to understand how such practices emerge within, and are shaped by, particular social and political contexts, and how psychotherapeutic knowledge has, in turn, impacted on the modern world, changing the way we understand ourselves in relation to each other.

This chapter aims to:

- outline the development of the psychodynamic approach, including the influence of Freud's Oedipus complex theory and the therapeutic concept of transference

- introduce the cognitive behavioral therapies, outlining their evolution away from the 'unconscious mind' towards observable behavioral responses

- introduce the person-centered and humanistic approaches, with their emphasis on personal growth and self-actualisation.

---

1 Psychoanalysis and the birth of the psychodynamic traditions

Various forms of **psychotherapy** predated **psychoanalysis**, but Sigmund Freud's work offered a new form of therapeutic 'talking cure', which arguably shaped all subsequent forms of psychotherapy. Freud was a medically trained Viennese doctor who self-described as a neurologist. Freud encountered the idea of unconscious suggestion and psychotherapy through the work of his contemporary, Hyppolyte Bernheim, a French neurologist with an interest in the power of hypnotism. His curiosity for the subject was augmented by a study trip to the Parisian Salpêtrière hospital in 1895, under the mentorship of the celebrated neurologist Jean-Marie Charcot. Charcot was conducting research into a nervous illness associated with convulsions, emotional outbursts and odd or dramatic physical gestures, classed at the time as hysteria. He conducted experiments with hypnosis on hysteria patients, and claimed that the ability to be hypnotised was itself a symptom of hysteria. He believed there was a hereditary disposition towards susceptibility to hysteria, but challenged other doctors who saw it as a disease of the female reproductive system, arguing that it could also affect male patients who had undergone some form of trauma (Goldstein, 1987; Libbrecht and Quackelbeen, 1995). These cases enthralled the young Freud who, on this return to Vienna, began to elaborate on Charcot's ideas. Inspired by the case of his friend Josef Breuer's patient, Freud contended that hysteria was caused by underlying mental conflicts related to sexual trauma.

In 1880 Breuer began treating Anna O (a pseudonym for Bertha Pappenheim), shown in Figure 3.1. Anna suffered from symptoms including paralysis, aphasia (loss of speech), amnesia and visual disturbances, and was eventually diagnosed with hysteria. During her consultations with Breuer, Anna O became preoccupied by reminiscences: discussing memories of significant relationships from her past, particularly her childhood, appeared to have a cathartic effect, and therefore a therapeutic benefit.

Psychotherapy
The use of a wide range of techniques, usually involving regular interpersonal meetings with a therapist, to work through emotional or behavioural difficulties in order to improve mental health or well-being.

Psychoanalysis
A form of long-term, one-to-one talking therapy developed by Sigmund Freud and his followers since the 1890s. It focuses on examining unconscious feelings, thoughts and desires, particularly through analysing transference.

Figure 3.1 Anna O

Freud also became intrigued by Anna O's expression of erotic feelings towards Breuer, which made Breuer highly uncomfortable. Freud posited that these desires were not in fact about Breuer specifically, but were redirected projections of impulses towards other significant people in her life. By analysing and interpreting this 'transference', as he came to call it, Freud suggested that patients might better understand and cope with their unconscious conflicts (Pick, 2015).

Psychoanalytic theory
A set of concepts and ideas underlying psychoanalytic practice, including theories about the structure of the conscious and unconscious mind, the emotional legacies of childhood relationships with parents, and sexual development.

This focus on transference was core to **psychoanalytic theory** and is the main feature distinguishing the so-called psychodynamic therapies (which adopt a more widespread and less intensive derivative of traditional psychoanalysis; the psychodynamic approach will be covered in Chapter 9). In 1896 Freud first used the term 'psychoanalysis' to distinguish this new approach from suggestion-based psychotherapies and went on to develop his thinking through a series of written case histories, which came to be known by their subjects: Little Hans, Dora, The Rat Man and The Wolf Man (Gay, 1988; Shamdasani, 2017).

Methodology: The 'case study' in the history of psychotherapy

Different traditions in psychotherapy have radically different philosophical underpinnings and divert from each other with regard to their norms of clinical practice. But if we look at them comparatively, the central role of the case study, or case history, is a striking continuity. Case histories are empirical records of research into the development of a person, usually in a real-life setting. This is one aspect that characterises psychotherapy as being different from experimental psychology, as the latter makes use of a very different type of evidence, which is reproducible through experiments.

The recording and publishing of case histories is not unique to psychotherapy, however, having been a common trope in medical writing for centuries. Just as in medicine, they provide a format for communicating clinical work to colleagues, and a textual basis for training new recruits to the profession. John Forrester pointed out the dual purpose of the case history for Freud and his followers: it served to show how people conform to common drivers and motivations, but 'what many find most seductive in psychoanalysis is its promise to give an account of the divergences, the detours, the idiosyncrasies of the individual's life' (Forrester, 2017, p. 11). Freud wrote five long-form case studies in a literary style, which became an important part of the canon of psychoanalysis and laid out key theoretical concepts in context. Although case histories are still used in psychoanalysis, this long-form genre became less common after the theoretical concepts became accepted (Sealey, 2011).

Person-centred therapy also made use of large-scale analysis of multiple cases to find patterns that applied across all examples. From these, Carl Rogers abstracted six core concepts of 'what it means to become a person': the experience of feeling, the discovery of self in experience, openness to experience, trust in one's organism, an internal locus of evaluation, and willingness to be a process (Rogers, 1967).

Rogers' book *Counselling and psychotherapy* (1942) broke new ground as it contained a long transcript of the case of one client, Herbert Bryan, covering the eight sessions he had with Rogers.

The recording of interviews became commonplace among the person-centred tradition and was seen to be important not only as a way of transmitting the approach to others, but also as a matter of transparency and external validation. By laying bare the full account of an interview, the reader could assess whether they agreed with Rogers' approach and conclusions about the case (Raskin, 1996).

Cognitive and behavioural therapists also make use of case studies, for example by recording sessions for peer review and commentary. Unlike in the original psychoanalytic cases, where idiosyncrasy and diversions were a key feature, case studies are now sometimes presented as composites, partly because of modern concerns about confidentiality and to protect the identity of the individuals, but also because of the increasing focus on exemplary details rather than on individual stories in their own terms.

Oedipus complex
A concept suggested by Freud describing a young child's unconscious desire towards one of their (usually same-sex) parents and consequent feelings of rivalry and jealousy towards the other parent. Regarded as a key developmental stage.

Psychosexual development
Freud's framework for describing the development of a child's sexuality in five stages as their sexual drives become associated with different body parts. The stages are: oral, anal, phallic, latency and genital.

Initially, Freud thought hysteria patients were recapitulating memories of sexual abuse from childhood, which became known as his so-called 'seduction theory'. He came to question this, however, and suspected that instead of memories, some of the unconscious material that was being presented may instead have been fantasy. This precipitated his invention of the **Oedipus complex** to denote the love-relationships and rivalries that young children struggle with in relation to their parents; expressions of infantile sexuality that would go on to shape relationships later in life. (His appropriation of Sophocles' *Oedipus Rex* was one of many Classical references borrowed and refigured for explanatory purposes, and which added to the literary texture of his theories.) Freud also began to trace the stages of a child's **psychosexual development** and claimed that the origins of anxieties in adult life had their roots in how these stages were negotiated in the person's early years (Gay, 1988).

If there is one aspect of psychotherapy that historians have attended to, it is psychoanalysis, and Freud himself in particular. Some, notably Carl Schorske, have pondered the particular reasons why such a concept of mind would emerge at that moment. Schorske situated Freud as part of an efflorescence of creative cultural production which broke away from the past towards a new modernist way of thinking that was less concerned with rationality and more with the emotional side of the psyche. While Freud was listening to the patients who lay on his therapy couch in Berggasse, literary figures such as Hugo von Hoffmannsthal and Arthur Schnitzler were frequenting nearby coffeehouses, along with revolutionary artists such as Gustav Klimt. At the turn of the century, Vienna was the cultural crucible in which a new, modern concept of 'psychological man' was forged (Schorske, 1980).

Others have focused more on continuities, showing how Freud's ideas emerged from tropes that existed in nineteenth-century science, from evolutionary theory to German sexology (Makari, 2008; Sulloway, 1979). More critical historians have questioned the scientific credentials of Freud's practice, characterising his interpretations of patients' unconscious material as spurious. Such critics suggested that the relationship between the analyst and the patient was tainted by the power of suggestion, and drew attention to the careful ways in which Freud created psychoanalysis as a brand with its own centrally controlled training (Borch-Jacobsen and Shamdasani, 2012; Gellner, 1985).

Psychoanalysis quickly gained momentum, first at Freud's own Wednesday evening meetings, beginning in 1902, which attracted visitors and trainee analysts from across Europe, including well-known names such as Carl Jung, Sabina Spielrein, Alfred Adler and Sandor Ferenczi. This was later formalised as the Vienna Psychoanalytic Society. A process of training, which required new analysts to undergo a personal analysis carried out by an existing psychoanalyst became the only route to legitimate practice. This resulted in a complex network of psychoanalysts linked to each other not only as colleagues with collegial relationships, but also through emotional and transferential relationships (Falzeder, 2015).

Despite his attempts to unify the movement, it was not long before personal splits and theoretical rifts also began to emerge among Freud's early disciples. Jung was the first to break away in 1913, challenging Freud's focus on sexuality and developing a theory of a shared **collective unconscious**. This theory drew on symbolic collective archetypes of myth and fairytale and had a heavier emphasis on cultural, spiritual and ancestral dimensions than Freud's focus on the individual unconscious (Shamdasani, 2003). Jung's ideas went on to inspire a range of psychotherapeutic approaches, from a Jungian school of analytic psychology through to artistic and creative therapies (Samuels, 1985). Alfred Adler also broke away, forming his own school

Collective unconscious
A concept suggested by Carl Jung to describe unconscious structures of the mind shared by all members of a species or group. These included instincts and universal symbols identified in myth and folklore, which he termed 'archetypes'.

of individual psychotherapy which, while it maintained a psychodynamic commitment to the idea of transference, overturned some Freudian motifs, notably abandoning Freud's signature therapy couch in favour of two chairs (Ansbacher and Ansbacher, 1964).

Freud's influence continued to loom large, however, and informed a variety of innovations in psychiatric and psychotherapeutic thinking later in the twentieth century. Many analysts, including Freud himself, emigrated to western Europe and the Americas after Nazism swept across central Europe. They made significant contributions to the psychoanalytic societies that had already begun to emerge there. In London during the Second World War, vociferous debates about the nature of the child's unconscious broke out between followers of Anna Freud and those of Melanie Klein respectively, with child analysis becoming an increasingly important practice in its own right (Zaretsky, 2005). The post-war period also became a time of experimentation with group analysis and saw the development of concepts about the nature of group dynamics and their implications for politics and society at the wider level (Bion, 2014). In the US, psychoanalysis became heavily integrated into the medical profession, and flourished in the post-war decades (Hale, 1995). More recently, historians have come to examine the misappropriation of psychoanalytic ideas, and sometimes even practice, for coercive political purposes during the cold war and under authoritarian regimes, reminding us of the potential that psychotherapy has for misuse (Damousi and Plotkin, 2012; Müller, 2016; ffytche and Pick, 2016).

To this day, on both sides of the Atlantic, Freudian and psychodynamic approaches based on ideas about transference and unconscious conflicts continue to inform psychotherapeutic training and practice, as well as wider culture and intellectual life, from film studies to literary theory. But from the mid-twentieth century, the psychoanalytic tradition was subject to fierce competition from two other key schools of psychotherapy: cognitive and behavioural therapies, and humanistic therapies.

2   Cognitive and behavioural therapies

Cognitive behavioural therapy (CBT) is classically dated back to the work of Aaron Beck, whose book *Cognitive therapy of depression* (Beck *et al.*, 1979) among others, is a foundational text for the field. Others fly the flag for Albert Ellis, a contemporary and colleague of Beck's, who was arguably the first to coin the tripartite term 'cognitive behavioural therapy' in 1969, in an article in the *International Journal of Psychiatry* (Ellis, 1969). Others still, particularly in Britain, make the case that the foundation of CBT also rested on earlier practices of behaviour therapy developed in the 1950s, which included processes such as desensitisation and exposure and – most controversially – aversion. Some proponents of CBT have also looked back to historical antecedents to argue that current methods are part of a much longer tradition in western thought. Examples include the early twentieth-century rational therapy of the Swiss psychotherapist Paul DuBois, and even the classical writings of Stoic philosophers such as Epictetus (Dryden and Still, 2012). This section of the chapter will outline these different trajectories while summarising some of the emerging historiography on CBT.

2.1   The emergence of behaviour therapies

Behaviour therapies emerged in the 1950s, predominantly in the US and Britain. They arose out of a particular approach to human nature that saw it as similar to that of other animals: just as in any other species, behaviours are learnt through a process of **conditioning**. Animal behaviourists were able to show that behaviours could also be 'unlearnt', and therefore, so too could unwanted or maladaptive patterns of behaviour, such as anxieties, phobias and compulsions. Conditioning rested on the premise that it is behaviour (rather than underlying thoughts, feelings and experiences) that should be the target for change. It focused on changing present behaviours rather than on analysing past experiences. This made behaviourism a more immediate approach to mental distress and meant that results were observable.

There were two main theories of conditioning. The first, classical conditioning, was associated with the Russian physiologist Ivan Pavlov and the American psychologist John Watson (O'Donnell, 1985). It posited that behavioural responses were conditioned by the creation of associations in the brain and nervous system, such as a dog which

Cognitive behavioural therapy
A collection of therapeutic techniques that has gained prominence since the 1960s. CBT aims to address maladaptive beliefs and behaviours and is based on both behaviour modification and cognitive approaches. There is often overlap between the use of the terms 'cognitive behavioural therapy', 'cognitive behavioural therapies' and 'cognitive therapy'.

Conditioning
A process of learning by association whereby particular behaviours or beliefs become reinforced through repeated association with a stimulus (classical conditioning) or through reward or punishment (operant conditioning).

salivated on hearing a buzzer because it associated this sound with the imminent arrival of food. The second theory, operant conditioning, was associated with B.F. Skinner (1953) and focused on how behaviours could be modified through reward and punishment.

Behaviour therapies emerged from a particular theoretical strain in the human sciences, but their success was also in part due to a number of other factors particular to the mid-twentieth century. This period saw vociferous debates about the philosophical assumptions that undergirded psychoanalysis, as a new generation of psychologists and psychiatrists wanted to ground psychotherapies in (what they saw as) a more scientific and experimental approach. **Behaviourism** was a particularly alluring world view to those who wanted to explicitly break away from a psychology that rested on human introspection and towards one built on observation and measurement. This was at a time when optimism about the possibilities of applied science was at its height (Marks, 2015). By not addressing the difficult problems of both conscious and unconscious processes and focusing on what could be externally observed, behavioural psychology – and therefore behaviour therapy – was presented as a rigorous, experimentally provable alternative. Its proponents also argued that it could be delivered within a particular timeframe and was therefore more efficient and cost-effective than psychoanalytic approaches. But the fact that many people were still fascinated by the human experience of consciousness – and, indeed, of the unconscious – limited the popularity of behaviourism.

Behaviourism
A theory of human and animal psychology, popular in the mid-twentieth century, that focuses on observable behaviours that can be explained and changed through learning and conditioning, rather than through unconscious drives and conflicts.

Pause for reflection

Thinking back to the principles of psychotherapy, can you think of any other reasons why behaviourism may have been less popular than other therapies? How might people have perceived the nature of behaviourist principles, with the prioritisation of rapid behaviour changes over personal introspection?

One reason for behaviour therapy's limited success was its association with 'mind control' and coercion. Hans Eysenck – an outspoken London-based German clinical psychologist, and a strong proponent of behavioural therapies – openly admitted that behavioural therapy shared the same techniques as those used in brainwashing. The difference, he claimed, was that the former was being used for a benevolent purpose (Eysenck, 1964). While it might be difficult to understand the association with brainwashing in relation to, for example, desensitising phobic patients, the use of aversion treatments with homosexual or cross-dressing subjects is a dark passage in the overall history of the CBT tradition. Regardless of whether or not the treatment conformed to the ethical norms of the day, it should not be overlooked as part of the history of psychotherapy and reminds us that the clinical setting is always vulnerable to the possibility of coercion. Although testimonies of these cases have been publicly reported, there is little discussion of them today. This suggests that some level of acknowledgement and reconciliation is needed to move beyond the difficult chapters of the profession's past (Dickinson, 2014)

2.2 The rise of cognitive behavioural therapy

Figure 3.2 Aaron Beck

CBT emerged in the 1960s, associated most closely with Aaron Beck (shown in Figure 3.2) and Albert Ellis (Beck *et al.*, 1979; Ellis, 1969). There were some important differences in their approaches: Ellis' rational emotive behaviour therapy took a more confrontational, challenging approach to the client's irrational beliefs, while Beck's preferred method enabled clients to see the irrationality for themselves. However, the approaches shared the core theoretical claim that people's difficulties are produced by strongly held, maladaptive beliefs and automatic thoughts, which were most likely learnt in familial and social environments. The merging of these 'cognitive' approaches with behavioural approaches happened gradually over the course of the 1960s and 1970s. Beck and Ellis were also interested in their therapies changing behaviour, as well as thoughts. Despite the apparent theoretical shift away from behaviourism in terms of the focus on internal thoughts and beliefs, some behavioural therapists embraced these new techniques. They saw that the fundamental emphasis of both approaches was still about learning and conditioning.

In the 1960s, both Beck and Ellis developed their techniques through practice by a process of client observation and by questioning the psychoanalytic theory of depression, in which they had previously been schooled. Their understanding of emotional disorders was built around the idea that depressive or anxious states were caused by a flaw in thought processing. Clients could be reasoned out of these unhelpful patterns of thinking through a process of interpersonal or group therapy, along with written exercises, reading and even (in Ellis' case) therapeutic song lyrics for clients to sing to popular tunes.

This should also be viewed against the background of the 'cognitive revolution' in psychology in the 1960s, when information processing metaphors, driven by early computer technology, were used to challenge the previously dominant behaviourist approach to the mind (Baars, 1986). That said, neither Beck nor Ellis were actively reading developments in non-clinical academic psychology at the time, and it cannot be claimed that cognitive therapy was a direct application of cognitive science. It is perhaps no accident, though, that the image of the brain as an information processing machine came to be a prevalent concept in cultural discourse at the same time that cognitive therapy emerged.

Unlike psychoanalysis, it has only been in very recent years that CBT has begun to be historicised. Historian Rachael Rosner, through carefully researching Beck's archival papers and extensive oral history interviews, has challenged the orthodox narrative that paints cognitive therapy as a rejection of psychoanalysis. As psychoanalysis – deemed outdated and inefficient – was phased out by the psychology department at the University of Pennsylvania where Beck worked, he had to generate new, scientifically valid approaches that would satisfy his superiors. His formulation of cognitive therapy allowed this, but while Beck agrees that he became disillusioned by the limitations of psychoanalysis during this time, he himself still saw cognitive therapy as essentially neo-Freudian. This may be disturbing to the identity of many CBT practitioners who see their approach as fundamentally different from, and superior to, psychoanalysis (Rosner, 2014).

Rosner has also written about Beck's approach to 'manualising' therapy by delivering it in a way that was amenable to randomised control trials and evidence-based medicine. It became increasingly important to show that a particular psychotherapeutic approach could be evaluated to the same gold standard as other types of medicine. This developed as the Food and Drug Administration became a more powerful regulatory body, following the public outcry over the thalidomide crisis in the 1960s. It was in parallel with this that Beck designed methods to prove CBT's efficacy (Rosner, 2018). In England and Wales, where the government-funded NHS already favoured randomised control trial data, CBT would become the gold standard.

The National Institute for Health and Care Excellence (NICE), after it was established in the UK in 1999, set out national guidelines for the treatment of particular conditions based on cost–benefit analysis and evidence of efficacy. Consequently, clinical psychologists set about providing evidence to ensure that CBT was included in the guidelines for the treatment of depression, alongside pharmacological interventions (NICE, 2004; Marks, 2015). But it took another few years before substantial government investment was made into the expansion of CBT, predominantly as a result of the initiative of the 'happiness' economist and Labour peer Richard Layard, who was concerned at the population-level effect of long-term anxiety and depression on national unemployment (Marks, 2015; Layard, 2011; Pickersgill, 2019). The invention and rise of cognitive behavioural therapies have been inextricably bound up with the increasing importance of evidence and economic efficiency in healthcare and, although the UK and the US have different systems for funding access to psychotherapy, their focus on randomised control trials goes some way to account for why they readily foster these approaches.

The success of cognitive and behavioural therapies has seen a number of other approaches – from mindfulness meditation to eye-movement desensitisation and reprocessing therapy – take shelter under the umbrella of 'third-wave' CBT. This suggests that the repertoire of psychotherapy is now much broader than merely a talking cure, with a wide range of approaches making use of the label.

3 Person-centred and humanistic approaches

The person-centred tradition, sometimes also referred to as the 'humanistic' tradition as it drew from **humanistic psychology**, emerged predominantly in the 1940s and became one of the most popular alternatives to psychoanalytic and psychodynamic psychotherapies in the twentieth century. It was built on the philosophical principles of optimism about human nature and potential; non-directive and non-authoritarian approaches to the therapeutic encounter; and hope that emotional insight would reduce conflict at both an interpersonal and international level (relevant in the wake of the Second World War and to the anxieties of the cold war). Like most traditions in psychotherapy, the person-centred approach is strongly associated with a founding father – Carl Rogers is at the centre of most of the historical literature, which is still predominantly written by practitioners from within the field (such as Kirschenbaum, 1979; Kirschenbaum and Henderson, 1989; Rogers, 1967).

Rogers drew from an eclectic range of influences. Historian Christopher Harding has pointed out that he spent time training for Christian ministry (Harding, 2018). Immediately after his BA in History from the University of Wisconsin in 1924, Rogers began at the Union Theological Seminary in New York, and spent time as a visiting pastor in Vermont in 1925. He quickly became disillusioned with the seminary's teaching and this crisis of faith led to his conversion to **clinical psychology**, which he formally began to study at Columbia University in the same year (Jones-Smith, 2016). Nevertheless, Rogers maintained an interest in Christian thought and, in 1965, he put himself in public dialogue with the theologian Paul Tillich. To Rogers, the most important emotional resources available to a person came from the human rather than the divine. Nevertheless, such dialogues showed a willingness to engage with spiritual ideas, as well as the resonances and parallels that person-centred counselling had with Christian thought and pastoral practice (Harding, 2018).

Rogers' own person-centred philosophy later in life had secular origins, drawing heavily from thought in biology and the sciences. The son of a farmer, Rogers had spent his childhood poring over agricultural science books, learning about control trials for crops and the underlying biological principles of plant and livestock management. By his own

Humanistic psychology
An approach to psychology and psychotherapy that focuses on individual uniqueness, human agency, and personal growth and fulfilment. It challenges the deterministic aspects of behaviourism and psychoanalysis.

Clinical psychology
A professional specialism in psychology. It is an 'applied' branch of psychology in that clinical psychologists work directly with clients, offering therapy but also performing many other roles in mental health services.

reckoning, this early self-schooling was highly influential on his later career (Rogers, 1967). The curative power of psychotherapy, for Rogers, lay in its capacity to help an individual gain insight into their authentic self, and to remove obstacles to achieving their potential through **self-actualisation**. This type of language was especially resonant in the mid-twentieth century owing to the popularity of existentialist thinkers. However, Rogers appears to have encountered ideas about personal growth and potential through reflection on biological thought, including the work of the Nobel Prize-winning Hungarian biochemist Albert Szent-Györgyi, who argued that the universe, and all organic life, had a tendency towards increased order, growth and development (Szent-Györgyi, 1957). For Rogers, this creative drive forward was a fundamental part of human nature, and it was this force that needed to be facilitated in the therapeutic encounter (Raskin, 1996).

Self-actualisation
A concept associated with humanistic psychology by which an individual is enabled to fulfil their potential and meaning in life, and to realise their personal talents.

Activity 3.1: Psychotherapeutic approaches and historical context

Allow about 15 minutes

Do psychoanalysis, cognitive behavioural therapies and person-centred approaches have fundamentally different ideas about how the human mind works? Do these reflect the historical period and culture from which they emerged?

Discussion

Modern psychotherapists sometimes draw on an eclectic range of models and techniques, adapting their approaches to the needs of the client. It is worth reflecting on the different ideas that these traditions developed about the mind's structure and function. Psychoanalytic and psychodynamic approaches placed great emphasis on unconscious drivers and transference, whereas CBT and person-centred approaches emerged in contrast to these ideas, focusing more on conscious thoughts, feelings and behaviours. What might unite all of these different approaches? They all value the process of talking through the client's experiences with a trained therapist, and all have a focus on trying to understand the mental obstacles and conflicts that may be causing an individual difficulties or impeding an authentic life. While psychodynamic approaches have the strongest focus on early childhood experiences and the way they shape later life, both CBT and humanistic approaches also ask how beliefs and ideas learnt in childhood can affect a person, especially if they cause difficulties in functioning or impede self-actualisation.

Historians have shown that Freud's ideas emerged at a particular moment in late nineteenth-century Vienna, when European ideas about hypnosis and suggestion were popular and provided a basis for thinking about the unconscious. Psychoanalytic ideas have been more popular in some cultures than others, and have enjoyed a rise and fall in popularity. CBT emerged as a challenge to psychoanalysis at a time when economics and politics put an emphasis on the measurability of effectiveness, as they still do. Person-centred approaches reached the height of their popularity in the US in the 1960s and 1970s, when ideas about personal fulfilment and potential had widespread social currency. This may suggest that ideas about psychotherapy are specific to certain times and places rather than being universal and timeless truths, and that it is important to consider the wider social, cultural and economic reasons why some approaches become more influential in particular contexts.

Rogers had a number of allies who shared his general world view. In 1963, along with existential psychotherapist Rollo May and esteemed psychologist Abraham Maslow, he co-founded the Association for Humanistic Psychology. He also collaborated with colleagues of a communitarian and democratic orientation and began to experiment with and develop group therapies, including encounter groups. These became highly popular in the 1970s and remain a key tool in the psychotherapeutic toolbox to this day (Rogers, 1973).

One of Rogers' own mentees, Nathaniel Raskin, reflected on the humanistic movement in the 1990s to account for its successes and failures. From the 1960s, Rogers benefited from operating outside of a university context, which gave him freedom to develop his practice without the restrictions of delivering teaching. Raskin argues that, as a result, person-centred approaches didn't have the institutional support or respect that other traditions, particularly behavioural therapies, were able to mobilise. Organisationally, the movement was also unusual, holding regular meetings without hierarchical positions and elected officers. Instead it opted for a more volunteer-based system and the inclusion of egalitarian, unstructured 'community meetings' at conferences, in the spirit of Rogers' anti-authoritarian approach (Raskin, 1996).

Despite this unorthodox approach, Rogers and others – notably G.T. Barrett-Lennard – had always been keen to make their approaches viable for academic psychology through measurement, testing and inventories, in order to provide sets of data for theory-building and evaluation. One such method was the Q-technique, developed by William Stephenson in the 1950s, to measure human subjectivity. This involved the client ordering statements about their personality from 'least characteristic of me' to 'most characteristic of me' at different points during the therapeutic process. Using this technique, Rogers showed that a person's perceived sense of self changed as a consequence of therapy, and was more likely to become aligned with their ideal self (Rogers and Dymond, 1954; Raskin, 1996). That said, by the turn of the twenty-first century, the comparative lack of enthusiasm for empirical trials among the person-centred community had resulted in it being less influential in socialised healthcare and insurance-based services than cognitive and behavioural approaches.

There are, nonetheless, degrees to which psychotherapy, and counselling more broadly, have been shaped by Rogers' philosophy, particularly in the move towards understanding service users as 'clients' rather than 'patients', and democratic ideas around collaboration between service users and service providers. The shift in focus away from concepts of medicalised illness towards the idea of 'problems of living' has also profoundly resonated with the rising well-being agenda. Rogerian language was arguably more accessible than psychoanalysis and behaviourism, as it relied less on jargon and complex theories of the mind and development. This vernacular approach facilitated the dissemination of humanistic psychology outside the clinic. The motifs and attitudes of the person-centred movement were taken up widely in late twentieth-century US and elsewhere, as they coincided with a wider cultural impetus for personal growth and self-improvement, and challenges to traditional social hierarchies and authority. These cultural themes are still prevalent, and humanistic psychology is a key part of the story of psychotherapy (Grogan, 2012).

Conclusion

This chapter has reconstructed some of the key moments and movements in the history of psychotherapy as a practice. It has examined the precursors to modern-day psychotherapy, including the widespread fascination with hypnosis and unconscious suggestion in the nineteenth century. Until Freud, psychotherapy was focused more on unconscious suggestions made by authority figures than on analysing the content of a patient's own words. The birth of psychoanalysis saw a shift towards free association and the examination of unconscious transference from the patient's early relationships towards the analyst, which forms the basic underlying idea for the psychodynamic tradition in psychotherapy.

Behavioural and cognitive therapies departed from psychoanalysis, rejecting the idea of an unconscious mind. In the 1950s, behaviour modification emerged to treat phobias and anxiety, drawing on learning and conditioning theories to change an individual's associations and responses to stimuli. It was also deployed for unethical purposes including the 'treatment' of homosexuality. In the 1960s, CBT approaches began to emerge in the US, which focused on rationally challenging the automatic thoughts that contribute to negative patterns of thinking. CBT became successful worldwide, partly because it was amenable to randomised control trials that could provide an evidence base for its efficacy.

This chapter has traced the history of the humanistic approaches, which first emerged in response to the Second World War. It showed how Carl Rogers' person-centred ideas developed through engagement with various influences, from religion and biology to democratic thought, and the impact that these ideas had on popular culture in post-war US and elsewhere.

Finally, this chapter discussed the types of evidence that different schools of psychotherapy have drawn on, both to build new theories and practices and to defend and popularise their approaches.

Further reading

- This collection of chapters gives a brief overview of the development of a variety of different psychotherapeutic traditions: Dryden, W. (ed.) (1996) *Developments in psychotherapy: historical perspectives.* London: Sage.

- This open-access article discusses debates about the history of psychotherapy and its meanings, and some of the recent literature published on the topic:

  Marks, S. (2017) 'Psychotherapy in historical perspective', *History of the Human Sciences*, 30(2), pp. 3–16. doi:10.1177/0952695117703243.

- The following text provides an accessible introduction to psychoanalysis as a practice and theoretical framework. It includes an overview of its historical development:

  Pick, D. (2015) *Psychoanalysis: a very short introduction.* Oxford: Oxford University Press.

References

Ansbacher, H. and Ansbacher, R. (eds.) (1964) *The individual psychology of Alfred Adler: a systematic presentation in selections from his writings*. New York: Harper Perennial.

Baars, B. (1986) *The cognitive revolution in psychology*. New York and London: The Guilford Press.

Beck, A., John Rush, A., Shaw, B. and Emery, G. (1979) *Cognitive therapy of depression*. New York: The Guilford Press.

Bion, W. (2014) *The complete works of Wilfred Bion*. Edited by C. Mawson. London: Karnac Books.

Borch-Jacobsen, M. and Shamdasani, S. (2012) *The Freud files: an inquiry into the history of psychoanalysis*. Cambridge: Cambridge University Press.

Carroy, J. (2000) 'L'invention du mot de psychothérapie et ses enjeux' [The invention of the word psychotherapy and its issues], *Psychologie Clinique*, 9, pp. 11–30.

Chaney, S. (2017) 'The action of the imagination: Daniel Hack Tuke and late Victorian psycho-therapeutics', *History of the Human Sciences*, 30(2), pp. 17–33.

Damousi, J. and Plotkin, M. (2012) *Psychoanalysis and politics: histories of psychoanalysis under conditions of restricted political freedom*. New York: Oxford University Press.

Dickinson, T. (2014) *'Curing queers': mental nurses and their patients, 1935–1974*. Manchester: Manchester University Press.

Dryden, W. and Still, A. (2012) *The historical and philosophical context of rational psychotherapy: the legacy of Epictetus*. London and New York: Karnac Books Ltd.

Ellis, A. (1969) 'A cognitive approach to behaviour therapy', *International Journal of Psychiatry*, 8(6), pp. 896–900.

Eysenck, H. (1964) 'The nature of behaviour therapy', in Eysenck, H. (ed.) *Experiments in behaviour therapy*. Oxford: Pergamon Press, p. 1–15.

Falzeder, E. (2015) *Psychoanalytic filiations: mapping the psychoanalytic movement*. London: Karnac Books.

ffytche, M. and Pick, D. (eds.) (2016) *Psychoanalysis in the age of totalitarianism*. London and New York: Routledge.

Forrester, J. (2017) *Thinking in cases*. Cambridge: Polity Press.

Gay, P. (1988) *Freud: a life for our times*. London: J.M. Dent & Sons.

Gellner, E. (1985) *The psychoanalytic movement: the cunning of unreason*. London: Paladin.

Goldstein, J. (1987) *Console and classify: the French psychiatric profession in the nineteenth century*. New York: Cambridge University Press.

Grogan, J. (2012) *Encountering America: humanistic psychology, sixties culture and the shaping of the modern self*. New York: Harper.

Hale, N. (1995) *The rise and crisis of psychoanalysis in the United States: Freud and the Americans, 1917–85*. New York: Oxford University Press.

Harding, C. (2018) 'Buddhism, Christianity, and psychotherapy: a three-way conversation in the mid-twentieth century', *European Journal of Psychotherapy & Counselling*, 20(1), pp. 62–75.

Jones-Smith, E. (2016) *Theories of counselling and psychotherapy: an integrative approach*. London: Sage.

Kirschenbaum, H. (1979) *On becoming Carl Rogers*. New York: Delacorte Press.

Kirschenbaum, H. and Henderson, V. (eds.) (1989) *The Carl Rogers reader*. London: Robinson.

Layard, R. (2011) *Happiness: lessons from a new science*. 2nd edn. London: Penguin.

Libbrecht, K. and Quackelbeen, J. (1995) 'On the early history of male hysteria and psychic trauma. Charcot's influence on Freudian thought', *Journal of the History of the behavioural sciences*, 31(4), pp. 370–384.

Makari, G. (2008) *Revolution in mind: the creation of psychoanalysis*. London: Gerald Duckworth & Co.

Marks, S. (2015) 'Psychologists as therapists: the development of behavioural traditions in clinical psychology', in Hall, J., Pilgrim, D. and Turpin, G. (eds.) *Clinical psychology in Britain: historical perspectives*. Leicester: British Psychological Society, pp. 194–207.

Müller, K. (2016) 'Psychoanalysis and American intelligence since 1940: unexpected liaisons', in ffycthe, M. and Pick, D. (eds.) *Psychoanalysis in the age of totalitarianism*. London: Routledge, pp. 55–70.

National Institute for Health and Care Excellence (NICE) (2004) *Depression: management of depression in primary and secondary care*. London: National Institute for Clinical Excellence.

O'Donnell, J. (1985) *The origins of behaviorism: American psychology, 1870–1920*. New York: NYU Press.

Pick, D. (2015) *Psychoanalysis: a very short introduction*. Oxford: Oxford University Press.

Pickersgill, M. (2019) 'Access, accountability, and the proliferation of psychological therapy: on the introduction of the IAPT initiative and the transformation of mental healthcare', *Social Studies of Science*, 49(4), pp. 627–650.

Raskin, N.J. (1996) 'Person-centred psychotherapy: twenty historical steps', in Dryden, W. (ed.) *Developments in psychotherapy: historical perspectives*. London: Sage, pp. 1–28. .

Rogers, C. (1942) *Counselling and psychotherapy: newer concepts in practice*. Massachusetts: Houghton Mifflin Company. Available at: https://archive.org/details/counselingandpsy029048mbp/page/n25 (Accessed: 28 November 2019).

Rogers, C. (1967) *On becoming a person: a therapist's view of psychotherapy*. London: Constable.

Rogers, C. (1973) *Carl Rogers on encounter groups*. New York: Harper and Row.

Rogers, C. and Dymond, R. (1954) *Psychotherapy and personality change: co-ordinated research studies in the client-centered approach*. Chicago: Chicago University Press.

Rosner, R. (2014) 'The "splendid isolation" of Aaron T. Beck', *Isis*, 105(4), pp. 734–758.

Rosner, R. (2018) 'Manualizing psychotherapy: Aaron T. Beck and the origins of *Cognitive Therapy of Depression*', *European Journal of Psychotherapy & Counselling*, 20(1), pp. 25–47.

Samuels, A. (1985) *Jung and the post-Jungians*. London and New York: Routledge.

Schorske, C. (1980) *Fin-de-siècle Vienna: politics and culture*. New York: Knopf.

Sealey, A. (2011) 'The strange case of the Freudian case history: the role of long case histories in the development of psychoanalysis', *History of the Human Sciences*, 24(1), pp. 36–50.

Shamdasani, S. (2003) *Jung and the making of modern psychology: the dream of a science*. Cambridge: Cambridge University Press.

Shamdasani, S. (2005) '"Psychotherapy": the invention of a word', *History of the Human Sciences*, 18(1), pp. 1–22.

Shamdasani, S. (2017) 'Psychotherapy in society: historical reflections', in Eghigian, G. (ed.) *The Routledge history of madness and mental health*. London: Routledge, pp. 363–378.

Skinner, B.F. (1953) *Science and human behavior*, New York: Macmillan.

Sulloway, F. (1979) *Freud: biologist of the mind*. Cambridge, MA: Harvard University Press.

Szent-Györgyi, A. (1957) *Bioenergetics*. New York: Academic Press.

Zaretsky, E. (2005) *Secrets of the soul: a social and cultural history of psychoanalysis*. New York: Vintage Books.

Chapter 4

Diagnosis, classification and the expansion of the therapeutic realm

David Harper

Contents

Introduction

'Blue' by Nevova Zdravka

As you saw in the preceding chapters, a medical framework is one of the dominant ways of understanding the kinds of psychological distress and behaviours that are collectively referred to as 'mental health problems', 'mental disorders' and 'mental illnesses'. This chapter will focus on the assessment and categorisation of mental health problems via the medical practice of diagnosis, using the sets of categories and criteria found in diagnostic manuals. In the UK, service users are given a psychiatric diagnosis from the *International classification of diseases* (ICD), currently in its eleventh revision (ICD-11; World Health Organization (WHO), 2018). This international manual covers both mental and physical health. Another manual, published by the American Psychiatric Association (APA), is also extensively used internationally: the *Diagnostic and statistical manual of mental disorders* (DSM), currently in its fifth edition (DSM-5; APA, 2013). This chapter will focus on the latter manual because it has a significant international impact (e.g. on research and on other manuals, such as the ICD) and because it has been the focus of significant scholarship and research.

In medicine, a diagnosis is used to:

- categorise the type of problem a person has
- identify treatment options and their likely outcome
- provide access to other kinds of support
- inform research
- inform the planning of health services.

The following quotations are from two people who received a psychiatric diagnosis. The first, Mike Shooter, is a psychiatrist who chose to speak openly about his experiences of depression, while the second is a mental health service user.

> When I was told that I was depressed it gave me a framework of understanding and a first grip on what was happening, not just for me but for my wife and children who had been equally frightened by my behaviour.
>
> (Shooter, 2010, p. 366)

> You only have to look at the definitions given in ICD 10 and DSM IV and read comments such as 'limited capacity to express feelings … callous unconcern for others … threatening or untrustworthy' … [o]ne thing that these comments have in common is that they are not helpful in any way.
>
> (Castillo, 2003, p. 128)

This chapter explores why such opposing opinions exist, outlining why some service users find diagnosis helpful and why others find it unhelpful.

This chapter aims to:

- provide a basic explanation of psychiatric diagnosis and the systems of psychiatric classification found in diagnostic manuals

- explain what medicalisation is and understand its role in the categorisation of certain problems in living as 'illnesses' and 'disorders'

- understand the ways in which diagnoses have changed over time and some of the reasons for these changes

- evaluate some of the conceptual, ethical and practical problems involved with diagnosis.

1   The first two editions of the DSM

Medicalise
To treat mental health concerns as though they are medical conditions that can therefore be diagnosed and treated.

Categorical system of diagnosis
A system of organising diagnoses that assumes that mental health problems are distinct – that they have clear boundaries – and can, therefore, be differentiated from each other using diagnostic criteria.

Neurosis
A psychiatric term that refers to a psychological state that causes distress but is not characterised by being out of touch with reality. Depression and anxiety are common examples.

The DSM is based on the premise that mental health concerns can be **medicalised**. Prior to the first edition of the DSM, a number of different diagnostic systems were in use. Often these were focused on gathering basic statistics about patients in asylums and concentrated predominantly on psychoses. In 1946 the US War Department published a classification system called *Medical 203* (War Department Technical Bulletin, Medical 203, 1946) organised around a **categorical system of diagnosis**. This was a broad system that focused on two 'types' of problems: those seen as primarily organic in origin and those seen as more psychological in origin. The term 'disorder' was used to refer to major categories but, for subcategories, the term 'reaction' was used. This reflected a broadly psychodynamic tradition in US psychiatry that saw problems arising from a dynamic interaction of biology, personality and social circumstances.

Published in 1952, the first edition of the DSM (APA, 1952) was designed to be consistent with the ICD-6 (WHO, 1949) – the term 'reaction' was used both in the DSM and ICD. The DSM was heavily influenced by *Medical 203* and was essentially a nine-page list of categories and codes followed by a longer section providing definitions and symptom descriptions. The categories were organised based on presumed causes. Sections with presumed organic and biological causes, such as 'mental deficiency', were differentiated from disorders seen as having psychological origins, including 'psychotic disorders', 'psychoneurotic reactions' and 'personality disorders' (which had been included in *Medical 203* as 'character and behaviour disorders').

The second edition of the DSM (DSM-II) was published in 1968 (APA, 1968) and was designed to be consistent with the new ICD-8 (WHO, 1968), the development of which had been heavily influenced by US psychiatrists. Both used the term 'reaction' much less, and anxiety and depression were categorised as **neuroses** rather than 'reactions'. By the end of the 1950s most psychiatrists worked in outpatient clinics and private practice (Cromby, Harper and Reavey, 2013), so DSM-II covered a broader range of problems than the first edition, including a new section specifically devoted to 'behaviour disorders of childhood and adolescence'. Although some categories were still influenced by causal theories, the foreword to DSM-II noted that, where there was some controversy about the nature or cause of a disorder, 'the Committee has attempted to select terms which it thought would least bind the judgment of the user' (APA, 1968, p. viii).

In summary, the DSM arose out of the need to collect statistics on the prevalence and demographics of various disorders, and to develop a classification system consistent with the ICD for use across the US. The system was influenced by ideas about the causes of certain problems and by the populations with which it was to be used.

2   Challenges to psychiatry's legitimacy: the road to DSM-III

As discussed in Chapters 1 and 2, the 1960s and 1970s saw psychiatry face a number of challenges to its legitimacy, both within its own ranks (e.g. psychiatrists such as Thomas Szasz and R.D. Laing) and from scholars and activists in civil rights movements. Questions were being raised about links between mental health and social conditions, the notion of mental illness itself and its relationship with restrictive social norms. Some researchers took up the challenge to examine the scientific basis of psychiatry, chiefly the **validity** and **reliability** of psychiatric diagnosis.

2.1   Empirical challenges: the validity and reliability of diagnosis

Psychologists sought to apply to diagnosis the criteria they used when evaluating the validity of psychometric tests. For example, did diagnosis predict outcomes? Were interview-based diagnoses corroborated by other methods? In a review of research relevant to the different types of validity, psychologist Joseph Zubin noted that 'just now, diagnosis is at its lowest ebb' (Zubin, 1967, p. 395). He took a middle position between those who saw the diagnostic system as excellent, requiring only better training of diagnostic interviewers, and those who thought that diagnosis was not 'possible or even desirable' (Zubin, 1967, p. 395). Instead, he concluded that the system simply represented a 'good starting point from which to improve approaches to classification' (Zubin, 1967, p. 395) and he recommended the adoption of a dimensional rather than categorical approach and more reliable interview methods.

Psychologists Frederick Thorne and Peter Nathan (1969) reviewed studies that had compared patients' DSM-II diagnoses with their responses to a 100-item symptom checklist administered by a psychiatrist. They found that the distribution of symptoms generally did 'not conform to patterns postulated in the official classification system' since they were 'distributed across the whole range of disorders in mixed patterns' (Thorne and Nathan, 1969, p. 382). Only 'functional psychosis' was clearly differentiated, while the symptoms of 'psychoneurosis' were found in all diagnostic categories and 'personality

Validity

The utility of a diagnostic system (does it do what it intends to do?); the degree to which the classification system provides a way of conceptualising problems that corresponds to service-users' experiences and provides a means of accurately classifying them.

Reliability

The degree to which clinicians agree on a diagnosis for a service user.

disorder' was 'essentially undifferentiable' from other categories (Thorne and Nathan, 1969, p. 382). Moreover, some of the supposedly classical symptoms of categories were so rare or occurred in such mixed patterns that they had 'little or no diagnostic predictive power' (Thorne and Nathan, 1969, p. 382).

However, not only did the DSM categories lack validity, other studies suggested that psychiatrists could not use them reliably. In a joint US– UK study of the psychiatric diagnosis of schizophrenia, Kendell *et al.* (1971) found that US psychiatrists had a much broader construct of schizophrenia than their UK colleagues, and so were much more likely to diagnose it. Spitzer and Fleiss's review of studies of diagnostic reliability acknowledged the 'obvious unreliability of psychiatric diagnosis' (Spitzer and Fleiss, 1974, p. 344) and argued that reliability could be improved through the use of detailed, specific criteria and structured diagnostic interview schedules.

2.2   Campaigning and diagnosis: the fall of one category and the rise of another

The 1970s saw two different campaigns by activist groups: one that aimed to remove homosexuality from the DSM, and another that aimed to introduce war trauma.

The DSM and homosexuality

Homosexuality had long been regarded as pathological within psychoanalysis and psychiatry, and it had been included as a 'sexual deviation' in the personality disorder category in both DSM-I and DSM-II. Many psychologists and behaviour therapists used sexual aversion therapy with gay men, which involved the use of electric shocks (Cromby, Harper and Reavey, 2013). However, the gay rights movement gathered momentum following the 1969 Stonewall riots in New York against homophobic policing, after which lesbian and gay activists disrupted several APA conventions. Kutchins and Kirk (1999) reported that Robert Spitzer, a psychiatrist and professor of psychiatry at Columbia University in New York, met gay psychiatrists and apparently became convinced of the need to change the classification, though he proposed retaining a category for those who were unhappy with their homosexuality. Following further discussions within the APA, in 1973 its board of trustees voted to remove homosexuality from DSM-II but also to introduce a new category of 'sexual orientation disturbance' for those unhappy with their sexuality. Attempts by psychoanalysts and other psychiatrists to overturn the decision failed when they lost an APA referendum in 1974. DSM-III relabelled the category as 'ego-dystonic homosexuality'. Apart from the obvious issue that such 'disturbances' of sexuality were only being applied to homosexuals, this category also ignored the impact of widespread prejudice and discrimination. While 'ego-dystonic homosexuality' was dropped, the category of 'sexual disorder not specified' (including ongoing and significant distress about one's sexual orientation) was included until the publication of DSM-5.

Vietnam veterans, trauma and the DSM

Following the Vietnam war, many campaigners and sympathetic psychiatrists felt that veterans were not being adequately diagnosed or treated for the psychological effects of combat, particularly distress resulting from a war that had been the subject of so much debate in the US. A new diagnostic category would be a means to provide the treatment needed, and to secure this treatment from the Veterans Administration in the US. Once the process to produce DSM-III had begun in 1974, psychiatrists and Vietnam veteran activists lobbied Spitzer (who was leading the effort to develop DSM-III) to introduce a category that might adequately address the needs of these veterans. As a result, Spitzer set up the Committee on Reactive Disorders, and the new category of 'post-traumatic stress disorder' (PTSD) was included in DSM-III (Kutchins and Kirk, 1999).

Pause for reflection

Why do you think one group of campaigners sought to de-medicalise homosexuality while another group sought to medicalise trauma resulting from war?

3 DSM-III and DSM-III-R: Spitzer's revolution

Robert Spitzer appointed a dozen committees which made recommendations about different categories. A key principle was that 'DSM-III reflects an increased commitment in our field to reliance on data as the basis for understanding mental disorders' (APA, 1980, p. 1). For Spitzer, detailed descriptive diagnoses were the foundation on which a scientific psychiatry could begin to test out theories of **aetiology**.

DSM-III, published in 1980 by the APA (APA, 1980), introduced a number of major changes designed to address problems of reliability:

- *Category boundaries*: DSM-III drew clear boundaries around categories, advising clinicians to make multiple diagnoses if necessary, even within the same category.

- *Specific diagnostic criteria*: For 163 of the 228 categories, specific criteria were included which needed to be satisfied before a diagnosis could be given.

- *An atheoretical approach*: Since the aetiology of many conditions was considered unclear, DSM-III proposed defining categories in descriptive terms that did not imply a particular causal explanation. The term 'disorder' was much more frequently used; thus, DSM-II's 'neuroses' were now labelled as 'affective disorders' (including depression) and 'anxiety disorders'.

- *A multi-axial system*: In order to provide a full, detailed assessment, different kinds of information needed to be gathered, and these were conceptualised along five different axes.

- *Field trials*: A series of field trials were conducted to provide feedback on the new criteria and to assess whether they led to increased reliability.

The multi-axial system was a marked diversion from DSM-II. Diagnoses of mental disorders were made using the first two axes: Axis II included 'personality disorders' and 'specific developmental disorders' (e.g. 'developmental reading disorder'), while Axis I included all other disorders. This meant that a person could be given a diagnosis on both Axes I and II. Since psychiatric service users could also have

Aetiology
A medical term that refers to theories about the causes of disorder or disease.

'physical disorders and conditions', these were identified on Axis III. The last two axes were intended primarily for researchers: Axis IV enabled the identification of relevant psychosocial stressors, while Axis V provided a rating system to assess the extent to which a person's problems affected their everyday adaptive functioning.

There has been debate about whether DSM-III was really atheoretical. For example, including PTSD, a category clearly based on a causal theory (i.e. that distress is the result of traumatic events), seems contrary to this aim. Moreover, the kinds of symptoms included in DSM-III tended to be those more consistent with biological models (Frances, 2013). Indeed, some categories were labelled as 'organic', implying a biological cause. The group of psychiatrists supporting Spitzer's approach certainly advocated a medical model, although they did not seem to think this was a theoretical approach or that it involved presuppositions: 'the medical model is without a priori theory but does consider brain mechanisms to be a priority' (Compton and Guze, 1995, p. 200). It seemed that it was only non-biological models, especially psychodynamic approaches, from which DSM-III had distanced itself. Despite this, traces of US psychiatry's psychodynamic legacy could still be seen in the DSM; for example, in subcategories such as 'narcissistic' and 'borderline' personality disorders.

DSM-III prompted a series of research studies which identified problems with some of the new categories and criteria. This prompted Spitzer to revise the manual, leading to the publication of DSM-III-R in 1987. By this time, administering structured interviews to service users was generally considered to increase the reliability of diagnosis, therefore Spitzer, together with some colleagues, developed one for DSM-III-R. There has been a structured clinical interview for each subsequent edition of the DSM.

Ultimately, DSM-III marked a radical diversion from previous DSMs, with its increased concern about the reliability of diagnosis and its move away from psychodynamic concepts. The claim that it was atheoretical was somewhat undermined by the introduction of the PTSD category and of symptoms more consistent with the medical model, as well as its retention of personality disorder subcategories with a psychodynamic heritage.

4   DSM-IV to DSM-5: the end of an era?

DSM-IV was much less radical in scope than DSM-III, but DSM-5 rejected many of the principles enshrined by Spitzer in DSM-III.

4.1   DSM-IV and DSM-IV-TR

DSM-IV was published in 1994 (APA, 1994). Its goals, as described by its chair, psychiatrist Allen Frances, were modest: they were 'to introduce rigour, objectivity, and transparency in how decisions were made' (Frances, 2013, p. 70). Conceptually and structurally, DSM-IV largely followed DSM-III, though it attempted to address the issue of cultural variation in mental health problems. Although the DSM is a US system, it is used in many countries and, of course, the US population itself is culturally varied. Culture researchers therefore argued that the manual needed to acknowledge that its construction of mental health was culturally shaped, but DSM-IV took a more minimalist approach. It included an appendix with an outline of a cultural formulation and a glossary of so-called 'culture-bound syndromes'. These could refer to the way in which a DSM disorder was expressed differently in different cultures, or to an indigenous 'folk' category of distress. An example given by DSM-IV was 'amok', which referred to 'a dissociative episode characterized by a period of brooding followed by an outburst of violent, aggressive, or homicidal behavior directed at people and objects' (APA, 1994, p. 845). This had apparently been reported primarily (although not exclusively) in Southeast Asia.

A further edition (DSM-IV-TR) was published six years later, in 2000, though the revisions were primarily textual rather than conceptual.

4.2   DSM-5: the end of Spitzer's revolution?

Those involved in planning DSM-5 challenged key tenets of Spitzer's approach. They identified a number of problems stemming from the changes implemented in DSM-III. These problems included the narrow and overly rigid categories introduced in DSM-III. As noted in the introduction to DSM-5: 'the once plausible goal of identifying homogenous populations for treatment and research resulted in narrow diagnostic categories that did not capture clinical reality, symptom heterogeneity within disorders, and significant sharing of symptoms across multiple disorders' (APA, 2013, p. 12). DSM-5 argued that apparently high rates of comorbidity were a result of overly narrow categories that required clinicians to make more than one diagnosis, something that could be circumvented by using broader categories.

However, during the DSM-5 planning process, the government-funded National Institute for Mental Health (NIMH) had proposed an entirely different way forward: the Research Domain Criteria (RDoC) project. Thomas Insel (the NIMH director), and his colleagues, proposed that the answer lay not in the conceptualisation of clinical categories but in the identification of problems in the brain itself, in 'neural circuitry' (Insel *et al.*, 2010). However, the team acknowledged this was a high risk, long-term option with no guarantee of a successful outcome. The competing approaches of the DSM-5 planners and the RDoC project suggested that there was a growing divide between practitioners and biomedically oriented psychiatric researchers.

DSM-5 was published in 2013 (APA, 2013) and led to widespread debate among academics, professionals, service users and in the media. DSM-5's feedback website received over 13,000 comments and thousands of organised petitions (APA, 2013). DSM-5 argued for the need to adopt a more **dimensional system of diagnosis** rather than a categorical approach. In a categorical approach you either meet criteria for a category or you do not, whereas in a dimensional approach, problems are viewed as lying along a spectrum and are thus a matter of degree. A dimensional system for personality disorders had originally been proposed by the authors of DSM-5 but, since this proposal had 'not been widely accepted' (APA, 2013, p. xliii), the personality disorder categories in Section II were largely unchanged; the proposed dimensional approach to personality disorder was, instead, included in Section III, 'emerging measures and models'. This section also included much more extensive detail on cultural formulation, and one of the appendices included a glossary of cultural concepts of distress. DSM-5 aimed for a simplified system of diagnosis and it abandoned the multi-axial system introduced in DSM-III. Axes I–III were now combined and axis IV was dropped (in favour of ICD codes for environmental factors). Axis V (the rating system to assess a person's everyday functioning) was abandoned due to its lack of conceptual clarity and questionable psychometric characteristics. A final change was that DSM-5 was referred to by Arabic rather than Roman

Dimensional system of diagnosis

A system of organising diagnoses that assumes that mental health problems are best understood as existing along a spectrum or dimension (e.g. how much they disrupt one's life). Different types of dimensions have been proposed for different forms of distress.

numerals (e.g. 'DSM-III'). This was to enable incremental updates in the future; thus, if and when DSM-5.1 is published, it may include updates only on some categories and will not be a wholesale revision as previous editions have been.

In summary, DSM-IV largely followed the approach of DSM-III, focusing more on the process of decision-making. DSM-5, on the other hand, challenged the conceptual framework of the third edition, although its more radical proposal to move to a dimensional system was thwarted.

5   Debates about DSM-5 and psychiatric diagnosis

The publication of DSM-5 led to widespread debate. This section will discuss some of the issues raised, issues which have been encountered throughout the history of the DSM.

5.1   Reliability and validity redux: the appropriateness of a medical lens and the role of social norms

DSM-III had aimed to improve the reliability of diagnosis and its field trials suggested that, through using structured clinical interviews, levels of reliability ranging from fair to satisfactory could be achieved between raters. However, this meant that symptoms had to be defined that were simple and obvious, with 'personal and contextual factors' omitted (Frances, 2013, p. 25). This raised the risk that the reliability of diagnosis had been prioritised over the validity of the categories. Some have argued that the use of the structured clinical interview for DSM-IV (commonly referred to as the SCID) has not improved reliability (Kutchins and Kirk, 1999). However, even if structured interviews did improve reliability, they are only used by researchers; they are not in everyday use by psychiatrists. Moreover, reliability is no guide to validity. We can all agree on the characteristics of a unicorn or of Santa Claus but that does not mean that either exists in the real world.

The problem of reliability reared its head again when the DSM-5 field trials were published by Freedman *et al.* (2013). Figure 4.1 shows their reliability results for categories for adults. DSM-5 aimed to develop categories that could be applied by ordinary clinicians with relatively little training and using unstructured clinical interviews. Reliability is measured by the kappa ($\varkappa$) coefficient, where a score of -1 indicates complete disagreement and a score of 1 indicates complete agreement. Spitzer and Fleiss's (1974) article implies that a kappa value of 0.4–0.7 is no better than fair agreement, but the DSM-5 field trial team labelled this range as running from 'good agreement' to 'very good agreement', as shown by the blue and green bars respectively in Figure 4.1. This decision was treated with derision by Allen Frances, the chair of DSM-IV, who argued that 'DSM-5 announced it would accept agreements among raters that were sometimes barely better than two monkeys throwing darts at a diagnostic board' (Frances, 2013, p. 175).

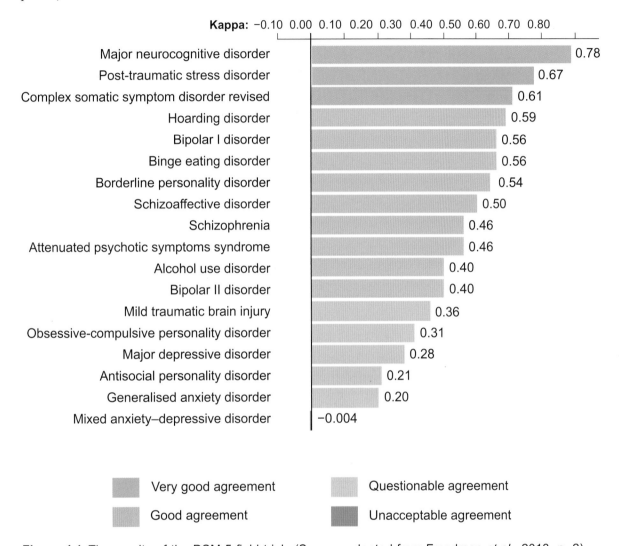

Figure 4.1 The results of the DSM-5 field trials (Source: adapted from Freedman *et al.*, 2013, p. 2)

The poor reliability of DSM-5 categories was matched by their poor level of validity. This chapter began by explaining that psychiatric diagnosis is an attempt to use a medical approach to assess problems in living. Medical diagnosis is essentially a process of identifying patterns and comparing problems with the descriptions found in diagnostic manuals. In medicine, clinicians base diagnoses on signs and symptoms. These are often used interchangeably but they are quite different. A sign refers to something that is observable to others or some kind of objective evidence, such as the results of laboratory tests (e.g. of blood or urine). A symptom, on the other hand, refers to a person's subjective self-report of something that is not observable by others and for which no objective test is available (e.g. a headache). Throughout the history of the DSM it has been rather embarrassing that, in comparison with many medical diagnoses, for most 'functional' psychiatric diagnoses there are no signs, only symptoms. This issue led to a remarkable public spat between the DSM-5 director David Kupfer and the NIMH director Thomas Insel. Just 18 days before the publication of DSM-5, Insel announced that the NIMH would be 're-orienting its research away from DSM categories' because of their 'lack of validity' since they were not based on 'any objective laboratory measure' (Insel, 2013). Four days later, Kupfer released a statement noting that 'We've been telling patients for several decades that we are waiting for biomarkers. We're still waiting.' (Kupfer, 2013).

Sixty years after the publication of DSM-I, psychiatrists appeared to agree that there were still no signs (i.e. objective measures) for most psychiatric diagnoses. As a result, disorders were constructed by clustering symptoms together largely on the basis of consensus among groups of psychiatrists. However, the psychiatrists involved in each edition of the DSM often grouped these symptoms and categories in different ways. Although both Insel and Kupfer identified a problem, neither entertained the idea that the conceptual framework used in medicine might not be applicable to problems in living – this issue will be discussed in greater detail in Chapter 8.

A continuing challenge for diagnosis has been that some socio-demographic groups are more likely to be given some diagnoses than others (Cromby, Harper and Reavey, 2013). How might we understand, for example, the fact that, according to DSM-5, women are more likely to be given a diagnosis of major depressive disorder while men are more likely to be given diagnoses of substance use disorders? Does this reveal bias on the part of clinicians? Are men and women exposed to different kinds of life events? Is it more socially acceptable for men to express distress through substance misuse and for women by becoming depressed, or are there other reasons?

Moreover, because diagnosis involves subjective judgement, it can be influenced by social norms. It could be argued, for example, that diagnosis involves comparing what a person says with an implicit idea of what it means to be 'normal'. A lot depends, therefore, on the kinds of implicit assumptions the diagnoser makes. For example, DSM-5 warns about the dangers of cultural bias in diagnosing paranoid personality disorder. Rates of paranoia are higher in some BAME groups. It has been argued that, because these groups have often experienced racism, a wariness of others is an understandable response rather than a sign of pathology (Cromby, Harper and Reavey, 2013).

5.2 Medicalisation and the expansion of the therapeutic realm

One of the repeated criticisms of the DSM has been that it has led to an increasing medicalisation of problems in living. As noted in Section 1, medicalisation, in its broadest sense, occurs when phenomena are viewed through a medical lens. However, the term is also used by researchers in a narrower way, to refer to how problems in living not previously approached in a medical manner can be treated as if they were illnesses. There are a number of ways in which this can happen in psychiatric diagnostic manuals such as the DSM:

- *The use of overly broad categories*: If diagnostic categories are overly broad and use definitions that leave lots of room for subjective judgement, then some clinicians may apply a given diagnosis more than other clinicians. For example, the broad categories in DSM-I and DSM-II led to the problems found in the US–UK study of schizophrenia diagnosis, as discussed in Section 2.1.

- *Ignoring normal rates in the general population*: In order to decide whether an experience is abnormal, manual developers should survey the general population, since many of us experience mild forms of symptoms which often resolve themselves. For example, in the past, delusions (false and unusual beliefs) have been considered a clear indication of schizophrenia; however, they are much more common in the general population than previously thought. A study of 7000 people in the Netherlands found that 12 per cent had delusions but significant problems were experienced in only 3.3 per cent of these cases (van Os *et al.*, 2000).

- *Reduced thresholds*: If the duration, intensity or number of symptoms required for a diagnosis is reduced, then more people will be diagnosed with that disorder. Prior to DSM-5, for example, clinicians were prevented from diagnosing major depressive disorder if the person had recently been bereaved, because of the risk of pathologising a normal grief response. DSM-5 removed this exclusion, raising concerns that rates of both diagnosis and antidepressant prescriptions would increase.

- *'Disease mongering'*: This occurs when new disorders are proposed for experiences that had not previously been considered a mental health problem. For instance, DSM-IV introduced 'premenstrual dysphoric disorder' (PMDD) as an example of a 'depressive disorder not otherwise specified'. This referred to 'markedly depressed mood', 'marked anxiety', 'marked affective lability', and 'decreased interest in usual activities' associated with a woman's menstrual cycle (APA, 1994, p. 350). In DSM-5, PMDD is a formal subcategory of depressive disorders. Several researchers and activists have argued that the category pathologises a common experience for many women (Ebeling, 2011). Moreover, it means that women may be inappropriately given antidepressant medication, with all its concomitant side effects.

Recent decades have seen substantial rises in the rates of certain diagnoses, such as attentional deficit hyperactivity disorder and depression, along with the prescription of associated medications such as Ritalin and antidepressants, respectively. There are lots of factors which appear to drive medicalisation: mental health awareness campaigns; the media; government policies (e.g. moves to offer medication and other treatments for mild problems as a preventative measure); advocacy groups campaigning for problems to be seen as illnesses; changing social norms; and the desire of the public for a technical fix to problems in living. Pharmaceutical companies are a key influence and, in their adverts to consumers in the US, they often include checklists of symptoms (mirroring DSM criteria) and recommendations to visit a doctor for assessment if a person experiences those symptoms (Ebeling, 2011).

Since medication is a common treatment for many psychiatric diagnoses, any changes in diagnostic manuals have the potential to increase or decrease the market for pharmaceutical companies' products. Ebeling (2011, p. 827) discusses the way in which the pharmaceutical company which produced the antidepressant Prozac 'heavily influenced the codification of PMDD as a disease state' by funding research in this area by a psychiatrist member of the DSM-IV PMDD work group. It relabelled the antidepressant Prozac as 'Sarafem' and sold it as a specific treatment for PMDD (Ebeling, 2011). Chapter 17 will discuss the controversial influence of the pharmaceutical industry on research into the effectiveness of antidepressants.

Activity 4.1: The pros and cons of medicalising mental health
Allow about 10 minutes

In the Introduction, you considered two opposing views on the medicalisation of mental health. Now that you have worked through most of the chapter, try to list a few reasons why some people might consider medicalisation to be a helpful approach to mental health, and a few reasons why others might consider it unhelpful. Only move on to the activity discussion once you have compiled your list.

Discussion

Those outlining the advantages of medicalisation might note that it:

- quickly and efficiently enables access to medical treatments
- can increase the reliability of diagnoses through its use of rigid categories
- provides clear, succinct categories that can be tested and modified.

Those outlining the drawbacks might note that it:

- restricts the ability to explore contextual and individual factors
- can reduce the validity of diagnosis, particularly as new disorders might be proposed for experiences not previously regarded as mental health problems
- can result in overly broad diagnostic categories
- can lead to the prescription of unnecessary medication.

5.3   The continuing impact of the DSM

The DSM continues to have a significant impact on research. Additionally, although the NIMH appears to be distancing itself from the DSM, many other research funding bodies continue to fund studies based on its diagnostic categories. This has an impact on clinical practice: in the UK, the National Institute for Health and Care Excellence publishes clinical guidelines on particular 'conditions' which draw on research findings using ICD and DSM categories.

Mental health services are increasingly organised by diagnostic categories. The high levels of comorbidity (a medical term used to denote when two or more conditions co-occur) that arise when categories such as those of the DSM are used can create problems; to which service should a person with a diagnosis of both depression and personality disorder be referred, for instance? There is an increasing proliferation of diagnosis-specific adaptations of therapies, such as cognitive behavioural therapy (CBT) for psychosis, CBT for anxiety, and so on. The use of diagnosis by health insurers and the NHS can cause a range of dilemmas. What if a clinician thinks that a person needs help but their problems do not map easily on to diagnostic categories? What if someone does not wish to receive a diagnosis? What if a professional feels that the use of diagnosis is pathologising? How can couple and family therapists record their work using a system that provides categories only for individuals?

The debate about DSM-5 has again prompted questions about how we understand mental health and the role of social norms. The reliability problem has returned, while diagnosis has expanded further into everyday life. Rates of diagnosis and medication for some problems have increased. This has led to questions being raised about the influence of the pharmaceutical industry. Diagnostic manuals such as the DSM continue to have an impact on both research and mental health services.

Conclusion

Psychiatric diagnosis involves the application of a medical framework to problems in living. By comparing people's reported problems against the criteria found in diagnostic manuals such as the DSM, the closest-matching diagnostic category or categories can be identified. This chapter has explored whether a medical framework can appropriately be applied to mental health. It has also examined the process of medicalisation, by which problems in living can come to be viewed as mental illnesses. In the case of PTSD, the medicalisation of the condition was welcomed by activists for Vietnam veterans, whereas gay and lesbian activists campaigned to de-medicalise homosexuality and feminists have criticised the inclusion of PMDD in the DSM.

The content of the DSM has changed over the sixty years between its first and fifth editions. It has changed from being a brief list of categories designed to produce statistics on the characteristics of adult patients in asylums to a larger, more detailed manual with a much broader scope. The DSM now covers the entire lifespan – including problems of varying severity – across a broader range of settings and serves a wider range of functions.

This chapter has identified shifts in the theoretical models that have informed the DSM – from the broadly organic and psychodynamic approach of the first two editions, through to the more biomedical approach of the third edition. Finally, it looked at the fifth edition's departure from Spitzer's principles, with its focus on clinical rather than research utility and the conflict between the DSM-5 and RDoC projects. This chapter has also examined a number of the conceptual, ethical and practical problems of psychiatric diagnosis, including its reliability, validity and the appropriateness of a medical framework. Whatever your views about diagnosis, it seems likely that it will continue to have a significant influence on mental health for some time to come.

Further reading

- This chapter provides a useful insight into the process of diagnosis, including the conceptual coherence and validity of diagnostic systems:
  Boyle, M. (1999) 'Diagnosis', in Newnes, C., Holmes, G. and Dunn, C. (eds.) *This is madness: a critical look at psychiatry and the future of mental health services*. Ross-on-Wye: PCCS Books, pp. 75–90.

- This is a short, accessible introduction to some of the debates in the chapter. Chapters 3–6 are particularly useful:
  Johnstone, L. (2014) *A straight talking introduction to psychiatric diagnosis*. Ross-on-Wye: PCCS Books.

References

American Psychiatric Association (APA) (1952) *Diagnostic and statistical manual of mental disorders* (DSM-I). Washington: American Psychiatric Association Publishing.

American Psychiatric Association (APA) (1968) *Diagnostic and statistical manual of mental disorders* (DSM-II). 2nd edn. Washington: American Psychiatric Association Publishing.

American Psychiatric Association (APA) (1980) *Diagnostic and statistical manual of mental disorders* (DSM-III). 3rd edn. Washington: American Psychiatric Association Publishing

American Psychiatric Association (APA) (1994) *Diagnostic and statistical manual of mental disorders* (DSM-IV). 4th edn. Washington: American Psychiatric Association Publishing.

American Psychiatric Association (APA) (2013) *Diagnostic and statistical manual of mental disorders* (DSM-5). 5th edn. Washington: American Psychiatric Association Publishing.

Castillo, H. (2003) *Personality disorder: temperament or trauma?*. London and Philadelphia: Jessica Kingsley Publishers.

Compton, W.M. and Guze, S.B. (1995) 'The neo-Kraepelinian revolution in psychiatric diagnosis', *European Archives of Psychiatry and Clinical Neuroscience*, 245(4–5), pp. 196–201.

Cromby, J., Harper, D. and Reavey, P. (2013) *Psychology, mental health and distress*. Basingstoke: Palgrave Macmillan.

Ebeling, M. (2011) "Get with the Program!': pharmaceutical marketing, symptom checklists and self-diagnosis', *Social Science & Medicine*, 73(6), pp. 825–832.

Frances, A. (2013) *Saving normal: an insider's revolt against out-of-control psychiatric diagnosis, DSM-5, big pharma and the medicalization of ordinary life*. New York: HarperCollins.

Freedman, R., Lewis, D.A., Michels, R., Pine, D.S., Schultz, S.K., Tamminga, C.A., Gabbard, G.O., Shur-Fen Gau, S., Javitt, D.C., Oquendo, M.A., Shrout, P.E., Vieta, E. and Yager, J. (2013) 'The initial field trials of DSM-5: new blooms and old thorns', *American Journal of Psychiatry*, 170(1), pp. 1–5. doi:10.1176/appi.ajp.2012.12091189.

Insel, T. (2013) 'Post by former NIMH Director Thomas Insel: transforming diagnosis', *The National Institute of Mental Health*, 29 April. Available at: https://www.nimh.nih.gov/about/directors/thomas-insel/blog/2013/transforming-diagnosis.shtml (Accessed: 26 February 2020).

Insel, T., Cuthbert, B., Garvey, M., Heinssen, R., Pine, D.S., Quinn, K., Sanislow, C. and Wang, P. (2010) 'Research domain criteria (RDoC): toward a new classification framework for research on mental disorders', *American Journal of Psychiatry*, 167(7), pp. 748–751.

Kendell, R.E., Cooper, J.E., Gourlay, A.J., Copeland, J.R., Sharpe, L. and Gurland, B.J. (1971) 'Diagnostic criteria of American and British psychiatrists', *Archives of General Psychiatry*, 25(2), pp. 123–130.

Kupfer, D. (2013) 'Statement by David Kupfer, MD: Chair of DSM-5 Task Force discusses future of mental health research'. Washington, DC: American Psychiatric Association. Available at: https://www.madinamerica.com/wp-content/uploads/2013/05/Statement-from-dsm-chair-david-kupfer-md.pdf (Accessed: 26 February 2020).

Kutchins, H. and Kirk, S.A. (1999) *Making us crazy: DSM – the psychiatric bible and the creation of mental disorders*. London: Constable.

Shooter, M. (2010) 'What my diagnosis means to me', *Journal of Mental Health*, 19(4), pp. 366–368. doi:10.3109/09638231003728174.

Spitzer, R.L. and Fleiss, J.L. (1974) 'A re-analysis of the reliability of psychiatric diagnosis', *British Journal of Psychiatry*, 125(587), pp. 341–347. doi:10.1192/bjp.125.4.341.

Thorne, F.C. and Nathan, P.E. (1969) 'The general validity of official diagnostic classifications', *Journal of Clinical Psychology*, 25(4), pp. 375–383.

van Os, J., Hanssen, M., Bijl, R.V. and Ravelli, A. (2000) 'Strauss (1969) revisited: a psychosis continuum in the general population?', *Schizophrenia Research*, 45(1–2), pp. 11–20.

War Department Technical Bulletin, Medical 203 (1946) 'Nomenclature of psychiatric disorders and reactions', *Journal of Clinical Psychology*, 2(3), pp. 289–296.

World Health Organization (WHO) (1949) *International classification of diseases* (ICD-6). 6th rev. edn. Geneva: World Health Organization.

World Health Organization (WHO) (1968) *International classification of diseases* (ICD-8). 8th rev. edn. Geneva: World Health Organization.

World Health Organization (WHO) (2018) *International classification of diseases* (ICD-11). 11th rev. edn. Geneva: World Health Organization.

Zubin, J. (1967) 'Classification of the behavior disorders', *Annual Review of Psychology*, 18(1), pp. 373–406.

Part 2

Presenting problems

Chapter 5
Understanding sadness and worry

Naomi Moller and Gina Di Malta

Contents

Introduction

'Alone' by Russell Hughes

It would take me close to 30 minutes to coax myself out of bed. The only reason I would even get up was because I had to walk my dog and go to my full-time job.

I'd manage to drag myself into work, but I couldn't concentrate. There'd be times when the thought of being in the office would be so suffocating that I'd go to my car just to breathe and calm myself down.

Other times, I'd sneak into the bathroom and cry. I didn't even know what I was crying about, but the tears wouldn't stop. After ten minutes or so, I would clean myself up and return to my desk.

I'd still get everything done to make my boss happy, but I'd lost all interest in the projects I was working on, even though I was working at my dream company.

(Byers, 2018)

This chapter focuses on experiences of sadness and worry – or as they are termed in diagnostic systems, 'depression' and 'anxiety'. It will provide an overview of these two most common of mental health difficulties. A core argument is that, despite lots of theorising and research, there is still disagreement about how depression and anxiety should be defined, understood and 'treated'.

This chapter explores why such opposing opinions exist – it outlines why some clients find diagnosis helpful and why others find it unhelpful.

This chapter aims to:

- discuss how depression and anxiety are understood: are they pathological responses, or can they be considered adaptive?

- explore the prevalence of depression and anxiety and, relatedly, whether they are cultural phenomena or fixed, universal patterns of human response

- explore the possible causes of depression and anxiety, from genes/faulty neurotransmitters, through to difficult life experiences or bad relationships, or simply a 'screwed-up' modern world

- highlight which counselling theories are relevant for working with anxiety and depression.

---

1 What are depression and anxiety?

This section explores how depression and anxiety can be understood. Before going any further, try Activity 5.1, which encourages you to consider your own ideas and assumptions about these concepts.

Activity 5.1: When do sadness and worry become pathological?

Allow about 10 minutes

Take out a piece of paper and write down the words 'sadness' and 'worry' in the middle. Then spend 3–5 minutes writing down all the words and phrases that come to mind. Now turn the page over, write down the words 'depression' and 'anxiety' and spend another 3–5 minutes free-associating. Look at the two sets of words – how are they similar and how are they different?

Discussion

One thing that might have come up is that sadness and worry are usually understood as part of a normal/unproblematic spectrum of emotions. In contrast, the words 'depression' and 'anxiety' may imply something that is abnormal or **pathological**, and therefore open to diagnosis and medical intervention. Where do you think the boundary is between 'ordinary' sadness and depression, and how does a person know when they have passed from one to the other?

1.1 Depression and anxiety diagnoses

The numbers of **depression** and **anxiety** diagnoses increase with each iteration of the diagnostic manuals – the *International classification of diseases* (ICD), currently in its eleventh revision (ICD-11), and the *Diagnostic and statistical manual of mental disorders* (DSM), currently in its fifth revision (DSM-5).

Pathological
Involving/caused by disease or illness (physical or mental); implies a medical understanding of mental distress.

Depression
The experience of low or very low mood. As a diagnosis, the term describes a cluster of physical, emotional and cognitive symptoms, of which a core feature is low mood.

Anxiety
The experience of severe worry or nervousness. As a diagnosis, the term describes a cluster of symptoms, of which a core feature is the person's sense of feeling overwhelmed by worry or nervousness.

The DSM-5 cluster for depression includes the following diagnostic categories (among others):

- *Major depressive disorder (MDD)*: Significantly affects a person's life (it is probably the most well-known diagnosis and is sometimes referred to as 'clinical depression').

- *Persistent depressive disorder*: Refers to a chronic but relatively lower level of depression.

- *Disruptive mood dysregulation disorder*: Used to refer to depression in children.

Bipolar disorder – historically referred to as 'manic depression' and associated with significant upswings in mood as well as severe lows – now forms its own separate cluster of diagnoses.

The DSM-5 cluster for anxiety includes the following diagnostic categories:

Generalised anxiety disorder

Involves experience of excessive or uncontrollable worry about many things in everyday life.

- ***Generalised anxiety disorder** (GAD)*: The most generic and common anxiety diagnosis.

- *Phobias*

- *Social anxiety disorder*

- *Panic disorder*

- *Agoraphobia*

- *Obsessive-compulsive disorder*

Post-traumatic stress disorder (discussed in Chapter 6) used to be included in the list of anxiety disorders, but in DSM-5 it is now included (alongside other disorders) in a distinct category of 'trauma and stressor-related disorders'.

To further understand how depression and anxiety are distinguished from 'unproblematic' emotional responses, have a look at the DSM-5 diagnostic criteria for MDD and GAD below.

Diagnostic criteria for MDD and GAD

Major depressive disorder

A Five (or more) of the following symptoms have been present during the same 2-week period and represent a change from previous functioning; at least one of the symptoms is either (1) depressed mood or (2) loss of interest or pleasure.

1   Depressed mood most of the day, nearly every day, as indicated by either subjective report (e.g., feels sad, empty, hopeless) or observation made by others (e.g., appears tearful). (Note: In children and adolescents, can be irritable mood.)

2   Markedly diminished interest or pleasure in all, or almost all, activities most of the day, nearly every day (as indicated by either subjective account or observation).

3   Significant weight loss when not dieting or weight gain (e.g., a change of more than 5% of body weight in a month), or decrease or increase in appetite nearly every day. (Note: In children, consider failure to make expected weight gain.)

4   Insomnia or hypersomnia nearly every day.

5   Psychomotor agitation or retardation nearly every day (observable by others, not merely subjective feelings of restlessness or being slowed down).

6   Fatigue or loss of energy nearly every day.

7   Feelings of worthlessness or excessive or inappropriate guilt (which may be delusional) nearly every day (not merely self-reproach or guilt about being sick).

8   Diminished ability to think or concentrate, or indecisiveness, nearly every day (either by subjective account or as observed by others).

9   Recurrent thoughts of death (not just fear of dying), recurrent suicidal ideation without a specific plan, or suicide attempt or specific plan for committing suicide.

Generalized anxiety disorder

A Excessive anxiety and worry (apprehensive expectation), occurring more days than not for at least 6 months, about a number of events or activities (such as work or school performance).

B The individual finds it difficult to control the worry.

C The anxiety and worry are associated with three (or more) of the following six symptoms (with at least some symptoms having been present for more days than not for the past 6 months):

Note: Only one item required in children.

1   Restlessness or feeling keyed up or on edge.
2   Being easily fatigued.
3   Difficulty concentrating or mind going blank.
4   Irritability.
5   Muscle tension.
6   Sleep disturbance (difficulty falling or staying asleep, or restless, unsatisfying sleep).

(Source: American Psychiatric Association, 2013, pp. 160–161 and 222)

Looking at these lists of symptoms, it is possible to see some overlap; for example, both MDD and GAD are associated with sleep difficulties, concentration issues and tiredness. Perhaps for this reason, research examining the frequency of depression and anxiety in the population suggests that these conditions co-occur about 50–60 per cent of the time (Moscati, Flint and Kendler, 2016; Judd *et al.*, 1998).

1.2   Can depression and anxiety be adaptive?

The debate about the potential adaptive advantages of depression and anxiety is anchored in the idea that, if an aspect of human response is common in the population, then it may have created an evolutionary advantage (Nettle and Bateson, 2012). In other words, for some humans, depression and anxiety may have increased the likelihood that they would survive and reproduce (Bergstrom and Meacham, 2016). Section 3.1 also discusses genetics and heritability.

Anxiety, it has been argued, is adaptive because it increases a person's vigilance to potential threats. Even if actual danger is rare, the cost of a failure to detect it is high, which suggests there is value in anxious engagement with the world (Bateson, Brilot and Nettle, 2011). Meacham and Bergstrom (2016) suggest that the adaptive propensity to anxiety becomes problematic because of individuals' prior history, as depicted in Figure 5.1.

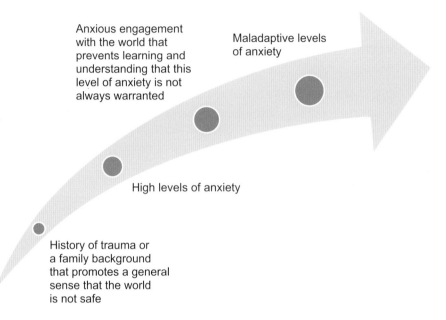

Anxious engagement with the world that prevents learning and understanding that this level of anxiety is not always warranted

Maladaptive levels of anxiety

High levels of anxiety

History of trauma or a family background that promotes a general sense that the world is not safe

Figure 5.1 How adaptive predisposition to anxiety can lead to maladaptive (clinical) levels of anxiety in some individuals

Some researchers have suggested that depressive symptoms may confer evolutionary advantages in the context of relationships with other people (Gilbert, 2006; Keller, 2008; Nettle, 2009). The argument is that depression prompts people to withdraw from stressful situations and allows time to analyse them. It may also prompt partners and family to help. Alternative theories include that proposed by Miller and Raison (2016), who suggest that historically adaptive immune system processes are fostering depression in the modern world.

This area is still being researched. For the purposes of this chapter, perhaps the best answer is: yes, it is possible that depression and anxiety may sometimes be adaptive responses. This does not mean, however, that those experiencing depression or anxiety will feel grateful to learn that their crushing experience may be an 'adaptive' one.

2   How common are depression and anxiety?

As noted above, people with anxiety are often also depressed, and vice versa. This is an example of comorbidity – when two (or more) medical conditions co-occur. The frequency with which anxiety and depression are comorbid has been determined by research that seeks to establish the prevalence of depression and anxiety. However, before considering these statistics, it is important to consider how they are derived.

The most common way to measure depression or anxiety is through the use of self-report questionnaires. One example is the GAD-7, an anxiety questionnaire backed by strong research evidence, that is widely used in both research and clinical practice (Spitzer *et al.*, 2006; Plummer *et al.*, 2016).

Activity 5.2: Completing the GAD-7

Allow about 10 minutes

Imagine that you have just arrived at an NHS counselling centre, have been handed a clipboard and a pen and been asked to complete the GAD-7. What do you think this might be like? Complete the GAD-7 below by circling the number that most accurately represents your experience for each of the statements. (If you don't want to imagine being the client, imagine that the questionnaire is being completed by someone in the public eye; for example, an actor or a politician.)

In the past two weeks how often have you been bothered by any of the following problems?	Not at all	Several days	More than half the days	Nearly every day
Feeling nervous, anxious or on edge	0	1	2	3
Not being able to stop or control worrying	0	1	2	3
Worrying too much about different things	0	1	2	3
Trouble relaxing	0	1	2	3
Being so restless that it is hard to sit still	0	1	2	3
Becoming easily annoyed or irritable	0	1	2	3
Feeling afraid as if something awful might happen	0	1	2	3

Discussion

If you are sitting in a waiting room before your first counselling session you might be feeling really anxious just because of that. Perhaps you are worried in case you see someone you know. Or you might think that you need to score highly on the questionnaire in order to receive counselling. All these things might lead to an artificially high GAD-7 score. Alternatively, you might know that you are so anxious you could scream but feel too ashamed to put the truth down in numbers. In other words, there are lots of reasons why the GAD-7 score you end up with may not be 'accurate'.

It is useful to reflect on the experience of filling in a measure such as the GAD-7 because it demonstrates that there are lots of social and situational factors – including the stigmatisation of mental health – that influence how someone scores (Schnyder *et al.*, 2017). Even when researchers are clear that a self-report measure provides 'good' evidence, it is important to remember the complexity of measuring something as personal and subjectively experienced as 'anxiety'.

2.1   The prevalence of depression and anxiety

So how common are depression and anxiety? The Global Burden of Disease (GBD) network is an international group of more than 3600 researchers in over 145 countries who work together to understand health globally. This work includes estimating the prevalence and impact (e.g. mortality and disability) of anything that affects health, including depression and anxiety. According to the GBD, in 2017 there were 264 million people globally (3.6 per cent of the global population) with depression, and 284 million (3.9 per cent of the global population) with anxiety disorders (Institute for Health Metrics and Evaluation, 2019).

What about UK-only estimates? The Adult Psychiatric Morbidity Survey (McManus *et al.*, 2016) provides population estimates for the prevalence of common mental health disorders. According to the survey, one in six people (17 per cent) in England were identified as currently suffering with what are referred to as common mental health disorders; of these, 5.9 per cent were identified as having GAD and 3.3 per cent as having depression. It seems that depression and anxiety are common both in England and worldwide.

2.2   Are depression and anxiety global or cultural phenomena?

One issue pertinent to the broader question of the validity of a diagnosis relates to what evidence exists to suggest that depression and anxiety exist globally. As you learnt in Chapter 4, diagnoses are conceptually linked to medical understandings of mental health, and an implicit assumption is that shared human biology means globally similar expressions of mental health disorders. If depression or anxiety 'look' different in different places (and across different times), this potentially provides evidence that they are instead cultural or social phenomena. (Of course, another possibility is that both culture and biology may have a role.)

Culturally-bound syndrome
A cluster of mental health symptoms recognised only in particular cultural contexts.

One way to examine whether the essence that is labelled 'depression' or 'anxiety' is the same globally is to explore how people in different cultural contexts talk about and experience mental health difficulties. Historically, research has led to the identification of **culturally-bound syndromes**, or forms of mental health difficulties found only in particular cultural contexts. More recently, it has been suggested that rapid globalisation and the interconnectedness that is possible through digital culture are reducing the potential for locally unique manifestations of mental distress, such that 'culturally-influenced syndromes' may be a better term (Ventriglio, Ayonrinde and Bhugra, 2015). Examples of such conditions include distinct, generationally and culturally specific manifestations of depression found in Japan. Kato *et al.* (2016, p. 10) outline the local understanding of a 'modern type depression' found in the younger generation in Japan, which is associated with 'occasional depressive symptoms mainly during work/school', a hatred of social order and hierarchical social relations, and not being a naturally hard worker. One could consider whether not being a hard worker might be understood differently in a British context.

Another approach to considering whether what is understood as depression and anxiety is the same globally is to systematically consider the extent to which DSM-5/ICD-11 conceptualisations of depression are valid for non-western populations. Haroz *et al.* (2017) examined research based on first-person accounts of depression from non-western countries. They considered the symptoms that people identified and compared these with the symptoms as described in ICD-11 and DSM-5. The authors found support for some of the traditional western diagnostic features of depression, but they also found that people commonly talked about symptoms not included in the western understandings of depression, including social isolation/loneliness, crying, anger and general physical pain.

The research described in this section suggests that the cultural and social context of mental health is important and supports the idea that mental health difficulties are at least partly a product of culture (Chapter 19 will further explore this idea).

3   Theoretical perspectives on depression and anxiety

Depression and anxiety may be common, but a key question remains: Why do some people develop these conditions while others don't? Understandings of depression and anxiety are important in counselling because, ideally, 'treatment' should logically follow from theory (e.g. if depression is understood as being caused by chemical imbalances in the brain, then the logical treatment is a medication that adjusts these chemical levels).

One way to think about the various theories that aim to explain anxiety and depression is to consider the levels of explanation at which they exist, as depicted in Figure 5.2 (social factors in mental health are also discussed in Chapter 19).

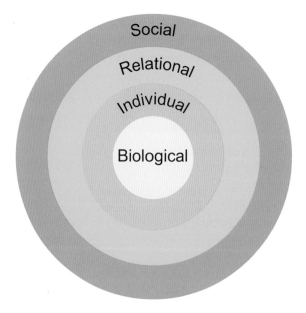

Figure 5.2 Levels of explanation of anxiety and depression

This section will describe the biological, individual and social factors that influence whether someone develops anxiety or depression, and the theories that seek to understand these factors. The levels of explanation are partly about scale (think about a powerful satellite camera zooming in on the earth): you see a town (social) and then a person (individual) and then the magic camera dips below the skin to peer at individual cells (biological). The role of relational factors in mental health difficulties, including depression and anxiety, is the focus of Chapter 7, so is not discussed further here.

3.1 Biological factors

One of the most common understandings of depression is that it is caused by low levels of the neurotransmitter 'serotonin' in the brain, yet this idea has been widely discredited (Cowen and Browning, 2015). Nonetheless, several biological mechanisms for depression and anxiety have been researched – for example, a considerable amount of research attention has been given to considering possible genetic foundations (Mullins and Lewis, 2017; Flint and Kendler, 2014; Gottschalk and Domschke, 2017). The rationale for looking at genetics is the body of evidence showing that both depression and anxiety are partly inherited; researchers estimate that, for adults, the heritability of either condition is 30–40 per cent (this is the proportion of variance in anxiety/depression that can be explained by genetic rather than environmental factors; Nivard *et al.*, 2015). However, it has been difficult for researchers to identify the specific genetic pathways involved in depression and anxiety, although the trend in genetics research to do massive sample studies is potentially beginning to change this (Howard *et al.*, 2018; Meier and Deckert, 2019; Wray *et al.*, 2018).

The story of one woman reveals how significantly genetics can impact mood. Following an article about her in the *British Journal of Anaesthesia* (Habib *et al.*, 2019), there were international news stories about Scottish pensioner Jo Cameron who, due to a rare genetic mutation, has very low pain sensitivity and anxiety. According to *The Guardian* newspaper:

> When a van driver ran her off the road two years ago, she climbed out of her car, which was on its roof in a ditch, and went to comfort the shaking young driver who cut across her. She only noticed her bruises later. She is relentlessly upbeat, and in stress and depression tests she scored zero.
>
> (Sample, 2019)

Medical conditions are also known to influence mood (directly, not just in that being sick is likely to make a person feel low). For example, a symptom of an underactive thyroid (hypothyroidism) is depression, while an overactive thyroid (hyperthyroidism) is associated with anxiety (the thyroid is a hormone-producing gland in the neck). Certain medications also seem to cause depression or anxiety (e.g. Celano *et al.*, 2011).

More recently, research on biological factors in depression and anxiety has focused on the gut microbiome, exploring the extent to which there is a healthy distribution of microorganisms in the digestive system. As discussed by MacQueen, Surette and Moayyedi (2017), this is a research area still in its infancy, but that has not prevented a surge in public interest in using probiotics to address both mood and physical health complaints.

Neurobiology
The study of the biology of the nervous system. In psychology specifically, it tends to mean the study of brain processes and structures and their impact on human behaviour.

Perhaps, however, the greatest research focus in this area has been on the **neurobiology** of depression and anxiety – this is the study of what structures and processes in the brain are implicated in these disorders. A lot of this research is focused on trying to understand what and how medications (e.g. antidepressants) might successfully effect change in anxiety and depression. The promise of this research is the potential to greatly improve the success rates of antidepressants and anti-anxiety medications; yet, as argued by one group of researchers in the area, 'the history of the past 50 years does not give cause for unrestrained optimism' (Willner, Scheel-Krüger and Belzung, 2013).

3.2   Individual factors

Research examining rates of depression and anxiety has found that some subgroups of people are more at risk of these disorders. When the people in these subgroups all share a personal characteristic (e.g. they are all women) it can be argued that this characteristic may be a causal factor in depression and/or anxiety. There can be a variety of reasons why each individual factor may be associated with increased risk of depression and anxiety. The explanations in Table 5.1 draw on biological, psychological and social understandings, known collectively as 'biopsychosocial' explanations.

Individual characteristics associated with depression and anxiety

Epidemiology has identified several individual characteristics involved in depression and anxiety, some of which are presented in Table 5.1.

Table 5.1 Individual factors involved in depression and anxiety

Individual factor	Biopsychosocial explanation
Being female or transgender	Females are twice as likely as males to report symptoms of depression. While this may in part be due to differences in gender socialisation, it is also explained by hormonal factors (such as activating sex hormones) which increase vulnerability to depression in women/girls. For example, a subgroup of women are susceptible to depression due to normal hormonal changes during premenstrual, peripartal and perimenopausal phases. In addition to hormonal factors, women are more likely to face severe adversity, such as childhood sexual abuse, violence, and structural gender inequity. They also face stressors such as combined responsibilities at home and work, single parenthood, and caring for aging parents and children (Kuehner, 2017). Sexual minorities, particularly transgender individuals, are also at a higher risk. This may be in part as a result of stressors induced by a hostile or homophobic environment. In addition, a significant proportion have had to struggle with the isolation of gender identity issues and sometimes trauma (Bockting *et al.*, 2013).
Old age	Being an older adult is associated with a higher risk of depression and anxiety. This is due to factors such as increased loneliness, health difficulties and reduced activity (Courtin and Knapp, 2017).

Epidemiology
The study of how often and why diseases occur in different populations.

Black, Asian and minority ethnic (BAME) groups in the UK	BAME groups in the UK are more likely to be diagnosed with mental health problems. They are also more likely to be hospitalised and to experience a poor outcome in treatment. This may be explained by the failure of mainstream mental health services to understand and adapt services to non-white British communities. It may also be due to factors such as poverty and racism (Mental Health Foundation, 2019; Breland-Noble and Miranda, 2017).
History of maternal depression	This factor is linked to genetics, but it is also explained by psychological theory: struggling with depression can lead to a mother's detachment from her baby, inability to be responsive to her child's needs, and apathy, which is a precursor to the infant developing depression and anxiety in later life (e.g. Madigan *et al.*, 2018).
Personality traits	Perfectionism is associated with high risk. Individuals who view themselves or the world with pessimism or who engage in rumination are particularly vulnerable. Some well-known personality dimensions such as neuroticism and introversion are associated with depression (e.g. Janowsky, Morter and Hong, 2002).

Pause for reflection

As identified in Table 5.1, being part of the non-dominant culture or a minority group is associated with higher risk of depression and anxiety. In society, how might issues of power affect minority groups?

Exploring individual risk factors for depression and anxiety provides a useful way to understand these conditions. However, beyond individual characteristics, there is a question about why and how a particular female/older/BAME person developed depression. The core theories of counselling practice (which are explored in Part 3 of this book) each provide an understanding of how mental health difficulties (in general) emerge; some of these core theories also provide understandings that explain why particular individuals develop depression and anxiety.

Psychological theories of depression and anxiety

When psychologists and other mental health professionals come into contact with depressed or anxious clients, they seek to understand why they are depressed or anxious. In drawing up their explanation – or formulation (discussed in Chapter 8) – they may draw on some of the following (non-exhaustive) themes.

Learnt responses to environmental triggers

Depression and anxiety can be understood as behavioural responses learnt through past interactions with a person's environment. Depression, for instance, can be understood as passivity resulting from the inability to prevent past unpleasant experiences (this is known as **learned helplessness**; Maier and Seligman, 1976). Similarly, an anxiety such as a phobia may be learnt through vicarious conditioning; for example, a child who witnesses their mother react with fear at the sight of a spider is susceptible to developing a phobia of spiders (Bandura and Rosenthal, 1966).

Learned helplessness
Behaviour exhibited by a person after enduring repeated aversive stimuli beyond their control, characterised by the person's acceptance of their powerlessness.

Related therapeutic approaches include cognitive behavioural therapy (CBT). As Chapter 3 explained, where behaviours have been learnt, behavioural therapy can be used to 'unlearn' them. In the case of phobia, techniques such as exposure – where an individual is gradually exposed to the feared object to increase their tolerance to it – can be used. If an individual is low in energy or apathic due to depression, techniques such as **behavioural activation**, using a schedule of activities, are applied to interfere with the negative pattern. (Chapter 10 will further explore the CBT approach.)

Behavioural activation
A technique used to get a depressed person re-engaged in daily activities.

Negative thinking styles

Depression and anxiety can be understood as pervasive negative thinking, which affects emotions, physiology and patterns of behaviour. Individuals who tend to think negatively are at greater risk of developing these conditions. These thinking styles may develop from negative **schemas** originating from a range of experiences and include, for instance, the tendency to attribute failure to oneself as opposed to the circumstances. Anxiety is understood as a result of chronic

Schema
A cognitive framework or concept that helps a person to organise and interpret information.

worrying about what is out of one's control. These thinking styles impact feelings and behaviours in ways that are likely to confirm original beliefs and maintain symptoms of anxiety and depression.

Related psychological approaches include CBT. As outlined in Chapter 3, the CBT model proposes that targeting cognitions and behaviours can help break the negative cycles that perpetuate negative feelings and lead to depression or anxiety. CBT consists of testing assumptions and integrating new information to improve how a person feels. Therapy progresses by challenging deeper core beliefs that have led to negative thinking. For instance, a person may believe that they are unacceptable or worthless (leading to sad thoughts and feelings), or that the world is a dangerous place (leading to fearful thoughts and feelings) (e.g. Leahy, 2006; Ellis, 1980).

Reactions to stressful experiences (adjustment)

Depression and anxiety can be viewed as a normal consequence of being exposed to stressful experiences such as the death of a loved one, divorce or marital problems, or the loss of a job. Difficult experiences may lead to a sense of loss or failure, fostering hopelessness and depression; or they may affect an individual's sense of control, leading to anxiety.

Precipitating factor
A factor that causes or contributes to the occurrence of a disorder.

Related psychological approaches include humanistic approaches. Many psychological theories acknowledge the impact of stressful events as **precipitating factors** in the development of symptoms of depression and anxiety. Humanistic approaches focus on acceptance, allowing space and providing support for the individual to adjust to change (Chapter 11 covers humanistic approaches).

Conflict resulting from unprocessed or preverbal emotions

Depression and anxiety can emerge from unresolved and unconscious conflicts. Such conflicts arise from residual emotions originating from negative experiences in infancy or childhood. At this early time, a person has both a limited vocabulary and capacity to understand their environment and experiences, which prevents effective processing of negative emotions. An example of this may be residual anger that was perceived as unsafe to express, and as a result is turned inwards at the self, leading to depression.

Related psychological approaches include psychodynamic therapy. As outlined in Chapter 3, psychodynamic theory proposes that some individuals encounter real or symbolic conflicts (and resultant losses) early in their development and may experience anger or rage as a result. This 'unacceptable' (in their family context) anger is then turned inwards as an attack towards the self. Psychodynamic approaches base treatment on insights that can be gained from talking through issues, and interpretations made by the therapist. Individuals gradually become more aware of, and able to talk about and understand, these inner conflicts. Preverbal experiences can be explored by working with the unconscious mind and by applying techniques such as free association – a way of working that aims to make unconscious processes conscious and to enable the individual to process residual emotions from negative childhood experiences (Chapter 9 will explore psychodynamic approaches).

Maladaptive rigid behaviours

Depression and anxiety can arise when an individual is unable to adapt to change because they rigidly respond to their environment or over-rely on a particular belief system. Adapting to change can be particularly challenging when such responses formed coping strategies previously important for the individual's survival, and which therefore became part of their sense of identity. These could be implicit reactions in the family environment which conferred approval or safety and were not questioned by the individual. As contexts change, rigid behaviours have the potential to become maladaptive, leading to depression or anxiety.

Related psychological approaches include person-centred therapy. This approach would further describe difficulty adapting to change as a person clinging to a particular self-image – one that emerged as a response to conditional acceptance at a time when they depended on a caregiver for safety. As a result, the individual is unable to respond to their own experience and becomes unable to grow and change. The emerging awareness of this **incongruence** becomes a source of anxiety as it challenges their sense of identity. Person-centred therapy aims to offer a genuine relationship based on empathy, warmth and acceptance to allow the person to trust and respond to their own experiences as opposed to internalised self-expectations (e.g. Cooper *et al.*, 2013; Chapter 11 will further explore person-centred therapy).

Incongruence
A person-centred term that refers to an inconsistency between how a person would like to be and how they see themselves.

Integrative, including pluralistic, approaches

Integrative approaches combine multiple theories to create an understanding that may best reflect the client's presenting issues (the problems that cause a person to seek counselling). When integrating theories to develop a treatment plan, collaborative integrative approaches, such as pluralistic therapy, also take into account the client's own understanding of their depression or anxiety, as well as their strengths and resources. As well as being empowering for clients, this approach can be useful for considering the many possible causes and understandings of depression and anxiety (Cooper and McLeod, 2010; Chapter 12 will cover integrative and pluralistic approaches in depth).

Pause for reflection

Think of a problem that has affected your mental health, or that of a friend or family member. Which psychological approach seems to fit your understanding of this problem?

3.3   Social factors

The GAD-7 that you considered in Activity 5.2 prompts consideration of what it is about a particular individual that explains why they are anxious. However, looking only at individual factors in mental health misses critical understanding and risks a person feeling they are to blame for the way they are feeling. At a macro level, structures in society influence mental health and have the potential to alleviate or maintain psychological problems such as anxiety and depression. For example, a large body of evidence suggests that economic hardship has an impact on mental health and suicide rates. NHS England programmes, such as Increasing Access to Psychological Therapies, report that recovery rates are much lower in highly deprived areas (Delgadillo *et al.*, 2016). This is likely due to stresses incurred from financial problems and challenging environments. Some political decisions such as austerity – reducing social spending and increasing taxation – have exacerbated mental health risks for those with already precarious employment or housing situations, or with existing health problems. For example, austerity in Britain and Europe has been associated with worsening mental health and increased suicide rates (Stuckler *et al.*, 2017). Other political decisions, particularly the allocation of funding to social and health services, also have long-term effects on mental health (e.g. Allen *et al.*, 2014).

Conclusion

This chapter has focused on three questions:

- What are depression and anxiety?

- How common are they?

- What causes these conditions?

It is clear that widely accepted definitions of anxiety and depression exist, even while still being contested. Further, even if estimates of prevalence depend on contested definitions and differing ways of assessing frequency, there is, nonetheless, evidence that depression and anxiety are common enough to constitute a significant global health burden.

Lastly, there are multiple theories that seek to explain the factors that cause anxiety and depression at biological, individual and social levels (and even the relational level, which will be explored in Chapter 7). Yet significant questions remain, including: Can depression and anxiety be adaptive, and if so, how? To what extent do definitions and understandings of depression and anxiety developed in high-income, western settings apply globally? To what extent do the various understandings of the causes of depression and anxiety fit together?

Further reading

- This article reviews the evidence against simplistic understandings of depression as caused by serotonin levels in the brain while also suggesting that it may still be worth studying how this neurochemical influences mood:

  Cowen, P.J. and Browning, M. (2015) 'What has serotonin to do with depression?', *World Psychiatry*, 14(2), pp. 158–160.

- This short paper discusses how the revised ICD-11 attempted to consider the impact of culture on mental health:

  Gureje, O., Lewis-Fernandez, R., Hall, B.J. and Reed, G.M. (2019) 'Systematic inclusion of culture-related information in ICD-11', *World Psychiatry*, 18(3), pp. 357–358.

- This paper argues that psychiatric systems like the DSM-5 are increasingly medicalising emotional experience that is understandable and unproblematic:

  Horwitz, A.V. (2015) 'The DSM-5 and the continuing transformation of normal sadness into depressive disorder', *Emotion Review*, 7(3), pp. 209–215.

References

Allen, J., Balfour, R., Bell, R. and Marmot, M. (2014) 'Social determinants of mental health', *International Review of Psychiatry*, 26(4), pp. 392–407.

American Psychiatric Association (APA) (2013) *Diagnostic and statistical manual of mental disorders* (DSM-5). 5th edn. Washington: American Psychiatric Association Publishing.

Bandura, A. and Rosenthal, T.L. (1966) 'Vicarious classical conditioning as a function of arousal level', *Journal of Personality and Social Psychology*, 3(1), pp. 54–62.

Bateson, M., Brilot, B. and Nettle, D. (2011) 'Anxiety: an evolutionary approach', *The Canadian Journal of Psychiatry*, 56(12), pp. 707–715.

Bergstrom, C.T. and Meacham, F. (2016) 'Depression and anxiety: maladaptive byproducts of adaptive mechanisms', *Evolution, Medicine, & Public Health*, 2016(1), pp. 214–218.

Bockting, W.O., Miner, M.H., Swinburne Romine, R.E., Hamilton, A. and Coleman, E. (2013) 'Stigma, mental health, and resilience in an online sample of the US transgender population', *American Journal of Public Health*, 103(5), pp. 943–951.

Breland-Noble, A.M., and Miranda, J. (2017) 'Racial and ethnic disparities in depressive illness and clinical care', in Cohen, N.L. (ed.) *Public health perspectives on depressive disorders*. Baltimore: John Hopkins University Press, pp. 313–331.

Byers, A. (2018) *What it's really like going through a deep, dark depression*. Available at: https://www.healthline.com/health/mental-health/what-major-depression-is-really-like#1 (Accessed: 7 February 2020).

Celano, C.M., Freudenreich, O., Fernandez-Robles, C., Stern, T.A., Caro, M.A. and Huffman, J.C. (2011) 'Depressogenic effects of medications: a review', *Dialogues in Clinical Neuroscience*, 13(1), pp. 109–125.

Cooper, M. and McLeod, J. (2010) *Pluralistic counselling and psychotherapy*. London: SAGE Publications.

Cooper, M., O'Hara, M., Schmid, P.F. and Bohart, A. (eds.) (2013) *The handbook of person-centred psychotherapy and counselling*. 2nd edn. Basingstoke: Palgrave Macmillan.

Courtin, E. and Knapp, M. (2017) 'Social isolation, loneliness and health in old age: a scoping review', *Health & Social Care in the Community*, 25(3), pp. 799–812.

Cowen, P.J. and Browning, M. (2015) 'What has serotonin to do with depression?', *World Psychiatry*, 14(2), pp. 158–160.

Delgadillo, J., Saria, M., Ali, S. and Gilbody, S. (2016) 'On poverty, politics and psychology: the socioeconomic gradient of mental healthcare utilisation and outcomes', *British Journal of Psychiatry*, 209(5), pp. 429–430. doi:10.1192/bjp.bp.115.171017.

Ellis, A. (1980) 'Rational-emotive therapy and cognitive behavior therapy: similarities and differences', *Cognitive Therapy and Research*, 4, pp. 325–340.

Flint, J. and Kendler, K.S. (2014) 'The genetics of major depression', *Neuron*, 81(3), pp. 484–503.

Gilbert, P. (2006) 'Evolution and depression: issues and implications', *Psychological Medicine*, 36(3), pp. 287–297.

Gottschalk, M.G. and Domschke, K. (2017) 'Genetics of generalized anxiety disorder and related traits', *Dialogues in Clinical Neuroscience*, 19(2), pp. 159–168.

Habib, A.M., Okorokov, A.L., Hill, M.N., Bras, J.T., Lee, M.C., Li, S., Gossage, S.J., van Drimmelen, M., Morena, M., Houlden, H., Ramirez, J.D., Bennertt, D.L.H., Srivastava, D. and Cox, J.J. (2019) 'Microdeletion in a FAAH pseudogene identified in a patient with high anandamide concentrations and pain insensitivity', *British Journal of Anaesthesia*, 123(2), e249–e253. doi:10.1016/j.bja.2019.02.019.

Haroz, E.E., Ritchey, M., Bass, J.K., Kohrt, B.A., Augustinavicius, J., Michalopoulos, L., Burkey, M.D. and Bolton, P. (2017), 'How is depression experienced around the world? A systematic review of qualitative literature', *Social Science & Medicine*, 183, pp. 151–162.

Howard, D.M., Adams, M.J., Shirali, M., Clarke, T.K., Marioni, R.E., Davies, G., Coleman, J.R.I., Alloza, C., Shen, X., Barbu, M.C., Wigmore, E.M., Gibson, J., 23andMe Research Team, Hagenaars, S.P., Lewis, C.M., Ward, J., Smith, D.J., Sullivan, P.F., Haley, C.S., Breen, G., Deary, I.J. and McIntosh, A.M. (2018) 'Genome-wide association study of depression phenotypes in UK Biobank identifies variants in excitatory synaptic pathways', *Nature Communications*, 9(1), p. 1470.

Institute for Health Metrics and Evaluation (2019) *Global Health Data Exchange: GBD results tool*. Available at: http://ghdx.healthdata.org/gbd-results-tool (Accessed: 5 December 2019).

Janowsky, D.S., Morter, S. and Hong, L. (2002) 'Relationship of Myers Briggs type indicator personality characteristics to suicidality in affective disorder patients', *Journal of Psychiatric Research*, 36(1), pp. 33–39.

Judd, L.L., Kessler, R.C., Paulus, M.P., Zeller, P.V., Wittchen, H.U. and Kunovac, J.L. (1998) 'Comorbidity as a fundamental feature of generalized anxiety disorders: results from the National Comorbidity Study (NCS)', *Acta Psychiatrica Scandinavica*, 98(393), pp. 6–11.

Kato, T.A., Hashimoto, R., Hayakawa, K., Kubo, H., Watabe, M., Teo, A.R. and Kanba, S. (2016) 'Multidimensional anatomy of 'modern type depression' in Japan: a proposal for a different diagnostic approach to depression beyond the DSM-5', *Psychiatry and Clinical Neurosciences*, 70(1), pp. 7–23.

Keller, M.C. (2008) 'The evolutionary persistence of genes that increase mental disorders risk', *Current Directions in Psychological Science*, 17(6), pp. 395–399.

Kuehner, C. (2017) 'Why is depression more common among women than among men?', *The Lancet. Psychiatry*, 4(2), pp. 146–158.

Leahy, R.L. (ed.) (2006) *Contemporary cognitive therapy: theory, research, and practice*. New York: The Guilford Press.

MacQueen, G., Surette, M. and Moayyedi, P. (2017) 'The gut microbiota and psychiatric illness', *Journal of Psychiatry & Neuroscience*, 42(2), pp. 75–77.

Madigan, S., Oatley, H., Racine, N., Fearon, R.M.P., Schumacher, L., Akbari, E. and Tarabulsy, G.M. (2018) 'A meta-analysis of maternal prenatal depression and anxiety on child socioemotional development', *Journal of the American Academy of Child and Adolescent Psychiatry*, 57(9), pp. 645–657.

Maier, S.F. and Seligman, M.E. (1976) 'Learned helplessness: theory and evidence', *Journal of Experimental Psychology: General*, 105(1), pp. 3–46.

McManus, S., Bebbington, P., Jenkins, R., Brugha, T. (eds.) (2016) *Mental health and wellbeing in England: adult Psychiatric Morbidity Survey 2014*. Leeds: NHS Digital. Available at: https://www.gov.uk/government/statistics/adult-psychiatric-morbidity-survey-mental-health-and-wellbeing-england-2014 (Accessed: 28 February 2020).

Meacham, F. and Bergstrom, C.T. (2016) 'Adaptive behavior can produce maladaptive anxiety due to individual differences in experience', *Evolution, Medicine, & Public Health*, 2016(1), pp. 270–285.

Meier, S.M. and Deckert, J. (2019) 'Genetics of anxiety disorders', *Current Psychiatry Reports*, 21(3), p. 16.

Mental Health Foundation (2019) *Black, Asian and Minority Ethnic (BAME) communities*. Available at: https://www.mentalhealth.org.uk/a-to-z/b/black-asian-and-minority-ethnic-bame-communities (Accessed: 6 December 2019).

Miller, A.H. and Raison, C.L. (2016) 'The role of inflammation in depression: from evolutionary imperative to modern treatment target', *Nature Reviews. Immunology*, 16(1), pp. 22–34.

Moscati, A., Flint, J. and Kendler, K.S. (2016) 'Classification of anxiety disorders comorbid with major depression: common or distinct influences on risk?', *Depression & Anxiety*, 33(2), pp. 120–127.

Mullins, N. and Lewis, C.M. (2017) 'Genetics of depression: progress at last', *Current Psychiatry Reports*, 19(8), pp. 1–7.

Nettle, D. (2009) 'An evolutionary model of low mood states', *Journal of Theoretical Biology*, 257(1), pp. 100–103.

Nettle, D. and Bateson, M. (2012) 'The evolutionary origins of mood and its disorders', *Current Biology*, 22(17), pp. R712–R721.

Nivard, M.G., Dolan, C.V., Kendler, K.S., Kan, K.J., Willemsen, G., van Beijsterveldt, C.E.M., Lindauer, R.J.L., van Beek, J.H., Geels, L.M., Bartels, M., Middeldorp, C.M. and Boomsma, D.I. (2015) 'Stability in symptoms of anxiety and depression as a function of genotype and environment: a longitudinal twin study from ages 3 to 63 years', *Psychological Medicine*, 45(5), pp. 1039–1049.

Plummer, F., Manea, L., Trepel, D. and McMillan, D. (2016) 'Screening for anxiety disorders with the GAD-7 and GAD-2: a systematic review and diagnostic metaanalysis', *General Hospital Psychiatry*, 39, pp. 24–31.

Sample, I. (2019) 'Scientists find genetic mutation that makes woman feel no pain', *The Guardian*, 28 March. Available at: https://www.theguardian.com/science/2019/mar/28/scientists-find-genetic-mutation-that-makes-woman-feel-no-pain (Accessed: 3 September 2019).

Schnyder, N., Panczak, R., Groth, N. and Schultze-Lutter, F. (2017) 'Association between mental health-related stigma and active help-seeking: systematic review and meta-analysis', *The British Journal of Psychiatry*, 210(4), pp. 261–268.

Spitzer, R.L., Kroenke, K., Williams, J.B. and Löwe, B. (2006) 'A brief measure for assessing generalized anxiety disorder: the GAD-7', *Archives of Internal Medicine*, 166(10), pp. 1092–1097.

Stuckler, D., Reeves, A., Loopstra, R., Karanikolos, M. and McKee, M. (2017) 'Austerity and health: the impact in the UK and Europe', *European Journal of Public Health*, 27(suppl_4), pp. 18–21.

Ventriglio, A., Ayonrinde, O. and Bhugra, D. (2015) 'Relevance of culture-bound syndromes in the 21st century', *Psychiatry and Clinical Neurosciences*, 70 (1), pp. 3–6.

Willner, P., Scheel-Krüger, J. and Belzung, C. (2013) 'The neurobiology of depression and antidepressant action', *Neuroscience and Biobehavioral Reviews*, 37(10), pp. 2331–2371.

Wray *et al.* (2018) 'Genome-wide association analyses identify 44 risk variants and refine the genetic architecture of major depression', *Nature Genetics*, 50 (1), pp. 668–681.

Chapter 6
Trauma and crisis

Andrew Reeves and Christina Buxton

Contents

Introduction

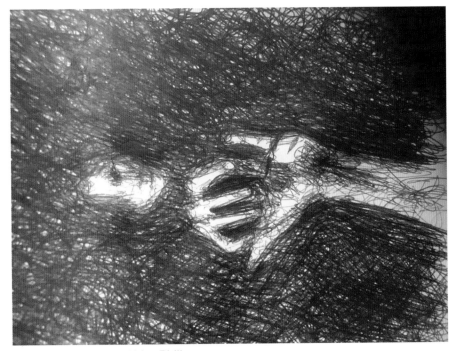

'A helping hand' by Abby Philips

Client presentations are becoming more complex, and trauma is increasingly something that mental health and counselling services are asked to respond to. The changing nature of mental health delivery in response to trauma and crisis has seen different professional groups coming into the frame. For many years, counsellors were probably seen as the last professional group able to respond to people in crisis (with psychiatrists, psychologists, social workers and mental health nurses being the professionals involved), but today it is much more usual for clients with trauma to present to counsellors, and trauma-related issues such as post-traumatic stress disorder (PTSD), self-injury and suicide are much more commonplace in counselling practice.

This chapter will consider how 'trauma' and 'crisis' are understood, including the diagnostic structures of these conditions and some of the presenting issues most commonly associated with the trauma response, including self-injury and suicide risk. The concept of risk itself will be considered more generally, as well as how those supporting others need to carefully attend to their management of risk in the helping context.

This chapter aims to:

- describe how trauma and crisis are understood, including how traumatic events are defined and presented in diagnoses

- offer an account of the risk factors of trauma and the effects of trauma on individuals

- describe what is meant by 'suicide' and 'self-injury' and consider how they can emerge as risks following traumatic experiences

- discuss how risk can be worked with in counselling, unpacking the concept of positive risk-taking and outlining the potential impact on therapists of working with trauma.

1   Understanding trauma and crisis

The term 'trauma' was originally used by the ancient Greeks to describe a physical wound or injury; however, today it has become synonymous with **psychological trauma**, referring to the psychological reactions experienced after a traumatic event or events. Freud was one of the first to attribute the term 'trauma' to a 'wound of the mind' (Caruth, 1996, p. 4). Freud (1922) describes psychological trauma as not a simple healable event, but an existential crisis that threatens our understanding of ourselves and the world in which we exist. Caruth (1996) positions trauma as much more than a wound of the mind: it erases the reality and truth an individual once believed in. Experiencing psychological trauma is, therefore, something that not only causes considerable problems with our psychological functioning, but also irrevocably shatters our beliefs about ourselves, others and the world around us, altering our sense of self and our identities (Janoff-Bulman, 1992). The charity MIND defines **crisis** as:

> when you feel your mental health is at breaking point, and you need urgent help and support. For example, you might have feelings or experiences that feel very painful or difficult to manage such as suicidal feelings, self-harm, panic attacks, flashbacks, hypomania or mania, or psychosis (such as paranoia or hearing voices). … Some people feel in crisis as part of ongoing mental health problems, or due to stressful and difficult life experiences such as abuse, bereavement, addiction, money problems or housing problems. Or there might not be a particular reason.

(MIND, 2019)

The experience of trauma will not necessarily move someone into a state of mental health crisis; however, high levels of trauma can be an important predisposing factor (as will be discussed in Section 3).

Psychological trauma
A psychological response to an experience of traumatic event(s).

Crisis
An experience of feeling your mental health is at breaking point and that urgent help/support is needed.

Activity 6.1: Traumatic events in the media

Allow about 10 minutes

There are many traumatic events reported in the media on a daily basis, such as natural disasters, terrorist activities and tragic accidents. Think of one or two such events and try to answer the questions below. (In the spirit of self-care, choose events that bear no resemblance to things you have experienced in your own life.)

1   Who has been affected by the event?

2   How might their lives be different after the event?

3   How might they think about the world now? Is it safe or unsafe? 'Good' or 'bad'? Are people kind or unkind?

4   What kinds of emotional and behavioural responses might they have?

5   How might this event change the way they see themselves?

Discussion

Traumatic events have impacts beyond the people directly involved – family members, partners, children, even work colleagues can also be affected. People who have experienced trauma may now feel that the world is no longer safe. They may feel worried and scared but also really low.

1.1   Types of traumatic events

Attempts have been made to classify traumatic events by how likely they are to cause problematic reactions. Shapiro (1995) distinguished between two kinds of trauma associated with different types of events:

- *Small-t traumas*: Associated with distressing life events that involve negative emotional reactions and provoke unpleasant thoughts and memories, such as the loss of a pet or family fights.

- *Large-T traumas*: Associated with overwhelming, highly distressing events, such as torture, rape and war, which are viewed as hallmark events for a traumatic reaction.

In making this distinction, Shapiro was drawing a line between events that are life-threatening and those that are not. However, some critics of this distinction say that it negates the often devastating effects that ongoing small-t traumas can have on an individual's lived experience (e.g. James and MacKinnon, 2012).

Terr (1991) took a more developmental approach and originally made a distinction between type I and type II traumas experienced in childhood. These terms, however, are now used to refer more to the nature of the event(s), rather than to the age at which they were experienced:

- *Type I traumas*: Single, one-off unexpected traumatic events, such as car accidents and natural disasters.

- *Type II traumas*: Ongoing and repeated exposure to traumatic events, as in the case of domestic violence and childhood abuse.

The events categorised by type II traumas are often perpetrated by those we (should) trust, and therefore involve a violation of personal boundaries. Type II traumas are also often associated with more complex responses, such as disjointed memories, emotional numbing, anger and dissociation (Herman, 1992).

1.2   Diagnostic definitions of traumatic events

The *Diagnostic and statistical manual of mental disorders*, currently in its fifth revision (DSM-5; American Psychiatric Association (APA), 2013) states that a traumatic event must involve 'death, threatened death, actual or threatened serious injury, or actual or threatened sexual violence' (APA, 2013, p. 271). It also states that this event must have been experienced in person, witnessed, or 'experienced' by learning that it has happened to someone close to the individual. However, it only considers violent or accidental events to be traumatic, which rules out death from a terminal illness. DSM-5 made it possible for individuals exposed to such events as a result of doing their job to be eligible for a diagnosis of PTSD. Previous editions of the DSM had not allowed for the idea that PTSD responses could result from a person's work-related exposure to traumatic experience. Although this phenomenon is recognised widely in occupational literature relating to the helping professions, the extension to the pool of people eligible for a PTSD diagnosis is not included in the more recent *International classification of diseases* (ICD), currently in its eleventh revision (ICD-11; World Health Organization (WHO), 2018).

ICD-11 retains a much simpler definition of a traumatic event, seeing it simply as 'an extremely threatening or horrific event or series of events' (WHO, 2018). Unlike DSM-5, this defines a traumatic event by the reaction that is expected to follow, rather than by the features of the event itself. ICD-11 also differs from DSM-5 in that it includes a reference to 'events' to capture those affected by multiple events, as in the type II traumas described above.

1.3   Trauma versus trauma diagnoses

It is important to note that not everyone who experiences a traumatic event(s) will develop problematic reactions. When we experience a traumatic event, our perception of that event will determine whether or not we will suffer psychological trauma as a result. What is a relatively innocuous occurrence for one person could bring about a profound, life-altering crisis for another, depending on the meaning attached to the event. Many people experience a traumatic event and do not go on to develop severe reactions. Indeed, most people who are exposed to a traumatic event have some level of understandable psychological problems for a number of days afterwards, but most return to their prior psychological state, with no, or limited, longer-term effects.

Pause for reflection

What might increase the likelihood of having a severe reaction to an event? Your answer might tell you something about how you currently view trauma. As you continue reading the chapter and encounter new ideas, consider which ones challenge your views.

If people have ongoing difficulty after a traumatic event, they may reach a threshold when they become eligible for a trauma-related diagnosis. As highlighted in Chapter 4, however, such diagnoses are seen by some to pathologise an understandable, 'normal' reaction to a distressing and threatening event. Additionally, despite formally becoming 'disordered' at this point (in that the person now has a diagnosis), the person's experience of their symptoms is unlikely to substantially change; rather, they will have reached a point where the number and type of symptoms they experience satisfy the criteria for a trauma-related disorder. It is important to consider the categorisations of both DSM-5 and ICD-11 (see Information box 6.1), as they not only conceptualise trauma disorders differently, but also recognise different time thresholds for trauma-related disorders.

Information box 6.1: Categorisations of trauma-related disorders

The categories of trauma-related disorders, according to both DSM-5 (APA, 2013) and ICD-11 (WHO, 2018), are outlined below in reference to the length of time that symptoms are experienced.

- *Acute stress reaction (ASR)*: Seen as a 'normal' stress response. Defined in both DSM-5 and ICD-11 as a stress response lasting for up to three days.

- *Acute stress disorder (ASD)*: Refers to ASR symptoms that do not subside within one month of the trauma, included only in DSM-5. It can be thought of as a diagnosis to describe early-stage responses to trauma.

- *Post-traumatic stress disorder (PTSD)*: Defined by DSM-5 as a trauma-related reaction persisting beyond one month, and in ICD-11 as a trauma-based reaction persisting for at least several weeks. It describes later-stage responses to trauma. Note that not everyone who meets the criteria for ASD goes on to develop PTSD and that people can develop PTSD without having experienced ASD.

- *Complex PTSD (CPTSD)*: Precipitated by the onset of PTSD. It is included only in ICD-11.

The usefulness of such diagnostic classifications is very much in debate. Some see them as reflecting an endemic societal power imbalance and therefore suggest that they be discarded altogether (Watson, 2019). Others propose alternative frameworks that exclude the 'disordered' label and other such pathologising language (Johnstone, 2019). However, the reality is that DSM-5 and ICD-11 currently provide the only widely recognised, legally and clinically accepted categorisations of human experience. As such, an awareness of the diagnostic categorisations related to trauma is essential.

2   Risk factors for trauma-related disorders

When someone is exposed to a traumatic event, the effects they experience can be varied, and the nature of the impact will depend in part on the presence or absence of various risk factors.

2.1   Trauma risk factors

Many factors have been identified that can influence whether or not someone is likely to experience psychological trauma as a result of a traumatic event. These are grouped into three areas and are outlined in Figure 6.1.

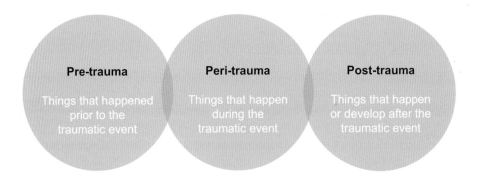

Figure 6.1 Categories of risk factors for trauma-related disorders

'Pre-trauma' risk factors have consistently been shown to predict the severity of reactions to a traumatic event. These factors include having previously experienced a traumatic event (Kessler *et al.*, 2014) and having previously experienced a mental health problem (Wild *et al.*, 2016). Being female, belonging to a black, Asian or other minority ethnic group, and having a lower level of education are also risk factors for developing more severe traumatic reactions (Xue *et al.*, 2015).

Dissociation is an influential peri-traumatic risk factor predicting the severity of a traumatic outcome. Dissociation occurs when a person is disconnected from themselves and their immediate environment. A person can dissociate either physically (by feeling that things are not really happening; like they are in a dream or a trance) or cognitively (by feeling disconnected from the emotions or sensations that accompany experiences). These reactions are not deliberate; they form a part of our instinctive survival mechanisms (Myrick and Brand, 2015). Evidence for both forms of peri-traumatic dissociation shows that a more complex traumatic response will likely result when dissociation is experienced (Kumpula *et al.*, 2011).

In relation to 'post-trauma' risk factors, experiencing a mental health problem has been associated with the development of more severe post-trauma reactions (e.g. Galatzer-Levy *et al.*, 2013). A lack of social support is also associated with a higher number and greater severity of trauma symptoms (Robinaugh *et al.*, 2011). In addition, where social support is absent, these symptoms tend to last longer (Sayed, Iacoviello and Charney, 2015). Together, this evidence shows the importance of positive social relationships for good mental health (an idea further unpacked in Chapter 7).

Pause for reflection

What are your reactions to the diagnostic classifications of trauma and crisis outlined in the chapter so far? How would you feel having such categorisations applied to you or someone close to you? Academically and clinically, such classifications provide useful information, but they can also be seen to ignore the human element of experiencing crisis. It is important to remember that behind such systems is always someone who is suffering and in distress.

2.2   Impacts of trauma

DSM-5 and ICD-11 categorise impacts of trauma into sets of symptoms that define the effects of trauma. Problematically, while both manuals specify the nature and number of symptoms required for the diagnosis of a trauma-related disorder, there are some differences in the way they understand these symptoms. Possible trauma effects include:

- *Intrusions*: Aspects of the event that intrude into a person's daily life through disturbing memories, dreams and flashbacks.

- *Avoidance*: Attempts to avoid reminders of the event, including people and places.

- *Negative thoughts and feelings*: Ongoing negative changes in a person's emotions and to the way they think about themselves, such as increased self-blame, guilt and emotional disconnection from others.

- *Being nervous/angry/irritable*: Changes to the way a person reacts to the world around them, such as increased anger, irritability or being 'jumpy' and constantly on edge.

The negative effects of exposure to traumatic events, as captured by the diagnostic frameworks, are widely considered to be the hallmark features of psychological trauma. The diagnostic frameworks tend to be primarily based on symptoms rather than on how a person's ability to function in their life is affected. Yet these effects ripple out into all aspects of an individual's functioning, resulting in issues with intimate relationships (Taft *et al.*, 2011) and with familial and wider social relationships (Riggs and Riggs, 2011). As the effects spread further, they adversely impact on employability, quality of life and wider social and community functioning. In order to fully appreciate the impact that trauma can have, it is therefore important to take account of the ways in which these effects shape an individual's life in a much wider context, rather than to view them simply as the sum total of the diagnostic symptoms. To consider this point further, read the case illustration below (which is a fictional client story).

Case illustration: Alfie, the army and trauma

I joined the army when I was 16. I've never been one for study, so joining the army offered a good job for someone like me. The initial training was hard. I swear those drill sergeants got a kick out of pushing us all to the limit, both physically and mentally.

When I finished training, I was chosen as part of a unit to go to Iraq. I was so proud – what an honour! All the guys I trained with were so jealous; after all, this is why we had done all that training. We saw some real action there too – when bullets are whizzing by you can't help but wonder if this might be the end. But then the adrenaline kicks in and you just get on with it; after all, you have a job to do and others depend on you doing it well. The whole time I was there it felt like living on a knife edge.

I completed two tours in Iraq and then I was posted with the same regiment to Afghanistan. For the first time in my life I felt like I fitted in, like I was part of one big family. I made some good mates during those times and we had each other's backs. While I was on my last tour my best mate was badly injured in a skirmish. I headed toward him, shouting for cover. We were under heavy fire but I was not going to leave him there – he would have done the same for me. I managed to drag him back far enough to get him evacuated by the medics. I was gutted when I later heard that he had died as a result of his injuries.

That one affected me badly and I was sent home on leave for a few months. But at home it felt like no one really 'got' me anymore – old friends would come around, but I could not relate to them at all. They were so preoccupied with the small stuff in life, but I knew that kind of stuff really didn't matter. I felt lost without my army routine, I had little motivation to do anything. My parents irritated me, treating me like I was 16 again. They just didn't understand who I was anymore. I ended up sleeping most of the time and not going out, just to avoid having to pretend I was someone who I wasn't. I wanted to go back so much, I missed the army and my military family, I could be myself with them and they understood me. Being on leave felt like torture!

Activity 6.2: Alfie's experience

Allow about 20 minutes

Consider the following questions:

1   Using the list of possible trauma effects (at the beginning of Section 2.2), what aspects of Alfie's experiences would be classed as 'symptoms' of PTSD?

2   What aspects of the experiences that Alfie describes do you think represent the wider relational and social effects that are not captured by these criteria?

3   What aspects of the military culture that Alfie describes do you think contributed to his responses?

Discussion

Alfie has been in combat, exposed to the risk of death and has witnessed fellow soldiers being severely injured, so he meets the criteria for PTSD in terms of his experience. He also meets it in terms of time since exposure to trauma, as it has been a few months since he was in the firefight in which his friend was fatally injured.

Alfie talks about feeling irritable, constantly on edge and emotionally disconnected from others – all classic PTSD symptoms. He also, however, talks about a wider sense of disconnect from others who have not experienced military life, and a changed sense of identity – he feels like he no longer fits in at home. This is perhaps an example of the wider social impact of the trauma. One aspect of military culture that seems important for Alfie is that he experiences a strong emotional bond with his unit. While this could be understood as a potential protective factor for him (social support), the absence of that support when he is at home can be seen to create additional challenges.

3 Trauma, self-injury and the risk of suicide

In the scientific literature, self-injury and suicide are strongly linked to trauma, particularly so when a person moves into a mental health crisis. This section looks at how suicide and self-injury can be understood and defined.

3.1 Unpacking 'suicide' and 'self-injury'

De Leo *et al.* (2006, p. 12) define suicide as 'an act with fatal outcome, which the deceased, knowing or expecting a potentially fatal outcome, has initiated and carried out with the purpose of bringing about wanted changes', while WHO (2014, p. 12) defines suicide as 'the act of deliberately killing oneself'. In practice, however, it is probably more helpful to consider what is meant by 'suicidal' than to understand the definition of 'suicide'. Particularly in the context of trauma and crisis, thoughts of suicide – suicidal ideation – can be commonplace and it is challenging to determine the extent to which somebody might present a **suicide risk**. For example, if someone says 'sometimes I want to go to sleep and not wake up', this might communicate a different level of intent from if they say 'I am going to kill myself'.

Suicide risk
The degree to which a person is seen as being at risk of taking their own life.

When considering the research that explores issues around self-injury, it is important to note that various terms with slightly different definitions are often used (e.g. NICE, 2011; Reeves, 2017). Predominantly, the primary terms are 'self-injury' and 'self-harm'. These are often used interchangeably but they can refer to different behaviours:

- ***Self-injury***: Harm caused to oneself with direct and immediate consequence; for example, cutting, burning, hitting and ingesting dangerous substances (including medications) (e.g. NICE, 2011; Reeves, 2017).

Self-injury
Actions or behaviours that intentionally cause injury to oneself but are engaged in without suicidal intent.

- *Self-harm*: Harm caused to oneself with indirect and deferred consequences; for example, over-exercising, disordered eating, smoking, drinking alcohol and taking drugs, and sexual risk-taking (e.g. Reeves, 2017).

A further point is that someone can self-harm or self-injure regardless of whether they intend to kill themselves (Babiker and Arnold, 1997;

Royal College of Psychiatrists, 2010). This section only looks at self-injury, as it can potentially flag a suicide risk.

3.2   Trauma, suicide risk factors and assessing risk in practice

Prior experience of trauma is one risk factor for suicide (Sarchiapone *et al.*, 2007). Other risk factors (factors that make a client's suicide more likely) include gender, age, employment status and mental health distress. Protective factors (factors that make a client's suicide less likely) include having a supportive network, engagement with mental health services and a willingness to explore the emotional content of experiences (McLean *et al.*, 2008). Consider Information box 6.2, which provides statistics on suicide in the UK in relation to gender and age risk factors.

Information box 6.2: Gender, age and suicide risk in the UK

In the UK, the Office for National Statistics (ONS) tracks and reports deaths as a result of suicide. According to ONS (2019), in 2018 there were 6507 suicides registered in the UK, and three-quarters of those who died were men. (These statistics reflect a prevalence that has been true in the UK since the mid-1990s.) The ONS statistics show that, for both men and women, the age group with the highest suicide rate in 2018 was 45–49. ONS also reported that suicide rates are going up in young people, particularly young women.

It is important for suicide researchers to examine risk and protective factors, with the aim of improving suicide prevention programmes. However, in actual practice with service users, applying such factors in a particular circumstance generally does not provide the information needed to make better sense of someone's experience – it does not reliably reveal the risk level for a particular service user in a given time and place.

Clearly, if in doubt, practitioners should ask about suicide potential. The single biggest myth in working with suicide is that, by asking about it, risk is increased. Rather, at worst, asking about suicide will leave the level of risk unchanged; however, asking about suicide often leads to a decrease in risk, as it presents an opportunity for service users to articulate thoughts and feelings. In therapeutic relationships that are founded on a dialogic–relational approach (where talking-based help is embedded in a relationship), gaining insight into a person's thoughts around suicide is more about listening to what they say than about discerning risk and protective factors. This may seem an obvious statement but, in practice, being able to hear the level of suicide potential embedded in a person's narrative can be notoriously difficult. Figure 6.2 outlines some indicative ways people can talk about their suicidal thoughts, linked to the ways in which people might be asked about them in therapy.

Figure 6.2 A dialogic framework for understanding levels of, and responding to, suicide risk

While the differentiation between acceptable risk and risk that requires action might appear obvious in print, in the therapeutic relationship the line between these two can cause great anxiety. It can be complicated determining whether it is helpful and appropriate to contain the risk within the confidential nature of the relationship and to work with the person to help them understand their distress, or whether the level of risk is too high for that degree of containment and a referral to a specialist service or further assessment is needed.

4   Working with risk in counselling

'Risk' is a term widely used in mental health settings, although perhaps usually thought of in a binary way – someone is either at risk or they are not. The reality is that life is often much more complicated than that. The term 'risk' seems to have become a shorthand for risk of self-injury and/or suicide, but in reality, risk is a multifaceted concept. When supporting others, it is important not only to be familiar with what kind of risk is relevant to the situation, but also to have the skills to work actively with it. Furthermore, risk tends to be defined in the negative: the risk of harm or an undesired outcome. The reality is, however, that mental health support can be highly effective for those who present as 'at risk' when the risk is collaboratively identified, discussed and explored in therapy. This concept, increasingly described by the term 'positive risk-taking' (which means taking risks for positive outcomes), acknowledges that mental health work will commonly involve engaging with risk in a way that facilitates change, rather than simply avoiding the potential of harm.

The risk-averse way of working would, of course, simply be for mental health workers to refer clients on to more specialist services should risk be identified. It could be asserted that, if practitioners were to refer all 'risky' clients on to specialist services, then most clients who seek help would simply be referred on. Alternatively, if a suitable and collaborative approach can be agreed with the client – perhaps with the support of a 'keep safe plan' (discussed in Section 4.1) – risk itself need not be the critical problem. Rather, working with a person who has the ability to explore particular areas of vulnerability and distress can provide an important opportunity for the client to make the necessary changes they have identified.

4.1   Keep safe plans

Using a **keep safe plan** – sometimes also referred to as a 'crisis plan' – can be a really effective way to work collaboratively with people around risk. As discussed, the traditional model of working with risk is for the mental health worker, such as a counsellor, to 'manage' it and make (often unilateral) decisions about the best course of action to take. This usually requires obtaining informed consent from the client (where this is possible) before enacting any intervention plan. Consent remains central to any working plan, so it must be asked whether a

Keep safe plan
A plan developed collaboratively with a client who is experiencing suicidal thoughts, to keep the client safe.

'done to' approach can really capture the level of informed consent that can be achieved with a 'done with' approach. The process of developing a keep safe plan, embedded within the therapeutic process, is a good example of a 'done with' approach.

Reeves (2015) outlined some of the key aspects that should be considered and included in a keep safe plan (see Information box 6.3). The information is captured in-session in the context of a therapeutic dialogue. The plan is then reviewed on a weekly basis to ensure it remains the best response to the person's changing needs.

Information box 6.3: What to include in a keep safe plan

- The actual risk being considered (e.g. thoughts of taking an overdose)

- The times when the risks are likely to be at their highest (e.g. at night)

- 'Red flags' the client might be aware of that could trigger such thoughts (e.g. when they are alone)

- Factors that make the feelings worse, being as specific as possible (e.g. alcohol or drugs)

- Factors that make the feelings better, being as specific as possible (e.g. being around people)

- Who is available to offer informal support (e.g. family, friends)?

- Who is available to offer formal support (e.g. a crisis team, accident and emergency, a telephone helpline) and ensuring details such as telephone numbers are recorded on the plan?

- What might make accessing support less likely (e.g. not wanting to wake someone up)?

- What might make accessing support more likely (e.g. agreeing contact with someone in advance)?

- Intrapersonal mechanisms for self-care (e.g. meditation, breathing techniques, distraction)

- A date for review (which will usually be the next session).

(Reeves, 2015, p. 62)

As discussed, risk is often unhelpfully defined in a binary way (there is either risk or there is no risk), particularly in relation to situational risks, such as that of suicide. The keep safe plan outlined above demonstrates clearly the assertion made that risk is not binary; that is, aspects of the keep safe plan illustrate the different layers of risk that underpin suicide potential and how the likelihood of suicide occurring relates to many complex, and often subtle, factors.

4.2   Impacts on the practitioner of working with risk

Best practice in working with trauma-related issues or crisis – particularly when crisis is framed by self-injury or suicide risk – includes considering the potential impacts that working with these issues could have on the practitioner.

Practitioners are not immune to the effects of working with trauma and risk. It has been shown that many professions working with traumatised and high-risk people are vulnerable to its contagious effect. These professions include nurses (Wies and Coy, 2013), doctors (Nimmo and Huggard, 2013), social workers (Canfield, 2005) and community health workers (Lynch and Lobo, 2012). These effects have been given a variety of labels over the years, including 'secondary traumatic stress' (Figley, 1995), 'burnout' (Maslach, 1982), 'compassion fatigue' (Figley, 2002) and 'vicarious trauma' (McCann and Pearlman, 1990). Each label brings a new understanding of what happens to practitioners as a result of the work they do.

There is widespread acceptance that the effects of working with trauma and risk are insidious, pervasive and enduring. As well as experiencing many of the same trauma symptoms as the people with whom they work, practitioners report other common effects, including a sense of helplessness, feeling overwhelmed, reduced self-efficacy and an inability to empathise, with resultant negative beliefs about themselves and the world around them. Certain professions are thought to be more vulnerable to these effects. Those working therapeutically with psychological trauma are often at greater risk, as their work involves a deep empathetic engagement with pain and suffering and the need to listen to first-hand accounts of disturbing narratives (Hunter, 2012). This leaves the therapist emotionally exposed and psychologically vulnerable in ways others are not (Baird and Kracen, 2006). Table 6.1 summarises some of the factors that make it more or less likely that practitioners will experience a trauma response.

Table 6.1 Factors that contribute to or mitigate trauma responses in practitioners

Contributing factors	Mitigating factors
Limited regular self-care practices	Regular independent trauma-focused supervision
Higher levels of exposure to traumatic material in work	Being a self-aware and reflexive practitioner
Having your own trauma history	Having a sense of accomplishment and job satisfaction
Experiencing current traumatic life events	
	Having good social support
Feeling a limited degree of empathic engagement	Receiving trauma-specific training
Being younger in age	Utilising adaptive coping strategies
Having worked longer as a therapist	Having a sense of self-enhancing humour
Adopting maladaptive coping strategies	Maintaining boundaries between personal and work life
A lack of organisational/managerial support	

(Source: Reeves, 2017)

Conclusion

This chapter has stressed the multidimensional nature of trauma and crisis. Trauma is defined differently in different diagnostic systems, and criticisms of these definitions exist. One key criticism is that the risk factors for and the effects of trauma go far beyond those outlined in diagnostic trauma symptoms. The chapter has defined the concepts of 'self-injury' and 'suicide' and suggested that a relationship exists between the experience of trauma and the emergence of suicide ideation or self-injury. This chapter has presented an approach to working with risk – one that includes working 'positively' with risk in therapy. Finally, the chapter has discussed the potential negative impacts for professionals (in particular counsellors and therapists) of working with trauma and crisis. An awareness that even working with trauma – for example as a police officer responding to a violent crime, or as a counsellor working with a refugee who fled a war zone – creates risk for trauma responses, provides a chilling reminder of the toxic impacts of trauma on human beings. Reading about trauma can be hard too, so it seems appropriate to end the chapter with encouragement to take some time for self-care.

Further reading

- This text draws on theory and practice and shows the complexities of understanding trauma and the wider factors that influence individual experiences of it:
Herman, J.L. (1992) *Trauma and recovery: the aftermath of violence – from domestic abuse to political terror.* New York: BasicBooks.

- This resource offers a good introductory review of the main perspectives on PTSD and trauma, examining the forces that have shaped these, with views from the sceptics and the proponents:

Brewin, C. (2003) *Posttraumatic stress disorder: malady or myth?.* New Haven and London: Yale University Press.

- Reeves offers a comprehensive overview of different types of risk that present in counselling and psychotherapy and offers guidance on how to work positively with risk in helping relationships. Chapters 4 and 5 offer specific insight into working with suicide and self-harm:

Reeves, A. (2015) *Working with risk in counselling and psychotherapy.* London: SAGE Publications.

References

American Psychiatric Association (APA) (2013) *Diagnostic and statistical manual of mental disorders* (DSM-5). 5th edn. Washington: American Psychiatric Association Publishing.

Babiker, G., and Arnold, L. (1997) *The language of injury: comprehending self-mutilation.* USA: Wiley-Blackwell.

Baird, K. and Kracen, A.C. (2006) 'Vicarious traumatization and secondary traumatic stress: a research synthesis' *Counselling Psychology Quarterly,* 19(2), pp. 181–188.

Canfield, J. (2005) 'Secondary traumatization, burnout, and vicarious traumatization: a review of the literature as it relates to therapists who treat trauma', *Smith College Studies in Social Work,* 75(2), pp. 81–101.

Caruth, C. (1996) *Unclaimed experience: trauma, narrative and history.* Baltimore and London: The Johns Hopkins University Press.

De Leo, D., Burgis, S., Bertolote, J.M., Kerkhof, A.J. and Bille-Brahe, U. (2006) 'Definitions of suicidal behavior: lessons learned from the WHO/EURO Multicentre Study', *Crisis,* 27(1), pp. 4–15.

Figley, C.R. (1995) 'Compassion fatigue as a secondary traumatic stress disorder: an overview', in Figley, C.R. (ed.) *Compassion fatigue: coping with secondary traumatic stress disorder in those who treat the traumatized.* New York: Routledge, pp. 1–20.

Figley, C.R. (2002) 'Compassion fatigue: psychotherapists' chronic lack of self-care' *Journal of Clinical Psychology,* 58(11), pp. 1433–1441. doi:10.1002/jclp.10090.

Freud, S. (1922) *Beyond the pleasure principle.* Translated from the German by C.J.M. Hubback. London and Vienna: International Psycho-Analytical. Available at: www.bartleby.com/276/ (Accessed: 9 September 2019).

Galatzer-Levy, I.R., Nickerson, A., Litz, B.T. and Marmar, C.R. (2013) 'Patterns of lifetime PTSD comorbidity: a latent class analysis', *Depression and Anxiety,* 30(5), pp. 489–496. doi:10.1002/da.22048.

Herman, J.L. (1992) *Trauma and recovery: the aftermath of violence – from domestic abuse to political terror.* New York: BasicBooks.

Hunter, S.V. (2012) 'Walking in sacred spaces in the therapeutic bond: therapists' experiences of compassion satisfaction coupled with the potential for vicarious traumatization', *Family Process,* 51(2), pp. 179–192. doi:10.1111/j.1545-5300.2012.01393.x.

James, K. and MacKinnon, L. (2012) 'Integrating a trauma lens into a family therapy framework: ten principles for family therapists', *Australian and New Zealand Journal of Family Therapy,* 33(3), pp. 189–209. doi:10.1017/aft.2012.25.

Janoff-Bulman, R. (1992) *Shattered assumptions: towards a new psychology of trauma*. New York: The Free Press.

Johnstone, L. (2019) 'Do you still need your psychiatric diagnosis? Critiques and alternatives', in Watson, J. (ed.) *Drop the disorder! Challenging the culture of psychiatric diagnosis*. Monmouth: PCCS Books, pp. 8–23.

Kessler. R. *et al.* (2014) 'How well can post-traumatic stress disorder be predicted from pre-trauma risk factors? An exploratory study in the WHO World Mental Health Surveys', *World Psychiatry*, 13(3), pp. 265–274. doi:10.1002/wps.20150.

Kumpula, M.J., Orcutt, H.K., Bardeen, J.R., and Varkovitzky, R.L. (2011) 'Peritraumatic dissociation and experiential avoidance as prospective predictors of posttraumatic stress symptoms', *Journal of Abnormal Psychology*, 120(3), pp. 617–627. doi:10.1037/a0023927.

Lynch S.H. and Lobo M.L. (2012) 'Compassion fatigue in family caregivers: a Wilsonian concept analysis', *Journal of Advanced Nursing*, 68(9), pp. 2125–2134. doi:10.1111/j.1365-2648.2012.05985.x.

Maslach, C. (1982) *Burnout: the cost of caring*. Englewood Cliffs, NJ: Prentice-Hall.

McCann, I.L. and Pearlman, L.A. (1990) 'Vicarious traumatization: a framework for understanding the psychological effects of working with victims', *Journal of Traumatic Stress*, 3, pp. 131–149.

McLean, J., Maxwell, M., Platt, S., Harris, F.M. and Jepson, R. (2008) *Risk and protective factors for suicide and suicidal behaviour: a literature review*. Edinburgh: The Scottish Government.

MIND (2019) *Crisis services and planning for a crisis*. Available at: https://www.mind.org.uk/information-support/guides-to-support-and-services/crisis-services (Accessed: 23 October 2019).

Myrick, A.C. and Brand, B.L. (2015) 'Dissociation, dissociative disorders, and PTSD', in Martin, C., Preedy, V. and Patel, V. (eds.) *Comprehensive guide to post-traumatic stress disorder*. Switzerland: Springer, Cham, pp. 1–16.

National Institute for Health and Care Excellence (NICE) (2011) *Self-harm: longer-term management (NICE guideline CG133)*. Available at: http://guidance.nice.org. uk/CG133 (Accessed: 30 October 2019).

Nimmo, A. and Huggard, P. (2013) 'A systematic review of the measurement of compassion fatigue, vicarious trauma and secondary traumatic stress in physicians', *Australasian Journal of Disaster and Trauma Studies*, 1, pp. 37–44.

Office for National Statistics (2019) *Suicides in the UK: 2018 registrations*. Available at: https://www.ons.gov.uk/peoplepopulationandcommunity/birthsdeathsandmarriages/deaths/bulletins/suicidesintheunitedkingdom/2018registrations#main-points (Accessed: 30 October 2019).

Reeves, A. (2015) *Working with risk in counselling and psychotherapy*. London: SAGE Publications.

Reeves, A. (2017) 'Suicide and self-harm', in Feltham, C., Hanley, T. and Winter, L. (eds.) *The Sage handbook of counselling and psychotherapy*. 4th ed. London: SAGE Publications, pp. 498–505.

Riggs, S.A. and Riggs, D.S. (2011) 'Risk and resilience in military families experiencing deployment: the role of the family attachment network', *Journal of Family Psychology*, 25(5), pp. 675–687. doi:10.1037/a0025286.

Robinaugh, D.J., Marques, L.M., Traeger, L.N., Marks, E.H., Sung, S.C., Beck, J.G., Pollack, M.H. and Simon, N.M. (2011) 'Understanding the relationship of perceived social support to post-trauma cognitions and posttraumatic stress disorder', *Journal of Anxiety Disorders*, 25(8), pp. 1072–1078. doi:10.1016/j.janxdis.2011.07.004.

Royal College of Psychiatrists (2010) *Self-harm, suicide and risk: helping people who self-harm: final report of a working group* (College Report CR158). Available at: https://www.rcpsych.ac.uk/docs/default-source/improving-care/better-mh-policy/college-reports/college-report-cr158.pdf?sfvrsn=fcf95b93_2 (Accessed: 14 October 2019).

Sarchiapone, M., Carli, V., Cuomo, C. and Roy, A. (2007) 'Childhood trauma and suicide attempts in patients with unipolar depression', *Depression and Anxiety*, 24(4), pp. 268–272.

Sayed, S., Iacoviello, B. M. and Charney, D.S. (2015) 'Risk factors for the development of psychopathology following trauma', *Current Psychiatry Reports*, 17(8), pp. 1–7. doi:10.1007/s11920-015-0612-y.

Shapiro, F. (1995) *Eye movement desensitization and reprocessing: basic principles, protocols, and procedures*. New York: Guildford Press.

Taft, C., Watkins, L., Stafford, J., Street, A. and Monson, C. (2011) 'Posttraumatic stress disorder and intimate relationship problems: a meta-analysis', *Journal of Consulting and Clinical Psychology*, 79(1). pp. 22–33. doi:10.1037/a0022196.

Terr, L.C. (1991) 'Childhood traumas: an outline and overview', *American Journal of Psychiatry*, 148(1), pp. 10–20.

Watson, J. (2019) 'There's an intruder in our house! Counselling, psychotherapy and the biomedical model of emotional distress', in Watson, J. (ed.) *Drop the disorder! Challenging the culture of psychiatric diagnosis*. Monmouth UK: PCCS Books, pp. 223–236.

Wies, J.R. and Coy, K. (2013) 'Measuring violence: vicarious trauma among sexual assault nurse examiners', *Human Organization*, 72(1), pp. 23–30.

Wild, J., Smith, K.V., Thompson, E., Béar, F., Lommen, M.J.J. and Ehlers, A. (2016) 'A prospective study of pre-trauma risk factors for post-traumatic stress disorder and depression', *Psychological Medicine*, 46(12), pp. 2571–2582.

World Health Organization (WHO) (2014) *Preventing suicide: a global imperative*. Available at: https://www.who.int/mental_health/suicide-prevention/world_report_2014/en/ (Accessed: 14 October 2019).

World Health Organization (WHO) (2018) *International classification of diseases* (ICD-11). 11th rev. edn. Geneva: World Health Organization. Available at: https://icd.who.int/en (Accessed: 14 October 2019).

Xue, C., Ge, Y., Tang, B., Liu, Y., Kang, P., Wang, M. and Zang, L. (2015) 'A meta-analysis of risk factors for combat-related PTSD among military personnel and veterans', *PLoS One*, 10(3). doi:10.1371/journal.pone.0120270.

Chapter 7
Relationships and intimacy

Naomi Moller

Contents

Introduction

'Unsolved mysteries' by Eleana Pourgouri

Relationships are highly important to most of us; they are a source of joy, comfort and meaning. For this reason, relationship difficulties can have significant and wide-ranging impacts and are critical to consider in the context of mental health. This chapter explores the argument that relationship and intimacy issues are a major reason why people feel distress and consequently seek therapy. While there are some contexts where family therapy is offered on the NHS, relationship difficulties are often ignored in mental health systems. For example, consider that, in England, people can receive psychological therapy for depression arising from loss but not for bereavement alone, because the dominant framework for mental health services (the Improving Access to Psychological Therapies (IAPT) programme) focuses on 'diagnosed' mental health conditions.

So, why are relationship issues often ignored in mental health settings? As you learnt in Part 1 of this book, mental health difficulties are understood, and therefore defined, in particular ways. For example, psychiatric diagnoses, such as depression, are applied to individuals and are thought to be 'illnesses'. In contrast, relationship difficulties occur between people (they are not 'individual' problems) and, arguably, relationship difficulties are 'normal' (everyone has them). This point is considered in Section 1 of this chapter, which looks at types of relationship problems (it is further explored in Chapter 14, which describes the systemic approach to therapy). Sections 2 and 3 investigate how relationship difficulties impact people's mental health.

This chapter aims to:

- outline the nature of relationship difficulties

- explore the impacts of relationship difficulties, specifically loneliness, relationship conflict and breakdown, abuse and bereavement

- discuss how relationship difficulties can be understood in counselling by looking at attachment theory and theories of grief.

1 What are relationship difficulties?

The focus in this chapter is on meaningful emotional relationships with family, romantic/life partners and friends. The emotions we feel about the person with whom we have such a relationship can be positive, negative or very mixed, but this person certainly matters.

1.1 Defining relationship difficulties

Relationship difficulties can be categorised in lots of ways, one of which is to group them into areas of:

- loneliness

- relationship conflict and breakdown

- abusive relationships

- bereavement.

Pause for reflection

If you were going to draw up a list of 'relationship difficulties', what would you include? Would your categories be different? Would you include further categories? One potential criticism of the list above is that the 'relationship conflict and breakdown' category is too broad, and that relationship difficulties may not always be associated with conflict.

One thing immediately clear is that each category in this list covers a wide range of relationship problems. For example, the term 'abusive relationships' includes relationships in which children and vulnerable adults (e.g. older people) are abused as well as partner abuse, which may be termed 'domestic violence'. Not only can many types of people be a target of relationship abuse, but the range of behaviours that constitute abuse is also wide and varied. You might think of physical and sexual abuse but, as defined by Women's Aid (a national domestic abuse charity), abusive relationships can also include emotional and financial abuse, harassment and stalking, online abuse and 'coercive control', which is a pattern of intimidation, humiliation, isolation and control that the abuser enforces through the use or threat of physical or sexual violence (Women's Aid, 2019).

Another thing to note is that what is and is not seen as 'abusive' varies across place and time. For example, in the UK, it was not a crime for a man to rape his wife until 1991 ('R. v. R.', 1991); the practice of female genital mutilation (also known as female circumcision) is a cultural practice in some parts of the world but, in Britain, it is illegal and is defined as child abuse (*Female Genital Mutilation Act 2003*). These points illustrate that any definition of 'relationship difficulties' can be said to be cultural in that it will reflect current social, political and legal understandings.

1.2   Difficulties with sexual relationships

To dive further into the question of what might constitute 'relationship difficulties' that might lead a person to seek counselling, consider difficulties with sexual relationships. This topic has concerned mental health practitioners, as can be seen by the number of diagnoses around sex (see the lists below). Additionally, the evidence suggests that sexual concerns are not uncommon in society (McCabe *et al.*, 2016), and also that they may be becoming more common (e.g. reported increases in sexual dysfunction in young men; Park *et al.*, 2016). Research also suggests that difficulties in sexual relationships can be highly distressing (Worsley *et al.*, 2017) and can negatively impact on quality of life (Nappi *et al.*, 2016). That said, the existence of diagnoses for sexual dysfunction is not uncontroversial.

Pause for reflection

What do you think or feel about the idea of mental health diagnoses related to sex? Notice your immediate reactions and keep them in mind while you read through the rest of this section. Think about what assumptions you may have about 'proper' or 'healthy' sexual functioning.

The fifth edition of the *Diagnostic and statistical manual of mental disorders* (DSM-5) has a category of what is referred to as 'sexual dysfunctions' for both men and women (American Psychiatric Association (APA), 2013). For men, these include:

- delayed ejaculation disorder

- premature (early) ejaculation disorder

- erectile disorder

- male hypoactive sexual desire disorder.

For women, they include:

- female orgasmic disorder

- female sexual interest/arousal disorder

- genito-pelvic pain/penetration disorder.

One thing to note about these diagnoses is that they assume that certain types of sexual response are normal and certain types are abnormal (as explained in Chapter 4, this criticism has been made of diagnoses more broadly). For example, the sexual desire (male) or sexual interest/arousal (female) disorders both assume there is a problem worthy of treatment if someone does not feel sexual and is distressed by that. However, there is no single accepted understanding of what constitutes a 'normal' and 'abnormal' sexual response. For example, while the *International classification of diseases* (ICD-11) includes the new diagnosis 'compulsive sexual behaviour disorder' (World Health Organization (WHO), 2018), in DSM-5 there is (currently) no corresponding diagnosis for someone worried about being 'overly' sexual.

In addition, 'normal' is sometimes problematically quantified; for example, the definition of premature ejaculation specifies that the diagnosis is merited if ejaculation occurs 'within approximately one minute following vaginal penetration and before the individual wishes' (APA, 2013, p. 443). This definition suggests that anything over a minute is fine (interestingly, earlier versions of the DSM gave different times). It also places the 'problem' of premature ejaculation within a male–female sexual relationship and restricts it to penis-in-vagina sex (the category notes that the problem is recognised for other, non-vaginal sexual activities but says that 'specific duration criteria have not been established' for other contexts (APA, 2013, p. 443). Arguably,

Heteronormative
Implies the world view that heterosexuality is the 'normal' and/or preferred sexual orientation; potentially implicitly transphobic or homophobic.

then, the definition ignores non-heterosexual partners and prioritises penis-in-vagina sex as the most important thing to be worrying about. In doing so, the diagnosis potentially not only reflects but actually reinforces current and **heteronormative** social understandings of sex. There is no intent here to belittle any distress that men may naturally feel about premature ejaculation. However, consider that, socially, sexual stamina in men is highly prized (Vares and Braun, 2006) and that, in Britain, a sizeable minority of the male population uses medications to enhance sexual performance (Mitchell *et al.*, 2016). One may therefore question whether the diagnosis of premature ejaculation unhelpfully reinforces pressure on men to perform sexually.

2   What are the impacts of relationship difficulties?

This section will focus on understanding more about why relationship difficulties have multiple negative impacts on people, and thus might bring them to counselling.

2.1   Loneliness and its consequences

Loneliness can result when a person does not have enough high-quality relationships. Yet, loneliness is not one thing – people experience it differently and there are various types of loneliness. For example, the Campaign to End Loneliness (n.d.) talks about the following types:

- *Emotional loneliness*: Some people may feel lonely because they are missing a particular person (e.g. because a friend has moved away), or because, although they have a circle of friends, they don't have a partner to share their deepest feelings with.

- *Social loneliness*: People can feel lonely because they don't have a big enough circle of friends and acquaintances – a social network – even if they live with someone that they love.

- *Chronic loneliness*: Some people feel lonely only sometimes, but others feel lonely most of the time.

- *Situational loneliness*: Some situations can make people more likely to feel lonely; for example, a person might feel particularly lonely on holiday because they don't have family to spend the holiday with.

Loneliness is also both a feeling ('I feel lonely') and something that can be quantified; for example, by counting the number of relationships a person has. If someone has few social contacts, they can be described as 'socially isolated'. Clearly, feeling lonely is more likely to occur if a person is socially isolated, but the two are not the same (Coyle and Dugan, 2012). Loneliness may be associated more with the quality of social relationships than with how many social contacts a person has.

Risk factors for loneliness

Research suggests that some factors may be associated with the risk of feeling lonely (Dahlberg, Agahi and Lennartsson, 2018; Hawkley and Kocherginsky, 2018). These include individual characteristics such as being older, having less education and less income, and being female. Some social factors also matter, such as living alone and having fewer social opportunities available.

Information box 7.1: Loneliness in older adults

Two fifths of all older people (about 3.9 million) say the television is their main company.

(Age UK, 2014)

It is possible to feel lonely at any age but research in the UK suggests that, of the nine million people who feel lonely, four million are older adults (Age UK, 2014). Not all older adults are lonely, of course. It is estimated that 10 per cent of older adults in the UK feel lonely. This percentage has stayed pretty stable over time but, because the UK has an ageing population (in that there is an increasing number of older adults), the overall number of lonely older adults is growing (Victor, 2011). Being lonely as an older person is associated with specific risks. For example, social isolation and loneliness increase the risk of developing dementia (Holwerda *et al.*, 2014).

Why are older adults at greater risk of loneliness? One factor might be that they are more likely to live alone – according to the UK Office for National Statistics, 28 per cent of people in the UK now live alone but that percentage is higher for older adults (Office for National Statistics, 2017). Older people are also more likely to be widowed and, unsurprisingly, spousal death is associated with risk of loneliness (Dahlberg, Agahi and Lennartsson, 2018). Increasing age is also associated with things like reduced mobility and poorer overall health, both of which can make it harder for a person to get out and see others (Dahlberg, Agahi and Lennartsson, 2018).

The impact of loneliness

Loneliness matters and not just because it makes people feel bad. There is a clear connection between experience of loneliness and having poorer health. For example, Holt-Lunstad *et al.* (2015) found that loneliness:

- increases risk of mortality by 26 per cent

- is as bad for health as smoking 15 cigarettes a day.

It is horrible feeling lonely, so it is unsurprising that loneliness also increases the risk of experiencing mental health difficulties; for example, there is considerable evidence that loneliness makes people more prone to depression and anxiety (Beutel *et al.*, 2017; Cacioppo *et al.*, 2006).

2.2   The impact of relationship conflict and breakdown

One way to begin unpacking the impact that relationships have on our lives is to consider the effects of even simple everyday arguments.

Activity 7.1: Experience of relationship arguments

Allow about 10 minutes

Think about the last time you had an argument with someone you care about. Spend a few minutes writing down what it was like for you in the aftermath of the argument. Write about your feelings and thoughts.

Discussion

During an argument with a loved one, a person might feel angry and upset. Afterwards, other emotions can arise; people can worry about how they reacted or about what might happen to the relationship as a result of the argument. They can also find it harder to concentrate on normal activities, including work. All of these might be short-term impacts, but if the argument is bad enough there may be long-term consequences too.

Being lonely is hard but so is being in a difficult relationship. Estimates suggest that, in 2017, one in four couples in the UK were experiencing relationship distress (Relate, 2017). Minor disagreements are normal in relationships but major conflicts – whether persistent, blisteringly angry arguments or seething and cold silences – have consequences for those involved. For example, there is a great deal of evidence that relationship conflict and breakdown have significant negative impacts on physical health. Marital separation and divorce are linked to a higher risk of hospital-diagnosed infectious disease, cardiovascular morbidities and even increased risk of early death (Sbarra and Coan, 2017).

Relationship conflict and breakdown also negatively impact the mental health of both adults and children. For example, evidence has shown that people in problematic relationships are more likely to suffer from anxiety and depression than those in satisfying relationships (Røsand et al., 2012), and divorce has been linked to increased suicide risk soon after the event (Stack and Scourfield, 2015). Other studies have reported that frequent and intense relationship conflict between parents/caregivers can harm the physical and mental health of children (Harold and Leve, 2012).

The association between relationship distress and mental health difficulties is not, however, one way. For example, the breakdown of marriage predicts mental health problems, but mental health problems also predict marriage breakdown (Mojtabai *et al.*, 2017). This underlines the importance of considering mental health influences beyond the level of the individual, specifically those related to broader relational systems (which will be covered in Chapter 14).

2.3 Abusive relationships and childhood maltreatment

Many relationships involve conflict but a subset of troubled relationships can be classed as abusive. There is extensive research that seeks to identify the prevalence and impacts of these types of relational experiences. As just one example, researchers have found that having a 'severe' mental health illness is itself associated with a greater risk of experiencing domestic and sexual violence (Khalifeh *et al.*, 2015). As discussed in this section, having a history of abusive relationships is associated with a greater risk of developing mental health difficulties; the fact that the inverse is also true is yet another example of the bidirectional associations that exist between relationship experiences and mental health difficulties.

To further assess the impact of abusive relationships one can consider the research on childhood maltreatment; for example, childhood experience of neglect, abuse and trauma. As with the other types of relationship difficulties discussed in this chapter, there is increasing evidence that childhood maltreatment increases the risk of physical health problems in adulthood, including heart disease, cancer, chronic lung disease, bone fractures, autoimmune disease and liver disease (Nemeroff, 2016). Long-standing and extensive research literature also documents that experience of childhood maltreatment leads to a significantly higher likelihood of experiencing mental health difficulties in adulthood (Lindert *et al.*, 2014; Infurna *et al.*, 2016; Nemeroff, 2016). Consider a study by Nelson *et al.*, (2017) which examined the association between a history of childhood maltreatment and the development of depression in adulthood. The authors

Meta-analysis
A statistical method of combining the results of multiple individual studies, investigating the same research question, to provide findings that are more compelling because they are based on larger samples.

conducted a **meta-analysis**, which combined the results of 184 studies incorporating thousands of individuals, to examine the relationship between childhood maltreatment and adult depression. The authors found that nearly half of the participants who had depression reported a history of childhood maltreatment and that those reporting this history were 2.66 times 'more likely to develop depression in adulthood, had an earlier depression onset and were twice as likely to develop chronic or treatment-resistant depression' (Nelson *et al.*, 2017, p. 96).

2.4   Bereavement

All of us will at some point experience the death of someone we care about but, although the experience of grief is universal, that does not mean it isn't devastating. For example, there is lots of evidence showing that bereavement impacts physical health (Stroebe, Schut and Stroebe, 2007). Studies have also associated bereavement with increased risk of death, particularly for those who are widowed (Shor *et al.*, 2012). Moon *et al.* (2011) estimated that someone whose spouse has died has a 41 per cent increase in risk of mortality in the first six months after the death.

Individuals' experience of bereavement will depend on a host of factors including the quality of the relationship and the manner of death. That said, research suggests there are two types of death associated with long-lasting difficulties in adjustment: the death of a parent (experienced as a child) and the death of a child. For example, research suggests that experiencing the death of a parent is associated with a higher risk of hospitalisation for depression as an adult, especially if the death occurred in early childhood or resulted from an accident, violence or suicide (Berg, Rostila and Hjern, 2016). Similarly, even many years after child loss, bereaved parents experience poorer psychological well-being and declines in self-perceived physical general health and physical functioning (Infurna and Luthar, 2017). The death of a child is also associated with marital distress and divorce; in other words, it negatively impacts on the parents' relationship (Albuquerque, Pereira and Narciso, 2016).

3   Theories of relationship difficulties

This section will focus on theories that help counsellors understand and work effectively with difficulties in relationships. There are many theories that could be discussed (e.g. see Chapter 14 on systemic approaches); the focus here is on two types of theory, both of which are influential and have been extensively researched: attachment theory and theories of grief.

3.1   Attachment theory

Attachment theory is a very influential theory initially developed by British psychologist, psychiatrist and psychoanalyst John Bowlby. It seeks to describe how human infants become attached to their caregivers and what the long-term impacts of differences in the qualities of these attachments might be for later relationships (Bowlby, 1969, 1973, 1988).

A central idea in attachment theory is that the repeated experiences that infants and toddlers have with their caregivers create learning or expectations about the self, others and relationships. Research on attachment has suggested that different types of learning lead to distinctly different types of 'secure' and 'insecure' attachment, and these are associated with particular ways of being in relationships. To give you an idea of the different attachment types, complete Activity 7.2 to consider how they were described in one of the earliest attachment questionnaires (Hazan and Shaver, 1990).

Activity 7.2: Considering your own attachment type

Allow about 10 minutes

The statements below reflect the three general relationship styles described by attachment researchers. Read the statements then answer the questions that follow. (Note: The terms 'close' and 'intimate' refer to psychological or emotional closeness, not necessarily to sexual intimacy.)

Relationship style 1: I find it relatively easy to get close to others and I am comfortable depending on them and having them depend on me. I don't worry about being abandoned or about someone getting too close to me.

Relationship style 2: I am somewhat uncomfortable being close to others; I find it difficult to trust them completely and to allow myself to depend on them. I am nervous when anyone gets too close and, often, others want me to be more intimate than I feel comfortable being.

Relationship style 3: I find that others are reluctant to get as close as I would like. I often worry that my partner doesn't really love me or won't want to stay with me. I want to get very close to my partner, and this sometimes scares them away.

1 Which statement do you think most accurately reflects your attachment type?

2 The three attachment types are 'insecure-avoidant', 'insecure-anxious/ambivalent', and 'secure'. Can you guess which relationship style corresponds with which attachment type?

3 Think back to your relationships with caregivers as a child. Do you think that the way you generally feel and behave in intimate/important relationships is pretty similar to how it was back then? If there is a difference, what do you attribute this to? If you experience relationship difficulties today, do you think that they have their origins in what you learnt about relationships when you were a child?

Consider your answers to these questions before you check the discussion.

Discussion

The relationship styles correspond with the attachment types as follows:

- Relationship style 1: secure attachment

- Relationship style 2: insecure-avoidant attachment

- Relationship style 3: insecure-anxious/ambivalent attachment

As you think about how much your childhood experience of relationships with caregivers explains (or not) your current relationships, it is worth considering what research says about the link between childhood and adult attachment. While attachment theory has proposed the long-term importance of early experience in relationships, longitudinal research examining attachment from infancy through to early adulthood has found weak evidence of stability (Fearon and Roisman, 2017). That said, at least some of the discontinuity seems to be explained by changes in the caregiving environment – in other words, a child who was securely attached may become insecurely attached if a caregiver suddenly (for example) becomes unavailable due to their own problems. Potentially, the lack of strong evidence for attachment stability from infancy into adulthood could be explained by the increasing complexities of our relational networks and attachment system, with influences from external factors such as economic pressures on the family, and the increasing importance of peer (friend/romantic partner) relationships as we age into adulthood.

Even if no strong evidence exists for a direct link between the quality of an infant's attachment to their caregiver and the quality of important relationships in adulthood, this does not mean that there is no influence. Remember, a key idea in psychodynamic theory is that current relationship difficulties might be partly explainable by the history of relationship experiences in childhood. Remember too the evidence reviewed in Section 2 about the long-term impacts of, for instance, experiencing the death of a parent in childhood, the impact of family conflict and parent separation on children, and the impact of childhood maltreatment. In all of these contexts, attachment research evidence suggests that insecure attachments are more likely, which means that attachment status may help to explain *why* these terrible experiences lead to all the negative impacts. Research has also found evidence of both current and prospective links between attachment insecurity and the development of various types of mental health difficulties, including depression, anxiety and eating disorders (Stovall-McClough and Dozier, 2016). In summary, there are good theoretical and research grounds for thinking that attachment theory provides a useful framework for making sense of and working with relationship difficulties in counselling. The field of attachment research, which is both significant and evolving, is part of a broader domain of multidisciplinary research focused on understanding human relationships. As such, attachment theory also exemplifies how research outside the field of counselling and psychotherapy potentially has an important relevance for improving therapy practice.

3.2   Theories of grief

In his 1917 essay, 'Mourning and melancholia', Freud provided what can be considered as the first theory of grief. From Freud's perspective, the key goal of mourning was to allow the person to let go of their attachment to the person who had died, with grieving (thinking about the dead person and allowing sadness) being a painful process necessary for a bereaved person to move on with their life (Freud, 2001). Attachment theory also considered loss; Bowlby argued that loss of an attachment figure has a profound impact on a person's attachment security, and drew on attachment theory to propose a four-stage model of grief response (Bowlby, 1969, 1973, 1988). The grief model that became hugely influential, however, was that developed by Swiss-American psychiatrist Elizabeth Kubler-Ross. Her book, *On death and dying: what the dying have to teach doctors, nurses, clergy and their own families* (Kubler-Ross, 1969), is credited with revolutionising medical care of the dying, but it also had a big impact on public understanding of grief, with its proposal of a five-stage model of grief response: denial, anger, bargaining, depression, and acceptance.

Subsequent research has questioned the idea of a linear process, arguing that responses are more individual than Kubler-Ross's model suggests, and that people rarely follow the theorised linear progression through the stages of grief (Stroebe and Schut, 2001). Yet Kubler-Ross's model was not actually developed to explain grief reactions; it was developed to explain how people who are dying cope emotionally. In contrast, attachment theory and Freud's ideas about loss do cover grief, but they are examples of broader theories being applied to understand the specific situation of how people react when a loved one dies. Therefore, any theory developed solely to try and understand the range of grief responses could potentially provide more accurate/specific explanations. Perhaps the most influential model specifically developed to explain bereavement is the dual process model of grief developed by Stroebe and Schut (2010) which is further discussed below. Together, the theory and research on grief responses suggests a number of relevant questions for working with grief in counselling. These questions are now addressed in turn.

Can grief be diagnosed?

The simple answer is yes. ICD-11 (WHO, 2018) has, for the first time, included 'prolonged grief reaction' as a diagnosis, while DSM-5 (APA, 2013) has included 'persistent complex bereavement disorder' under the category of 'Conditions for further study'. Yet, grief is a normal part of being human, so the idea that it is possible to have grief diagnoses is controversial. The diagnoses come out of the fact that there is a long history of theory (from Freud onwards) and research focused on grief reactions that are understood as not normal (disordered or 'pathological'). This type of grief response is typically differentiated from 'normal' grief on the basis that it is 'prolonged' – the grief remains too intense for too long, or is complicated because it is accompanied by a concurrent mental health condition, such as depression or post-traumatic stress disorder (Maciejewski *et al.*, 2016). It is these types of grief responses that are associated with grief diagnoses.

Why do some people get 'stuck' in their grief?

An assumption about 'normal' grief is that, after time, someone who is bereaved experiences a lessening of their grief. In contrast, a marker of those experiencing persistent/complicated grief is that a person gets somehow stuck in the grieving process. As one researcher poignantly described it:

> We can speak of disturbed or 'complex grief' if the state of acute emotional distress persists. If one continues to experience disbelief about the irreversibility of the loss. If the death still feels as something that happened yesterday, even when months or years already passed since the loss. If one's emotional life is drenched

by yearning and longing, and this yearning and longing dominate and steer all thoughts, feelings, and actions.

(Boelen, 2016)

Research suggests that one in ten people who are bereaved experience prolonged or complicated grief (Lundorff *et al.*, 2017). Research also suggests that some factors may increase the risk of prolonged or complicated grief (Burke and Neimeyer, 2013); for example:

- an intimate/close relationship with the person who died (e.g. those experienced by spouses and parental caregivers)

- a violent and sudden/unexpected manner of death

- an impoverished social context after the bereavement (e.g. a lack of social support)

- certain characteristics of the bereaved person (e.g. a person's vulnerability, including history of insecure attachments or mental health difficulties).

What does healthy grieving look like?

A persistent idea in grief response theories is that the aim is to 'work through' grief by focusing consciously or actively on the emotional pain. However, more recent theory and research has suggested that this kind of active focus is only one part of grieving. In their dual process model of grief, Stroebe and Schut (2001, 2010) suggested that the mourning process involves oscillating between focusing on the grief and trying to move on from it (see Figure 7.1). This model assumes that periods of feeling incredibly sad about a death alternate with attempts to get on with life. It also assumes that distracting oneself from grief (e.g. by watching TV mindlessly) and denying/avoiding the grief are part of a typical grief process and that individuals will vary in how much they consciously focus on the pain versus try to move on from it. The model additionally implies that there are lots of different but equally good ways to engage in 'healthy' grieving'.

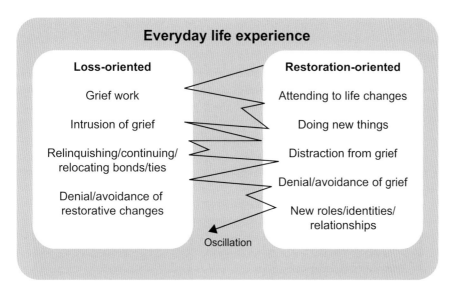

Figure 7.1 Dual process model of grief (Source: Stroebe and Schut, 2001, p. 59)

Should the focus be on letting go of or continuing bonds?

An integral idea in some bereavement theories has been that successful grieving requires moving on from the attachment, and essentially from the person who has died. More recently, however, researchers have examined how attachments are maintained past death and how this practice is supported in various cultural and religious traditions (an example might be the Mexican holiday called 'The Day of the Dead' in which families gather to remember those who have died). This has led to debates about which leads to a more adaptive response – letting go or working to maintain the bond.

Research findings have been mixed (Root and Exline, 2014). Stroebe, Schut and Stroebe (2007) have suggested that the answer may depend on the attachment status of the person who is bereaved, and the qualities of the relationship with the deceased. Nonetheless, research in this area suggests the potential benefits of continuing to think about a person who has died, even while accepting that they have gone. This idea was explored by psychotherapist and researcher Jane Speedy in a research paper, in which she included the following autobiographical poem about her own experience of bereavement.

A quietly spoken poem about a complete failure in relation to coming to terms with my brother's death …

There was silence and some subversion around our annual pact.

It had captured us this lifelong commitment

to spending our birthdays together

and was quite a transgression for siblings

there was already something deliciously odd about that

It started at school, do you remember?

I even missed a crucial Latin test once

the whole of which I later failed quite extravagantly

'no such thing as crucial Latin', you said.

and just before you died

we went to the roller-disco in Camden Town

do you remember?

It was sometime later that you mentioned

your vital meeting with the 'then prime-minister'

'no such thing as a vital Tory' I said

afterwards I tried to push on through February

my pockets filled with pebbles

and my eyes ablaze

somehow my own birthday

did not leave such a hollow stain on the calendar.

Februaries came and went

and *'time's healing powers'*

and the *'terms'* I was supposed to come to

and *'the natural course of things'* just passed me by

and then, one February morning

I was out collecting pebbles for my pockets

when you whispered:

'hang on. I've turned up every year

It is you that's broken our agreement.'

and so we remain bound together on our birthdays

which is quite a transgression for a dead person and his sister

this year you would have been fifty

we went to the 'Tate Modern'

where there was an exploding grand piano suspended from the ceiling

next to an excruciating treatise on post-modernism

which had us doubled-up

and we walked back across the millennium bridge clutching our sides

our pockets filled with memories.

(Speedy, in Speedy *et al.*, 2005, pp. 68–72)

Conclusion

The focus of this chapter has been on understanding why relationship difficulties might bring someone to counselling. A broad range of potential types of relationship difficulties have been proposed, including loneliness, relationship conflict and breakdown, abuse and bereavement. But, as the chapter has pointed out, such categories are likely to be culturally and temporally specific – in other words, the categories might look different in another place or at another time. Through a review of research on multiple types of relationship difficulties, the chapter has argued that problems in relationships lead to negative impacts for individuals in terms of both physical and mental health, which may be both severe and long lasting. Theories of grief and attachment theory provide different but equally influential understandings of why relationship difficulties might bring a person into counselling, yet both theory development and research continue because there are still lots of things we don't understand. One thing is crystal clear, however: relationships are important for all of us.

Further reading

- This paper argues that medicalised understandings of sexual difficulties are really unhelpful – in particular for women. The paper contrasts the medical understanding by redefining women's sexual problems from the perspective of women:

  McHugh, M.C. (2006) 'What do women want? A new view of women's sexual problems', *Sex Roles*, 54(5–6), pp. 361–369.

- This is a complex and technical paper by a leader in the field that summarises the pathways and impacts by which childhood experience of abuse and neglect increases risk for psychological and physical health problems in adulthood:

  Nemeroff, C.B. (2016) 'Paradise lost: the neurobiological and clinical consequences of child abuse and neglect', *Neuron*, 89(5), pp. 892–909.

- This paper by prominent grief researchers makes a strong argument that stage models of grief should be abandoned:

  Stroebe, M., Schut, H. and Boerner, K. (2017) 'Cautioning health-care professionals: bereaved persons are misguided through the stages of grief', *OMEGA-Journal of Death and Dying*, 74(4), pp. 455–473.

References

Age UK (2014) *Evidence review: loneliness in later life*. London: Age UK

Albuquerque, S., Pereira, M. and Narciso, I. (2016) 'Couple's relationship after the death of a child: a systematic review', *Journal of Child and Family Studies*, 25(1), pp. 30–53.

American Psychiatric Association (APA) (2013) *Diagnostic and statistical manual of mental disorders* (DSM-5). 5th edn. Washington: American Psychiatric Association Publishing.

Berg, L., Rostila, M. and Hjern, A. (2016) 'Parental death during childhood and depression in young adults – a national cohort study', *Journal of Child Psychology and Psychiatry*, 57(9), pp. 1092–1098.

Beutel, M.E., Klein, E.M., Brähler, E., Reiner, I., Jünger, C., Michal, M., Wiltink, J., Wild, P.S., Münzel, T., Lackner, K.J. and Tibubos, A.N. (2017) 'Loneliness in the general population: prevalence, determinants and relations to mental health', *BMC Psychiatry*, 17(97). doi:10.1186/s12888-017-1262-x.

Boelen, P.A. (2016) 'Improving the understanding and treatment of complex grief: an important issue for psychotraumatology', *European Journal of Psychotraumatology*, 7(1), 32609. doi:10.3402/ejpt.v7.32609.

Bowlby, J. (1969) *Attachment and loss. Volume 1: attachment*. New York: Basic Books.

Bowlby, J. (1973) *Attachment and loss. Volume 2: separation: anxiety and anger*. New York: Basic Books.

Bowlby, J. (1988) *A secure base: parent-child attachment and healthy human development*. New York: Basic Books.

Burke, L.A. and Neimeyer, R.A. (2013) 'Prospective risk factors for complicated grief: a review of the empirical literature', in Stroebe, M., Schut, H. and van den Bout, J. (eds.) *Complicated grief: scientific foundations for health care professionals*. US: Routledge, pp. 145–161.

Cacioppo, J.T., Hughes, M.E., Waite, L.J., Hawkley, L.C. and Thisted, R.A. (2006) 'Loneliness as a specific risk factor for depressive symptoms: cross-sectional and longitudinal analyses', *Psychology and Aging*, 21(1), pp. 140–151.

Campaign to End Loneliness (n.d.) *About loneliness*. Available at: https://www.campaigntoendloneliness.org/about-loneliness/ (Accessed: 28 February 2020).

Coyle, C.E. and Dugan, E. (2012) 'Social isolation, loneliness and health among older adults' *Journal of Aging and Health*, 24(8), pp. 1346–1363.

Dahlberg, L., Agahi, N. and Lennartsson, C. (2018) 'Lonelier than ever? Loneliness of older people over two decades', *Archives of Gerontology and Geriatrics*, 75, pp. 96–103.

Fearon, R.P. and Roisman, G.I. (2017) 'Attachment theory: progress and future directions', *Current Opinion in Psychology*, 15, pp. 131–136.

Female Genital Mutilation Act 2003, c. 31. Available at: https://www.legislation.gov.uk/ukpga/2003/31/contents (Accessed: 4 September 2019).

Freud, S. (2001) 'Mourning and melacholia', in Strachey, J. (ed.) *The standard edition of the complete psychological works of Sigmund Freud, Volume XIV (1914–1916): on the history of the psycho-analytic movement, papers on metapsychology and other works*. London: Vintage. pp. 237–258.

Harold, G.T. and Leve, L.D. (2012) 'Parents as partners: how the parental relationship affects children's psychological development', in Balfour, A., Morgan, M. and Vincent, C. (eds.) *The library of couple and family psychoanalysis. How couple relationships shape our world: clinical practice, research, and policy perspectives*. London: Karnac Books, pp. 25–55.

Hawkley, L.C. and Kocherginsky, M. (2018) 'Transitions in loneliness among older adults: a 5-year follow-up in the National Social Life, Health, and Aging Project', *Research on Aging*, 40(4), pp. 365–387.

Hazan, C. and Shaver, P.R. (1990) 'Love and work: an attachment-theoretical perspective', *Journal of Personality and Social Psychology*, 59(2), pp. 270–280.

Holt-Lunstad, J., Smith, T.B., Baker, M., Harris, T. and Stephenson, D. (2015) 'Loneliness and social isolation as risk factors for mortality: a meta-analytic review', *Perspectives on Psychological Science*, 10(2), pp. 227–237.

Holwerda, T.J., Deeg, D., Beekman, A., van Tilburg, T.G., Stek, M.L., Jonker, C. and Schoevers, R.A. (2014) 'Feelings of loneliness, but not social isolation, predict dementia onset: results from the Amsterdam Study of the Elderly (AMSTEL)', *Journal of Neurology, Neurosurgery and Psychiatry,* 85(2), pp. 135–142. Available at: http://jnnp.bmj.com/content/early/2012/11/06/jnnp-2012-302755 (Accessed: 28 February 2020).

Infurna, F.J. and Luthar, S.S. (2017) 'Parents' adjustment following the death of their child: resilience is multidimensional and differs across outcomes examined', *Journal of Research in Personality*, 68, pp. 38–53.

Infurna, M.R., Reichl, C., Parzer, P., Schimmenti, A., Bifulco, A. and Kaess, M. (2016) 'Associations between depression and specific childhood experiences of abuse and neglect: a meta-analysis', *Journal of Affective Disorders*, 190, pp. 47–55.

Khalifeh, H., Moran, P., Borschmann, R., Dean, K., Hart, C., Hogg, J., Osborn, D., Johnson, S. and Howard, L.M. (2015) 'Domestic and sexual violence against patients with severe mental illness', *Psychological Medicine*, 45 (4), pp. 875–886.

Kubler-Ross, E. (1969) *On death and dying: what the dying have to teach doctors, nurses, clergy and their own families*. Reprint. New York: Scribner, 2011.

Lindert, J., von Ehrenstein, O.S., Grashow, R., Gal, G., Braehler, E. and Weisskopf, M.G. (2014) 'Sexual and physical abuse in childhood is associated with depression and anxiety over the life course: systematic review and meta-analysis', *International Journal of Public Health*, 59(2), pp. 359–372.

Lundorff, M., Holmgren, H., Zachariae, R., Farver-Vestergaard, I. and O'Connor, M. (2017) 'Prevalence of prolonged grief disorder in adult bereavement: a systematic review and meta-analysis', *Journal of Affective Disorders*, 212, pp. 138–149.

Maciejewski, P.K., Maercker, A., Boelen, P.A. and Prigerson, H.G. (2016) '"Prolonged grief disorder" and "persistent complex bereavement disorder", but not "complicated grief", are one and the same diagnostic entity: an analysis of data from the Yale Bereavement Study', *World Psychiatry*, 15(3), pp. 266–275.

McCabe, M.P., Sharlip, I.D., Lewis, R., Atalla, E., Balon, R., Fisher, A.D., Laumann, E., Lee, S.W. and Segraves, R.T. (2016), 'Incidence and prevalence of sexual dysfunction in women and men: a consensus statement from the Fourth International Consultation on Sexual Medicine 2015', *The Journal of Sexual Medicine*, 13(2), pp. 144–152.

Mitchell, K.R., Prah, P., Mercer, C.H., Datta, J., Tanton, C., Macdowall, W., Copas, A.J., Clifton, S., Sonnenberg, P., Field, N. and Johnson, A.M. (2016) 'Medicated sex in Britain: evidence from the third National Survey of Sexual Attitudes and Lifestyles', *Sexually Transmitted Infections*, 92(1), pp. 32–38.

Mojtabai, R., Stuart, E.A., Hwang, I., Eaton, W.W., Sampson, N. and Kessler, R.C. (2017) 'Long-term effects of mental disorders on marital outcomes in the National Comorbidity Survey ten-year follow-up', *Social Psychiatry and Psychiatric Epidemiology*, 52(10), pp. 1217–1226. doi:10.1007/s00127-017-1373-1.

Moon, J.R., Kondo, N., Glymour, M.M. and Subramanian, S.V. (2011) 'Widowhood and mortality: a meta-analysis', *PLoSOne*, 6(8), p. e23465. doi:10.1371/journal.pone.0023465.

Nappi, R.E., Cucinella, L., Martella, S., Rossi, M., Tiranini, L. and Martini, E. (2016) 'Female sexual dysfunction (FSD): prevalence and impact on quality of life (QoL)', *Maturitas*, 94, pp. 87–91.

Nelson, J., Klumparendt, A., Doebler, P. and Ehring, T. (2017) 'Childhood maltreatment and characteristics of adult depression: meta-analysis', *The British Journal of Psychiatry*, 210(2), pp. 96–104.

Nemeroff, C.B. (2016) 'Paradise lost: the neurobiological and clinical consequences of child abuse and neglect', *Neuron*, 89(5), pp. 892–909.

Office for National Statistics (2017) *Families and households in the UK: 2017*. Available at: https://www.ons.gov.uk/peoplepopulationandcommunity/birthsdeathsandmarriages/families/bulletins/familiesandhouseholds/2017#how-does-the-number-of-people-who-live-alone-vary-by-age-and-sex (Accessed: 28 February 2020).

Park, B.Y., Wilson, G., Berger, J., Christman, M., Reina, B., Bishop, F., Klam, W.P. and Doan, A.P. (2016) 'Is internet pornography causing sexual dysfunctions? A review with clinical reports', *Behavioral Sciences (Basel, Switzerland)*, 6(3), p. 17.

'R. vs. R.' (1991) *BAILII*, 12 [Online]. Available at: https://www.bailii.org/uk/cases/UKHL/1991/12.html (Accessed: 4 September 2019).

Relate (2017) *The way we are now: the state of the UK's relationships.* Available at: https://www.relate.org.uk/sites/default/files/the_way_we_are_now_-_it_takes_two.pdf (Accessed: 28 February 2020).

Root, B.L. and Exline, J.J. (2014) 'The role of continuing bonds in coping with grief: overview and future directions', *Death Studies*, 38(1), pp. 1–8.

Røsand, G.B., Slinning, K., Eberhard-Gran, M., Røysamb, E. and Tambs, K. (2012) 'The buffering effect of relationship satisfaction on emotional distress in couples', *BMC Public Health*, 12(66). doi:10.1186/1471-2458-12-66.

Sbarra, D.A. and Coan, J.A. (2017) 'Divorce and health: good data in need of better theory', *Current Opinion in Psychology*, 13, pp. 91–95.

Shor, E., Roelfs, D.J., Curreli, M., Clemow, L., Burg, M.M. and Schwartz, J.E. (2012) 'Widowhood and mortality: a meta-analysis and meta-regression', *Demography*, 49(2), pp. 575–606.

Speedy, J., Margie, F., Jack, P. and Jones, J. (2005) 'Failing to come to terms with things: a multi-storied conversation about poststructuralist ideas and narrative practices in response to some of life's failures', *Counselling and Psychotherapy Research*, 5(1), pp. 65–74.

Stack, S. and Scourfield, J. (2015) 'Recency of divorce, depression, and suicide risk', *Journal of Family Issues*, 36(6), pp. 695–715.

Stovall-McClough, K.C. and Dozier, M. (2016) 'Attachment states of mind and psychopathology in adulthood', in Cassidy, J. and Shaver, P.R. (eds.) *Handbook of attachment: theory, research, and clinical applications.* New York and London: The Guildford Press, pp. 715–738.

Stroebe, M.S. and Schut, H. (2001) 'Meaning making in the dual process model of coping with bereavement', in Neimeyer, R.A. (ed.) *Meaning reconstruction and the experience of loss.* Washington, DC: American Psychological Association, pp. 55–73

Stroebe, M. and Schut, H. (2010) 'The dual process model: a decade on', *OMEGA: Journal of Death and Dying*, 61(4), pp. 273–289.

Stroebe, M., Schut, H. and Stroebe, W. (2007) 'Health outcomes of bereavement', *The Lancet*, 370(9603), pp. 1960–1973.

Vares, T. and Braun, V. (2006) 'Spreading the word, but what word is that? Viagra and male sexuality in popular culture', *Sexualities*, 9(3), pp. 315–332.

Victor, C. (2011) 'Loneliness in old age: the UK Perspective', *Safeguarding the Convoy: a call to action from the Campaign to End Loneliness.* Oxford: Age UK Oxfordshire.

Women's Aid (2019) *What is domestic abuse?*. Available at: https://www.womensaid.org.uk/information-support/what-is-domestic-abuse/ (Accessed: 4 September 2019).

World Health Organization (WHO) (2018) *International classification of diseases* (ICD-11). 11th rev. edn. Geneva: World Health Organization.

Worsley, R., Bell, R.J., Gartoulla, P. and Davis, S.R. (2017) 'Prevalence and predictors of low sexual desire, sexually related personal distress, and hypoactive sexual desire dysfunction in a community-based sample of midlife women', *The Journal of Sexual Medicine*, 14(5), pp. 675–686.

Chapter 8

Understanding psychological formulation

Lucy Johnstone

Contents

Introduction

'Configurations of self' by Alexander Church

Formulation is, at its simplest, a narrative that helps to make sense of someone's difficulties in the context of their relationships, social circumstances and life events. Everyone comes to therapy or mental health services with a life story, often a very difficult one. In formulation-based practice, the professional contributes their clinical experience and their knowledge of the evidence. The client brings their personal experience and the sense they have made of it. The end result of putting these two essential aspects together, in written or diagrammatic form, is called a formulation, or a personal narrative about why the client may be struggling in these ways and at this time.

Formulation has been described as 'a process of ongoing collaborative sense-making' (Harper and Moss, 2003, p. 8) and 'a way of summarising meanings, and of negotiating for shared ways of understanding and communicating about them' (Butler, 1998, p. 4). It is also an evidence-based hypothesis, or in more informal terms, a 'best guess' about the origins of someone's difficulties. It is 'the tool used by clinicians to relate theory to practice' (Butler, 1998, p. 2).

Unlike psychiatric diagnosis (which medicalises a person's difficulties), a formulation is not a judgment by an expert; it is an evolving, collaborative account that includes the person's strengths, and that suggests the best route towards recovery. Formulation-based approaches assume that, however unusual, confusing, risky, destructive, overwhelming or frightening a person's thoughts, feelings and behaviours are, 'at some level it all makes sense' (Butler, 1998, p. 2).

The ability to formulate is increasingly seen as a core skill for all mental health, counselling and related professions. All therapies are based on exploration of the meaning of people's experiences, and all therapists will engage in 'meaning-making' in a general sense. Formulation makes this an explicit, shared and structured process. This has advantages, such as checking understandings, marking progress, strengthening the therapeutic alliance and clarifying the best way forward (Division of Clinical Psychology (DCP), 2011). There is no set format for a formulation; this will vary according to the clinician and the therapeutic modality.

This chapter argues that formulation is an adaptable, collaborative and empowering way of drawing on evidence in order to conceptualise clients' distress. However, in order to ensure sensitive and effective practice, it is also important to be aware of the contexts, debates and limitations of formulation-based practice.

This chapter aims to:

- describe the core principles of formulation and formulation-based practice

- illustrate how formulation might be used in practice, particularly with reference to the trauma-informed approach

- outline some of the controversies and debates about formulation; in particular how formulation contrasts with psychiatric diagnosis, and the promising but currently limited body of research into its effectiveness.

1   Core principles of formulation and formulation-based practice

This chapter focuses on the *common* features of **formulation** from all therapeutic traditions, although the structure and content of formulations vary (Johnstone and Dallos, 2013). Some therapies (e.g. person-centred) do not use explicit formulations at all, while others (especially cognitive behavioural therapy, or CBT) often use formulation alongside diagnosis. Some (e.g. cognitive analytic therapy) prescribe a particular written format, while others more commonly use diagrams.

The characteristic assumptions on which these various approaches are based will shape the content and structure of the formulation. For example:

> a psychodynamic formulation: makes a statement about the nature of the patient's problems or difficulties, usually in terms of repeated maladaptive patterns occurring in relationships... Makes an inference as to how these are related to the patient's internal world, including unconscious conflicts... Links the above (if possible) with historical information in an explanatory model.
>
> (McGrath and Margison, cited in Johnstone and Dallos, 2013, p. 5)

Alternatively, CBT formulations are likely to emphasise negative cognitions, while systemic ones (based on systemic theory, discussed in Chapter 14) will focus on family relationships (these differences will be further discussed in Part 3 of this book). Figure 8.1 provides an example of a CBT model of formulation – Padesky and Mooney's (1990) 'hot cross bun' model, which seeks to explain the cascade of thoughts, emotions, physical sensations and behaviours in a person who is experiencing anxiety in social situations (CBT models are further unpacked in Chapter 10).

Formulation
The process of collaborating with a client to make sense of their difficulties in the context of their relationships, social circumstances and life events. The term is also used to refer to the written or diagrammatic summary of the process, which may be used in letters and reports.

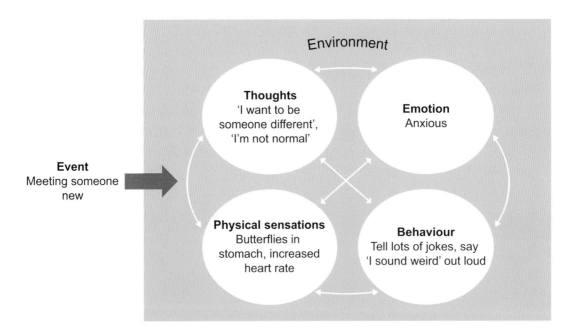

Figure 8.1 Hot cross bun CBT formulation model (Source: Padesky and Mooney, 1990, p. 13)

Figure 8.1 depicts the assumption in CBT that 'what we feel is closely connected to our thinking, our behavior, our biology and our environment' (Padesky and Mooney, 1990, p. 13). Thus, thinking 'I'm not normal' is likely to increase a person's feelings of anxiety as well as the physical sensations that accompany them. At the same time, noticing physical symptoms of anxiety might further increase anxious feelings and worried thoughts. One might note that this model ignores a person's broader relational and social context – something that is increasingly recognised as important in formulation (Section 2.3 looks at social factors in formulation). Nonetheless, even though the approach to formulation can be quite different in different models, there are common features. In addition to their focus on the meaning of experience, all formulations have the purpose of:

1   summarising the service user's core problems

2   indicating how the service user's difficulties may relate to one another, by drawing on psychological theories and principles

3   suggesting, on the basis of psychological theory, why the service user has developed these difficulties, at this time and in these situations.

(Johnstone and Dallos, 2013)

The main aim of a formulation is to provide the basis for an **intervention plan** tailored to the individual and their needs. This can be thought of as a personalised map for the best way forward.

Formulation has other uses and benefits as well, including (DCP, 2011):

- clarifying hypotheses and questions

- providing an overall picture

- noticing what is missing

- prioritising issues and problems for the client to work on

- minimising bias by making choices and decisions explicit

- putting medical interventions in context

- predicting responses to interventions

- thinking about lack of progress

- ensuring that a cultural perspective is incorporated.

A formulation can also be seen as an intervention in itself. If it is developed and shared sensitively, it can convey a message of relief and hope, help the client to feel listened to and understood, and strengthen the relationship with the therapist or other professional (DCP, 2011).

Formulation can offer a helpful midpoint between what are sometimes described as 'brain or blame' positions. People may feel they face a narrow choice between two opposing societal messages: 'You have a physical illness, therefore your distress is real and no one is to blame for it' versus 'Your difficulties are imaginary and/or are your own or someone else's fault; you ought to pull yourself together'. In contrast, the core message of a formulation is: 'You are having an understandable response to an abnormal situation. Anyone who had been through the same experiences might well end up feeling the same. You can recover'.

Intervention plan
A plan describing the best way forward for the client, which in counselling will be based on what the counsellor and the client should focus on in their work together.

2   Using formulation in practice

This section looks at the practice of creating, applying and revising formulations in therapy, and what factors need to be considered in this process. For demonstration purposes, the fictional character 'Lisa' is used throughout the section. The fictional example used here is drawn from one-to-one work with adults, but formulation can also be used with couples, families, children and young people. Lisa's case illustration below provides an outline of her circumstances and the initial formulation devised by her therapist.

Case illustration: Lisa's formulation

Lisa is a white woman aged 25. She is experiencing feelings of low mood after the end of a short-term relationship. She has also been self-harming. After a few weeks of getting to know Lisa, her therapist writes a provisional summary of what she has understood about the origins and meanings of Lisa's difficulties. She shows it to Lisa for feedback on whether or not it seems to 'fit'. The initial version of the formulation might look like the one below.

Initial formulation report

You came to see me because you have been feeling despairing and hopeless since your partner left. This is my best understanding of why the break-up has hit you so hard, based on what you have told me so far.

Your early life was dominated by your father's violence towards your mother. This, along with his harsh parenting, meant that you grew up feeling insecure and unconfident. Although your parents eventually separated, and you are close to your mother, it is not surprising that you have been left with anxieties about relationships. You find it particularly difficult to deal with anger and conflict, because of your dread of becoming or ending up with someone who behaves like your father. However, this means that you sometimes feel unable to stand up for your own needs.

As a child, you were so preoccupied with events at home that you found it hard to make friends, and some of your classmates took advantage of your lack of confidence by bullying you. You still have flashbacks to some of the most frightening incidents.

Despite your academic ability, you left school unqualified for anything but low-paid jobs, which leaves you short of money and unfulfilled in your work. You are anxious about being made redundant when your current contract comes to an end, and you feel unsafe in your flat and the surrounding area.

Your childhood has left you with a longing to be emotionally close to someone, along with a fear that you may be hurt if you get too intimate. If you are rejected or abandoned, as you were by your father, you are overwhelmed with feelings of self-hatred and hopelessness. You feel as if your deepest fear – that no one will ever accept and love you however hard you try – has been confirmed. The end of your relationship seems to have brought all these feelings to the surface again.

By constantly telling yourself that you are a useless failure, you seem to be replaying your father's harsh criticisms, being as hard on yourself as he was on you. Self-harm is one way to punish yourself, as well as offering some release from these overwhelming feelings.

Despite all this, you have many strengths. You are intelligent and have a talent for music. You are sensitive and self-aware, with a good understanding of how you have come to be in this situation. You have been able to find a few close friends who care for you. You have shown great determination in surviving your early life, and you have already started to take steps towards overcoming your difficulties.

We can see that the formulation is personal to Lisa and is expressed in ordinary language, based on what she has told her therapist. At the same time, it draws on a wider body of research about the impact of bullying and witnessing domestic violence; in other words, it is based on the best current evidence. These factors are integrated into a coherent narrative through the central thread of what they mean to Lisa herself. The formulation suggests a pathway forward, which will probably include building on the trusting relationship with her therapist and talking through the feelings from the past. It might also include practical steps, such as taking up new activities or, in the longer-term, changing jobs or going to college. The hope is that the formulation helps Lisa to view her experiences as understandable, to feel that she has been listened to, and to see that she has many strengths and that, with support, she can overcome her difficulties.

Lisa may wish to make some changes to the formulation so that her therapist understands her better. For example, Lisa may feel that the therapist has overlooked the guilt she felt for not being able to protect her mother; or she may want to remind the therapist that she always felt safe and loved when she was with her grandmother. The formulation will evolve as the therapy continues, and at the end of the sessions, Lisa and the therapist may collaborate on a more detailed version which reminds Lisa of the progress she has made and the future directions she plans to take.

Pause for reflection

Imagine that you are in Lisa's situation. How might you feel if you were offered this formulation? How might you feel if you were offered a diagnosis of clinical depression instead? Consider the positives and negatives of each option.

2.1   General best practice principles of formulation

Like any other intervention, and like therapy in general, formulation can be done badly as well as helpfully. For this reason, The British Psychological Society's Division of Clinical Psychology (DCP) has produced a set of guidelines called *Good practice duidelines for the use of psychological formulation* (DCP, 2011). The guidelines list criteria for the content of a formulation; for example, it should be expressed in accessible language, culturally aware, non-blaming and inclusive of strengths and achievements. They also list criteria for the process of developing a formulation; for example, the need to be collaborative and respectful of the client's views about accuracy and helpfulness. Therapists are expected to take a reflective stance, which helps to avoid formulating in insensitive, non-consenting or disempowering ways (DCP, 2011). Information box 8.1 describes some service-user reactions to formulation, both positive and negative.

Information box 8.1: Evaluating the effectiveness of formulation

As highlighted in Chapter 2, many service users have expressed strong dissatisfaction with their experiences of mental health services, in part for their failiure to ask about or address the trauma and adversity that are so often a part of service-users' history (Read *et al.*, 2017). It might be hoped that formulation could improve matters, but there is relatively little research into how service users experience this process.

On the positive side, some service users have found that formulation has increased their understanding and trust, bringing them empowerment and relief and enabling them to move forward ('It just all made sense. I got it because... it was true'; 'It was bang on, so I trusted that she understood'; 'I think if you know the reason something's happening it automatically becomes more controllable'; Redhead, Johnstone and Nightingale, 2015, pp. 7, 10). Others have reported experiencing formulation as saddening, frightening or overwhelming (Chadwick, Williams and Mackenzie, 2003; Morberg Pain, Chadwick and Abba, 2008).

To fully understand what formulation practices lead to the best outcomes, more and longer-term research would be useful.

2.2   Trauma-informed practice

The DCP guidelines state that formulation should consider 'the possible role of trauma and abuse' (DCP, 2011, p. 29). This refers to the large body of evidence that testifies to the impact of all kinds of trauma and adversity on people's mental health (Kezelman and Stavropoulos, 2012). As discussed in Chapter 6, for years it has been clear that trauma is common in the lives of people experiencing all forms of distress, from eating problems to experiences that may be 'diagnosed' as 'borderline personality disorder', 'depression', 'anxiety', 'phobias' and self-harm. This also applies to more serious problems that may be diagnosed as 'schizophrenia' or 'psychosis' (Read and Bentall, 2012). From a **trauma-informed perspective**, these too can be understood, or formulated, as responses to life struggles rather than as medical illnesses or 'disorders'. This radical shift in perspective is summarised by the slogan, 'Instead of asking "What's wrong with you?" ask "What's happened to you?"'.

The trauma-informed perspective draws on trauma studies, attachment theory and neuroscience in order to show how the mind, the body, relationships (particularly in early life) and the social world interact when a person is faced with threats (Herman, 2015; van der Kolk, 2015). As Chapter 6 described, the concept of 'trauma' includes sexual, emotional and physical abuse and neglect, bereavement and loss, domestic violence and bullying. There is increasing recognition of

Trauma-informed perspective
An approach to distress which is based on evidence about the impact of trauma and adversities on the mind and body.

the impact of background adversities, such as poverty, unemployment, racial discrimination and other forms of social inequality. Although trauma-informed approaches originated in the US, they are gradually gaining influence in the UK, and some services are adopting their ideas (Sweeney *et al.*, 2018).

As outlined in Part 1 of this book, psychiatric practice is based on the medical model. The language of diagnosis reflects this, as does the tendency to see doctors, nurses, medication and hospitals as offering the most appropriate 'treatments'. In contrast, the trauma-informed perspective sees what the medical model refers to as 'symptoms' as survival strategies. Our minds and bodies have creative ways of coping with emotionally overwhelming events and situations. We may go into an automatic fight/flight/freeze response to protect ourselves from danger. We may protect ourselves from overwhelming feelings and memories through the process of dissociation; for example, it is not a coincidence that people with a diagnosis of schizophrenia often hear the voice of someone who abused them, or that many people with 'paranoid delusions' have been victims of bullying and violence, which has made them extremely sensitive to threat (van Dam *et al.*, 2012). These experiences often indicate unresolved emotional trauma; the identity of the voices, or the content of the unusual beliefs, may be a clue to what has happened (Corstens and Longden, 2013). The trauma-informed approach recognises that, while all of these responses were essential at the time, they can become a problem in their own right. Therapists start by giving the client information about typical reactions to trauma and suggesting coping strategies. Only when the person has achieved a degree of safety and control in their emotions, bodies and relationships will the therapist support them to process the memories and emotions that may need to be revisited (Herman, 2015).

Trauma-informed formulations help to ensure that therapists' knowledge is integrated into the interventions people are offered. In addition, a trauma-informed approach recognises that services may unintentionally re-traumatise people through coercive practices such as forced drugging or, less obviously, by failing to ask about possible trauma, or by failing to offer appropriate support if it is disclosed (Fallot and Harris, 2009; Read *et al.*, 2017). The DCP guidelines therefore state that formulations developed within service settings should consider the 'possible role of services in compounding the difficulties' (DCP, 2011, p. 29).

We can see that Lisa's formulation draws on trauma-informed ideas. It starts from the assumption that her low mood, flashbacks and self-harm are meaningful responses to what she has experienced. Lisa's therapist can reassure her that these reactions are very common and understandable in people who have experienced trauma, and may suggest various strategies to help her gain more control over them. In the longer-term, when she feels safer, Lisa may feel ready to return to those earlier memories and express any underlying feelings of fear, guilt and shame. She may be able to start creating a new story, or formulation, in which she is able to see how well she did to survive.

Let's take the example a bit further. Suppose Lisa also reports hearing a hostile voice telling her she is a 'dirty slut', or suppose she feels a compulsive need to scrub her skin clean. It is not always immediately obvious what this kind of experience is about, but a trauma-informed therapist might suspect undisclosed trauma. Perhaps Lisa will eventually trust the therapist enough to reveal that she was sexually abused by a neighbour. If the hostile voice sounds very much like this neighbour's, or if Lisa describes feeling 'dirty' and defiled after the abuse, then the voices or the compulsive washing may begin to make more sense, and these new insights can be added to the formulation. This kind of understanding may be particularly helpful if Lisa is admitted to mental health services.

2.3   Social factors in formulation

One of the messages of the trauma-informed approach is that tragic events happen within a wider social context. Environments of poverty, violence, discrimination, inequality and exclusion are traumatic in themselves, and are breeding grounds for interpersonal abuses (Public Health Management Corporation, 2013). Formulations therefore need to include the influence of the social environment, or as the DCP guidelines put it, practitioners need to have 'a critical awareness of the wider societal context within which formulation takes place' (DCP, 2011, p. 20). Without this, we may primarily attribute the difficulties to the characteristics of the person, even if they are described in psychological rather than medical terms (Hagan and Smail, 1997). In other words, the implicit message may be one of blame, and the client may feel more inadequate than ever if they are unable to carry out the recommended individual-focused interventions.

Activity 8.1: Lisa's social circumstances

Allow about 20 minutes

Reread Lisa's formulation and then spend 10 minutes listing what you know about Lisa's context – the world in which she finds herself living. Then spend another 10 minutes considering how these aspects of her context may have influenced her mental health (both positively and negatively). If it helps, think about Lisa's context in terms of her home and family life; broader social life or contacts outside the family; her personal resources or strengths and vulnerabilities; and her material or economic resources (Hagan and Smail, 1997).

Discussion

To take her economic and employment context as an example, Lisa is facing very real job stresses, as she is only able to find insecure, minimum-wage, zero-hour contracts. Her economic and employment context is, therefore, potentially creating or exacerbating her anxiety. Lisa may also be genuinely at risk from further bullying or assaults in her part of town, so her community environment may be creating an additional risk of trauma. These factors in turn are the result of social and economic policies which, especially in recent years, have greatly increased poverty and inequality. If the formulation simply suggests Lisa tries anxiety management techniques without acknowledging the wider context, Lisa may perceive the message that her anxiety is an unreasonable response, and that she ought to be able to manage it better.

2.4   Formulation in therapy and mental health settings

Formulation is a core skill of the profession of clinical psychology. It is growing in influence and popularity and has been added to the regulatory requirements for counselling, educational, health, forensic, occupational, sports and exercise psychologists (Health Professions Council, 2015), as well as psychiatrists (Royal College of Psychiatrists, 2013) and mental health nurses (Nursing and Midwifery Council, 2010). It is also included in the professional occupational standards for cognitive, systemic and constructivist therapists (United Kingdom Council for Psychotherapy, n.d.). A recent document – the *Mental health core skills education and training framework* (Skills for Health, Skills for Care and Health Education England, 2016) – includes formulation as a core skill for all mental health and related professionals. Formulation has gained a firm foothold in mental health services for adults, children and adolescents, and may also be used in other health settings to place diagnoses of physical ill-health, learning disability, stroke, dementia, and so on within a holistic context (Johnstone, 2018).

The term 'formulation' can be used in several senses. It can refer to a specific written summary or report, such as the fictional one for Lisa. She will be given her own copy, and a copy will also go in her medical notes. Adapted versions can be used for a professional's letter to a GP, or other referrer, for legal reports and so on. There is no standard format but, typically, a summary of the individual's history and current problems would be followed by a formulation, and this would then be used as the basis for making recommendations about interventions.

Formulation reports are also commonly used in therapy training as a way of helping trainees think systematically about how they are making sense of the clients with whom they are working. The idea behind this use of formulation reports is that the act of making explicit the potentially unspoken assumptions about what is going on for a client will help a trainee therapist to be clearer about their 'sense-making' and how their understanding of the client is influencing how they are responding to them. As an example, Lisa's formulation suggests she calls herself a 'useless failure' because she has internalised her violent father's harsh criticisms of her. However, if she tells a trainee that there is no point in therapy because she is such a 'useless failure', the trainee might read this as Lisa 'resisting' therapy. Instead of responding to Lisa with empathy, the trainee might inadvertently withdraw from her, thereby missing the opportunity of making the link with Lisa's past experiences.

More broadly, it could also be said that in any therapy encounter there is an evolving formulation in that, even if no one writes it down, both client and therapist are mutually engaged in trying to make sense of the client's experiences. Parts of these formulations may be shared between the two people, but therapists and clients may also have ideas about what is going on that they have not (yet) shared with each other. For example, long before she tells her therapist about her history of abuse, Lisa may know that this experience is a key factor in understanding what is going on for her in the present. Equally, the therapist may begin to wonder about the potential of abuse weeks before Lisa talks about her history.

It is important to remember that formulations arise out of a conversation within a relationship and thus they can be seen as a process, not just an event. The evolving story is never complete; it is always open to revision. In an even wider sense, formulation can be seen as an entire approach to mental health and therapeutic work, in which the starting point is the assumption that even the most extreme and unusual expressions of despair and distress are, ultimately, meaningful communications about what has happened in people's lives.

3   Controversies and debates about formulation

The growing popularity of formulation – a term that was almost unknown outside clinical psychology until around 2000 – has brought its own controversies. One of the biggest debates is about the relationship between formulation and psychiatric diagnosis. In many settings, a medical diagnosis will be needed alongside a formulation; for example, in the case of someone with an intellectual disability, dementia or a physical illness. As psychiatric diagnosis is a contested practice, however, there are debates in mental health settings around the question of whether a formulation needs to be accompanied by a psychiatric diagnosis.

3.1   Formulation and psychiatric diagnosis

In our fictional example, Lisa is undoubtedly very unhappy, and it is likely that a GP or mental health professional would give her a diagnosis of depression. This might bring some short-term relief, because it sounds like an explanation and suggests that medication might be the solution. However, as discussed in previous chapters (Chapters 4 and 5 especially) there is no evidence that the experiences we call 'depression' are best seen as a medical illness with biological causes, such as chemical imbalances. Moreover, the diagnosis may have the additional disadvantage of confirming Lisa's deeply held belief that there is something different and flawed about her, and that the problem lies within her alone.

As this chapter has highlighted, psychological formulation is based on fundamentally different principles from those of psychiatric diagnosis. The difference between them is the contrast between the messages: 'You have a medical illness with primarily biological causes' and 'Your problems are an understandable emotional response to your life circumstances'. Once there is a reasonable explanation, or formulation, it's not required to add another – possibly contradictory – explanation in the form of a diagnosis, which would effectively tell Lisa: 'By the way, you also feel like this because you have 'x' disorder or 'y' diagnosis'. This is reflected in the DCP guidelines, which state that 'best practice formulations … are not premised on psychiatric diagnosis' (DCP, 2011, p. 17).

The debate has become more complicated in the context of increasingly vocal critics of diagnosis and the medical model of distress. That is why the DCP guidelines draw a distinction between psychiatric formulation and psychological formulation – the former is used to supplement diagnosis, while the latter is used as an alternative to diagnosis. The training curriculum for psychiatrists requires them to 'demonstrate the ability to construct formulations of patients' problems that include appropriate differential diagnoses' (Royal College of Psychiatrists, 2013, p. 25). Thus, a psychiatric formulation for Lisa might describe her as experiencing clinical depression/borderline personality disorder triggered by early trauma and recent life events. Although such psychiatric formulations provide some context for people's experiences, they are likely to have a primary focus on the 'illness' or 'disorder' and to sideline the 'triggers' – the actual life events and their meanings.

In real-world practice, some psychiatrists do offer psychological formulations, and some psychologists use psychiatric ones. Formulations are underpinned by ways of thinking that cut across professional groups, not 'turf wars'. However, the distinction between the two types of formulation is an important one, and arouses controversy because of the wider implications. By adopting formulation in its more limited sense, supporters of the existing psychiatric model can claim to be filling some of the gaps in diagnosis while retaining the basic system as it is. As two senior psychiatrists put it, 'the key is to produce a formulation that … complements the diagnosis by including information about important clinical variables that have relevance for the management plan. We should continue to make diagnoses complemented by formulations' (Craddock and Mynors-Wallis, 2014, p. 93). Trauma-informed psychological formulation, on the other hand, has the potential to take us beyond the medical model altogether.

Whatever our perspectives on this debate, we should be aware that formulation is not a straightforward or unproblematic alternative to diagnosis. Both practices have arisen within western contexts and may not translate well to other cultures. The Diversity box highlights some of the issues.

Diversity: Applying formulation across populations

Storytelling is a universal human skill – we all try to make sense of our experiences, both good and bad. However, the specific version of narrative construction called 'formulation' has arisen within western psychological models, which have their own cultural biases. These may include assumptions about the separation of the individual from the social group and from the natural world, and rejection of spiritual or religious understandings.

In collectivist cultures, the idea of engaging in one-to-one therapy may be alien, and distress may more typically be located within the contexts of extended family relationships, ties to village and social networks, relationships with the land, and so on. For example, formulations – or individualised understandings of distress – based on western post-traumatic stress models were found to be very unhelpful to Sri Lankan communities devastated by the 2004 tsunami, who 'conceived of the damage ... as occurring not inside their mind but outside the self, in the social environment' and already had their own spiritual healing practices (Watters, 2011, p. 100).

Can, or should, formulation practices be used with non-western groups, within or beyond the UK? Minority groups and indigenous populations nearly always experience higher rates of distress, but it does not follow that the dominant culture has the answers, either in terms of diagnosis or in terms of formulation. At the very least, awareness of the influence of colonisation, and the resulting intergenerational trauma and loss of culture and identity, is needed in all versions of formulation or narrative-construction with these populations.

3.2   Formulation and research

Counselling and psychotherapy practice today is often concerned with the need for practice to be 'evidence-based' (as will be unpacked in Chapter 17). It is sometimes claimed that formulation practice lacks evidence to support it. One response is to point out that formulation is essentially a structure for developing a hypothesis, which is at the heart of evidence-based practice (Sackett *et al.*, 2000). Formulation generates meaningful, personalised hypotheses about the origins of people's difficulties, which are evaluated and revised through the process of therapy and the general intervention plan that follows from the formulation.

Having said that, there is a lack of research into the effectiveness of this particular way of constructing hypotheses. In therapy settings, it is hard to disentangle the impact of the formulation from the implicit meaning-making process that is at the heart of all therapeutic work. Little is known about whether formulation-based practice in mental health services actually achieves specific outcomes, such as higher rates of recovery, less use of psychiatric drugs and increased satisfaction rates (Cole, Wood and Spendelow, 2015). However, **team formulation** (see Johnstone, 2013) seems to be highly valued by staff (Cole, Wood and Spendelow, 2015), and has the potential to improve staff–patient relationships (Berry, Barrowclough and Wearden, 2009) and achieve significant reductions in client distress (Araci and Clarke, 2016).

Team formulation
The process of facilitating a group or team of staff to develop shared formulations about the clients they are working with, ideally through regular weekly meetings.

Conclusion

This chapter has described the core principles of formulation and formulation practice. While formulation may be understood differently in different theoretical models, and conducted differently in different settings, there are agreed core principles of good practice. A central principle is that psychological formulation involves listening respectfully and sensitively to a client's evolving story, and engaging in shared meaning-making in order to co-construct a guide to the best way forward. Good practice guidelines for formulation emphasise the importance of considering the potential role of trauma and social factors in the formulation. The chapter also examined how formulation is used by practitioners in a range of settings, both within and beyond mental health and related services, and in training. Formulation-based practice has become more prominent but also more controversial in the face of criticisms of psychiatric diagnosis, for which it is sometimes seen as a replacement. For this reason, the final section of this chapter examined some of the controversies and debates about formulation and argued that more research is needed in order to evidence the benefits that are claimed about it.

Further reading

- The authors of this text discuss formulation and its relationship to narrative and storytelling, both within and beyond therapeutic settings:
  Corrie, S. and Lane, D.A. (2010) *Constructing stories, telling tales: a guide to formulation in applied psychology*. London: Karnac Books.

- These guidelines provide further detail about what good formulation practice should look like:

  Division of Clinical Psychology (DCP) (2011) *Good practice guidelines on the use of psychological formulation*. Leicester: The British Psychological Society. Available at: :http://www.bpsshop.org.uk/Good-Practice-Guidelines-on-the-use-of-psychological-formulation-P1653.aspx (Accessed: 27 February 2020).

- A key text on formulation, this book includes information on how formulation is conducted in different therapy modalitites. Chapter 1 introduces definitions and purposes of formulation, and Chapter 12 discusses controversies and debates about formulation:

  Johnstone, L. and Dallos, R. (eds.) (2013) *Formulation in psychology and psychotherapy: making sense of people's problems*. 2nd edn. London: Routledge.

- This journal paper summarises current formulation-based practice in the UK and argues that it should be seen as an alternative to psychiatric diagnosis:

  Johnstone, L. (2018) 'Psychological formulation as an alternative to psychiatric diagnosis', *Journal of Humanistic Psychology*, 58(1), pp. 30–46.

References

Araci, D. and Clarke, I. (2016) 'Investigating the efficacy of a whole team, psychologically informed, acute mental health service approach', *Journal of Mental Health*, 26(4), pp. 307–311. doi:10.3109/09638237.2016.1139065.

Berry, K., Barrowclough, C. and Wearden, A. (2009) 'A pilot study investigating the use of psychological formulations to modify psychiatric staff perceptions of service users with psychosis', *Behavioural and Cognitive Psychotherapy*, 37(1), pp. 39–48. doi:10.1017/S1352465808005018.

Butler, G. (1998) 'Clinical formulation', in Bellack, A.S. and Hersen, M. (eds.) *Comprehensive clinical psychology*. Oxford, UK: Pergamon, pp. 1–23.

Chadwick, P., Williams, C. and Mackenzie, J. (2003) 'Impact of case formulation in cognitive behaviour therapy for psychosis', *Behaviour Research and Therapy*, 14(6), pp. 671–680.

Cole, S., Wood, K. and Spendelow, J. (2015) 'Team formulation: a critical evaluation of current literature and future research directions', *Clinical Psychology Forum*, 275, pp. 13–19.

Corstens, D. and Longden, E. (2013) 'The origins of voices: links between life history and voice hearing in a survey of 100 cases', *Psychosis*, 5(3), pp. 270–285.

Craddock, N. and Mynors-Wallis, L. (2014) 'Psychiatric diagnosis: impersonal, imperfect and important', *British Journal of Psychiatry*, 204(2), pp. 93–95. doi:10.1192/bjp.bp.113.133090.

Division of Clinical Psychology (DCP) (2011) *Good practice guidelines on the use of psychological formulation*. Leicester: The British Psychological Society.

Fallot, R.D. and Harris, M. (2009) *Creating cultures of trauma-informed care (CCTIC): a self-assessment and planning protocol*. Washington DC: Community Connections.

Hagan, T. and Smail, D. (1997) 'Power-mapping—I. background and basic methodology', *Journal of Community & Applied Social Psychology*, 7(4), pp. 257–267.

Harper, D. and Moss, D. (2003) 'A different kind of chemistry? Reformulating 'formulation'', *Clinical Psychology*, 25, pp. 6–10.

Health Professions Council (2015) *Standards of proficiency: practitioner psychologists*. London, UK: Health Professions Council.

Herman, J.L. (2015) *Trauma and recovery: the aftermath of violence – from domestic abuse to political terror*. New York, NY: Basic Books.

Johnstone, L. (2013) 'Using formulation in teams', in Johnstone, L. and Dallos, R. (eds.) *Formulation in psychology and psychotherapy: making sense of people's problems*. 2nd edn. London: Routledge, pp. 216–242.

Johnstone, L. (2018) 'Psychological formulation as an alternative to psychiatric diagnosis', *Journal of Humanistic Psychology*, 58(1), pp. 30–46.

Johnstone, L. and Dallos, R. (eds.) (2013) *Formulation in psychology and psychotherapy: making sense of people's problems*. 2nd edn. London: Routledge.

Kezelman, C.A. and Stavropoulos, P.A. (2012) *Practice guidelines for treatment of complex trauma and trauma informed care and service delivery*. Milsons Point: Blue Knot Foundation. Available at: https://www.blueknot.org.au/resources/Publications/Practice-Guidelines (Accessed: 10 June 2019).

Morberg Pain, C., Chadwick, P., and Abba, N. (2008) 'Clients' experience of case formulation in cognitive behaviour therapy for psychosis', *The British Journal of Clinical Psychology*, 47(2), pp. 127–138. doi:10.1348/014466507X235962.

Nursing and Midwifery Council (2010) *Standards for competence for registered nurses*. London: Nursing and Midwifery Council (NMC). Available at: https://www.nmc.org.uk/standards/standards-for-nurses/pre-2018-standards/standards-for-competence-for-registered-nurses/ (Accessed: 27 February 2020).

Padesky, C.A. and Mooney, K.A. (1990) 'Clinical tip: presenting the cognitive model to clients', *International Cognitive Therapy Newsletter*, 6, pp. 13–14.

Public Health Management Corporation (2013) *Findings from the Philadelphia urban ACE survey*. Philadelphia: Institute for Safe Families. Available at: https://www.philadelphiaaces.org/philadelphia-ace-survey (Accessed: 18 December 2019).

Read, J. and Bentall, R.B. (2012) 'Negative childhood experiences and mental health: theoretical, clinical and primary prevention implications', *British Journal of Psychiatry*, 200, pp. 89–91.

Read, J., Harper, D., Tucker, I. and Kennedy, A. (2017) 'Do adult mental health services identify child abuse and neglect? A systematic review', *International Journal of Mental Health Nursing*, 27(1), pp. 7–19.

Redhead, S., Johnstone, L. and Nightingale, J. (2015) 'Clients' experiences of formulation in cognitive behaviour therapy', *Psychology and Psychotherapy: Theory, Research and Practice*, 88(4), pp. 453–467. doi:10.1111/papt.12054.

Royal College of Psychiatrists (2013) *A competency based curriculum for specialist core training in psychiatry*. Available at: https://www.rcpsych.ac.uk/docs/default-source/training/curricula-and-guidance/curricula-core-psychiatry-curriculum-april-2018.pdf?sfvrsn=881b63ca_2 (Accessed: 27 February 2020).

Sackett, D.L., Straus, S.E., Richardson, W.S., Rosenberg, W. and Haynes, R.B. (2000) *Evidence-based medicine: how to practice and teach EBM*. 2nd edn. London, UK: Churchill Livingstone.

Skills for Health, Skills for Care and Health Education England (HEE) (2016) *Mental health core skills education and training framework*. London: Department of Health.

Sweeney, A., Filson, B., Kennedy, A., Collinson, L. and Gillard, S. (2018) 'A paradigm shift: relationships in trauma-informed mental health services', *British Journal of Psychiatry Advances*, 24(5), pp. 319–333.

United Kingdom Council for Psychotherapy (UKCP) (n.d.) *Professional occupational standards: for the information of commissioners, trainers and practitioners*. London: UKCP.

van Dam, D.S., van der Ven, E., Velthorst, E., Selten, J.P., Morgan, C. and de Haan, L. (2012) 'Childhood bullying and the association with psychosis in non-clinical and clinical samples: a review and meta-analysis', *Psychological Medicine*, 42(12), pp. 2463–2474.

van der Kolk, B. (2015) *The body keeps the score: brain, mind, and body in the healing of trauma*. New York, NY: Viking.

Watters, E. (2011) *Crazy like us: the globalization of the western mind*. London: Robinson Publishing.

Part 3

Models of working

Chapter 9

The psychodynamic approach

David Kaposi

Contents

Introduction

'Free' by Jonathan New

Being haunted by the smell of burnt pudding; an inexplicable difficulty in walking; a sudden out-of-breath sensation; the inability to drink water – such were the complaints encountered by Sigmund Freud in his late nineteenth-century Viennese medical practice. As Chapter 3 outlined, in Freud's era and earlier, the way of dealing with such symptoms was to classify them as 'hysterical' and irrational nonsense; perhaps destructive in nature, giving rise to physical restraint or hypnotic suggestion, but nonsense nonetheless. The founding father of psychoanalysis and psychodynamic thought was not to follow tradition, though, but to do something truly revolutionary. Freud started to *listen* to his clients and took what they had to say about their symptoms seriously. This, in turn, led him to the trailblazing conclusion that his clients' symptoms were meaningful, if indirect, communications – they conveyed that his clients were 'suffer[ing] mainly from reminiscences' (Breuer and Freud, 2001[1895], p. 7).

As this chapter aims to highlight, listening to 'indirect communications' was by no means easy. These reminiscences refused to 'behave' like proper memories. Despite tormenting clients in the present, they somehow simultaneously appeared forgotten. Freud therefore had to facilitate his clients' efforts to recall them and to find a way to perceive their experiences beyond simply what they were consciously expressing.

This process ultimately revealed things that were hard for both Freud and his clients to accept: traumatic experiences that were related to loving and hateful sensual/sexual relations (Freud, 2001[1896]). What is more, these were relayed by invariably middle-class people of privileged backgrounds, which further suggested to Freud that the trauma may have been caused by a regular part of development, rather than by an extraordinary event or by social or economic deprivation.

Thus, the invention of the 'talking cure' (as described in Chapter 3) was also the discovery of a very special kind of listening process, and a special type of psychic reality. The distinguishing features of the contemporary psychodynamic approach remain in keeping with these discoveries, despite many important changes in theory and practice. The psychodynamic approach continues to posit that, to alleviate mental distress, the therapist must engage with a directly inexpressible, dynamic unconscious realm of mental life, which originates in the vicissitudes of highly charged early experiences of love and hate.

This chapter aims to:

- introduce the central psychodynamic concept of unconscious communication

- introduce the origins of the dynamic unconscious and explain how it can inform our understanding of mental health

- outline the process of psychodynamic therapy – how unconscious communication may manifest and how it can be dealt with in therapy

- discuss the psychodynamic approach's relationship to outcome research.

---

1   Core psychodynamic principles and their development

The development of the psychodynamic approach entailed a progressive expansion of the realm of **unconscious communication,** through which consciously inexpressible feelings of love and hate are communicated and understood.

Freud's treatment of reminiscences continued with the clients' memories themselves, which he took to mean something more than what appeared on the surface. First, he traced troubling memories of relatively recent origin back to early traumatic experiences. Then, he considered how these early experiences themselves expressed more than what they seemed to – Freud understood the memories of early experiences as representing not simply historical truth (objective events that happened between parent and child) but also traumatising infantile impulses (the fears and desires central to the Oedipus complex, as outlined in Chapter 3, Section 1). Finally, he realised that virtually any detail clients brought to therapy may be interpreted as the unconscious communication of early traumatic experiences (Freud, 2001[1916-1917]; see Information box 9.1).

Unconscious communication
Unintentional acts by which directly inaccessible psychic states are expressed.

Information box 9.1: The psychodynamic origins of mental distress

It is often said that the year 1897 was crucial in the formation of psychodynamic thought – and, indeed, in the way that subsequent generations of clinicians understood the role of trauma in mental health. Before 1897, Freud unquestioningly believed what his clients revealed about past traumas, and he hypothesised that the external cause of common mental distress was childhood sexual abuse. Afterwards, he became sceptical of clients' memories and accordingly asserted an internal cause of trauma: the child's own infantile sexual impulses (Herman, 2015; Freud, 2001[1925]).

Today, even clinicians who believe that the internal life/desires of the infant are crucial to subsequent development tend not to question that adult clients' traumatic memories refer (also) to events that actually happened. What is more, as you read in Chapter 8, there is now the general expectation across counselling and psychotherapy that any formulation of mental distress must account for past traumas. The idea of Freud questioning his clients'. memories may therefore seem unprofessional or heartless.

Yet, reading Freud's pre-1897 case histories, the interesting thing is that, when his clients hint at or disclose traumatic memories, they themselves appear at the same time reluctant to take these seriously. Thus, the crucial question may not simply be whether or not Freud's clients suffered sexual abuse in their childhood, or whether Freud was right in being sceptical, but why they found it difficult to perceive their own memories as being 'real'.

This continues to be relevant today. The question in therapy often concerns why traumatic episodes are recalled in a seemingly incongruent, detached manner. Why is the potential impact of a painful early experience occasionally flatly rejected? Why is the therapist often treated as someone who cannot really understand what happened? Such questions attend to the possibility that Freud's real insight lay neither in his idea that childhood sexual abuse is the causal factor in trauma, nor in his later idea that infantile sexual desires are the causal factor; rather, his legacy lies in his understanding of the crucial importance of a person's sense of alienation from and resistance to their own memories/ experiences in the formation of mental distress.

However, something else remained – something very peculiar. Freud observed clients unaccountably developing an extremely high or low opinion of their therapist. They might praise, and behave affectionately towards, them; for example, one particular client is even reported to have developed a phantom pregnancy and enacted a childbirth (Jones, 1974[1961]). Or, clients suddenly found fault with almost everything their therapist said – they might criticise their therapist's manners or taste, declare them completely useless and shout at them angrily (Freud, 2001[1916–1917]).

What was going on? Discounting his personal charm as an explanation, Freud suggested that this strange clinical phenomenon was another manifestation of unconscious communication. The cause of his clients' suffering was not simply represented in memories; rather, it got *transferred* into the room and *acted out* in the strange declarations of love or hate they felt towards the therapist (Freud, 2001[1915]). Freud's remarkable insight continues to be highly relevant to present-day practice. If a client or a service user reacts angrily to a comment, psychodynamic clinicians will consider what memories or experiences the comment may have tapped. What past event is being replayed in the present? With whom is the client angry?

In post-Freudian and contemporary psychodynamic practice, the recognition of **transference** became more than a mere addition to the concept of unconscious communication, and assumed a central position in understanding mental distress. For Freud, transference phenomena entailed rather crude and explicit acts by clients, such as those mentioned above, but in contemporary practice transference is something far subtler and also far more pervasive: the client's overall orientation to the very process of therapy, involving the therapist. The dreams, stories and memories clients bring to therapy remain important, of course. Yet they too are seen as part of the transference. It is in the very process of therapy that the client's suffering is understood to be repeated and re-enacted (O'Shaughnessy, 2015; Racker, 1968). You will see a case illustration example about this in Section 3.

Some may find the idea of transference astonishing, but post-Freudian and contemporary psychodynamic clinicians have taken it even further. For Freud, his own feelings were a distraction from the process of listening (Freud, 2001[1915]), whereas modern psychodynamic therapists understand their own conduct in terms of the client's **dynamic unconscious**. A psychodynamic therapist will try to

Transference
A client's overall conduct (emotional and behavioural responses) towards the therapist, which conveys information about their unconscious internal life.

Dynamic unconscious
A set of mental states that cannot directly be communicated, yet influence, motivate or even determine a person's observable behaviour and conscious affective states.

Countertransference
A therapist's overall conduct (emotional and behavioural responses) in the therapeutic process, which conveys information about the client's unconscious internal life.

understand what they feel, say and do in therapy in terms of the client's suffering. This clinical phenomenon is called **countertransference** (Stefana, 2017). Thus, if a client relates an upsetting early memory yet remains strangely detached, while the therapist somehow feels upset and even angry, the therapist will probably question: What does my anger reveal about the client's experience? Why are they unable to experience it? In other words, the therapist's countertransference would be interpreted in terms of the source of the client's suffering.

As suggested in Chapter 3, working with the dynamics of transference (and countertransference) came to be a distinguishing feature of the psychodynamic approach. Before moving on to look at *how* such work is carried out, it is important to look at *what* exactly may be acted out in therapy.

Pause for reflection

Can you think of examples in your own life of transference (being treated as though you are someone you are not) and countertransference (learning from your own reactions what might be troubling someone else)? Note which of these you found easier to think of.

---

2   The psychodynamic understanding of mental health

What is this mysterious dynamic unconscious? What is it that can only be communicated unconsciously, and acted out rather than simply remembered? The short answer is that it is an amalgam of highly charged, early (and often preverbal) experiences of relationships of love and hate/destruction. In a psychodynamic understanding of mental health, the past is crucially important.

In Freud's view, people are born with impulses, such as primitive love and primitive hate/destructiveness, that blindly and unstoppably drive their satisfaction. Conflict, however, is on the horizon as these impulses clash with reality (Freud, 2001[1930]).The most important manifestations of this reality are culture and morality, which are first transmitted by the family surrounding a child.

Freud posited a critical period of infant psychosexual development (see Chapter 3) around the age of 3–5 years, when the child's intimate love for and wish to possess one parent (usually the one of the opposite sex) clashes with their aggressive eliminatory tendencies, fear and love towards the other. This fundamental conflict (referred to as the Oedipus complex – see Chapter 3, Section 1 for a reminder of the definition) is then solved by the **repression** of the loving/possessive and aggressive/destructive impulses. This results in identification with the parent who had formerly been the target of destructive tendencies. According to this theory, common mental health issues derive from an unsatisfactory resolution of this fundamental conflict (Freud, 2001 [1940]).

Repression
An unintentional mental process by which an unacceptable, overwhelming or unbearable impulse is rendered unconscious.

Culture, morality and the oedipal triangle (consisting of the father, mother and child) were of critical interest to Freud in understanding how our repressed desires can lead to distress. Post-Freudian and contemporary psychodynamic thought, both in the UK and the US, has emphasised different aspects of mental development. The focus has changed from age 3–5 to the preverbal (and premoral or precultural) years of 0–3 and, correspondingly, from the triangular relationship to the infant's quasi-exclusive, dyadic relationship with their mother (or primary caregiver).

While for Freud it was the self's conflicts that were implicated in mental health, post-Second World War clinicians, such as Wilfred Bion, Margaret Mahler and Donald Winnicott, came to focus on the very *formation* of people's sense of self. For Freud, a complete and *self-contained* child is what faced reality. In contrast, for post-Freudian authors, the child and their impulses were not a given; rather, they were the achievement of interactions with the parental environment. Moreover, this environment also became involved in another crucial potential achievement: the infant's development of an inner and true (as opposed to outwardly compliant and false) sense of self – first, by 'containing' the all-encompassing, frightening affective states with which the infant struggles, and then by gradually letting the infant's independent self emerge by withdrawing in a non-traumatic way (Greenberg and Mitchell, 1983).

Contemporary psychodynamic therapists continue to attribute great significance to the directly inaccessible realm of highly charged affective states (e.g. love and hate/destruction), just like Freud. However, they also see these states as loving and hating relationships, with every affect implying a self–other relation. Nowadays these relationships are considered to be formed from birth onwards and involve sensual preverbal experiences and representations. It is these preverbal affective relations that are then enacted and transformed in childhood and later life – and in transference (Benjamin, 2017; Mitchell, 1988; Taylor, 2017[1999]).

Case illustration: Jamie and anxiety

Jamie is 33. He has sought counselling as he feels an 'anxious pressure' in his chest whenever he talks to his boss, a 67-year-old mild-mannered Englishman.

Jamie is from South America. His father's family fell victim to political oppression, with several members having disappeared in the early 1980s.

Jamie's parents are still together. He remembers often having to play the role of mediator between them. This is a role he sometimes has to fulfil even today, although he now does it with a growing sense of irritation.

Jamie does not remember ever having any conflict with his dad. He does, however, remember being frequently irritated by his mum in his teenage years. He describes his present relationship with his mum as normal, although he still sometimes gets angry with her, for instance when she won't hang up the phone when they have finished speaking. Jamie and his dad used to share a passionate interest in local historical sites. Since Jamie moved away from home at the age of 24, however, his interest in local history has subsided. He has started to feel that interacting with his dad is sometimes awkward.

2.1   The psychodynamic understanding of anxiety

To illustrate the psychodynamic understanding of mental health, this section will look at the example of anxiety. In psychodynamic thought, anxiety plays a crucial role in mental health. It is not considered merely one symptom among many but rather a fundamental experience which, from infancy, underpins our mental development. This is not surprising: where there are forces of love and hate/destruction, there will also be worry, and even fear.

Freud understood anxiety as precipitating repression – the very process that makes experiences inaccessible to conscious verbal recollection. According to Freud, anxiety signals a situation in which a person fears being overwhelmed by their emotions (often because they feel left to deal with them alone), so they push them permanently outside of their consciousness (Freud, 2001[1926], 2001[1933]). In the oedipal situation, a child may fear their own aggression towards their father/mother, and fear that this aggression will succeed in destroying that person, who they otherwise love very much. Alternatively, there may be debilitating fear of parental retaliation, which can be exacerbated by overt or covert aggression from the father/mother. Even in the best of cases, Freud claimed, the anxiety around these dangers is overwhelming enough to precipitate repression of the aggressive impulses, as well as the sensually loving ones (Freud, 2001[1940]).

This understanding of anxiety (as central to all aspects of our mental health) remained important for subsequent psychodynamic developments. Yet, once again, the emphasis in relation to its origins shifted with post-Freudian authors, who highlighted how anxiety emerges from the context of our earliest preverbal (as opposed to later oedipal) relationships. One influential development, associated with the

Paranoid-schizoid position

A mental configuration dominated by extreme anxiety around the self's survival or destruction. This results in the splitting of reality into isolated Bad and Good versions.

Depressive position

A psychic configuration arising from the realisation that the object of both hate and love is the same, and from the corresponding ability to tolerate ambiguity. This is related to the developing capacity to make (and anxiety about making) reparations to the imagined damage done to the other.

work of Melanie Klein, posits two important phases during the first year of the infant's life, each with a distinct set of concerns and types of anxiety. In the first – the **paranoid-schizoid position** – what is perceived to be at stake is the self's very survival. The first months of life are dominated by the infant 'splitting' reality into an omnipotent and satisfying Good version and an unambiguously threatening Bad version. From around six months of age, the infant moves from the paranoid-schizoid position to the **depressive position**, where they start to develop the capacity to bring together into one reality what were originally two diametrically opposite and mutually exclusive realities (Good versus Bad; love versus hate/destruction). The focus of anxiety also moves from the survival of the self to the dependence of the self on others and, with this, to the concern for others and the reparation of damaged relationships (Klein, (1998[1937]), 1997[1946]).

The Kleinian approach outlined above mainly concerns the internal, intra-psychic representations of these self–other relationships. Other authors have expanded on some social determinants of these fundamental anxieties (i.e. paranoid-schizoid and depressive) in the family environment (Fairbairn, 1994[1952]; Winnicott, 1990[1965]). This understanding of anxiety (as derived from the dynamics of internal and external relations) is further expanded by contemporary developments in empirical research on infants (Stern, 1985), which shows how infants' inevitable anxieties can be either alleviated or attenuated by caregivers, and vice versa. For instance, the breast or bottle can be presented to the infant in a playful or intrusive manner; feeding can be offered to either assuage hunger or to 'fob off' distress; loving attention can be given to, solicited from or imposed on the infant. Likewise, crying can express helplessness or intrusion, and eating can involve gusto, ambivalence or greed.

Activity 9.1: The psychodynamic understanding of mental health

Allow about 10 minutes

Considering the case illustration 'Jamie and anxiety' above, how would you understand Jamie's anxiety from a psychodynamic perspective?

1 Consider his position in the oedipal triangle, with his mum and dad.

2 Consider his position with regard to the paranoid-schizoid and depressive positions.

3   Finally, consider his early relationship with his mother.

Which of these are more and which are less important in Jamie's case?

Discussion

The obvious way to think about Jamie's problems would be in terms of the oedipal conflict, in relation to repressed aggression towards his father. There may also be insights, however, into an early intrusive/ overwhelming mother, and a corresponding difficulty for Jamie to negotiate the depressive position. In other words, Jamie may feel unable to substantively contribute to or repair his relationships other than in omnipotent ways.

3   Therapeutic process and technique in the psychodynamic approach

As this chapter has highlighted, the past matters for the psychodynamic approach precisely because it refuses to stay in the past. When traumatic aspects of past self–other relations cannot be integrated into a person's sense of self, they are unconsciously re-enacted in their present life. The task of psychodynamic therapy is to help people tolerate these aspects of the past and present by integrating them into their present self.

The first step of the psychodynamic therapy process is **free association**. Meeting with their therapist at least once a week, usually over the course of six months to five years or longer, it is the client who sets the agenda. They are encouraged to talk about whatever is on their mind, even if this should feel irrelevant, awkward or even immoral. Perhaps surprisingly, this is no simple thing to do. Consider Jamie's fictional experience outlined below.

Free association
A fundamental component of the process of psychodynamic therapy where the client is relatively free to exhibit spontaneous conduct, without influence from external structures such as guiding questions or directives from the therapist.

Case illustration: Jamie's first session

Jamie: Rrrrright, so I know about this free association thing obv-[pause]. Oh, sorry, hiya, how're you? Sooooo [pause], just thought I would start straightaway with this dream. I was in this big whale, and [pause] well, not just me but my whole family were there, Mum and Dad and also my sister. So we were there but somehow did not seem to realise that this is a serious situation and our life just [pause] kind of went on as if this was an everyday [pause] situation. We were having breakfast in fact, just like any weekday, I was having porridge and my sister just kind of popped in, as she usually does. Dad with his toaster. As I am telling this, it's as though it was really quite an everyday experience. Well, except for when the whale moved. It moved and then the table got turned upside down and all the porridge and toast flew in the air. We realised we were inside a whale and all the chit-chat stopped. Yeah [pause]. So [pause] I wonder what this means?

[Jamie looking straight at the therapist]

[Silence]

Jamie: Are you not gonna say anything?

[Silence]

Therapist: Hmm. Hi, Jamie.

Jamie: [Smiling] Huhh [pause]. Yeah, hi.

[Pause]

Therapist: Perhaps you are telling me [pause] you find it difficult to arrive here. Put on the spot, suddenly.

Jamie: Hmm. Yeah, you know, [pause] a bit.

At first, Jamie may appear to relish therapy. He himself refers to free association and volunteers a clearly interesting dream. Yet, at the same time, one may feel that his conduct is not quite *free*. Jamie may feel compelled to do what he does; his narration seems to leave no space for meandering thoughts or for unexpected feelings. Likewise, by demanding an immediate interpretation, he seems to allow no freedom for the therapist to respond. What exactly is going on?

To understand this, it is worthwhile returning to the concept of transference from Section 1. It may be that, at the moment, Jamie cannot verbally express what he is suffering from; he can only express it with his overall conduct in the therapeutic situation. As he launches into his dream, he barely acknowledges his therapist's presence or possible interest in him. Perhaps the therapist refuses to take up Jamie's blunt request to offer an interpretation because he instead considers what it is that Jamie is telling him through both the content of his dream and the peculiar way he relates it. Maybe Jamie is communicating that he is fearful of something in the therapeutic situation, and that his way of telling the dream is actually an attempt to *escape from* or *control* that something. His anxiety does not exist in isolation from the current situation – it involves the therapist himself.

It is evident, then, that transference provides crucial insight into a person's dynamic unconscious. However, as Section 1 explained, for contemporary practice the therapist's feelings about and conduct towards the client may too be understood in terms of unconscious communication. Psychodynamic therapists scrutinise their own countertransference very carefully, precisely to learn more about the affective relations that might be troubling their clients (Feldman, 2009; Joseph, 1989).

Take the statement of Jamie's therapist, for instance: '[Y]ou find it difficult to arrive here. Put on the spot, suddenly.' This may in part be prompted by the therapist's understanding of Jamie's dream and general demeanour, but it may also come because it is actually the therapist who suddenly feels overly self-conscious. He has barely met Jamie, who is already demanding his interpretation. The therapist finds this very uncomfortable. Registering their own discomfort at being suddenly 'put on the spot', a psychodynamic therapist will ask: What is this person unconsciously communicating to me? What does the way they make me feel tell me about them and their anxiety?

Activity 9.2: The technique of psychodynamic therapy

Allow about 10 minutes

How do therapists work with the material brought into therapy by clients or service users, made accessible through transference and countertransference?

Reread Jamie's therapy extract in the case illustration above and specifically focus on what the therapist does. How does the therapist work with what he may understand to be Jamie's overwhelming anxiety at the start of this first session? In particular, think about the following issues:

1   What is the therapist's first intervention?

2   How would you characterise this intervention?

3   How does Jamie seem to react?

The rest of this section offers answers to these questions.

Freud's main therapeutic tool for excavating the dynamic unconscious was **interpretation**. The therapist would in effect say, 'You seem to talk about this, but I think you actually mean that'. The interpretative stance continues to be crucial for communicating the therapist's understanding to clients. However, contemporary practitioners would also be sensitive to aspects of interpretation that may render it ineffective or even anti-therapeutic. This is because interpretation is by its nature a confrontation. While such confrontation is necessary to bring about positive change, it may also increase anxiety to an intolerable level. For an interpretation to work, therefore, it has to happen in an environment where the client feels safe – from themselves as much as anything else (Benjamin, 2017; Taylor, 2017 [1999]).

Using psychodynamic terms, providing this safe environment is referred to as 'containing' or **holding**. It is perhaps this that Jamie's therapist is doing when he responds simply with 'Hi, Jamie'. This is not a social pleasantry – it gently communicates the therapist's understanding of Jamie's anxiety. It also promises that the coming session will not form what Jamie is perhaps dreading: a mechanical exchange of client material and therapist interpretation. Instead, there will be a meaningful relationship between two people.

Interpretation
The therapeutic act of elaborating, elucidating or teasing out obscure, unintended or unconscious meaning.

Holding
A therapeutic technique involving non-interpretative and often nonverbal acts directly aimed at reducing a client's anxiety. It is a post-Freudian concept that traditionally takes the baby–mother dyad as its model for the therapy situation.

Jamie seems responsive to this; he smiles and becomes less anxious. This is perhaps why the therapist then offers a straightforward interpretation. The previous gesture of holding or containment seems to have resonated with Jamie, and so does the interpretation: yes, perhaps he does feel a bit 'put on the spot'. There is clearly more to this interpretation, of course; there is the slower, calmer pace – the tentativeness – communicating that there may be something *free* in the room. In any case, it strikes a chord with Jamie and may also spark a therapeutic relationship.

4   The efficacy and scope of the psychodynamic approach

This is all very well, you might say, but does it work? Do psychodynamic therapists make people happier? What if, despite their best efforts, they actually make people feel worse? These are very important questions, but the answers to them are not straightforward.

Imagine, for instance, that Jamie's first session is difficult and emotionally charged: throughout, he complains about how aggressive his boyfriend has been over the course of their relationship. Now imagine that Jamie returns to therapy the following week announcing: 'I feel so much better! I learnt a lot here. We can finish therapy today, right?' So, did a single therapy session work?

As touched on above, psychodynamic clinical experience suggests that, for therapy to work, regular sessions are required for an extended period, possibly even for years. The therapist probably feels, therefore, that Jamie needs more than one session – but Jamie insists that he does not.

As you can see from even such a short vignette, for psychodynamic therapists the outcome of therapy is no straightforward matter. As the conclusion and outcome of psychodynamic therapy is inevitably bound up with the process of therapy itself and the dynamics of transference and countertransference, for a long time the profession had viewed outcome research with a sceptical eye and had distanced itself from it. However, beginning in the twenty-first century there has been a change in this respect, as researchers from a psychodynamic perspective made a twofold contribution to empirical knowledge of therapeutic outcomes. The first was to look at outcome evidence gathered from short-term (i.e. up to 24 sessions) or longer-term psychodynamic therapy. The second was to transform the research methodology of outcome trials themselves and the way research evidence is thought about.

Methodology: Researching the processes of therapy

Research typically focuses on whether (a particular form of) therapy results in positive outcomes for the client. Yet it may address a different question: How does therapy work/operate? Or, to phrase the question another way: What are the processes that characterise therapy and how do they engender a positive change in mental health?

As Section 3 highlighted, psychodynamic therapists have a very rich understanding of these questions. They focus on the minute details of what is going on in therapy. In recent years, empirical research has been directed to these subtle and often nonverbal characteristics of therapy sessions. Interestingly, these empirical endeavours appear to validate the two crucial yet apparently elusive processes that psychodynamic therapists regard as fundamental: transference and countertransference.

Research into detailed transcripts of therapy delivery suggests that a lot more is happening in these sessions than verbatim reports, such as Jamie's, are able to capture. Detailed transcripts capture nonverbal events, such as micro-silences, subtle hesitations, emphases on certain syllables and sudden intakes of breath. It may be that therapists are attuned to clients' and service-users' nonverbal and sometimes almost imperceptible communicative acts, but they don't always consciously register them. What they do consciously register is the general atmosphere created by these communications (i.e. transference) or their own reactions to them (i.e. countertransference) (Forrester and Reason, 2006; Peräkylä *et al.*, 2008).

Thus, there is now empirical support suggesting that transference and countertransference are consequences of actual but unconscious communicative acts by service users.

Regarding the overall success of psychodynamic therapy unrelated to specific diagnoses, a number of meta-analyses have argued in favour of the psychodynamic approach (e.g. Leichsenring and Rabung, 2011). Indeed, a seminal review of available meta-analyses asserted that research evidence not only supports the general efficacy of psychodynamic therapy but also demonstrates a therapeutic effect at least as large as other therapies, such as cognitive behavioural therapy (Shedler, 2010).

Less broad approaches naturally tend to arrive at more nuanced conclusions. Rather than using meta-analysis, the most detailed review to date examined individual but high-quality studies. It tentatively highlighted support for the use of psychodynamic therapy in treating depressive symptoms (including what had up to that point been dubbed 'treatment-resistant depression'), anxiety, eating disorders and the contested diagnoses of personality disorders. There appeared to be less evidence for the effective treatment of post-traumatic stress disorder, obsessive-compulsive disorder and psychosis (Fonagy, 2015).

There is thus a growing inclination to test psychodynamic theories and practices at the 'independent tribunal' of rigorous outcome research. Importantly though, as mentioned above, a different yet equally significant trend within the psychodynamic perspective is to seek to be at the forefront of research, not simply by submitting to the existing agenda of outcome research but by improving this agenda: asking better-quality questions and coming up with improved methods of assessing outcome (Taylor, 2008).

One methodological argument from a psychodynamic perspective concerns the time required for change in mental health. A well-documented finding is that post-therapeutic effects of psychodynamic therapy may remain dormant for as long as two years before manifesting in substantial change. Often, clients not only maintain therapeutic gains but continue to improve after the therapy's termination. This has recently prompted psychodynamic researchers to argue that any measurement of outcome needs to take into account a longer time frame (Fonagy *et al.*, 2015; Shedler, 2010).

Pause for reflection

When Jamie suggested, 'We can finish therapy today, right?', how do you think the therapist may have responded?

A related issue is the nature of mental change. Some researchers have argued that psychodynamic therapy results in change that is more comprehensive and qualitatively different from that which is usually measured by standard outcome research. It may be that these more complex mental changes lead to more sustainable outcomes. To assess this, researchers arguably need more complex ways of assessing therapy outcomes, possibly including qualitative methods (Leuzinger-Bohleber *et al.*, 2019).

Finally, a broader and more complex view of research evidence also coincides with a more comprehensive view of what clients and service users bring to therapy. While the currently prevailing clinical and research positions (based on the medical model) focus on treating discrete and isolated symptoms, the psychodynamic perspective argues that these symptoms cannot be treated in isolation: it is the whole person that comes to therapy, so this should be reflected in the way outcome success is evaluated (Taylor, 2008).

In summary, the psychodynamic approach has for decades stood apart from rigorous and independent outcome research. More recently, though, the approach has not only submitted itself to research trials but has also started to develop arguments for improved and more valid trials. Thus, there is now hope that what many see as the transformative potential of the psychodynamic approach may not only be validated within the consulting room, but also beyond it.

Conclusion

The contemporary psychodynamic approach remains grounded in the ideas and practices of Freud. As this chapter has covered, psychodynamic therapists maintain that:

- people's struggles stem from the vicissitudes of their loving and hateful impulses in the oedipal triangle (ages 3–5)

- in these experiences, impulses conflict with reality and, due to overwhelming anxiety, get pushed out of consciousness

- the most troubling aspects of someone's past can only be communicated unconsciously – through dreams, memories, everyday perceptions or instances of transference

- it is making these unconscious materials conscious in therapy sessions that alleviates suffering.

The chapter has also outlined how, since the original discoveries of Freud, subsequent psychodynamic therapists/theorists not only elaborated on these ideas but did so in unexpected ways. In particular, they expanded Freud's acknowledgment of the basic role of our *relatedness* to the self and the (real or imagined) social environment. Accordingly, contemporary psychodynamic therapists also think that:

- people's struggles (and impulses) stem from nonverbal affective self–other relations, starting as early as birth

- overwhelming anxieties prevent these relations from forming part of a person's sense of self

- these relations will be unconsciously repeated in the therapeutic process

- it is engaging these unconscious relations in the dynamics of transference and countertransference that makes it possible to alleviate suffering.

Further reading

- This text is a sophisticated but succinct introduction to psychodynamic theory:

  Frosh, S. (2002) *Key concepts in psychoanalysis*. London: The British Library.

- This is an introduction to the psychodynamic approach with a focus on practice:

  Jacobs, M. (2010) *Psychodynamic counselling in action*. 4th edn. London: SAGE.

- Freud at his best (and shortest!), on sex and culture:

  Freud, S. (2001[1912])) 'On the universal tendency of debasement in the sphere of love', in *The standard edition of the complete psychological works of Sigmund Freud. Volume 11*. London: Vintage, pp. 179–190.

References

Benjamin, J. (2017) *Beyond doer and done to: recognition theory, intersubjectivity and the third*. London and New York: Routledge.

Breuer, J. and Freud, S. (2001[1895]) 'Studies on Hysteria' in *The standard edition of the complete psychological works of Sigmund Freud. Volume 2 (1893–1895): studies on hysteria*. London: Vintage Books.

Fairbairn, W.R.D. (1994[1952]) *Psychoanalytic studies of the personality*. London: Routledge.

Feldman, M. (2009) *Doubt, conviction and the analytic process: selected papers of Michael Feldman*. Edited by B. Joseph. London: Routledge.

Fonagy, P. (2015) 'The effectiveness of psychodynamic psychotherapies: an update', *World Psychiatry*, 14(2), pp. 137–150.

Fonagy, P., Rost, F., Carlyle, J.A., McPherson, S., Thomas, R., Pasco Fearon, R.M., Goldberg, D. and Taylor, D. (2015) 'Pragmatic randomized controlled trial of long-term psychoanalytic psychotherapy for treatment-resistant depression: the Tavistock Adult Depression Study (TADS)', *World Psychiatry*, 14(3), pp. 312–321.

Forrester, M. and Reason, D. (2006) 'Conversation analysis and psychoanalytic psychotherapy research: questions, issues, problems and challenges', *Psychoanalytic Psychotherapy*, 20(1), pp. 40–64.

Freud, S. (2001[1896]) 'The aetiology of hysteria', in *The standard edition of the complete psychological works of Sigmund Freud. Volume 3*. London: Vintage, pp. 191–221.

Freud, S. (2001[1915]) 'Observations on transference-love', in *The Standard edition of the complete psychological works of Sigmund Freud. Volume 12*. London: Vintage, pp. 157–171.

Freud, S. (2001[1916–1917]) 'Introductory lectures on psycho-analysis', in *The standard edition of the complete psychological works of Sigmund Freud. Volumes 15–16*. London: Vintage.

Freud, S. (2001[1925]) 'An autobiographical study', in *The standard edition of the complete psychological works of Sigmund Freud. Volume 20*. London: Vintage, pp. 7–74.

Freud, S. (2001[1926]) 'Inhibitions, symptoms and anxiety', in *The standard edition of the complete psychological works of Sigmund Freud. Volume 20*. London: Vintage, pp. 87–156.

Freud, S. (2001[1930]) 'Civilization and its discontents', in *The standard edition of the complete psychological works of Sigmund Freud. Volume 21*. London: Vintage, pp. 59–145.

Freud, S. (2001[1933]) 'New introductory lectures on psychoanalysis', in *The standard edition of the complete psychological works of Sigmund Freud. Volume 22*. London: Vintage, pp. 5–184.

Freud, S. (2001[1940]) 'An outline of psycho-analysis', in *The standard edition of the complete psychological works of Sigmund Freud. Volume 23*. London: Vintage.

Greenberg, J. and Mitchell, S. (1983) *Object relations in psychoanalytic theory*. London: Harvard University Press.

Herman, J.L. (2015) *Trauma and recovery: the aftermath of violence – from domestic abuse to political terror*. New York: Basic Books.

Jones, E. (1974[1961]) *The life and work of Sigmund Freud*. Edited by L Trilling and S. Marcus. London: Penguin Books.

Joseph, B. (1989) *Psychic equilibrium and psychic change: selected papers of Betty Joseph*. Edited by M. Feldman and E. Bott Spillius. London and New York: Routledge.

Klein, M. (1998[1937]) 'Love, guilt and reparation', in Klein, M. *Love, guilt and reparation, and other works 1921–1945*. London: Vintage, pp. 306–343.

Klein, M. (1997[1946]) 'Notes on some schizoid mechanisms', in Klein, M. *Envy and gratitude and other works 1946–1963*. London: Vintage, pp. 1–24.

Leichsenring, F. and Rabung, S. (2011) 'Long-term psychodynamic psychotherapy in complex mental disorders: update of meta-analysis', *The British Journal of Psychiatry*, 199(1), pp. 15–22.

Leuzinger-Bohleber, M., Kaufhold, J., Kallenbach, L., Negele, A., Ernst, M., Keller, W., Fiedler, G., Hautzinger, M., Bahrke, U. and Beutel, M. (2019) 'How to measure sustained psychic transformations in long-term treatments of chronically depressed patients: symptomatic and structural changes in the LAC Depression Study of the outcome of cognitive-behavioural and psychoanalytic long-term treatments', *The International Journal of Psychoanalysis*, 100(1), pp. 99–127.

Mitchell, S. (1988) *Relational concepts in psychoanalysis: an integration*. Cambridge, Mass. and London: Harvard University Press.

O'Shaughnessy, E. (2015) *Inquiries in psychoanalysis: collected papers of Edna O'Shaughnessy*. Edited by R. Rusbridger. London and New York: Routledge.

Peräkylä, A., Antaki, C., Vehviläinen, S. and Leudar, I. (eds.) (2008) *Conversation analysis and psychotherapy*. Cambridge: Cambridge University Press.

Racker, H. (1968) *Transference and countertransference*. London: Karnac Books.

Shedler, J. (2010) 'The efficacy of psychodynamic psychotherapy', *American Psychologist*, 65(2), pp. 98–109.

Stefana, A. (2017) *History of countertransference: from Freud to the British object relations school*. London: Routledge.

Stern, D. (1985) *The interpersonal world of the infant: a view from psychanalysis and developmental psychology.* New York: Basic Books.

Taylor, D. (2008) 'Psychoanalytic and psychodynamic therapies for depression: the evidence base', *Advances in Psychiatric Treatment*, 14(6), pp. 401–413.

Taylor, D. (ed.) (2017[1999]) *Talking cure: mind and method of the Tavistock clinic.* London: Karnac.

Winnicott, D.W. (1990[1965]) *The maturational processes and the facilitating environment studies in the theory of emotional development.* London: Karnac Books.

Chapter 10

Cognitive behavioural therapy

Simon P. Clarke

Contents

Introduction

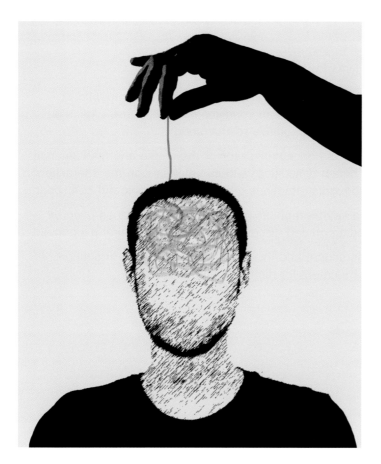

'Obfuscation' by Victor Guerrero

Cognitive behavioural therapy (CBT) is a psychotherapeutic approach characterised by its emphasis on the role of reasoning processes to treat mental health difficulties. It has been applied to a range of problems, from anxiety, depression and psychosis to addictions, relationship difficulties, neuropsychological conditions and physical health. It is the most widely-researched psychotherapy in terms of quantitative and medical research, with its success often attributed to the way it has methodologically allied itself with evidence-based medicine through its extensive use of the randomised controlled trial. CBT has incorporated 'common-sense' conceptualisations of everyday difficulties in a manualised treatment format that is replicable in different service contexts. There has been an increasing tendency towards computerised forms of CBT (which will be explored in

Chapter 15), along with a widespread application to primary healthcare in the UK through the Improving Access to Psychological Therapies (IAPT) initiative.

This chapter aims to:

- explore how CBT has developed as a psychotherapeutic approach, from its basis in conditioning to its current focus on principles such as cognitive restructuring

- consider CBT's conceptualisation of the cause and maintenance of mental health difficulties, with its emphasis on the interaction between thoughts, emotions, physical sensations and behaviour

- identify the key therapeutic principles and techniques used by CBT, including guided discovery and the behavioural experiment

- discuss the scope, and the limits, of the evidence in support of CBT as a treatment for mental health difficulties.

1 Core CBT principles and their development

CBT is best thought of as an umbrella term for a family of techniques that are unified by the importance given to **cognitive processes** in the cause and maintenance of mental health difficulties (Hofmann *et al.*, 2012). More specifically, CBT looks at the relationship between emotions, cognitive processes, physical sensations and behaviour (Padesky and Mooney, 1990). It is typically assumed that certain events trigger specific emotional and physical responses, which are then appraised in ways that lead to behaviour that reinforces the original emotional and physical responses (Beck, 1976). It is also assumed that these appraisals are often based on faulty reasoning (sometimes called 'reasoning errors') and so maintain mental health difficulties (Beck and Haigh, 2014). This process is demonstrated in Figure 10.1, which shows an example model of a panic attack.

Cognitive process
A discrete function of mental activity, such as attention, memory, language use, perception, problem-solving and creativity.

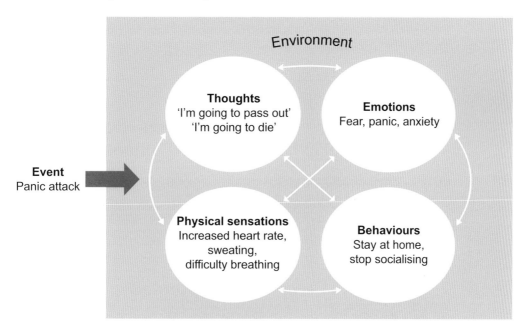

Figure 10.1 The hot cross bun CBT model of a panic attack (Source: based on Padesky and Mooney, 1990)

Activity 10.1: Thoughts, emotions, physical sensations and behaviours

Allow about 15 minutes

Think of a mildly stressful event that has happened to you recently and try to understand it using the diagram in Figure 10.1. How did you feel? What was going on in your body? What thoughts were going through your head at the time? How did you react?

Discussion

The diagram in Figure 10.1 is sometimes referred to as the hot cross bun model (first introduced in Chapter 8, Figure 8.1) because it represents the cross-sectional influence between thoughts, emotions, physical sensations and behaviours that is central to CBT formulations of mental health difficulties. As this chapter will show in the case illustration of Deborah below, however, it is often how these factors are related in the client's experience that determine why a particular problem continues. The relationships between these four areas are often very complex in a person's experience and need careful exploration through the use of idiosyncratic formulations, such as vicious cycle diagrams (outlined in Section 2).

1.1 The development of the CBT approach

Modern CBT represents an amalgamation of behaviour therapy and cognitive therapy. As Chapter 3 provided a detailed outline of the growth of talking therapy, this section will provide a shorter, more focused outline of the development of CBT to the present day.

Behaviourism

Positive reinforcement
The reinforcement of a behaviour through consistently positive consequences.

Negative reinforcement
The reinforcement of a behaviour through the consistent removal of adverse consequences.

Chapter 3 outlined the roots of behaviour therapy, which lie in conditioning (learning) theories (see Chapter 3, Section 2.1 for a reminder of the definition of conditioning). These theories were initially developed through Watson's (1913) and Pavlov's (2010[1927]) experiments in behaviour modification and then further developed by Skinner (1938) through the use of operant conditioning and the application of **positive reinforcement** and **negative reinforcement**. Applying these theories to psychological difficulties such as anxiety,

Wolpe (1958) argued that it was possible to remove symptoms of fear and anxiety, as exhibited through phobias, using a method called 'systematic desensitisation' (based on Pavlov's classical conditioning). In this approach, increasingly intense phobic stimuli were introduced alongside anxiety-inhibiting techniques such as relaxation. As a therapeutic technique, systematic desensitisation evolved into **graded exposure**, whereby the therapist and client formulate a hierarchy of feared situations. The therapist then encourages the client to face the first situation on the hierarchy until their anxiety decreases enough to allow them to progress to the next feared situation, and so on, until all situations have been confronted and the fear is eliminated. Later developments incorporated other strategies alongside exposure, including relaxation training and social skills training (Hayes, 2004a).

Graded exposure
A technique in which the therapist gradually exposes the client to a feared situation/experience (real or imagined), making sure the client can control their fear at each exposure step.

Cognitive therapy

Modern CBT evolved out of psychoanalysis and behaviourism through the work of Aaron 'Tim' Beck (Rosner, 2012). Beck had initially trained as a psychoanalyst but, by the early 1960s, he had become disenchanted with what he saw as the authoritarianism of psychoanalysis and believed that key psychoanalytic concepts were not empirically supported (Rosner, 2014). Beck's interests in cognitive theory (particularly the work of George Kelly) and experimental psychology led him to formulate his own 'cognitive' theory of depression (Beck, 1967) incorporating elements of behaviour theory and psychoanalysis (Rosner, 2012).

The relationship between psychoanalysis and early CBT, very much downplayed by CBT researchers, has recently become a topic of historical interest (Rosner, 2012, 2014; this relationship was discussed in detail in Chapter 3). Beck's burgeoning cognitive theory was developed alongside clinical observations and experimental studies on depression. The overarching approach was underpinned by the argument that people could be persuaded out of unhelpful thinking patterns through a combination of therapeutic reasoning (i.e. the therapist facilitating the client to see logical inconsistencies in their unhelpful belief) and the application of behavioural 'experiments' that encouraged people to empirically test out their unhelpful thought processes (Beck, 2011).

Randomised controlled trial

A clinical research methodology, considered by many to be the 'gold standard' of evidence-based medicine, in which participants are randomly allocated to either an experimental condition (which receives the intervention of interest) or a control condition (which receives an alternative treatment for comparison).

Evidence-based medicine

A hierarchical system for medical research evidence, with the randomised controlled trial and meta-analysis at the top and expert opinion at the bottom, used to determine the efficacy of different treatments based on the quality of evidence.

Cognitive restructuring

The process of changing a person's negative thoughts, assumed to be the main change mechanism in CBT.

While Beck's (1967) early work predominantly focused on depression, beginning in the 1970s CBT gradually branched out into other areas of mental health difficulties, including anxiety, post-traumatic stress disorder, physical health and severe mental health difficulties such as eating disorders and psychosis (Beck, 2011). Although the model was adapted for each area of mental health, the core tenets remained: that psychological difficulties are maintained by reasoning errors (i.e. faulty interpretations of the original situation that lead to automatic biases in appraising similar situations negatively), and that the focus of therapy should be on helping people to correct these errors through a combination of therapeutic discussion and empirical observation (Rosner, 2014).

Beck's (1967) approach was also supported by an incipient empirical research programme that included the development of research materials, such as the Beck Depression Inventory (one of the most widely used questionnaires for depression), and the successful delivery of some of the largest psychotherapy **randomised controlled trials** (RCTs) ever attempted (Rosner, 2014). By the 1980s, CBT had accumulated the largest body of research evidence of any psychotherapeutic approach (Beck and Dozois, 2011). There was also a significant crossover between clinical and university departments, leading to the association of CBT with **evidence-based medicine** and quantitative research methodologies (Rosner, 2012).

From 'second-wave' to 'third-wave' approaches

Since CBT has become the dominant psychotherapeutic approach in the western world, a new range of mindfulness-based cognitive therapies have emerged. Referred to as 'third wave' by Hayes (2004a) to denote their identified lineage with behavioural ('first wave') and cognitive behavioural ('second wave') therapies, mindfulness-based cognitive therapies also base their approaches on experimental research and identify negative thinking as the main mechanism by which mental health difficulties are maintained.

Unlike those of the so-called 'second wave', however, 'third-wave' approaches highlight the lack of empirical evidence suggesting that **cognitive restructuring** is the primary change mechanism (Longmore and Worrell, 2007). Instead, continuing to expand and extend the range of CBT, they advocate a range of different strategies based on mindfulness-based approaches and concepts, which Hayes and

Hofmann (2017) call 'cognitive diffusion' (i.e. changing one's relationship to negative thoughts, rather than the thoughts themselves).

Pause for reflection

What do you think might be the benefits of 'accepting' rather than 'challenging' negative thoughts?

---

2   The cognitive behavioural understanding of mental health

This section will outline the CBT approach in terms of the way it conceptualises mental health problems. It will also show how CBT uses formulation to help understand a person's difficulties. As for the other modalities within this book, the focus will be on anxiety as the main presenting problem. Key CBT concepts will be illustrated through the case of Deborah.

Beck's (1976) cognitive theory of emotion proposes that it is not events or situations that generate specific negative emotional responses, but rather the *meaning* that a person attaches to an event. If the interpretation of an event is negative, the emotional response will also be negative; if the interpretation of an event is more positive, the emotional response will also be more positive. Typically, anxiety is likely to result if the situation is negatively interpreted as a sign of threat or danger (Clark, 1989). One of the purposes of a CBT formulation is to show how certain situations are interpreted cognitively, and how this interpretation generates specific emotional, physiological and behavioural responses that, over time, may become unhelpful (Beck, 2011). These processes can be further demonstrated in reference to the fictional case of Deborah below.

Case illustration: Deborah and panic disorder

Deborah is a 32-year-old single mother who was first assessed at home because she was unable to leave her house. At the time she was seen, she was having three to five panic attacks per week. During these attacks, which seemed to her to come 'out of the blue', she felt a sudden increase in several physical sensations, including a pounding heart and feeling hot, dizzy, short of breath, confused and shaky. Her first panic attack happened in a supermarket six years previously when she noticed that she was feeling short of breath and dizzy. When she started getting pains in her chest, she thought that these symptoms meant that she was having a heart attack and was going to pass out then die – a belief that persisted in her further panic attacks. Not surprisingly, she then felt very afraid. She thought that if she could get out of the supermarket, then she would be safe. 'So I did, and I was,' she later relayed in therapy. Deborah tried going into another shop, and it happened again. 'I didn't let it get so bad before I came out of the shop,' she explained. This happened again a third time. As a result of this experience, Deborah avoided these shops, but continued to experience panic attacks. She said, 'Gradually, I did less and less until I couldn't go out of the house except with my mother'.

The cognitive theory of emotion specifies that the meaning a person attaches to what is happening to them will be the result of a complex interaction between that person's history (both early and more recent), their mood and the context (Beck, 1976). A range of situations, events or stimuli can trigger an episode of anxiety (Clark, 1989). In Deborah's case, it was entering a supermarket that first triggered a panic attack, but it was the memory of the event that triggered further anxiety reactions afterwards. It was also her catastrophic interpretation that she was going to pass out and die in the supermarket that initially heightened her anxiety. Going into the supermarket was interpreted as being potentially fatal and therefore a threat, influencing subsequent behaviours.

These processes are included in the formulation of Deborah's difficulties. For understandable reasons, during a panic attack Deborah misinterprets normal bodily symptoms of anxiety and mistakenly believes that she is about to have a heart attack or pass out. This unhelpful belief increases her anxiety, which in turn increases her bodily sensations, seeming to confirm that she is having a heart attack or going to faint. Her attention becomes focused on the physical symptoms and this then reinforces her unhelpful interpretation. These processes are illustrated in Figure 10.2.

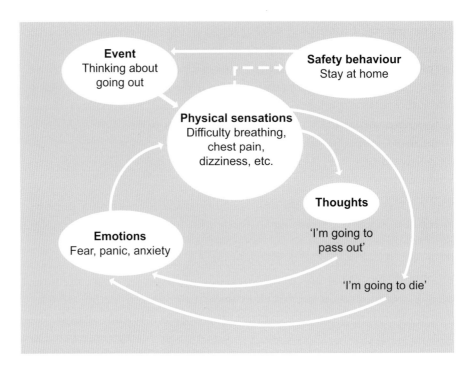

Figure 10.2 Deborah's panic vicious cycle

One of the main issues with unhelpful beliefs in anxiety is that they are often associated with behavioural avoidance, or what CBT therapists call 'safety seeking behaviours' (Salkovskis, 1991). These behaviours may work in the short term to relieve the immediate sensations of anxiety, but in the long term they can lead to chronic avoidance (Clark, 1989). Deborah initially removes herself from the anxiety-provoking experience by leaving the supermarket. As Figure 10.2 illustrates, in order to avoid further anxiety attacks, she stays at home and stops going out. This behaviour (staying at home) means that she exits the cycle, leading to a reduction in negative thoughts, symptoms and emotions (which then reinforces the avoidance behaviour). Although this might work in the short term, Deborah's quality of life is significantly diminished in the long term as she is unable to go out and perform everyday tasks, therefore becoming more socially isolated. Additionally, it leads to the interpretation that staying home is 'safe' and going out is 'dangerous'. She therefore never gets an opportunity to challenge her unhelpful interpretation and the vicious cycle is maintained, to the detriment of her overall quality of life.

The CBT model argues that cognitive factors, such as attention (focusing on physical symptoms) and automatic memory (remembering what happened in the supermarket), are critical in maintaining vicious behavioural cycles when such factors are based on faulty or unhelpful interpretations of what is happening (Beck, 1976). However, the specific processes contributing to vicious behavioural cycles may differ across different anxiety disorders (Clark, 1989). For example, someone with panic disorder might misinterpret anxiety-related bodily sensations as signals of imminent danger, while a person with obsessive-compulsive disorder (OCD) might misinterpret intrusive thoughts, images and impulses as indicative of their responsibility for serious harm to themself or others. The person with panic disorder might use an avoidance safety behaviour to control physical sensations and mental states, while someone with OCD might use avoidance but also washing, checking, neutralising, suppressing thoughts and seeking reassurance.

In summary, formulation in CBT provides a pragmatic outline of the presenting problem that can be used to illustrate how the client's thinking patterns have become unhelpful and why they continue to cause difficulties. The emphasis of the CBT formulation is the relationship between thinking, emotions, physical reactions and behaviour, showing how these different elements link up in the client's experience to maintain their difficulties in specific situations (Beck, 2011). If the formulation is accurate, then it has specific implications for treatment (Padesky and Beck, 2003). In the case of Deborah, instead of leaving the panic situation she needs to try to challenge her belief that she is going to pass out and die if she has a panic attack. As the next section will explore, CBT has developed a number of techniques to facilitate this process.

Activity 10.2: Safety behaviours

Allow about 10 minutes

One of the key ideas of the CBT approach is that mental health difficulties are often extreme expressions of normal processes. In other words, we all use safety behaviours at times to relieve insecurities and anxieties. Think about your 'safety behaviours'. What do you do to avoid stressful situations? How successful are these behaviours for you?

Discussion

You may have considered avoiding everyday stressors such as a family member or friend who makes you feel low, or a difficult meeting or conversation. Perhaps you considered distraction techniques, which move attention away from yourself and on to something else (e.g. changing the conversation or pretending that you have a call to make). You may even have considered something with bigger implications, such as avoiding people entirely, or failing to show up for a presentation you had arranged to give. Once you consider the range of such behaviours it is easy to see that they inevitably form a part of most people's lives, but they can also limit your quality of life in some situations.

---

3 Therapeutic process and technique in CBT

The main focus in CBT is eliciting the client's appraisal of the events that trigger their anxiety, and then changing the underlying faulty belief that is assumed to be maintaining the problem (Beck, 1976). For example, anxiety is often linked to the idea that there is some imminent threat, and the likelihood of this threat occurring is often grossly overestimated (Clark, 1989). Again, the specific processes may differ across conditions and individuals.

CBT begins with the client and therapist getting to know each other and building a rapport (Beck, 2011). The therapist asks the client about the way their problems are affecting them. Once a general impression has been gained, assessment proceeds by the therapist obtaining a brief relevant history orientated around questions such as: 'How did the problem start?', 'What happened next?', 'How have you tried to deal with the problem?' (Clark, 1989). At some point during this assessment process, the therapist and client negotiate short-, medium- and long-term goals of therapy (Padesky and Beck, 2003). Throughout the course of therapy, the therapist needs to remain constantly aware of the state of the **therapeutic alliance**, responding empathically and using summaries and emotional reflection (Kazantzis, Dattilio and Dobson, 2017). Key meaning-oriented questions focused specifically around the client's cognitions such as 'What went through your mind *at that moment*?' and 'What did you think *at that time* was the worst thing that could happen?' can be used as appropriate (Salkovskis, 1991). A more specific assessment is then required to develop and explore a shared understanding of how the problem works (Beck, 2011). The context is primed using the most recent example, framed by relevant questions (e.g. 'When was this?', 'What were you doing at that time?', 'What else was happening?', 'How did you feel just before it became problematic?').

Therapeutic alliance
Refers to all the collaborative aspects of the relationship between a client and a therapist that are relevant for the therapy outcome.

Diversity: Cultural sensitivity and CBT

One of the core therapeutic mechanisms in CBT is challenging negative thoughts. However, this can become a problem when the therapist is not sensitive to the cultural background of the client (Beck and Naz, 2019), or if they try to apply the CBT model too rigidly (Omylinska-Thurston *et al.*, 2019).

Consider the following example: a client with OCD has developed excessive cleaning rituals, often using harsh materials such as bleach, which are causing severe skin rashes. They say they do this because they have negative intrusive thoughts about having sex with people other than their partner and these thoughts conflict with their devout religious faith. The client has interpreted these thoughts as evidence of being 'sinful' and is washing their hands as a form of penance, in the hope of eliminating the thoughts.

A culturally insensitive CBT response would be for the therapist to try to change the negative thoughts and appraisals, without considering the difficulties this might present for the client. This could have the result of making the client feel like they have to choose between their faith and their therapy.

A more culturally sensitive version of CBT might take the following approach: after conducting a thorough assessment, the therapist offers to meet the client's religious leader to discuss their current difficulties. The client agrees and the therapist meets with them, together with the religious leader. The religious leader explains that, according to their religion, having negative thoughts does not automatically mean that you are a bad person; rather, it is how you respond to such thoughts that is important. The religious leader also says that punishing oneself is not considered an appropriate way of dealing with such thoughts, according to their faith. The therapist then works with the client to gently reframe their belief that these thoughts mean they are sinful. The therapist helps them develop alternative strategies for managing the negative thoughts.

Once an initial assessment has been conducted, the therapist and client work together in a process of **guided discovery** (Padesky and Beck, 2003). A range of techniques can be used to support this process, including thought records (getting the client to measure and record the occurrence and context of negative thoughts), behavioural experiments (see below) and Socratic dialogue. The Socratic method is defined by Beck and Dozois (2011, p. 401) as 'a method of guided discovery in which the therapist asks a series of carefully sequenced questions to help define problems, assist in the identification of thoughts and beliefs, examine the meaning of events, or assess the ramifications of particular thoughts or behaviours'. The aim of the semi-structured collaborative work of guided discovery is to explore whether or not there are *alternative ways* to make sense of the difficult situation (Clark and Egan, 2015). During this process, the client is encouraged to gather evidence, test hypotheses generated with the therapist and collaboratively evaluate the evidence of their investigations (Beck, 1976).

The end result of this 'shared understanding' is the development of a cognitive behavioural formulation, which can be written out in diagrammatic format (e.g. Deborah's panic vicious cycle in Figure 10.2). The person is helped to identify where (and how) they may have become 'trapped' or 'stuck' in their way of thinking, and then to identify and consider other ways of looking at their situation. In particular, they are encouraged to examine more helpful ways of reacting to specific situations or stimuli, and in general (Padesky and Beck, 2003). CBT focuses on targeting the factors that maintain the problem and establishing the meanings, misinterpretations and beliefs that drive or motivate them (Beck, 2011). At this stage in therapy, the therapist helps the client to identify their anxious responses as 'theory A', an understandable set of beliefs which focus on the danger they fear, while also devising a potential alternative explanation, which is identified as 'theory B' (Clark *et al.*, 1998). This process can be outlined for Deborah, as shown in the case illustration below.

Guided discovery
The process through which a therapist helps a client to reflect on the ways they process information, particularly in terms of the logic (or illogic) of their core beliefs.

Case illustration: Guided discovery with Deborah

Therapist: Tell me what was happening right before your panic attack came on.

Deborah: I was trying to get the kids out to spend their pocket money – we were a bit pushed for time.

Therapist: What went through your mind right when the attack started?

Deborah: I thought I was having a heart attack.

Therapist: And what did you feel then?

Deborah: I started to feel dizzy, light-headed, sick and sweaty and my chest started to hurt.

Therapist: And how did that make you feel?

Deborah: Terrified.

Therapist: It sounds like it was horrible for you. When you felt terrified, what did that do to the physical symptoms?

Deborah: It made them worse.

Therapist: Okay. On a scale of 0 to 100 per cent, with 100 per cent being most likely, how likely did you think it was a heart attack?

Deborah: I would say probably about 90 per cent.

Therapist: Okay. Bearing in mind what we discussed last session, what other explanations could there be for the chest pains?

Deborah: Erm, I guess it could have been a stitch.

Therapist: And using the scale again, how likely do you think it was a stitch?

Deborah: Probably 10 or 15 per cent.

Therapist: Okay. And what explanations could there be for it being a stitch?

Deborah: I was rushing around a lot.

Therapist: Okay. When you started to feel the chest pains, what did you do then?

Deborah: I sat down to catch my breath.

Therapist: And how did that make you feel?

Deborah: I felt calmer.

Therapist: And what happened to the chest pains?

Deborah: They started to go.

Another key therapeutic technique used to support this process is the **behavioural experiment**. Behavioural experiments are direct, experiential information-gathering exercises which are designed to help the person examine the efficacy of their beliefs (Bennett-Levy *et al.*, 2004). Returning to the example of Deborah, she noticed that her chest pain tended to occur or worsen if she had to walk quickly or climb stairs. During discussion about this observation and what it might mean, it became clear that she was uncertain about whether this happened before, during or after exercise. In order to test this out, she and her therapist went for a brisk walk, taking ratings of chest pain intensity as they went. Deborah discovered that the chest pain tended to improve when she was walking quickly but increased when she stopped. Having established this, meaning and interpretation could be explored in terms of the shared formulation and theories A and B.

> **Behavioural experiment**
> A collaborative intervention between the therapist and the client whereby a potentially negative or harmful belief is either confirmed or disproved through designing an experiment to test the belief.

Throughout CBT there is an emphasis on the need to generalise from the therapy sessions to the rest of the person's life. This is done in several ways, most commonly through the use of 'homework' (Beck, 2011). At the end of each therapy session, the therapist and client discuss and agree ways in which the latter can continue the process of discovery, understanding and change in their everyday environment, outside of sessions. This homework is then carefully reviewed as the first agenda item of the next session, with the emphasis being on what has been learnt (Padesky and Beck, 2003). In some instances, some of the treatment is carried out in the person's home or in vivo; for example, in places where they tend to feel anxious (crowded places for people with social anxiety, or places where the trauma occurred for people suffering from post-traumatic stress disorder). However, this treatment is carried out in careful consultation with the client (Bennett-Levy *et al.*, 2004).

> ## Pause for reflection
>
> What do you think might be the benefits of setting tasks between therapy sessions? If you were the client, how would you feel about being set 'homework'?

4   The efficacy and scope of the CBT approach

CBT is the most researched psychotherapeutic approach currently available (David, Cristea and Hofmann, 2018). From the outset, Beck developed his cognitive approach with close links to experimental research (Rosner, 2014), and evidence for CBT has been developed in line with RCTs for medicine. According to this evidence, CBT has demonstrated efficacy in a range of problem areas including anxiety, depression, eating disorders, chronic pain and psychosis (Butler *et al.*, 2006; Hofmann *et al.*, 2012). In clinical guidelines, such as those of the National Institute for Health and Care Excellence (2009), CBT is often considered the primary treatment for a range of disorders, owing to the amount and the quality (defined in evidence-based medicine terms) of research evidence available.

However, while there is a range of strong evidence for CBT in terms of **efficacy**, some have pointed out issues with the quality of the evidence for CBT's **effectiveness**. Issues include weak comparison groups and limited follow-up time points, as most CBT trials are usually no longer than 12 months (Wampold *et al.*, 2017). In relation to follow-up time points, psychodynamic therapists have questioned whether CBT provides only 'symptom substitution', and if the client's difficulties may reoccur in a different guise (Leuzinger-Bohleber *et al.*, 2019). Another issue with the evidence is that clinical trials are applied under 'ideal' conditions, with highly trained, closely supervised clinicians working with clients who have been carefully selected according to the narrow criteria required for research trials (Carey and Stiles, 2016). Some argue it is highly unlikely that these conditions could be replicated in real clinical practice, especially in contexts such as the UK National Health Service where resources are limited (Slade and Priebe, 2001). Further, CBT trials have not always reported on the outcomes relating to minority groups; there is a vast over-representation of white, middle-class participants in research trials (Stewart and Chambless, 2009). A final issue is that negative side effects arising from CBT treatment (such as a reduction in well-being and the worsening of symptoms) have often been downplayed in CBT trials (Schermuly-Haupt, Linden and Rush, 2018).

Efficacy
The ability of a treatment to function well in 'ideal' conditions (e.g. a research trial with carefully selected patients and highly trained, experienced practitioners).

Effectiveness
The degree to which a treatment functions well in the 'real world'.

Another major issue with CBT research evidence is the assumption that cognitive restructuring is the primary mechanism for symptom improvement.

Typically, CBT interventions provide an integration of both cognitive and behavioural techniques, which CBT researchers tease apart through moderation and mediation analysis (Hayes and Hofmann, 2017). In his review of the CBT literature, Hayes (2004b) identified three areas that represented empirical anomalies between theory and data in the CBT literature:

- The cognitive components of an intervention are not strong predictors of behavioural change.

- A change in symptoms often preceded the implementation of cognitive techniques.

- Changing thoughts and beliefs appeared to be superfluous to the therapeutic outcome.

In their review of the evidence around depression and anxiety, Longmore and Worrell (2007) found little evidence for the 'C' in CBT contributing to a positive therapeutic outcome, concluding that there exists 'a substantial body of research showing that cognitive interventions are not a necessary component of the therapy' (Longmore and Worrell, 2007, p. 184).

In response to these issues, many CBT researchers and practitioners have focused their efforts on factors such as the therapeutic relationship, core hypothesised mechanisms and the impact on practice (see the Methodology box below).

Methodology: Issues with evidence in CBT

The principal method of testing the efficacy of treatments in medical research is through the use of the randomised controlled trial (RCT). This is based on a hierarchy of evidence types in which the 'highest' forms are meta-analyses and systematic reviews of RCTs. RCTs typically work by aggregating the mean averages of different groups (typically experimental/treatment and control) at post-treatment stage to assess whether any change has occurred. However, this approach has led to the following issues in CBT research:

- *Lack of individual-level effects*: Comparing the mean averages of two different groups does not show individual-level variations in treatment, which can lead to false reporting of effects in CBT research (Evans, Margison and Barkham, 1998). For example, an intervention might show 'no change' because there was no statistical difference between groups; however, this could have been because 50 per cent of participants showed improvement and the other 50 per cent deteriorated!

- *Lack of validity in group-based designs*: Clients are recruited into RCTs on the basis of a diagnostic category. However, psychiatric categories are highly disputed, particularly in conditions labelled as 'schizophrenia'. This has led to some disputes about the validity of CBT evidence for conditions such as psychosis (Thomas, 2015).

- *Difficulty establishing treatment integrity*: While some trial reports show the treatment protocol to which therapists were supposed to adhere, there is sometimes wide variation in how the trial is delivered in practice. One of the main issues with CBT research is that trials do not always report the level of adherence to (or deviation from) the treatment protocol (Johnsen and Friborg, 2015).

- *Unclear mechanisms of CBT*: RCTs show whether an intervention works or not; they do not show the elements of the intervention that make it effective (Carey and Stiles, 2016). This has led to questions around the main mechanisms behind CBT's effectiveness (Hayes, 2004b).

Many CBT researchers and clinicians, aware of these limitations, have adopted different approaches. For example, there has been a renewed focus on process, with researchers developing increasingly sophisticated methods to tease apart the different mechanisms underlying CBT (Hayes and Hofmann, 2017). Other CBT researchers and clinicians have begun focusing on the therapeutic relationship in CBT practice (Kazantzis, Dattilio and Dobson, 2017), which has often been neglected in CBT research. Finally, other researchers have looked at individual-level data in CBT interventions in routine clinical practice (Sheldon, Clarke and Moghaddam, 2015).

Conclusion

This chapter introduced the CBT approach, showing how CBT developed out of Beck's integration of cognitive psychology, psychoanalysis and behaviourism. It showed that CBT treatment develops through collaborative formulation based on the principle that the client's thinking patterns have become unhelpful and need to be changed through a collaborative therapeutic process. Application of a CBT formulation was illustrated in relation to Deborah, who was experiencing panic disorder.

The chapter also examined some of CBT's key treatment techniques, such as the Socratic method and the behavioural experiment. Key applications of the techniques were illustrated through the Deborah case study.

This chapter explored research evidence for CBT, showing that there is a high volume of research trials demonstrating CBT's efficacy, but issues remain with the quality of the evidence and around clarity regarding the core mechanisms underlying therapeutic change. The chapter concluded by examining the attempts of some CBT approaches to address these issues by focusing on process, mechanisms and application to real-world scenarios.

Further reading

- This classic text presents Beck's original theories in a very accessible way:

  Beck, A.T. (1976) *Cognitive therapy and the emotional disorders.* New York: International Universities Press.

- This book presents a very thorough and useful overview of various CBT techniques and practices, some of which are mentioned in this chapter:

  Beck, J. (2011) *Cognitive behavior therapy: basics and beyond.* 2nd edn. New York: The Guilford Press.

- This book provides a comprehensive outline of the theory and practice of developing behavioural experiments in CBT, including providing numerous examples for the reader of different experiments for different presenting problems:

  Bennett-Levy, J., Butler, G., Fennell, M., Hackman, A., Mueller, M. and Westbrook, D. (eds.) (2004) *Oxford guide to behavioural experiments in cognitive therapy.* New York: Oxford University Press.

Acknowledgement

This chapter has been substantially revised from an earlier version by Paul Salkovskis.

References

Beck, A.T. (1967) *The diagnosis and management of depression*. Philadelphia, PA: University of Pennsylvania Press.

Beck, A.T. (1976) *Cognitive therapy and the emotional disorders*. New York: International Universities Press.

Beck, J. (2011) *Cognitive behavior therapy: basics and beyond*. 2nd edn. New York: Guilford Press.

Beck, A.T. and Dozois, D.J. (2011) 'Cognitive therapy: current status and future directions', *Annual Review of Medicine*, 62, pp. 397–409.

Beck, A.T. and Haigh, E.A.P. (2014) 'Advances in cognitive theory and therapy: the generic cognitive model', *Annual Review of Clinical Psychology*, 10 (1), pp. 1–24.

Beck, A. and Naz, S. (2019) 'The need for service change and community outreach work to support trans-cultural cognitive behaviour therapy with Black and Minority Ethnic communities', *The Cognitive Behaviour Therapist*, 12, E1. doi:10.1017/S1754470X18000016.

Bennett-Levy, J., Butler, G., Fennell, M., Hackman, A., Mueller, M. and Westbrook, D. (eds.) (2004) *Oxford guide to behavioural experiments in cognitive therapy*. New York: Oxford University Press.

Butler, A.C., Chapman, J.E., Forman, E.M. and Beck, A.T. (2006) 'The empirical status of cognitive-behavioral therapy: a review of meta-analyses', *Clinical Psychology Review*, 26(1), pp. 17–31. doi:10.1016/j.cpr.2005.07.003.

Carey, T.A. and Stiles, W.B. (2016) 'Some problems with randomized controlled trials and some viable alternatives', *Clinical Psychology and Psychotherapy*, 23, pp. 87–95. doi:10.1002/cpp.1942.

Clark, D. (1989) 'Anxiety states: panic and generalized anxiety', in Hawton, K., Salkovskis, P.M., Kirk, J. and Clark, D.M. (eds.) *Cognitive behaviour therapy for psychiatric problems: a practical guide*. New York, NY: Oxford University Press, pp. 52–96.

Clark, G.I. and Egan, S.J. (2015) 'The Socratic method in cognitive behavioural therapy: a narrative review', *Cognitive Therapy and Research*, 39(6), pp. 863–879. doi:10.1007/s10608-015-9707-3.

Clark, D., Salkovskis, P., Hackmann, A., Wells, A., Fennell, M., Ludgate, J., Ahmad, S., Richards, H. and Gelder, M. (1998) 'Two psychological treatments for hypochondriasis: a randomised controlled trial', *British Journal of Psychiatry*, 173(3), pp. 218–225. doi:10.1192/bjp.173.3.218.

David, D., Cristea, I. and Hofmann, S.G. (2018) 'Why cognitive behavioral therapy is the current gold standard of psychotherapy', *Frontiers in Psychiatry*, 9, p. 4. doi:10.3389/fpsyt.2018.00004.

Evans, C., Margison, F. and Barkham, M. (1998) 'The contribution of reliable and clinically significant change methods to evidence-based mental health', *Evidence-Based Mental Health*, 1(3), pp. 70–72.

Hayes, S.C. (2004a) 'Acceptance and commitment therapy, relational frame theory, and the third wave of behavioral and cognitive therapies', *Behavior Therapy*, 35(4), pp. 639–665. doi:10.1016/S0005-7894(04)80013-3.

Hayes, S.C. (2004b) 'Acceptance and commitment therapy and the new behavior therapies: mindfulness, acceptance, and relationship', in Hayes, S.C., Follette, V.M. and Linehan, M.M. (eds.) *Mindfulness and acceptance: expanding the cognitive-behavioral tradition*. New York, NY: The Guilford Press, pp. 1–29.

Hayes, S.C. and Hofmann, S.G. (2017) 'The third wave of cognitive behavioral therapy and the rise of process-based care', *World Psychiatry*, 16(3), pp. 245–246. doi:10.1002/wps.20442.

Hofmann, S.G., Asnaani, A., Vonk, I.J., Sawyer, A.T. and Fang, A. (2012) 'The efficacy of cognitive behavioral therapy: a review of meta-analyses', *Cognitive Therapy and Research*, 36(5), pp. 427–440. doi:10.1007/s10608-012-9476-1.

Johnsen, T.J. and Friborg, O. (2015) 'The effects of cognitive behavioral therapy as an anti-depressive treatment is falling: a meta-analysis', *Psychological Bulletin*, 141(4), pp. 747–768. doi:/10.1037/bul0000015.

Kazantzis, N., Dattilio, F.M. and Dobson, K.S. (2017) *The therapeutic relationship in cognitive-behavioral therapy: a clinician's guide*. New York, NY: The Guilford Press.

Leuzinger-Bohleber, M., Kaufhold, J., Kallenbach, L., Negele, A., Ernst, M., Keller, W., Fiedler, G., Hautzinger, M., Bahrke, U. and Beutel, M. (2019) 'How to measure sustained psychic transformations in long-term treatments of chronically depressed patients: symptomatic and structural changes in the LAC Depression Study of the outcome of cognitive-behavioural and psychoanalytic long-term treatments', *International Journal of Psychoanalysis*, 100(1), pp. 99–127.

Longmore, R.J. and Worrell, M. (2007) 'Do we need to challenge thoughts in cognitive behaviour therapy?', *Clinical Psychology Review*, 27(2), pp. 173–187.

National Institute for Health and Care Excellence (NICE) (2009) *Depression in adults: recognition and management: clinical guideline CG90*. Available at: https://www.nice.org.uk/guidance/cg90 (Accessed: 6 May 2020).

Omylinska-Thurston, J., McMeekin, A., Walton, P. and Proctor, G. (2019) 'Clients' perceptions of unhelpful factors in CBT in IAPT serving a deprived area of the UK', *Counselling and Psychotherapy Research*, 19(4), pp. 455–464. doi:10.1002/capr.12249.

Padesky, C.A. and Beck, A.T. (2003) 'Science and philosophy: comparison of cognitive therapy and rational emotive behavior therapy', *Journal of Cognitive Psychotherapy*, 17(3), pp. 211–224.

Padesky, C.A. and Mooney, K.A. (1990) 'Clinical tip: presenting the cognitive model to clients', *International Cognitive Therapy Newsletter*, 6, pp. 13–14.

Pavlov, P.I. (2010[1927]) 'Conditioned reflexes: an investigation of the physiological activity of the cerebral cortex', *Annals of neurosciences*, 17(3), pp. 136–141. doi:10.5214/ans.0972-7531.1017309.

Rosner, R.I. (2012) 'Aaron T. Beck's drawings and the psychoanalytic origin story of cognitive therapy', *History of Psychology*, 15(1), pp. 1–18. doi:10.1037/a0023892.

Rosner, R.I. (2014) 'The "Splendid Isolation" of Aaron T. Beck', *Isis*, 105(4), pp. 734–758.

Salkovskis, P.M. (1991) 'The importance of behaviour in the maintenance of anxiety and panic: a cognitive account', *Behavioural Psychotherapy*, 19(1), pp. 6–19. doi:10.1017/S0141347300011472.

Schermuly-Haupt, M-L., Linden, M. and Rush, A.J. (2018) 'Unwanted events and side effects in cognitive behavior therapy', *Cognitive Therapy and Research*, 42, pp. 219–229. doi:10.1007/s10608-018-9904-y.

Sheldon, K., Clarke, S. and Moghaddam, N. (2015) 'Clinical effectiveness of a pain psychology service within an outpatient secondary care setting', *Mental Health Review Journal*, 20(3), pp. 166–176.

Skinner, B.F. (1938) *The behavior of organisms: an experimental analysis*. New York: Appleton-Century-Crofts.

Slade, M. and Priebe, S. (2001) 'Are randomised controlled trials the only gold that glitters?', *British Journal of Psychiatry*, 179(4), pp. 286–287.

Stewart, R.E. and Chambless, D.L. (2009) 'Cognitive-behavioral therapy for adult anxiety disorders in clinical practice: a meta-analysis of effectiveness studies', *Journal of Consulting and Clinical Psychology*, 77(4), pp. 595–606. doi:10.1037/a0016032.

Thomas, N. (2015) 'What's really wrong with cognitive behavioral therapy for psychosis?', *Frontiers in Psychology*, 6, p. 323. doi:10.3389/fpsyg.2015.00323.

Wampold, B.E., Flückiger, C., Del Re, A.C., Yulish, N., Frost, N., Pace, B., Goldberg, S., Miller, S., Baardseth, T., Laska, K. and Hilsenroth, M. (2017) 'In pursuit of truth: a critical examination of meta-analyses of cognitive behavior therapy', *Psychotherapy Research*, 27(1), pp. 14–32. doi:10.1080/10503307.2016.1249433.

Watson, J.B. (1913) 'Psychology as the behaviorist views it', *Psychological Review*, 20(2), pp. 158–177.

Wolpe, J. (1958) *Psychotherapy by reciprocal inhibition*. Stanford, CA: Stanford University Press.

Chapter 11
The humanistic approach

Michael Sims and Gina Di Malta

Contents

Introduction

'Broken pieces' by Coral Locke

Humanistic psychology is a movement – originating from nineteenth-century humanist values – that believes humans are meaning-making, purposeful beings who bear responsibility for their actions in the world. This psychological perspective gained popularity in the twentieth century as a reaction to the perceived reductionism (the belief that human behaviour can be explained by breaking it down into smaller component parts) dominant in psychological approaches at the time. Humanistic therapies were based on a holistic view of human beings (emphasising the whole rather than constituent parts), putting a particular emphasis on human potential and people's innate drive for creativity and growth. This chapter will look at developments and concepts in humanistic psychology. It will examine the person-centred perspective as an anchor in humanistic approaches and it will review the evidence and developments of the person-centred approach in today's context.

The person-centred approach was created by Carl Rogers, a founding father of humanistic psychology, which theoretically and practically advocates the fundamental principles of humanistic psychology, such as actualisation and free will. Uniquely to the person-centred approach, Rogers (1957) developed a theory of therapy to enhance human development.

This chapter aims to:

- introduce the historical inception and continuous development of humanistic approaches

- anchor contemporary forms of practice in the enduring relevance of the person-centred approach, particularly with reference to concepts of the actualising tendency and the core conditions for positive personality change

- outline person-centred formulation

- review the evidence, criticisms and developments of person-centred therapy.

1   Core humanistic principles and their development

The inception of humanistic psychology and its approaches evolved from **phenomenology** and existentialist thinking, with key writers including Heidegger (1889–1976), Merleau-Ponty (1908–1961) and Sartre (1905–1980). These philosophers developed ideas around the meaning of human existence, the consequences of living an inauthentic life and the responsibility ensuing from having **free will** and **agency**. These philosophical concepts came to greatly influence humanistic psychology. The humanistic-existentialist writer James Bugental (1964) summarised five core principles of humanistic psychology. Human beings:

- supersede the sum of their parts; they cannot be reduced to components

- exist within a uniquely human context

- are aware, and are aware of being aware

- possess a consciousness that always includes an awareness of oneself in the context of other people

- have the ability to make choices, and therefore have responsibility

- are intentional, aim at goals, are aware that their behaviours cause future events, and seek meaning, value and creativity.

In the 1940s and 1950s, humanistic approaches to therapy – underpinned and informed by humanistic psychology – started to take hold in the US. At the time, the two main approaches to psychology were psychoanalysis/psychodynamic therapy and behaviourism. It wasn't until the 1950s that the three founding fathers of humanistic psychology – Carl Rogers, Abraham Maslow and Clark Moustakas – met in Detroit to develop the 'third force' in psychology. This humanistic third force was a counter reaction and a challenge to the psychodynamic approach, which put emphasis on deterministic unconscious forces, and to behaviourism – which ignored human consciousness and was reliant on animal studies. The humanistic approach embodied a tangible alternative view of humans as autonomous, free-thinking and multifaceted, capable of creation and destruction, and with the ability to make choices in their lives. The

Phenomenology
The study of subjective experience.

Free will
The ability to act without the constraint of necessity or fate.

Agency
The ability to control and direct one's own life towards a chosen goal.

three men established the ground work and developed the significant principles and theories that are commonplace today.

One fundamental humanistic concept developed at the time was that of 'actualisation': a process of realising oneself. For Abraham Maslow (1954), the concept was expressed as 'self-actualisation' (see Chapter 3, Section 3, for a reminder of the definition), which is the highest developmental achievement in his famous 'hierarchy of needs' theory (outlined in Figure 11.1).

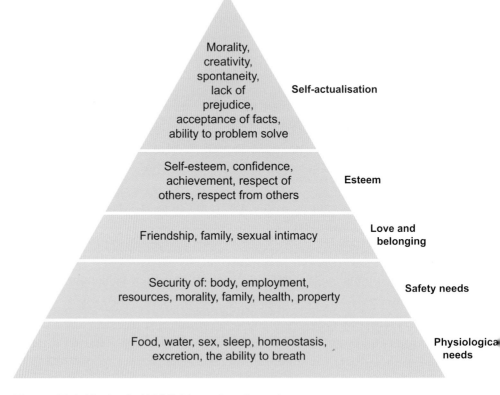

Figure 11.1 Maslow's (1954) hierarchy of needs

The hierarchy of needs pyramid depicts the motivational movement that people undergo. They first seek to meet important basic physiological needs (such as the need for food and shelter). Once these are met, people seek safety, then love and belonging, until they are ultimately able to seek the achievement of the higher needs of esteem and self-actualisation. Maslow believed that humans have an inner force for growth-optimisation, driving them to reach their full potential, and he saw self-actualisation as the end goal. The self-actualised person would demonstrate qualities of acceptance for themself and others and an authentic openness to experience; would have creative and fulfilling relationships; and would generally feel 'okay' in the world.

For Carl Rogers (1959), actualisation manifested in his concept of the 'actualising tendency' (Chapter 3 introduced Rogers' conceptual ideas). In his theory of personality, Rogers notably stated that this was 'the inherent tendency of the **organism** to develop all its capacities in ways which serve to maintain or enhance the organism' (Rogers, 1959, p. 196). Like Maslow, Rogers believed that people actualise to enhance their way of life. However, Rogers' view of actualisation differed from Maslow's, as Rogers didn't see actualisation as an end goal, or something one strives to achieve. Rogers believed actualisation was an ongoing process and in a constant state of flux. Regardless of the specific theory, the concept of actualisation is fundamentally grounded in people's drive and capability to seek and achieve their potential. It is a characteristic tenet underlying humanistic therapies.

Organism
Also referred to as the 'organismic self' or 'real self', it is the self a person is born with, which is considered authentic. The organism naturally strives towards growth and self-actualisation.

1.1 Humanistic therapies

Since its significant beginnings, the humanistic approach, although single in name, has developed and consists of many subgroups and disciplines. This section will briefly describe some of the traditional humanistic therapeutic approaches. The remainder of this chapter will be focused on a detailed description of Carl Rogers' person-centred therapy and its recent developments.

Gestalt therapy

The word *gestalt* comes from the German language and means 'whole'. Gestalt therapy was developed by Frederick (Fritz) Perls (1969). As per the humanistic tradition, it sees individuals as having the potential for growth. Contrary to behaviourism, it is also based on a general assumption of holism, maintaining that meaning cannot be found from breaking things down into parts, but rather by appreciating the whole of the self in its context. In contrast to behaviourists, Gestalt psychologists believe that human behaviour and perceptions rely on hidden processes in the mind. In order to argue this point, they used ambiguous imagery. Figure 11.2 presents a famous image of the 'Rubin goblet' (Rubin, 1915), which can be seen as a vase-like object or as two faces. The premise is that the same stimulus can result in two different perceptions, therefore suggesting that there is more to human perception and behaviour than what can be observed and measured.

Figure 11.2 Gestalt image: the Rubin goblet

Gestalt therapy involves helping an individual to become more aware of these hidden internal processes. Clients are assisted in removing barriers to this self-awareness and are encouraged to understand themselves as a part of the social world (comprised of relationships, culture, family, etc.). Therapy focuses on 'here-and-now' thoughts, feelings and behaviours to understand how individuals relate to others.

Existential therapy

Existential therapy is a group of psychotherapies guided by existentialist philosophy, which is aimed at making sense of human existence. One common assumption of these therapies is that inner conflict arises from the non-acceptance of existential givens; for example, death, being fundamentally alone in the world, being free to choose, and a lack of inherent meaning in life. Different existential psychologists have emphasised various philosophical viewpoints. Rollo May (1961), for instance, proposed that the awareness of one's own mortality makes vitality and passion possible. Existential therapists borrow techniques from an array of therapies including psychodynamic, Gestalt, person-centred and cognitive behavioural therapy (CBT). However, they tend to be characterised by the use of phenomenology, putting the focus on subjective experience. The goal of existential therapy is for the individual to live a more authentic life by accepting existential givens and creating their own meaning.

Process-experiential and emotion-focused therapy

This empirically supported neo-humanistic approach, developed by Laura North Rice and Leslie Greenberg in the late 1990s, sees emotion as a source of meaning and direction. The theory starts with the assumption that a person's facets and experiences all have something of value to offer. Similarly to Gestalt therapy, these facets are thought to enable growth and change to happen naturally when integrated into one's awareness. Therapy consists of supporting a client to find the words to accurately express a part of themselves that has been supressed from consciousness, or that they fear will be rejected (Elliott and Greenberg, 2007). The outcome of therapy is for clients to improve their relationship with themselves and their experience. Energy formerly used to avoid their experience is freed up for growth potential.

Activity 11.1: Therapeutic factors

Allow about 5 minutes

Note down the commonalities between the different humanistic therapies presented above. What common therapeutic factors can you identify?

Discussion

You may, of course, have come up with different factors, but we can note that all of these therapies are grounded in the common factors of free will, human potential, the development of self-awareness and ascribing meaning to human experience.

Person-centred therapy

As explained in Chapter 3, the person-centred approach (also known as client-centred therapy, non-directive therapy and Rogerian counselling) was established by Carl Rogers (1951, 1957, 1959, 1961, 1980) and has become one of the most influential humanistic therapies. This may be in part because its central therapeutic tenets – the core conditions – are relational elements that have since transpired across all psychological schools of thought (e.g. Norcross and Lambert, 2018).

These are considered necessary in most contemporary psychological therapies.

The person-centred approach has also moved into and informed other areas and disciplines, including education, group work, conflict resolution, organisational consultancy and even politics (Tudor and Worrall, 2006; Thorne and Sanders, 2012). Hence, the rest of this chapter will focus on the person-centred approach and its recent developments.

2   The person-centred understanding of mental health

Before looking at the application to the concept of mental health, it would be helpful to recap on the person-centred approach to understanding the individual person. Rogers had a foundational belief that all individuals have the innate capacity for growth, maturity and the ability to fulfil their potential, given the right relational environment (Rogers, 1951, 1957). In his theory of the 'actualising tendency' (Rogers, 1959), Rogers conceptualised this as the person's continual process of 'becoming'. He believed that people have an inherent core that is trustworthy and an innate capacity to move forward in a prosocial way. This belief in an individual person's ability to move forward and find their own direction in life is essentially the foundation of his theory of therapy (Rogers, 1957) and his theory of personality (Rogers, 1959). Rogers proposed that, given the ideal environment and relationships – in which the individual feels genuinely empathically understood and unconditionally accepted – the individual will actualise into a fully functioning person.

For Rogers, the fundamentals of a fully functioning person consist of a **self-concept** (image of one's self) that is *congruent* with (or matches) the person's experience. From this basis, the individual will function from an 'internal locus of evaluation' – a place of autonomy within the person, so they therefore trust their own decision making. Other attributes of a fully functioning person include:

Self-concept
An idea of one's self comprised of values and beliefs about it, which fundamentally incorporate conditions of worth. It is the fundamental means by which a person understands and experiences their self.

- being free of defensive behaviours

- having all experience available to awareness and symbolised accurately (e.g. in words or images) in one's awareness

- living life harmoniously with others while experiencing unconditional positive self-regard (a genuine unconditional acceptance of one's self).

In simple terms, the person feels okay with themselves, the people around them and with the life they are living. From this basic notion of a fully functioning person, one can explore the person-centred understanding of mental health. Rogers believed that each individual has a basic need for approval from others, and at times it can conflict with one's instinctual feelings and responses to a situation. In theoretical person-centred terms, there is a tension between the organism and the self-concept.

This point can be further illustrated with the example of a baby engaging with the world. The baby is crying due to feeling hungry; if their need of hunger is met, the baby experiences their environment positively and learns to trust their feelings. In Rogerian terms, the baby learns to trust their 'organismic promptings', that is the signalling from the organism. However, as the baby grows up, they may start to experience some of their behaviour and feelings as more or less acceptable than others, depending on their caregiver's approval of them (or lack of). This discerning or conditional acceptance from those around them (e.g. their parents) culminates with the development of what Rogers termed **conditions of worth**. For a child to gain continual approval, or positive regard, from their parents, they begin to internalise these conditions of worth, therefore adopting and behaving in ways approved by the parents. These behaviours may conflict with a child's own organismic response. For example, they may want to hit another child who has just taken their toy, but they begin to suppress this feeling of anger and negative behaviour to 'fit' the condition of worth specifying that they must be a 'good' child. As the child grows and begins to take on more of these conditions of worth, they start to develop a self-concept, which may conflict with the organismic self.

Conditions of worth
Conditional dynamics within a relationship, usually between a parent/caregiver and a child, which the child takes on in order to receive love from the parent/caregiver. If the child does not meet a parental condition, then love is withheld.

2.1   The person-centred understanding of anxiety

It is probably fair to assume that everyone reading this chapter has had some experience of anxiety over the course of their life. Anxiety is a natural human response to how we sometimes engage with our ever-changing environments, and the level of anxiety we feel generally depends on our ability (or inability) to cope with this change (Anxiety UK, 2018). You may be experiencing some anxiety right now; for instance, you might be going out this evening to meet a new person and feeling anxious about how they will perceive you, or you might be feeling anxious about writing an upcoming assignment.

The person-centred perspective regards anxiety as a natural human response, so using diagnosis to label a client is considered anti-therapeutic. Some person-centred therapists therefore reject the medical model of mental health. Rogers believed that the client is the best person to know what is wrong, and he respected that they are the expert in themselves. Theoretically, Rogers suggested that anxiety is no more and no less than a process of *incongruence* in a person. Rogers viewed anxiety/incongruence as a conflict between the person's felt experience (the organism) and their self-concept. This results in psychological tension, the degree of which depends on the level of threat to the self-concept (Rogers, 1957, 1959).

The (fictional) case of Sarah below illustrates this process. Sarah holds a self-concept of a confident, articulate and intelligent woman, but her experiences do not always match. People often experience such a mismatch as feeling 'outside of' themselves. You may have heard people say, 'That's so out of character' or 'That just wasn't me!'. The self's response to this mismatch is to become even more rigid and tight – a defence mechanism that keeps the self-concept from breaking down – which compounds the incongruence and anxiety.

Case illustration: Sarah and anxiety

Sarah is a 36-year-old white woman who identifies as bisexual. Sarah is currently in a relationship with a woman with whom she shares a flat. She works as a primary school teacher near where she lives in Central London. Sarah sees herself as a confident, articulate and intelligent woman.

Sarah started to experience difficulty when speaking in class and in team meetings. Before she was about to speak, she'd notice her hands beginning to sweat and her heart beginning to race. She'd stumble on her words and would feel herself going red in the face. Sarah went to her local GP with the presenting problem and got signed off work with general anxiety.

The high levels of incongruence a person generally feels is usually the result of denied and/or distorted feelings; for example, jealousy, rage, sadness, hate, or sexual feelings. These are repressed because the individual deems them unacceptable, either in their own eyes or from a societal perspective. The purpose of person-centred therapy is therefore to help people become more aware of their feelings, facilitating a relationship that supports the client to integrate them into their self-concept and to gain greater self-acceptance.

2.2   Person-centred formulation

The person-centred approach to formulation is mixed. Some argue the nature of formulation is obstructive to the person-centred approach (Rogers, 1951; Joseph, 2017; Proctor et al., 2006), whereas others are more sympathetic to the concept (Freeth, 2007; Sommerbeck, 2003, 2014). The argument against forumlation comes from the person-centred ethos of experiencing a client's world from their own perspective, understanding and language, rather than adopting or placing an external value judgement on them. Whatever your stance on person-centred formulation, however, the very concept of understanding the client, and why they have come to therapy, is fundamental to Rogers' (1957) theory of therapy and, arguably, all forms of therapy.

As described in Chapter 8, formulation consists of three main questions that underpin the therapy structure: What has caused the problem(s)?; What factors are maintaining the problem(s)?; What might facilitate change? These questions are important in all types of therapy as they provide a framework and guidance for therapeutic steps and interventions, enabling the therapist and the client to work collaboratively. Returning to the case illustration of Sarah, the therapist would need to know why Sarah has come to therapy and what her presenting issue is. Then they would need to apply this information and relate it to the three main formulation factors to help Sarah achieve the best outcome from therapy.

An example of this process is outlined below.

- **What has brought Sarah to therapy and why?**

  She is experiencing anxiety due to having to speak in her current job role as a teacher.

- **What has caused the problems?**

  By applying Rogers' theory of personality, one can infer that the anxiety is a form of incongruence resulting from a conflict between Sarah's organismic experience (an aversion to speaking to people in her professional capacity) and her self-concept (that she is articulate, confident and intelligent, and therefore speaking to people should not cause her a problem).

- **What factors are maintaining the problems?**

  The conditions of worth that maintain Sarah's self-concept, which cause incongruence between Sarah's organismic experience and her self-concept.

- **What might facilitate change?**

  The therapist offers Rogers' core conditions of empathy, unconditional positive regard and congruence, which counters Sarah's conditions of worth, bringing them into her awareness and positively changing her self-concept.

Pause for reflection

Take a moment to reflect on Sarah's experience of anxiety. What are some of the conditions of worth she could have internalised that have led to her current anxiety?

---

3   Therapeutic process and technique in the person-centred approach

The 'doing' of person-centred therapy is based in the creation of Rogers' theory of therapy. As previously stated, Rogers believed that everyone has the capacity to understand not only what's wrong but also how to change it, and that this understanding can be achieved through a therapeutic relationship that fosters the development of clients' own self-awareness. Rogers' (1957, 1959) process of therapeutic change, based on this fundamental belief, is not purely focused on symptom reduction in the client – it is about an actual change in their personality structure, towards becoming a fully functioning person.

Rogers (1957) proposed an optimum therapeutic relationship to help facilitate the development of a client's self-awareness. This consisted of six necessary and sufficient conditions that would enable positive personality change in the person. Rogers considered them 'necessary' in that they were needed for therapy to work, and also 'sufficient' because nothing else was needed. This was a provocative and radical position for his time.

Information box 11.1: The necessary and sufficient conditions of therapeutic personality change

For constructive personality change to occur, it is necessary that these conditions exist and continue over a period of time:

1   Two persons are in psychological contact.
2   The first, whom we shall term the client, is in a state of incongruence, being vulnerable or anxious.
3   The second person, whom we shall term the therapist, is congruent or integrated in the relationship.
4   The therapist experiences unconditional positive regard for the client.
5   The therapist experiences an empathic understanding of the client's internal frame of reference and endeavours to communicate this experience to the client.
6   The communication to the client of the therapist's empathic understanding and unconditional positive regard is to a minimal degree achieved.

> No other conditions are necessary. If these six conditions exist, and continue over a period of time, this is sufficient. The process of constructive personality change will follow.
>
> (Rogers, 1957, pp. 95–96)

Out of the above six conditions, there are three famous 'core conditions': congruence (condition 3), unconditional positive regard (condition 4) and empathy (condition 5), arguably the foundational blocks of therapy. Rogers believed these to be the active conditions provided by the therapist which facilitated change in the client. The other conditions (conditions 1, 2 and 6) are centred predominately on the client: they are feeling anxious (condition 2), they want to engage in therapy (condition 1) and they perceive the offering of the core conditions (condition 6). All conditions are needed, and then positive personality change will occur. Rogers worked tirelessly over the course of his career to promote and present the core conditions as the fundamental therapeutic change agents. It is these qualities that facilitate a therapeutic relationship and counteract a person's incongruence (condition 2) from their conditions of worth.

Informed by his own practice and research, Rogers believed that, for a client to move from incongruence to congruence, they need to experience a person in a greater state of congruence than themselves. Therefore the therapist needs to meet condition 3. Rogers was adamant that this required the therapist to be genuine and authentic in the relationship, and to not appear 'fake' or as though they are hiding behind a façade/mask.

Empathy (condition 5) is the process of understanding a client from their own perspective or, in person-centred terms, from their 'frame of reference'. It is having an accurate sense of the client's own private world and being able to communicate this appreciation to them with unconditional acceptance. This condition allows the client to experience themselves within an accepting space, and to safely explore their internal and external world without fear of being misunderstood.

Unconditional positive regard (condition 4) is the unconditional acceptance or non-judgment of the client in their totality. Rogers also used the term 'non-possessive love' to describe his concept of unconditional positive regard toward the client, irrespective of how they were presenting or what they were bringing to therapy. It is this ability of the therapist to unreservedly accept the client that counters the *conditionality* of their conditions of worth and challenges their self-concept.

Pause for reflection

Think about the times you have received empathy and unconditional positive regard from others in your life. What did this feel like? Did you feel understood, accepted and heard? Was there a sense of genuineness from the person who offered them?

The case illustration below demonstrates how these potent core conditions can be translated into therapy to facilitate change to Sarah's self-concept.

Case illustration: Sarah's person-centred therapy session

Sarah: I don't understand it; I've never not been able to speak in public before.

Therapist: So, this feels almost like an alien concept to you.

Sarah: Yeah, like it's not even a part of who I am.

Therapist: Like it doesn't fit.

Sarah: That's it, completely; it doesn't fit. And then to feel so scared and anxious as well.

Therapist: Feelings you don't normally feel.

Sarah: Absolutely not. Dad said I should never be scared and that I'm a strong kid and no one should ever push me around.

Therapist: So, Dad was adamant you should not be scared, and you should be strong.

Sarah: Yeah, and when I went to university, he was keen for me to join the debating club to develop my self-confidence and ability to speak publicly, which I did.

Therapist: And that was an okay experience for you.

Sarah: If I'm honest I was scared. Actually I was terrified – my hands would sweat and I'd get a churning stomach, but once I'd been in it for a few months I got over the fear.

Therapist: So, the fear is anxiousness?

Sarah: Something like that. What I do know is that, before I'd go to speak, I'd have to give myself a pep talk and I've stopped doing that lately. In fact, thinking about it, it ties in with this anxiety.

Therapist: So, the pep talk helped you feel okay.

Sarah: Yes, and I'd say, 'Come on Sarah, what would Dad think?'

Therapist: Feels like Dad is tied up in this.

Sarah: Dad was so proud of me, it's hard to explain how good that felt.

Therapist: Dad's approval was everything.

Sarah: Like you wouldn't believe.

Therapist: And you still need it.

Sarah: Well no, of course not, I'm a grown woman now. [pause] Oh my god, I think I do.

Therapist: You think you do.

Sarah: Yes, I really do. I can't do this without Dad.

Therapist: You can't do this without your Dad.

Sarah: No. You know, I never really wanted to be a teacher; Dad said it was a good, worthy job. Reliable. You can't beat an education, he'd say.

Activity 11.2: The core conditions

Allow about 10 minutes

Work through the case illustration above, noting down how the core conditions of empathy, unconditional positive regard and congruence are being offered to Sarah and how she responds to them.

Discussion

Perhaps this activity has enabled you to further appreciate the impact of the core conditions – how the genuine/congruent offering of empathy and unconditional positive regard can positively affect relationships in a person's life. It might indicate how important the core conditions are to person-centred counsellors and how intrinsic they are to the therapeutic relationship.

---

4   The efficacy and scope of the person-centred approach

Over the years, the scope and efficacy of person-centred therapy has encountered challenges as it has grown and developed. Rogers was a pioneer of psychotherapy research: he founded psychotherapy **process research** with his early use of recording technology in the 1940s and investigated the person-centred approach with controlled outcome research in the early 1950s (Elliott and Farber, 2010). While both quantitative and qualitative research were part of his legacy, the pursuit of hard quantitative evidence, beginning at the start of the twenty-first century, has increasingly become a political necessity as part of national efforts to regulate counselling and psychotherapy.

While this is in place to protect the public from poor practice, it also had the consequence of restricting the range of therapies to those that can easily be manualised and assessed with standard **positivist methods** (Elliott, 2016). Methods such as randomised controlled trials – considered the 'gold standard' for determining causal effects of treatments – are highly structured, make assumptions about the length of treatment, require categorising clients into diagnostic groups, and rely on **standardised outcome measures** which transpose people's lived experiences into averages (e.g. McCormack, Sundling and Badian, 2017). These rigorous methods assume a 'one-size-fits-all' approach to the processes and outcomes of therapy and they contrast with the fundamental assumption of humanistic approaches that each individual and experience is unique. Due to practitioners' reluctance to engage with such methods, person-centred therapy has been criticised for lacking 'acceptable' evidence, and over the years has suffered political setbacks. The approach had been decommissioned from publicly funded services in the UK and Germany, and was 'gradually and increasingly disappearing from sight' (Hofmeister, 2010 , p. 7).

It is only in recent years, following rigorous work undertaken by advocates of the person-centred approach, that person-centred therapy has found its place within the UK National Health Service (NHS) as part of its current clinical model Improving Access to Psychological Therapies (IAPT), which began in 2008. Specifically, Sanders and Hill (2014) developed counselling for depression (CfD), a person-centred therapy treatment available through the NHS and approved by the National Institute for Health and Care Excellence (NICE). CfD is a

Process research
The examination of therapeutic processes in relation to their influence on outcomes in order to identify the most effective methods to bring about positive change.

Positivist method
An approach to science with origins in the nineteenth century. It regards only 'factual' phenomena observable to the senses as trustworthy building blocks of science. The approach is often understood to support present-day quantitative methods.

Standardised outcome measure
A clinical tool used in practice and research to accurately and consistently assess a person's symptoms or diagnosis.

model of person-centred and process-experiential therapy as it utilises processes from emotion-focused therapy (discussed in Section 1.1) and involves the practitioner being more active in working with a client's emotions than they would in classical person-centred therapy (e.g. Murphy, 2019). The evidence base indicates that this active component is essential in treating depression (Elliott *et al.*, 2013). Advocates of the person-centred approach urge practitioners to advance it by remaining engaged with research (e.g. Elliott, 2016; Cooper *et al.*, 2013; Tudor and Worrall, 2006; Wilkins, 2016).

Recent person-centred therapy research – including Hill and Elliot (2014), Gibbard and Hanley (2008) and King *et al.* (2000) – has focused its efforts on examining the effectiveness of person-centred therapy. A meta-analysis by Robert Elliott *et al.* (2013) provided an examination of over 200 person-centred and experiential studies since the 1940s. This rigorous statistical approach offers a summary of existing studies. Results suggested that person-centred and experiential therapy brings about a large pre–post therapy change for clients, and that this change is maintained over time. Clients show considerable improvements, or gains, compared to those who receive no therapy. These gains are generally equivalent to those of other therapies, including CBT. However, some treatments labelled 'supportive' or 'non-directive' showed significantly smaller pre–post change than CBT. Elliott *et al.* found that these treatments turned out to be non-*bona fide* person-centred treatments used by researchers with an allegiance to CBT, meaning that the results may have been subject to bias. Person-centred therapy was more effective than other therapies for relational and interpersonal issues, depression and trauma. On the other hand, it was found to be less effective for treating anxiety. The researchers also found that person-centred therapy was the most effective therapy for psychosis and schizophrenia. Surprisingly, they note that these results are in contrast with current NICE guidelines, which recommend CBT for psychosis and contraindicate 'supportive counselling' (NICE, 2014, p. 24).

There are also increasing qualitative and mixed-methods studies looking at the client–therapist relationship that demonstrate the benefits and value of person-centred therapy and how it informs the ever-growing therapeutic world. Tickle and Murphy (2014) used a theory-building case study to examine the concept of 'mutuality', when both the client and the therapist experience Rogers' core conditions (rather than the therapist unidirectionally providing it and the client receiving it) (Murphy, Cramer and Joseph, 2012). Other emerging person-centred developments include the construct of relational depth – a state of profound engagement between two people in which each is fully genuine and experiences high levels of empathy and unconditional positive regard for the other (Mearns and Cooper, 2018). Qualitative research using **semi-structured interviews** has brought rich phenomenological descriptions of relational depth and has established that such experiences, while relatively rare, exist among clients and therapists (Cooper, 2005; Knox, 2008). Growing evidence suggests that clients also experience a positive shift during these moments, and researchers propose to assess its association with therapy outcomes in a large **pre–post study** using a validated measure for the construct (Di Malta, Evans and Cooper, 2019).

Semi-structured interview
An interview used in qualitative research that enables and supports a subjective exploration into the topic being researched. The interviewer uses a set of prepared questions and follows up on answers with prompts.

Diversity: Client groups in person-centred therapy

One criticism over the years has been that person-centred therapy is only suitable for the 'worried well' (referring to middle-class white people who can afford therapy) and that it doesn't take into account cultural diversity, class and ethnicity (Kovel, 1976; Ryan, 1995; Tudor and Worrall, 2006). However, over the last few decades, many person-centred practitioners and theorists have challenged this view. They have developed more explicitly inclusive practice within the approach through increasingly working with marginalised/disenfranchised groups and individuals – including LGBTQ+ communities, non-white communities and people with disabilities – to facilitate unique person-centred therapeutic ways of working to meet all the client's needs (e.g. Lago and Charura, 2016; Joseph, 2017).

Pre–post study
A research method to test the effectiveness of an intervention, whereby a standardised outcome measure is used at the beginning and again at the end of treatment to measure change.

The person-centred approach has been criticised throughout its lifespan (e.g. see the Diversity box), and continues to be criticised by competing theoretical models and styles of therapy. Some argue that the approach is light on theory, does not consider wider societal concerns, and does not have strong empirical research. These claims have consistently been challenged and are still being addressed by the ever-growing development of the person-centred approach (e.g. Lago and Charura, 2016; Joseph, 2017).

Conclusion

Humanistic therapies carry fundamental prosocial values which have changed the face of the western psychotherapy world. At the heart of humanistic therapies lies a recognition that vulnerability, as well as the power of creative growth, exists within each of us. This shift comes with a respect that is humbling and an openness to the whole being of the individual seeking help.

The person-centred offering is to share in a uniquely human relationship – a relationship in which the therapist fundamentally trusts the client's ability to 'right themselves' through the therapist's capacity to unconditionally enter their world and offer a genuine empathic understanding. When received and perceived by the client, this facilitates positive therapeutic growth.

Since the inception of Rogers' theories, humanistic therapies have developed, and there have been advances in research and practice – for example, the emergence of evidence-based practice and the embracing of broader cultural diversity – but fundamentally, the processes are still the same.

Further reading

- This book offers an accessible introduction to the person-centred approach, covering theory, contexts and contemporary practice: Lago, C. and Charura, D. (eds.) (2016) *The person-centred counselling and psychotherapy handbook: origins, developments and current applications*. Berkshire: Open University Press and McGraw-Hill Education.

- This book covers the ongoing dialogue between person-centred therapeutic practice and the mental health profession:

  Joseph, S. (ed.) (2017) *The handbook of person-centred therapy and mental health: theory, research and practice*. Monmouth: PCCS Books.

References

Anxiety UK (2018) 'Anxiety conditions'. Available at: https://www.anxietyuk.org.uk/get-help/anxiety-information/ (Accessed: 5 May 2020).

Bugental, J. (1964) 'The third force in psychology', *Journal of Humanistic Psychology*, 4(1), pp. 19–26.

Cooper, M. (2005) 'Therapists' experiences of relational depth: a qualitative interview study', *Counselling and Psychotherapy Research*, 5(2), pp. 87–95.

Cooper, M., O'Hara, M., Schmid, P. and Bohart, A. (2013) *The handbook of person-centred psychotherapy and counselling*. 2nd edn. Basingstoke: Palgrave Macmillan.

Di Malta, G., Evans, C. and Cooper, M. (2019) 'Development and validation of the relational depth frequency scale', *Psychotherapy Research*, 30(2), pp. 213–227.

Elliott, R. and Farber, B.A. (2010) 'Carl Rogers: Idealistic pragmatist and psychotherapy research pioneer', in Castonguay, L.G., Muran, J.C., Angus, L, Hayes, J.A., Ladany, N. and Anderson, T. (eds.) *Bringing psychotherapy research to life: Understanding change through the work of leading clinical researchers*. American Psychological Association, pp. 17–27. doi: 10.1037/12137-002.

Elliott, R. and Greenberg, L.S. (2007) 'The essence of process-experiential/emotion-focused therapy', *American Journal of Psychotherapy*, 61(3), pp. 241–254.

Elliott, R. (2016) 'Research on person-centred/experiential psychotherapy and counselling: summary of the main findings', in Elliott, R., Lago, C. and Charura, D. (eds.) *Person-centred counselling and psychotherapy*. Maidenhead: McGraw-Hill/Oxford University Press, pp. 223–232.

Elliott, R., Watson, J.C, Greenberg, L.S., Timulak, L. and Freire, E. (2013) 'Research on humanistic-experiential psychotherapies', in Lambert, M.J. (ed.) *Bergin & Garfield's handbook of psychotherapy and behavior change*. 6th edn. New York: Wiley, pp. 495–538.

Freeth, R. (2007) *Humanising psychiatry and mental health care: the challenge of the person-centred approach*. Oxford: Radcliffe Publishing.

Gibbard, I. and Hanley, T. (2008) 'A five-year evaluation of the effectiveness of person-centered counseling in routine clinical practice in primary care', *Counseling and Psychotherapy Research*, 8(4), pp. 215–222.

Hill, A. and Elliott, R. (2014) 'Evidence-based practice and person-centred and experiential therapies', in Sanders, P. and Hill, A. (eds.) *Counselling for depression: a person-centred and experiential approach to practice*. London: SAGE, pp. 5–20

Hofmeister, B. (2010) 'The person-centred approach in Germany: to cut a long story short', *Person-Centred and Experiential Psychotherapies*, 9(1), pp. 1–13.

Joseph, S. (ed.) (2017) *The handbook of person-centred therapy and mental health: theory, research and practice*. Monmouth: PCCS Books.

King, M., Sibbald, B., Ward, E., Lloyd, M., Gabby, M. and Byford, S. (2000) 'Randomised controlled trial of non-directive counselling, cognitive-behaviour therapy and usual general practitioner care in the management of depression as well as mixed anxiety and depression in primary care', *Health Technology Assessment*, 4(19), pp. 1–83. Available at: https://www.ncbi.nlm.nih.gov/pubmed/11086269 (Accessed: 5 May 2020).

Knox, R. (2008) 'Clients' experiences of relational depth in person-centred counselling', *Counselling and Psychotherapy Research*, 8(3), pp. 182–188.

Kovel, J. (1976) *A complete guide to therapy: from psychotherapy to behaviour modification*. New York: Pantheon Books.

Lago, C. and Charura, D. (eds.) (2016) *The person-centred counselling and psychotherapy handbook: origins, developments and current applications*. Berkshire: Open University Press and McGraw-Hill Education.

Maslow, A.H. (1954) *Motivation and personality*. New York, NY: Harper & Row.

May, R.E. (1961) *Existential psychology*. New York: Random House.

McCormack, B., Sundling, V. and Badian, R. (2017) 'Person-centred research: a novel approach to randomized controlled trials', *European Journal for Person Centered Healthcare*, 6(2), pp. 209–218.

Mearns, D. and Cooper, M. (2018) *Working at relational depth in counselling and psychotherapy*. 2nd edn. London: SAGE.

Murphy, D., Cramer, D. and Joseph, S. (2012) 'Mutuality in person-centered therapy: a new agenda for research and practice', *Person-centered and experiential psychotherapies*, 11(2), pp. 109–123.

Murphy, D. (2019) *Person-centred experiential counselling for depression*. London: SAGE.

National Institute for Health and Care Excellence (NICE) (2014) *Psychosis and schizophrenia in adults: prevention and management*. Available at: https://www.nice.org.uk/guidance/cg178/resources/psychosis-and-schizophrenia-in-adults-prevention-and-management-pdf-35109758952133 (Accessed: 5 May 2020).

Norcross, J.C. and Lambert, M.J. (2018) 'Psychotherapy relationships that work III', *Psychotherapy*, 55(4), pp. 303–315.

Perls, F.S. (1969) *Gestalt therapy verbatim*. Gouldsboro, ME: The Gestalt Journal Press.

Proctor, G., Cooper, M., Sanders, P. and Malcolm, B. (eds.) (2006) *Politicizing the person-centred approach: an agenda for social change.* Ross-on-Wye: PCCS Books.

Rogers, C.R. (1951) *Client-centered therapy: its current practice, implications and theory.* Boston, MA: Houghton-Mifflin Company.

Rogers, C.R. (1957) 'The necessary and sufficient conditions of therapeutic personality change', *Journal of Consulting Psychology*, 21(2), pp. 95–103.

Rogers, C.R. (1959) 'A theory of therapy, personality, and interpersonal relationships: as developed in the client-centered framework', in Koch, S. (ed.) *Psychology: a study of a science: Vol. 2 Formulations of the person and the social context.* New York: McGraw-Hill, pp. 184–256.

Rogers, C.R. (1961) *On becoming a person.* London: Constable.

Rogers, C.R. (1980) *A way of being.* New York: Houghton Mifflin Company.

Rubin, E. (1915) *Synsoplevede Figurer: Studier i psykologisk Analyse. Første Del.* Copenhagen and Christiania: Gyldendalske Boghandel, Nordisk Forlag.

Ryan, R.M. (1995) 'Psychological needs and the facilitation of integrative processes', *Journal of Personality*, 63(3), pp. 397–427.

Sanders, P. and Hill, A. (2014) *Counselling for depression: a person-centred and experiential guide to practice.* London: SAGE.

Sommerbeck, L. (2003) *The client-centred therapist in psychiatric contexts.* Ross-on-Wye: PCCS Books.

Sommerbeck, L. (2014) 'Refutations of myths of inappropriateness of person-centred therapy at the difficult edge', in Pearce, P. and Sommerbeck, L. (eds.) *Person-centred practice at the difficult edge.* Monmouth: PCCS Books, sections 3803–4086.

Thorne, B. and Sanders, P. (2012) *Carl Rogers.* 3rd edn. London: Sage.

Tickle, E. and Murphy, D. (2014) 'A journey to client and therapist mutuality in person-centred psychotherapy: a case study', *Person-Centered & Experiential Psychotherapies*, 13(4), pp. 337–351.

Tudor, K. and Worrall, M. (2006) *Person-centred therapy: a clinical philosophy.* London: Routledge.

Wilkins, P. (2016) *Person-centred therapy: 100 key points.* 2nd edn. Abingdon and New York, NY: Routledge.

Chapter 12
The pluralistic approach

Julia McLeod and John McLeod

Contents

Introduction

'Multiple selfs' by Victor Guerrero

Training, research and practice in counselling and psychotherapy have been largely dominated by therapy approaches that focus on specific change processes. For example, person-centred therapy (Chapter 11) primarily seeks to use authentic empathic reflection to promote self-acceptance; psychodynamic therapy (Chapter 9) uses the interpretation of transference and countertransference to enable insight about emotional responses and relationship patterns; and cognitive behavioural therapy (CBT; Chapter 10) employs various re-learning techniques to facilitate cognitive and behavioural change in respect of dysfunctional behaviour. Some counsellors and psychotherapists have viewed such 'unitary' models of therapy as too restrictive, and have sought to develop eclectic and integrative forms of practice that allow the combination of ideas and techniques from different approaches.

Pluralistic therapy is a collaborative, strengths-oriented integrative approach that is built on an appreciation that there are a wide range of different ways of understanding mental health difficulties, and a wealth of potentially helpful ways of dealing with such difficulties (Villaggi *et al.*, 2015). The key idea in pluralistic therapy is that the client or service user is a person who is actively trying to address the problems in living that are troubling them, and has their own ideas about what is likely to be helpful or unhelpful in relation to that endeavour (Bohart and Tallman, 1996). Pluralistic practitioners work alongside clients to identify and implement therapeutic activities that draw on the knowledge and experience of both client and therapist.

This chapter aims to:

- introduce the ideas and principles that underpin a collaborative pluralistic approach to working with mental health difficulties, including the concept of a decision-space and the importance of cultural resources and feedback opportunities

- consider the ways in which pluralistic practice differs from other approaches, particularly the psychodynamic approach, the humanistic approach and CBT

- explore the practical implementation of a pluralistic stance when helping a person suffering from anxiety

- consider the evidence around using the pluralistic approach in therapy and the ways in which this evidence can be integrated into practice.

1 Core pluralistic principles and their development

The concept of pluralism refers to the philosophical idea that there is no single truth. Core questions about how people should live their lives are always a matter for dialogue and debate – defining characteristics of being human include curiosity, creativity, imagination and reflexivity. A pluralistic stance is reflected in many aspects of social and political life, such as a commitment to democracy, equality and human rights; respect for those with different beliefs and lifestyles; and dialogue across faith communities.

Pluralistic therapy (Cooper and McLeod, 2011) is organised around ongoing engagement in shared decision making between the client and therapist. In facilitating such a process, a pluralistic therapist invites their client to engage in conversation and dialogue around their goals for therapy, how these goals can be broken down into achievable tasks, and the best methods or techniques that might be deployed to enable the accomplishment of these tasks. The client and therapist work together to develop a shared understanding that takes account of the ideas, values and assumptions of both participants. These activities are supported by regular review and monitoring of the extent to which the client and therapist are on the 'same page', or moving in the same direction. Pluralistic practice is informed by a moral and ethical position that highlights respect and openness to the uniqueness of the other person (McLeod, 2017).

In seeking to find the combination of ideas and methods that are most effective for each individual client, pluralistic therapy can be categorised as a form of **integrative therapy**. Historically, a number of contrasting styles of therapy integration have been proposed, such as theoretical integration, eclecticism, assimilative integration, and the common factors/contextual model (McLeod, 2019). Pluralistic therapy incorporates elements of these existing integrative approaches; for example, by drawing on different theories (theoretical integration) and deploying a wide repertoire of interventions (eclecticism). The pluralistic approach offers a distinctive form of therapy integration through its emphasis on the client as a contributor to decisions about the direction of therapy, and through its openness to embracing non-therapy methods for facilitating learning and change in the shape of

Integrative therapy
An approach that combines ideas and methods from different therapy theories.

cultural resources such as nature, spirituality and art (McLeod and Sundet, 2016).

From the point of view of the counsellor, working pluralistically requires a commitment to ongoing professional learning and development. For example, therapists who find personal meaning in person-centred or psychodynamic ideas and methods, or have received extensive training in these approaches, may be highly skilful in working relationally with clients and using immediate moment-by-moment processes to facilitate awareness and change. However, in order to work responsively and effectively with a client who believes that a more structured problem-solving programme of behaviour change is better for them, a relationally oriented therapist may decide that they need to learn about CBT. Conversely, a CBT therapist may be an expert in supporting behaviour change but may realise that their capacity to facilitate meaning making, personal growth and insight is somewhat limited. They may therefore decide to become more responsive to their clients by learning about how these therapeutic processes are handled in person-centred, psychodynamic and other relationally focused therapies. This does not mean that pluralistic therapists need to be experts in everything. The aim is to create a therapeutic palette, repertoire, toolkit or menu that is sufficiently wide to allow the practitioner to engage constructively with the needs of the particular client population with whom they work.

In terms of its relationship with single-theory approaches to therapy, such as person-centred, psychodynamic and CBT, a pluralistic orientation adopts a pragmatic stance that regards these approaches as assemblages of concepts and techniques that can be dismantled and used in new combinations (Polkinghorne, 1992). The therapist functions as a 'bricoleur' who uses whatever materials are at hand to work alongside their client to design and implement a satisfactory resolution to their problem (Bohart, 2015; Smedslund, 2012). So, if a client acknowledges difficulty putting their feelings and concerns into words, a therapist might make use of person-centred empathy skills. The client themselves may suggest that playing the therapist a recording of a particular piece of emotionally significant music might be a valuable way of conveying their inner feelings. At a later stage of therapy with the same person, the therapist might negotiate the use of in-session role play as a means of building skills in handling difficult social situations.

Pause for reflection

Think of a time in your own life when you were able to overcome a difficult personal issue. What ideas, activities and relationships did you find helpful or unhelpful?

2   The pluralistic understanding of mental health: the case of anxiety

A pluralistic approach to mental health is open to insights from a range of disciplines, including philosophy, sociology, social anthropology, neuroscience and the humanities. Pluralistic practitioners seek to combine different sources of knowledge in their work with clients: ethical, scientific, personal, cultural and practical (McLeod, 2017).

Anxiety is a mental health issue that troubles many people (Remes *et al.*, 2016). A pluralistic perspective on anxiety is as open as possible to different ways of making sense of this type of experience. Different patterns of anxiety are associated with, for example, particular social situations (e.g. being in crowded places), performance settings (e.g. exam anxiety), health concerns, and political issues (e.g. climate change anxiety). There are also different ways in which anxiety can be understood in theoretical terms. CBT theory views anxiety as a form of learnt fear response that is maintained through avoidance behaviour and rumination. Psychodynamic theory regards anxiety as a sign that threatening memories and emotions from repressed past events have been triggered. Person-centred theory looks at anxiety as a failure of personal growth. Existential philosophy understands anxiety as an inevitable aspect of life, and a reminder of the inevitability of death. Biological psychiatry posits that anxiety is a biochemical imbalance in the brain, shaped by genetic factors.

Each of these theories has generated different interventions for managing or eliminating anxiety (Glock, Hilsenroth and Curtis, 2018). In pluralistic therapy, the theories behind each therapeutic approach are not regarded as scientific 'truths'. Instead, they provide narrative structures that offer the individual alternative ways to make sense of how their problem developed, what it means, and how it might be alleviated (Hansen, 2006). Rather than responding to a client from only a single theoretical model, pluralistic therapists invite the person to consider how their problem might make sense through different theoretical 'lenses'. Alongside the professional theoretical knowledge available to the therapist, pluralistic practice involves bringing the common-sense assumptions and perspectives of the client into the decision-making process. The concept of **cultural resources** is central to a pluralistic way of working. It refers to the exploration of healing

Cultural resources
Any activity available in the everyday life of a client that has the potential to make a positive contribution to enabling them to overcome their emotional and psychological concerns.

practices and sources of support that are available within the cultural world of the client. The following Diversity box highlights some of the ways in which cultural dimensions of anxiety can be used to make sense of the experience of clients, and as sources of potentially helpful therapeutic activities.

Diversity: Cultural aspects of anxiety

Pluralistic therapy encompasses paying attention to how a client's difficulties are shaped by the social and cultural context within which they live. There is substantial evidence that therapy that is sensitive to the cultural identity, beliefs, 'indigenous' healing practices and culture of the service user or client is more effective (Hall *et al.*, 2016) and that approaches that do not take cultural beliefs into account may even be harmful (Wendt, Gone and Nagata, 2015). For example, hikikomori is a form of social anxiety, mainly found in young men, in which the person withdraws into their own home for long periods of time and has no interest in attending school, college or work. Although this pattern was first identified in Japan, it has increasingly been observed in other countries (Kato *et al.*, 2012). This particular form of anxiety may involve obsessive use of computer games and social media as a way of coping with stressful aspects of contemporary social life (such as unrewarding and competitive workplaces, changing norms around gender identity, and general hopelessness around the future of the human race). It is notable that these cultural themes initially emerged in Japan, a country marked by high rates of technological and environmental change, low marriage and birth rates, and work practices that call for significant personal sacrifice in the interests of the employer. Working therapeutically with hikikomori calls for a willingness on the part of the therapist to develop innovative ways of reaching out to such clients – ways that acknowledge these cultural realities.

Beyond specific 'culture-bound' syndromes such as hikikomori, cultural meanings are relevant in all forms of anxiety (Koydemir and Essau, 2018). For example, women experiencing perinatal mental health problems often describe crippling anxiety around the responsibility and challenge of caring for a helpless small baby

– worries that may be grounded in cultural images of the 'good mother' (Hollway, 2010).

For male clients suffering from hikikomori, or female clients struggling with the demands of being a mother, it can be helpful to develop a shared understanding of the cultural meaning of their anxieties. This kind of cultural awareness can also make it possible to identify cultural resources that have the potential to make a crucial contribution – alongside therapy – to the client's recovery.

Decision-space
Episodes in a therapy session where client and therapist share their ideas about how therapy should proceed, and explore options around how to take their work forward.

A pluralistic approach to anxiety involves creating a **decision-space** that allows the client's concerns to be viewed from different angles. This kind of 'pluralisation' of the problem can be helpful for people because the reason for entering therapy is that someone is 'stuck' – the ways of dealing with their problem that they have tried to implement on their own initiative have ceased being effective. Exploring different perspectives allows the client to see that there are other solutions and approaches that might be useful. These could include strategies that the individual has used at earlier points in their life, ideas and techniques suggested by the therapist on the basis of their knowledge of therapy theory and practice, or novel activities that emerge in the process of their work together. The process of exploring the client's perspective, by highlighting things that might be done to alleviate their current problems, both energises and instils hope in the client and conveys a sense that the therapist considers them to be a person of value whose knowledge and experience is worth listening to. The fictional case illustration of Nancy offers an example of this process.

Case illustration: Nancy's first pluralistic therapy session

Nancy decided to enter therapy because she felt tense, worried and anxious most of the time. She would constantly check whether she had some kind of illness or disease, to the point where her GP suggested that she should see a counsellor. She was terrified of most social situations and avoided meeting new people. She believed that her body was repulsive and assumed that anyone who looked at her would see her as fat and ugly. She had been to university and was a highly accomplished designer, but she found it impossible to cope with the social demands of spending time in an office. She was currently unemployed and in a cycle of isolation, depression and comfort eating.

At the start of therapy with a pluralistic practitioner, Nancy was invited to talk about her goals for therapy, what her day-to-day life was like, how her problems had developed, and the sources of meaning and support available to her. Between them, Nancy and her therapist used this information to construct a formulation by way of a timeline diagram. The process of creating this diagram triggered further memories for Nancy around significant events and turning points in her life that seemed to be linked to her current difficulties. Nancy and her therapist worked together, adding information as it became available and relevant.

Toward the end of the session, the therapist asked Nancy whether she was ready to explore how these ideas might lead to specific therapeutic tasks that they could pursue in subsequent weeks. Figure 12.1 offers a simplified version of Nancy's timeline. The circles and arrows were added by the therapist in the closing phase of the session; they suggest relationships between Nancy's life events and the difficulties she is currently experiencing, which might be worth focusing on in therapy.

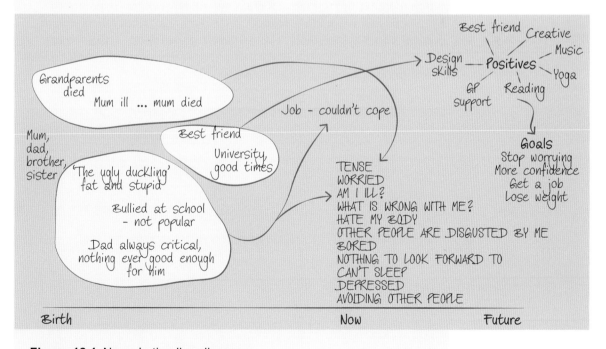

Figure 12.1 Nancy's timeline diagram

Activity 12.1: Understanding Nancy's problems from a pluralistic perspective

Allow about 10 minutes

A pluralistic approach encourages the practitioner to consider the relevance of different ways of 'knowing' in relation to a client's problems. Consider Nancy's difficulties from the following perspectives:

- Personal knowledge: What is your own emotional response to Nancy? How might you use these feelings to deepen your understanding of Nancy, and to shape your way of working with her?

- Theoretical knowledge: What theoretical perspectives might provide ways of making sense of Nancy's difficulties?

- Cultural knowledge: What are the cultural meanings that might be influencing Nancy's story?

- Practical knowledge: What kinds of therapy interventions might be appropriately applied to the different themes within Nancy's life?

Discussion

A perspective that might be useful is the therapist's appreciation of the cultural context of their client's life. One salient cultural aspect of Nancy's situation could be related to her feelings about her body and physical attractiveness, and her relationship with food. These issues tend to be grounded in powerful cultural assumptions about what it means to be a woman.

3 Therapeutic process and technique in pluralistic practice

A pluralistic approach does not involve simply adding person-centred, CBT and psychodynamic ideas and interventions together like ingredients in a salad bowl. What distinguishes pluralistic technique is an intentional, structured and purposeful process of shared decision making, in which the therapist and the client each draw on their relevant experience and knowledge to identify activities that the client might try out in order to move on in their life.

In the first session of therapy, or in pre-therapy intake or assessment meetings, a pluralistic therapist explains that there are many ways in which people can be helped, and that their aim is to work together to find the best way forward for the client. They also seek to convey the principle that, because the client is the one who knows whether therapy is helpful to them, it is important for them to give feedback to the therapist on whether their way of working is effective. The client is also told that, throughout therapy, it will be extremely useful to share any ideas about methods and activities that might be relevant. The therapist is also interested in getting a sense of their world and the potential resources that might be available within it. It is not assumed that these initial conversations will yield a complete or definitive understanding of the individual's ideas, goals and strengths. Instead, the aim is to initiate a thread of conversation and enquiry that will continue through later sessions.

A pluralistic therapist initiates conversations to clarify the goals of the client, how these goals can be broken down into step-by-step achievable tasks, and the methods that might be implemented to accomplish these tasks. For example, a client may identify the goal of reducing or eliminating the occurrence of panic attacks in their life. In exploring this issue with their therapist, it may emerge that tackling the problem might involve three key tasks: understanding how and why panic happens, being able to identify warning signs, and acquiring ways of stopping a panic attack developing once warning signs have been detected. After these tasks are agreed, it becomes possible to look at how to pursue them. For instance, understanding panic could be facilitated by reading a book or handout, watching a YouTube video, talking to a close friend who has overcome panic in their life, or listening to the therapist explain different theories. It is possible that the client would find all of these methods to be relevant. Similarly, the other main tasks, such as building a repertoire of strategies for 'stopping panic in its tracks' might be addressed in a variety of ways. The aim is to personalise and individualise the therapy process as much as possible by identifying the goals, tasks and change methods that make most sense to the individual and are effective for them.

Even though some of the elements of the therapy process, such as using mindfulness or a model of panic, may be drawn from standardised, evidence-based therapy protocols (e.g. Clark and Beck, 2011), these elements are selected and adapted according to the needs of the individual. In addition, pluralistic therapy is open to the inclusion of ideas and activities that are not derived from standard models or protocols, but rather are suggested by the client, improvised during sessions, or involve the use of cultural resources.

Collaborative case formulation

A specific, planned therapy event in which the client and therapist develop a shared understanding of how the client's difficulties developed, and create an action plan for how they might be addressed.

A key moment in pluralistic therapy is the process of **collaborative case formulation**, in which the client and the therapist allocate time to explicitly building a shared understanding of the individual's difficulties and goals, along with an action plan. While there are many ways of approaching this aspect of the work, as in the case illustration of Nancy, a pluralistic therapist would typically invite the person to sit alongside them to co-construct a timeline diagram on a large sheet of paper. The advantage of this technique, in contrast to only talking, is that visual representation allows the client to see patterns, causal connections and choice-points within the overall complexity and messiness of their life. The experience of sitting side by side and working together to create a diagram is a tangible way of emphasising that therapy involves sharing ideas from both sides. For some clients, it may be easier to talk about embarrassing or emotionally painful experiences when sitting alongside the therapist, rather than face to face. The production of a tangible document makes it possible to refer back to that piece of paper and, if necessary, change or alter it as new information or connections come to light. The client may also want to take a picture of the diagram or take it home with them so that they can reflect on it in their own time. Although pluralistic case formulation is informed by theory and research into case formulation and case conceptualisation within CBT and other therapy approaches, it comprises a more collaborative, theoretically integrative and creative version of such practices (McLeod and McLeod, 2016).

As therapy proceeds, a pluralistic approach makes use of strategies for ensuring that the collaboration remains in alignment with shared understanding and plans. One way of maintaining alignment is to agree an agenda at the start of each session. Another strategy is the use of **metacommunication**, which involves pausing the ongoing flow of therapeutic conversation and inviting reflection on the intentions and covert reactions of each participant. For example, a therapist might make a statement that invites the client to share their thoughts and feelings, such as:

> I was aware that you were talking about that awful panic attack you had yesterday, and then you seemed to change the topic and began to tell me about being at the football game. I was wondering what was behind that shift. Is there a connection between these two things, that I haven't grasped, or is something else happening?

Alternatively, they might offer a response that clarifies their own personal thoughts and feelings:

> I just wanted to say that I felt really moved when you talked about what happened yesterday – I felt close to you and it really helped me to understand what these awful, terrifying episodes are like for you. I know it's hard for you to talk about these experiences, but from my point of view they really make a big contribution to what we are trying to achieve together. But, what do you think?

Metacommunication
Moments in therapy where the ongoing flow of client–therapist conversation is paused, to allow discussion of whether what is happening is helpful.

A further strategy for maintaining alignment is to invite the client to submit feedback at the end of sessions. Such measures typically invite the client to rate the intensity or frequency of their symptoms, the degree to which therapy goals have been accomplished, and their views about the therapist. From a pluralistic perspective, these scales function as 'conversational tools' (Sundet, 2009): they provide an opportunity and scaffolding for discussions about whether the client feels that therapy is helping them, and whether a change of direction might be necessary.

Another characteristic of pluralistic therapy is that sessions are 'punctuated'. Agreed blocks of time are allocated to specific tasks, and to reviewing progress on these tasks. A session may focus on just one task or area, or on a series of tasks. This makes it easier to combine ideas and techniques from different therapy approaches or sources. For example, a behavioural strategy of gradual exposure to anxiety-eliciting situations (systematic desensitisation) is conceptually and practically very different from a psychodynamic strategy of using dream analysis to explore the deeper personal meaning of anxiety or panic. In pluralistic therapy, there is no expectation that it is necessary to develop a theory of how these quite different activities might fit together: if the individual finds them helpful, that is sufficient. For most service users, pluralistic therapy involves pursuing several tasks in parallel: exposure-based homework, reflecting on dreams, reading a self-help book and becoming more aware of emotions. In any one session, a particular task may be more salient, while others remain in the background. The aim is to keep the individual actively involved in their own process of learning and change, in a way that accepts that important aspects of this process can take place largely outside of sessions. Breaking down therapy into different tasks can also make it likely that at least one task will be resolved fairly quickly and easily. The experience of an 'early gain' can buttress the service-user's motivation and belief in therapy, which may be crucial when later stages of therapy involve tasks where the client may feel uncooperative.

Collaborative decision making in pluralistic therapy also encompasses practical arrangements. For example, a person may start off by attending therapy weekly, then at a later point shift to monthly meetings that are used as a way of maintaining gains and avoiding relapse. Alternatively, a service user may start with weekly one-hour sessions then negotiate either daily or three-hour sessions if they encounter emotionally disruptive personal memories or are in a state of crisis. Other practical arrangements that may be discussed include the participation of family members in sessions, and the concurrent use of other forms of help such as psychiatric care, group therapy, self-help groups and spiritual retreats. At the end of therapy, there may be collaboration around what needs to be done and said to finish things off and how much time is needed for this.

Activity 12.2: Using cultural resources

Allow about 5 minutes

An important aspect of pluralistic therapy is that, as well as drawing on ideas and methods from therapy theory and research, it acknowledges the potential value of everyday activities that may be helpful for the client (cultural resources).

Identify a cultural resource that you use in your own life to help you deal with anxiety. Think about the following questions:

1   How does this resource work?
2   In what ways does this activity function to reduce or prevent anxiety?
3   What kind of support might you need in order to make better use of this resource at times of stress?

Reflect on your responses to these questions in terms of what they suggest about the cultural resources that might be available to Nancy, and how her therapist might work with her to use these resources to overcome her anxiety.

For some people, the invitation to share their ideas and preferences is experienced as liberating and energising and is highly welcomed. Other people, however, do not want to be involved in making choices (Ogden, Daniells and Barnett, 2008). Instead, they expect and want their therapist to know what is best and to take care of them. There are many reasons why people may want their therapist to take the lead, such as cultural norms, lack of confidence in their own knowledge and opinions, previous experiences of opening up and then being betrayed, or merely a sense that time is short so they just want to get on with it. Valuable ideas around how to facilitate shared decision making can be found in the work of researchers in the field of healthcare (Stiggelbout, Pieterse and De Haes, 2015).

The development of a strong client–therapist collaborative relationship is a central aspect of pluralistic practice. While pluralistic therapists make use of the relationship perspectives discussed in Chapter 7, there is a greater emphasis on the idea that relationships are cemented through doing things together. A pluralistic approach also recognises that clients may have preferences around different types of relational connectedness that are most helpful for them at different times. For example, at a point of great vulnerability a client may need their therapist to offer caring presence, whereas at a phase of actively pursuing new life strategies they may be looking for someone who will challenge them.

Pluralistic therapy is intended to be helpful for people in two main ways. First, and most importantly, it aims to enable the client to find and engage with whatever ideas and activities are necessary to make it possible for them to attain their goals for therapy and move forward in their lives. A secondary aim is to do this in a way that allows the individual to develop a realistic sense of what works for them and what to do when difficulties emerge in the future, and to learn generic skills and develop awareness in respect of how to work together with other people to accomplish tasks. The ways in which these aims may be achieved can be illustrated by continuing the case of Nancy.

Case illustration: Nancy makes progress

During the first two sessions of therapy, Nancy identified her main goals for therapy as 'controlling and reducing how much I worry about everything', 'being more confident in social situations', 'getting a job' and 'losing weight'.

Based on their discussions during the creation of the timeline, Nancy generated a task list that consisted of:

- understanding how and why negative thoughts happened

- observing and analysing what these thoughts were, when they occurred and what they did to her

- learning and applying skills to reduce these thoughts.

Nancy avidly read information about CBT on the internet and in self-help books, and completed thought records. Nancy and her therapist worked together to devise behavioural homework experiments to see what happened when her new coping skills were applied in real-life situations. Nancy implemented, on the basis of her own personal experience, a yoga breathing exercise that helped her to remain grounded and in the moment. Alongside these activities, she re-established contact with a school and university friend 'who I know cares about me'.

In terms of both Nancy's own self-observation and her feedback on anxiety symptom measures, completed at the end of every session, by the end of session six her anxiety had reduced significantly. She described herself as being much more in control of her life. In the week leading up to session eight, she started to apply for jobs and signed up for an equine therapy programme. She announced: 'It's now time to talk about Mum. I have never really talked to anyone about what it was like to see her die – it's the main thing that I now need to do in therapy, so that I can start to look forward rather than being stuck in the past.'

Pause for reflection

What do you think Nancy's therapist might be thinking in terms of ending the therapy? What might the ending achieve, in relation to Nancy's goals, and how might the decision be made together?

4   The efficacy and scope of the pluralistic approach

Considerable research evidence exists to support the value of constituent elements of pluralistic therapy, such as responsiveness to client preferences (Swift *et al.*, 2019), use of feedback measures (Lambert, Whipple and Kleinstäuber, 2018; Mackrill and Sørensen, 2019), and client–therapist collaboration around tasks and goals (Tryon, Birch and Verkuilen, 2019). A study of pluralistic therapy for depression found that client outcomes were equivalent in effectiveness to rates in established forms of therapy such as CBT (Cooper *et al.*, 2015). Furthermore, clients reported that the distinctively collaborative pluralistic components of their therapy had been helpful for them (Antoniou *et al.*, 2017).

In pluralistic therapy, research is integrated into practice: information from process and outcome measures is used to inform ongoing collaborative reviews of what works for clients. This has also led to research into the design of client-friendly feedback measures, such as the therapy preference form (Bowens and Cooper, 2012) and the Cooper-Norcross Inventory of Preferences (Cooper and Norcross, 2016).

Pluralistic practice endeavours to personalise or tailor therapy to the needs and preferences of each client. This means that case study research – which is able to capture the complexity of the unfolding process of therapy within individual cases – represents a particularly relevant source of evidence (McLeod, 2013). A further valuable source of research-based insight comprises qualitative studies of client experiences of therapy and recovery that explore multiple change processes and activities used by individuals to overcome psychological problems.

Methodology: Pluralism in researching pluralistic therapy

Unlike long-established therapy approaches, such as psychodynamic and person-centred, pluralistic therapy was developed at a time when an extensive and methodologically diverse counselling and psychotherapy research literature already existed. This has meant that the basic principles of pluralistic therapy have been informed by different types of research evidence (McLeod, 2016).

The following studies provide examples of the types of evidence that can be used to shape a pluralistic response to anxiety:

- Timulak *et al.* (2017) carried out a mixed-methods (i.e. questionnaires and interviews) study of therapy for generalised anxiety disorder that evaluated techniques used by some pluralistic practitioners.

- Hjeltnes *et al.* (2015) conducted a study that used qualitative interviews to gain a deeper understanding of the client experience of therapy for anxiety issues.

- Smith *et al.* (2014) carried out a research-based case study of the process of change for a client with health anxiety.

- Campbell (2018) provided an intensive first-person account of the experience of anxiety.

- Woodgate, Zurba and Tennent (2017) analysed pictures of everyday situations that represented the experiences of young people living with anxiety.

Conclusion

This chapter has presented pluralistic therapy as a flexible and collaborative approach to enabling clients to identify and make use of their own strengths and resources. By accessing a wide array of ideas, methods and research evidence, pluralistic therapy provides a structure within which therapists can maximise their capacity to be helpful. Pluralistic practice is grounded in the values of inclusiveness and respect introduced by the humanistic approach (Chapter 11) and a commitment to client–therapist collaboration and shared decision making as exhibited, for example, in case formulation (Chapter 8). The philosophical basis of a pluralistic stance functions as a 'meta-theoretical' resource that opens up possibilities for practitioners to deepen their understanding of therapy through critical reflection. As an approach to therapy, pluralistic practice is defined in terms of a set of broad principles, rather than specific procedures, which encourages high levels of openness to innovation and creativity in both clients and practitioners.

Further reading

- This resource provides an analysis of how clients experience the goal-focused approach adopted in pluralistic therapy:
Di Malta, G., Oddli, H.W. and Cooper, M. (2019) 'From intention to action: a mixed methods study of clients' experiences of goal-oriented practices', *Journal of Clinical Psychology*, 75(10), pp. 1770–1789.

- This text focuses on similarities and differences between pluralistic and other models of therapy:

  McLeod, J. (2017) *Pluralistic therapy: distinctive features*. London and New York: Routledge.

- Chapter 21 of this resource provides an overview of the main ideas and techniques of a pluralistic approach:

  McLeod, J. (2019) *An introduction to counselling and psychotherapy: theory, research and practice*. 6th edn. London: Open University Press and McGraw-Hill Education.

References

Antoniou, P., Cooper, M., Tempier, A. and Holliday, C. (2017) 'Helpful aspects of pluralistic therapy for depression', *Counselling & Psychotherapy Research*, 17(2), pp. 137–147.

Bohart, A.C. (2015) 'From there and back again', *Journal of Clinical Psychology*, 71(11), pp. 1060–1069.

Bohart, A.C. and Tallman, K. (1996) 'The active client: therapy as self-help', *Journal of Humanistic Psychology*, 36(3), pp. 7–30.

Bowens, M. and Cooper, M. (2012) 'Development of a client feedback tool: a qualitative study of therapists' experiences of using the Therapy Personalisation Forms', *European Journal of Psychotherapy & Counselling*, 14(1), pp. 47–62.

Campbell, E. (2018) 'Reconstructing my identity: an autoethnographic exploration of depression and anxiety in academia', *Journal of Organizational Ethnography*, 7(3), pp. 235–246.

Clark, D.A. and Beck, A.T. (2011) *Cognitive therapy of anxiety disorders: science and practice*. New York: The Guilford Press.

Cooper, M. and McLeod, J. (2011) *Pluralistic counselling and psychotherapy*. London: SAGE.

Cooper, M. and Norcross, J.C. (2016) 'A brief, multidimensional measure of clients' therapy preferences: the Cooper-Norcross Inventory of Preferences (C-NIP)', *International Journal of Clinical and Health Psychology*, 16(1), pp. 87–98.

Cooper, M., Wild, C., van Rijn, B., Ward, T., McLeod, J., Cassar, S., Antoniou, P., Michael, C., Michalitsi, M. and Sreenath, S. (2015) 'Pluralistic therapy for depression: acceptability, outcomes and helpful aspects in a multisite study', *Counselling Psychology Review*, 30(1), pp. 6–20.

Glock, G., Hilsenroth, M. and Curtis, R. (2018) 'Therapeutic interventions patients with anxiety problems find most helpful: a case for integration?', *Journal of Psychotherapy Integration*, 28(2), pp. 233–241.

Hall, G.C.N., Ibaraki, A.Y., Huang, E.R., Marti, C.N. and Stice, E. (2016) 'A meta-analysis of cultural adaptations of psychological interventions', *Behavior Therapy*, 47(6), pp. 993–1014.

Hansen, J. (2006) 'Counseling theories within a postmodernist epistemology: new roles for theories in counseling practice', *Journal of Counseling & Development*, 84(3), pp. 291–297.

Hjeltnes, A., Binder, P.E., Moltu, C. and Dundas, I. (2015) 'Facing the fear of failure: an explorative qualitative study of client experiences in a mindfulness-based stress reduction program for university students with academic evaluation anxiety', *International Journal of Qualitative Studies on Health and Well-being*, 10, p. 27990.

Hollway, W. (2010) 'Conflict in the transitions to becoming a mother: a psycho-social approach', *Psychoanalysis, Culture & Society*, 15(2), pp. 136–155.

Kato, T.A. *et al.* (2012) 'Does the "*hikikomori*" syndrome of social withdrawal exist outside Japan? A preliminary international investigation', *Social Psychiatry and Psychiatric Epidemiology*, 47(7), pp. 1061–1075.

Koydemir, S. and Essau, C.A. (2018) 'Anxiety and anxiety disorders in young people: a cross-cultural perspective', in Hodes, M., Gau, S.S. and de Vries, P.J. (eds.) *Understanding uniqueness and diversity in child and adolescent mental health*. London: Academic Press, pp. 115–134.

Lambert, M.J., Whipple, J.L. and Kleinstäuber, M. (2018) 'Collecting and delivering progress feedback: a meta-analysis of routine outcome monitoring', *Psychotherapy*, 55(4), pp. 520–537.

Mackrill, T. and Sørensen, K.M. (2019) 'Implementing routine outcome measurement in psychosocial interventions – a systematic review', *European Journal of Social Work*. doi:10.1080/13691457.2019.1602029.

McLeod, J. (2013) 'Process and outcome in pluralistic transactional analysis counselling for long-term health conditions: a case series', *Counselling & Psychotherapy Research*, 13(1), pp. 32–43.

McLeod, J. (2016) *Using research in counselling and psychotherapy*. London: SAGE.

McLeod, J. (2017) *Pluralistic therapy: distinctive features*. Abingdon: Routledge.

McLeod, J. (2019) *An introduction to counselling and psychotherapy: theory, research and practice*. 6th edn. London: Open University Press and McGraw-Hill Education.

McLeod, J. and McLeod, J. (2016) 'Assessment and formulation in pluralistic counselling and psychotherapy', in Cooper, M. and Dryden, W. (eds.) *The handbook of pluralistic counselling and psychotherapy*. London: SAGE, pp. 15–28.

McLeod, J. and Sundet, R. (2016) 'Integrative and eclectic approaches and pluralism', in Cooper, M. and Dryden, W. (eds.) *The handbook of pluralistic counselling and psychotherapy*. London: SAGE, pp. 158–170.

Ogden, J., Daniells, E. and Barnett, J. (2008) 'The value of choice: development of a new measurement tool', *British Journal of General Practice*, 58(554), pp. 614–618.

Polkinghorne, D.E. (1992) 'Postmodern epistemology of practice', in Kvale, S. (ed.) *Psychology and postmodernism*. London: SAGE, pp. 146–165.

Remes, O., Brayne, C., van der Linde, R. and Lafortune, L. (2016) 'A systematic review of reviews on the prevalence of anxiety disorders in adult populations', *Brain and Behavior*, 6(7). doi: 10.1002/brb3.497.

Smedslund, J. (2012) 'The bricoleur model of psychological practice', *Theory & Psychology*, 22(5), pp. 643–657.

Smith, K., Shoemark, A., McLeod, J. and McLeod, J. (2014) 'Moving on: a case analysis of process and outcome in person-centred psychotherapy for health anxiety', *Person-Centered & Experiential Psychotherapies*, 13(2), pp. 111–127.

Stiggelbout, A.M., Pieterse, A.H. and De Haes, J.C. (2015) 'Shared decision making: concepts, evidence, and practice', *Patient Education and Counseling*, 98 (10), pp. 1172–1179.

Sundet, R. (2009) 'Therapeutic collaboration and formalized feedback: using perspectives from Vygotsky and Bakhtin to shed light on practices in a family therapy unit', *Clinical Child Psychology and Psychiatry*, 15(1), pp. 81–95.

Swift, J.K., Callahan, J.L., Cooper, M. and Parkin, S.R. (2019) 'Preferences', in Norcross, J.C. and Wampold, B.E. (eds.) *Psychotherapy relationships that work. Volume 2: evidence-based therapist responsiveness.* 3rd edn. New York: Oxford University Press.

Timulak, L., McElvaney, J., Keogh, D., Martin, E., Clare, P., Chepukova, E. and Greenberg, L.S. (2017) 'Emotion-focused therapy for generalized anxiety disorder: an exploratory study', *Psychotherapy*, 54(4), pp. 361–366.

Tryon, G.S., Birch, S.E. and Verkuilen, J. (2019) 'Goal consensus and collaboration', in Norcross, J.C. and Lambert, M.J. (eds.) *Psychotherapy relationships that work. Volume 1: evidence-based therapist contributions.* 3rd edn. New York: Oxford University Press, pp. 167–204.

Villaggi, B., Provencher, H., Coulombe, S., Meunier, S., Radziszewski, S., Hudon, C., Roberge, P., Provencher, M. and Houle, J. (2015) 'Self-management strategies in recovery from mood and anxiety disorders', *Global Qualitative Nursing Research*, 2. doi:10.1177/2333393615606092.

Wendt, D.C., Gone, J.P. and Nagata, D.K. (2015) 'Potentially harmful therapy and multicultural counseling: bridging two disciplinary discourses', *The Counseling Psychologist*, 43(3), pp. 334–358.

Woodgate, R.L., Zurba, M. and Tennent, P. (2017) 'A day in the life of a young person with anxiety: arts-based boundary objects used to communicate the results of health research', *Forum: Qualitative Social Research*, 18(3), p. 17.

Part 4

Counselling in practice

Chapter 13
The therapeutic relationship

Daragh Keogh and Ladislav Timulak

Contents

Introduction

'Reaching out' by Carly Merchant

Counselling and psychotherapy are fundamentally relational processes. Irrespective of the particular therapeutic model, whether therapy consists of a single appointment or twice-weekly appointments over many years, and whether therapy takes the form of individual, family or group work, therapy essentially involves a meeting of different individuals. Therapy happens in the context of this relational meeting, and the collaborative work of therapy is facilitated or impeded by the nature and quality of that relationship. Across almost all schools of therapy, the therapeutic relationship is thus seen as critical to successful therapeutic outcomes. In some schools, particularly those within the psychodynamic and humanistic traditions, the role of the therapeutic relationship is typically centre stage. However, as this chapter will show, even approaches that do not conventionally emphasise the central role of the relationship (e.g. cognitive behavioural therapy, or CBT) still recognise the critical importance of relational factors.

This chapter will look at what the research literature tells us about the role of the therapeutic relationship, summarising key findings and connecting these findings with implications for practice. For example, theoretical perspectives on the importance of the therapeutic relationship are supported by extensive research, with ratings of the therapeutic alliance in particular appearing to be a significant predictor of positive therapy outcomes (Flückiger *et al.*, 2018). The chapter will then briefly turn to how the relationship is conceptualised and used in the main schools of therapy, exploring differences and commonalities across these different approaches. The chapter will draw on emotion-focused therapy as a case example to illustrate how the therapeutic relationship is understood in this model. Along the way, we hope to prompt your own reflections on the nature of the therapeutic relationship, inviting you to imagine yourself as either the therapist or the client.

This chapter aims to:

- introduce the concept of the therapeutic relationship, exploring how this relationship differs from (but in some respects may also be similar to) relationships outside the context of therapy

- summarise key research findings regarding the therapeutic relationship (e.g. the finding that positive reports of the therapeutic relationship are predictive of positive therapy outcomes)

- provide an overview of the various ways in which different forms of therapy conceptualise and use the therapeutic relationship

- give an example of the therapeutic relationship within one particular theoretical model: emotion-focused therapy.

1   Characterising the therapeutic relationship

As mentioned above, therapy is a relational process. In many ways, the therapeutic relationship is similar to relationships in the world outside of therapy. For example, many of the qualities that clients value in the therapeutic relationship are the same qualities they value in personal relationships. This should not be that surprising; after all, how likely are you to confide in a therapist you do not trust, or feel supported by a therapist you believe does not like you? In other ways, however, the therapeutic relationship is very different from relationships outside of therapy. By definition, it is a professional relationship: typically, the therapist is paid to provide a service, and while clients are invited to share aspects of their inner world with their therapist, therapists are ethically required to be much more circumspect regarding what they share with their clients. This chapter will look at key research findings regarding the therapeutic relationship, and at the different ways that different theoretical approaches conceive of and utilise the therapeutic relationship. First though, Activity 13.1 encourages reflection on some of the ways the therapeutic relationship may be different from or similar to relationships in the wider world.

The contrasting fictional case illustrations below are suggestive of how the therapeutic relationship can be compared to relationships we have in everyday life.

Case illustrations: Benjamin, Olivia, Isabella and Mohammed experience therapy

Benjamin

Benjamin was directed to see the school counsellor as a consequence of being argumentative, oppositional and disruptive in class. He was surprised to discover that the counsellor was good humoured, easy to talk to and eager to understand what he had to say. He found it helpful to talk about the upsetting things that were going on at home, and he began to look forward to the weekly counselling appointments.

Olivia

Olivia found her initial meetings with her therapist highly anxiety-provoking. In addition to finding it difficult to figure out what to talk about, she found herself increasingly wondering if her therapist was thinking critically of her. Her increased anxiety led to her discontinuing therapy.

Isabella

Isabella sought therapy to explore her painful and confusing feelings regarding gender identity. She was initially apprehensive of confiding in her therapist, as the therapist's attire indicated they might come from the same cultural background. However, she quickly became comfortable with her therapist and together they began to explore Isabella's feelings about gender.

Mohammed

Mohammed experienced therapy as very helpful and he greatly valued his relationship with his therapist. However, he was embarrassed when his therapist stopped to say hello in the local supermarket – he did not want to tell his friends that this person was his therapist or explain to them why he was in therapy.

Activity 13.1: Comparing the therapeutic relationship to other types of relationship

Allow about 20 minutes

Having read the vignettes above, take some time to reflect on them. Make notes on how you imagine each client experienced the therapeutic relationship. Where the relationship was experienced positively or negatively, consider how this might be similar to or different from the experiences we regard as positive or negative in our everyday relationships.

Discussion

In Benjamin's case, it might be helpful to contrast his experience of the counsellor with how you imagine he more typically experiences the adults in his life. What aspects of the counsellor's manner surprised Benjamin? What impact did this have on his ability to attend therapy and to engage in the work of therapy? We all need to feel listened to and understood. In this respect, there is nothing especially distinct about these aspects of the therapeutic relationship; however, how powerful might it be to feel listened to and understood if this is something one does not experience in everyday life? We might think of these relationship factors as a product of the therapeutic space (e.g. the therapist does not have to deal with issues of classroom discipline), but equally, we can consider them a product of the individual therapist (e.g. another therapist might not have connected with Benjamin or earned his trust in the same way).

---

2 Key factors contributing to the therapeutic relationship

For over a century, extensive research has been carried out in the area of the therapeutic relationship (see the Methodology box for a description of some of the research methods currently used to study the relationship). In 1999, the American Psychological Association's (APA) Division of Psychotherapy commissioned a task force to summarise and report on all the available evidence relating to the therapeutic relationship. The task force conducted a series of reviews and meta-analyses of the available research evidence and summarised its findings and recommendations in a 2001 special issue of the journal *Psychotherapy* (Norcross, 2001), and in the book, *Psychotherapy relationships that work* (Norcross, 2002). Subsequently, these publications have been superseded by the work of the second (Norcross, 2011) and, most recently, the third (Norcross and Lambert, 2018, 2019) interdivisional APA Task Force on Evidence-Based Relationships and Responsiveness.

Methodology: Investigating the nature of the therapeutic relationship

A wide variety of research methods have been used to study the therapeutic relationship. A brief summary of some of the most commonly used methods is provided here.

Qualitative research

Qualitative researchers have interviewed clients and therapists about their experiences of, and perspectives on, therapy. Many of these studies enquired specifically about the therapeutic relationship. Qualitative studies can be especially useful when relatively little is known about a particular topic. An example of such research is *Clients' perception of the therapeutic alliance: a qualitative analysis* (Bachelor, 1995). In this study, the author qualitatively analysed descriptive accounts of therapy from 34 clients, finding that three relatively distinct types of perceived alliance were reported by clients (nurturing, insight-oriented or collaborative).

Process–outcome research

Many measures have been developed to quantify aspects of the therapeutic relationship. Process–outcome research studies have investigated the relationship between scores on these measures of the relationship (i.e. process) and how well clients do in therapy (i.e. **outcomes**). While outcome research can show whether or not therapy is effective, process–outcome research can help to determine what it is about therapy that is specifically helpful. An example of process–outcome research is 'The role of the therapeutic alliance in psychotherapy and pharmacological outcome: findings in the NIMH Treatment of Depression Collaborative Research Program' (Krupnick *et al.*, 2006). This study was part of a wider randomised controlled trial investigating differences between two different psychotherapies, medication and a placebo in the treatment of depression. In the study, Krupnick and colleagues were able to demonstrate that observer-based ratings of the therapeutic alliance (based on an analysis of video recordings of sessions) were correlated with positive outcomes, irrespective of which of the four treatment conditions participants were in.

Outcome
A result or effect of psychotherapy. It can be assessed using client reports of well-being or symptom-specific scores (measured before and after therapy), or using objective data such as body mass index in eating disorders or the presence/absence of substances in cases of substance addiction.

Meta-analysis

As outlined in Chapter 7, meta-analytic studies combine the findings from all available studies in a particular area of interest (e.g. all studies exploring the relationship between therapy outcomes and client experiences of empathy) in an endeavour to summarise the evidence pertaining to the relevant research question. While some of the detail gets lost when multiple studies are aggregated, meta-analyses provide the strongest evidence of the importance of particular phenomena. A noteworthy example in relation to the therapeutic relationship is 'The alliance in adult psychotherapy: a meta-analytic synthesis' (Flückiger *et al.*, 2018). This study analysed findings from 295 independent studies published between 1978 and 2017 covering more than 30,000 clients of face-to-face and internet-based psychotherapy. Some findings and recommendations from the study are discussed in Section 2.1.

In their presentation of the findings of the interdivisional APA Task Force on Evidence-Based Relationships and Responsiveness, Norcross and Lambert (2018, 2019) concluded that decades of clinical experience and research evidence conclusively show that the therapeutic relationship considerably and consistently contributes to therapy outcomes *independently* of the mode of treatment. They also argued that the conventional distinction between treatment/intervention and the therapeutic relationship is meaningless, proposing instead that treatment methods are inherently relational acts. In other words, rather than being distinct from the therapeutic relationship, any particular intervention is instead inherently an expression of the relationship. The relationship does not exist in isolation from the therapist's actions – anything the therapist does is impacted by the relational manner in which it is performed.

Norcross and Lambert emphasised the critical importance of being guided – not just by the empirical evidence regarding treatments that work but also by the evidence regarding *relationships* that work.

This section will look at research findings related to contributions to the therapeutic relationship made by two specific factors (the alliance and empathy), and the effect on outcomes. It will also summarise other findings of the APA task force and, finally, client perspectives on the therapeutic relationship.

2.1   The therapeutic alliance

One of the most researched concepts in psychotherapy is that of the therapeutic alliance (see Chapter 10 for a reminder of the definition). In essence, conceptualisations of this alliance seek to define what it is that constitutes an *effective* working therapeutic relationship. While there have been many different theoretical conceptualisations of the alliance, the best known is Bordin's (1979) concept of the 'working alliance'.

Bordin proposed that the working alliance is comprised of three elements:

- agreement between the client and the therapist on the goals of therapy

- agreement between the client and the therapist on the tasks of therapy (i.e. the means by which the goals can be achieved)

- the personal bond (characterised by reciprocated positive feelings such as trust and liking) between the client and the therapist.

In part because of its **pan-theoretical** utility (that is, the concept can be applied to any theoretical approach), the concept of the alliance has been widely studied and a variety of methods have been developed to measure it. Measures of the alliance are typically completed by therapists and/or clients, but they can also be completed by independent observers (e.g. by viewing video recordings of therapy sessions).

Pan-theoretical
Refers to any concept that relates to all psychotherapy theories/traditions rather than to any specific mode of therapy.

Despite the wide variety of measures and the varying sources of data, studies have repeatedly reported high correlations between positive reports of the therapeutic alliance and positive outcomes, with some studies indicating that client reports of the alliance may be an especially strong predictor (Martin, Garske and Davies, 2000; Horvath et al., 2011). At the time of writing, the most recent meta-analysis (Flückiger et al., 2018) reported that the correlation between alliance and outcomes was found irrespective of who reported on the alliance (e.g. client, therapist or observer), the measure used, the treatment approach adopted (e.g. person-centred or CBT), the client characteristics and the country in which the study was conducted. Results from a separate meta-analysis (Tryon, Birch and Verkuilen, 2018) provided further evidence to suggest that, when therapists and clients agree on psychotherapy goals and actively collaborate together, clients tend to have more positive treatment outcomes. (The importance of collaboration and goal agreement underpins formulation, which was introduced in Chapter 8, and is also central to the pluralistic approach, covered in Chapter 12.)

Based on their findings, Flückiger *et al.* recommended a number of practices likely to strengthen the therapeutic alliance and thus therapy outcomes. These recommendations included:

- working on building and maintaining the alliance over the course of therapy

- attending to body language and other forms of nonverbal communication

- negotiating agreement on treatment goals and tasks early in therapy

- responding to the client's motivation to change and capabilities early in therapy

- regularly assessing the client's perspective on the quality of the alliance

- directly and immediately addressing ruptures in the alliance.

2.2   The importance of empathy

The task force also reported on the important role of empathy, which was associated with, and predictive of, positive client outcomes (Elliott *et al.*, 2018). For example, empathy was predictive of treatment outcomes across therapeutic approaches, including those approaches that did not conventionally emphasise the role of empathy (e.g. CBT);

across treatment formats (e.g. individual or group treatments); and across levels of severity.

Interestingly, Elliott *et al.* (2018) note that it is the rating of perceived empathy (where the client perceives the therapist as empathic) that is predictive of outcomes, not therapist empathic accuracy per se. In other words, it is not sufficient for the therapist to empathise with and understand the client; rather, what is critical is for the client to feel this understanding. It is important, therefore, that therapists make efforts to understand their clients' experiences and to demonstrate this understanding through responses (verbal and nonverbal) that can be perceived by the client. Furthermore, Elliott *et al.* note that empathy involves attending not just to the client's words but also to their overall goals and to moment-to-moment experiences, including aspects of those experiences that are implicit (not yet verbally articulated).

2.3 Other factors contributing to productive therapeutic relationships

In addition to the therapeutic alliance and empathy, the task force identified several other factors that contribute to productive therapeutic relationships and thus to positive therapy outcomes for clients. These included the therapist's ability to:

- assess and enhance the client's early perceptions of the credibility of therapy (e.g. whether the therapy makes sense for the client; Constantino *et al.*, 2018)

- show positive regard towards the client, and congruence (genuineness) (Farber, Suzuki and Lynch, 2018; Kolden *et al.*, 2018)

- perceive potential alliance ruptures and repair any that arise (Eubanks, Muran and Safran, 2018)

- successfully manage any negative responses to their clients (Hayes *et al.*, 2018)

- productively and appropriately use immediacy (respond to what is happening in the here and now between the therapist and the client) and self-disclosure (Hill, Knox and Pinto-Coelho, 2018). While therapist self-disclosure is not commonplace, in some contexts it can be both appropriate and helpful; for example, the disclosure that the therapist can themselves feel vulnerable may help a vulnerable client feel less abnormal and more like others.

2.4   Client perspectives on the therapeutic relationship

Research into the therapeutic relationship has been criticised for typically using measures (e.g. the Working Alliance Inventory; Horvath and Greenberg, 1986) that are based on theoretical conceptualisations of the relationship (e.g. Bordin's working alliance) that may or may not fit with clients' own experiences and perspectives. What if clients don't experience the therapeutic relationship the same way as theorists conceptualise it? For example, what if they don't consider agreement on goals or tasks as core aspects of a positive therapeutic relationship? In response, a number of qualitative (and mixed-methods) studies have sought to investigate the therapeutic relationship as experienced by clients. One such study (Bachelor, 1995), based on a qualitative analysis of 66 descriptive accounts obtained from 34 clients, found that clients perceived their therapeutic alliance to be one of three distinct types: nurturant (46 per cent), insight-oriented (39 per cent) or collaborative (15 per cent).

In a different study, Bedi, Davis and Williams (2005) interviewed 40 participants, asking them to describe behaviours and verbalisations they thought had contributed to a positive therapeutic alliance. Results indicated that clients predominantly placed the responsibility for forming and strengthening the alliance on the therapist. They also revealed that many of the factors understood by the clients to be involved in alliance formation were basic; they included eye contact, smiling, warm and personalised greetings and farewells, paraphrasing, identifying client feelings, encouraging the client and referring to material from previous sessions. The authors observed that these key factors were so simple that their importance could easily be underestimated by therapists.

In a later study, Duff and Bedi (2010) reported that three therapist behaviours (making encouraging statements, making positive comments about the client and greeting the client with a smile) were found to account for 62 per cent of the variance in therapeutic alliance scores (which means that a big part of the differences in the scores can be predicted by these therapist behaviours). The authors concluded that 'seemingly small, strengths-fostering counsellor micro-behaviours can play a key role in strengthening therapeutic alliances' (p. 91).

Activity 13.2: Nonverbal communication

Allow about 10 minutes

Imagine you are a client attending your first session with a therapist.

1   Imagine an ideal therapist – someone who invites closeness, trust and collaboration. What facial expressions, tone of voice and aspects of body language do you think might be displayed by this ideal therapist?

2   Now imagine a therapist who does not invite closeness, trust or collaboration. Again, what facial expressions, tone of voice and aspects of body language do you feel might be displayed by such a therapist?

Discussion

This activity invited you to consider nonverbal communication and how it can make a person feel. Across the two examples, what facial expressions, tone of voice and aspects of body language were most salient for you? How do you think you would react if you encountered these aspects in the imagined therapist? Can you recall times in your own life when you encountered someone whose manner embodied these aspects? They might have been a friend, a doctor, a family member or someone in a position of authority.

Consider discussing this exercise with a peer or a friend to explore similarities and differences in your experiences.

3   Ways of understanding the therapeutic relationship

The chapter now turns its attention to how the therapeutic relationship is conceptualised and used within different psychotherapeutic perspectives. As discussed elsewhere in this book (e.g. in Chapter 12), while counselling and psychotherapy were traditionally developed within distinct schools or traditions, there is an ever-increasing trend towards integrative, eclectic, common factors or pluralistic models. This section, however, discusses the therapeutic relationship as conceptualised in the three main psychotherapeutic perspectives: psychodynamic, cognitive behavioural and humanistic. These approaches share certain factors, but there are fundamental differences on both a conceptual and practical level. A wide variety of approaches also exists, even within these distinctly different perspectives (e.g. within the psychodynamic paradigm, Lacanian analysis and supportive–expressive short-term psychotherapy conceptualise and work with the therapeutic relationship in radically different ways). The conceptualisations of the relationship described here are therefore prototypical and somewhat simplistic, rather than ones that universally apply to all variations of any particular school of thought.

Pause for reflection

From what you have read in previous chapters on psychodynamic (Chapter 9), cognitive behavioural (Chapter 10) and humanistic (Chapter 11) approaches, how do you imagine these therapeutic traditions differ in the way they employ the therapeutic relationship?

3.1 Psychodynamic perspectives

As presented in Chapter 3, of the three main traditions of psychotherapy, the psychodynamic tradition is the oldest. More so than with other theoretical approaches, and perhaps because of its origins in the hospital or clinic, the psychodynamic orientation has historically tended to view the therapeutic relationship as a relationship between doctor and patient. (It should be noted again that this is a historical and simplistic perspective; many contemporary psychodynamic approaches do not retain this perspective of the client as patient.) The psychodynamic tradition can also be viewed as seeing the therapeutic relationship as one in which the therapist, in the role of knowledgeable expert, facilitates change in the client, primarily by promoting insight via skilled interpretations of the nature of the client's difficulties (see Chapter 9 for a reminder of the definition of interpretation). Additionally – and to a varying degree depending on the particular variant of psychodynamic therapy – the psychodynamic tradition also emphasises the potential that a validating and supportive therapeutic relationship has for offering a **corrective emotional experience** to the client.

While therapist interpretation of the nature of a client's difficulties is a core intervention within the psychodynamic tradition, therapist interpretations of the way transference and countertransference manifest within the therapeutic relationship itself is especially important to the psychodynamic way of working. As Chapter 9 outlined, transference refers to any feelings, thoughts or behaviours the client experiences about or displays towards the therapist that originate in the context of childhood relationships with significant others (rather than the therapist) and repeat within therapy through displacement. For example, a client may experience an older male therapist as dominating or authoritarian, not because the therapist is actually acting

Corrective emotional experience
The idea that the client's experience of the therapeutic relationship can be healing in and of itself, perhaps because the therapist relates to the client's vulnerability in a healthy or adaptive way that is different from how the client's vulnerability has typically been responded to prior to, or outside of, therapy.

in a domineering way, but because the client has a painful relationship with a dominating and authoritarian father and is therefore susceptible to projecting those characteristics on to older males in positions of authority. Conversely, countertransference refers to feelings, thoughts or behaviours that the therapist experiences about or displays towards the client. Countertransference may be counter-therapeutic if it is not reflected on; for example, because it originates from unresolved issues in the therapist's own life. It can also, however, be therapeutic because, as unconscious reactions to the client's unconscious mind, it may provide clues to understanding the client's unconscious drives, conflicts and defences (Hayes *et al.*, 2018).

The therapeutic relationship can, therefore, be considered central to a psychodynamic way of working. Metaphorically speaking, the relationship is a playing field on which the client's unconscious drives, conflicts and defences play out. The therapist draws on their clinical training and expertise to cultivate a relationship with the client within which such transference and countertransference can occur. The therapist interprets this transference and countertransference and shares these interpretations at appropriate points with the client, thereby bringing into awareness phenomena of which the client may have hitherto been unaware. This ultimately allows for problematic relational patterns to be changed, as a consequence both of insight and also of being worked through and transformed in the context of the therapeutic relationship itself (as outlined in the case illustration of Jamie in Chapter 9).

3.2   Cognitive behavioural perspectives

As a reaction to what were perceived as being the unscientific perspectives and tendencies of psychoanalysis, the originators of cognitive behavioural approaches endeavoured to develop psychotherapeutic models based on findings from experimental and academic psychology (as outlined in Chapter 10). This led them to focus on the idea of therapy as the delivery of evidence-based interventions by skilled clinicians. Traditionally, the cognitive behavioural paradigm also focused on developing specific models of therapy for treating specific medically defined disorders, such as major depressive disorder and generalised anxiety disorder. As such, the view of the therapeutic relationship as one between a patient and a scientifically informed practitioner can, to some degree, be seen as a continuation of the psychodynamic doctor–patient perspective. More generally, however, while the CBT therapist can be seen as an 'expert' (e.g. by delivering an intervention rooted in science and research), they are also conceptualised as a 'teacher' (e.g. by giving and reviewing homework), teaching skills that the client can apply on a day-to-day basis in order to overcome, work through or manage their difficulties. To some extent, the therapeutic relationship within the CBT paradigm can therefore also be seen as a teacher–student relationship.

While the CBT tradition does not conventionally foreground it, a productive therapeutic relationship is certainly considered important to therapy (Gilbert and Leahy, 2007). Simply put, a good therapeutic relationship facilitates the effective teaching of skills. The relationship is thus conceptualised in terms of the therapist skill of interpersonal effectiveness. For example, in the Cognitive Therapy Scale Revised, which is used to rate the extent to which CBT therapy is CBT adherent, interpersonal effectiveness is identified as a key skill: 'The patient is put at ease by the therapist's verbal and nonverbal (e.g. listening skills) behaviour [and] should feel that the core conditions (i.e., warmth, genuineness, empathy and understanding) are present' (Blackburn *et al.*, 2001, p. 7). In other words, while not foregrounded theoretically, the quality of the relationship is deemed important. Additionally, other key CBT therapist skills, such as goal setting for therapy, agenda setting within sessions and ongoing collaboration and review of progress, can all also be seen as core processes contributing to the formation of strong therapeutic alliances (e.g. Bordin, 1979).

3.3 Humanistic perspectives

As discussed in Chapter 11, the humanistic paradigm can, in some ways, be seen as having evolved as a reaction to both the psychodynamic and cognitive behavioural perspectives on psychology, psychopathology and therapy. Broadly speaking, it rejected both the medical model (refusing to equate human suffering with sickness) and the experimental psychology paradigm (refusing to see humans as comparable to the animals on which much experimental psychology was conducted). Instead, the humanistic perspective views humans as essentially healthy, sees psychopathology as largely the consequence of exposure to prolonged, adverse (typically interpersonal) conditions, and trusts that humans generally possess an inbuilt capacity to move towards well-being when provided with optimal (typically interpersonal) conditions (Rogers, 1957, 1959, 1961). As such, humanistic therapies seek to distance themselves from doctor–patient or teacher–patient positions on the therapeutic relationship. Instead, the humanistic paradigm generally views the client – rather than the therapist – as the expert on the client's experiences. It generally seeks to cultivate a more egalitarian relationship between the therapist and the client, viewing therapeutic change as resulting not from something the therapist *does* (the intervention) but from how the therapist *is* (the relationship). The humanistic perspective places particular emphasis on the healing power of the relationship in and of itself.

Within the humanistic paradigm, the work of Carl Rogers has been especially influential. Rogers (1957) proposed a number of conditions for therapeutic growth, three of which – known as the core conditions (outlined in Chapter 11) – are therapist ways of being in the relationship: congruence or genuineness (where the therapist has an awareness of feelings and attitudes in the context of the relationship, combined with a capacity to communicate relevant aspects of this experience to the client in an honest and respectful way); unconditional positive regard for the client; and empathy. Within Rogers' person-centred therapy, a productive therapeutic relationship is conceptualised as one in which the client and therapist are in contact with each other and the core conditions are met. What ultimately facilitates therapeutic change is the client's experience of these relational qualities within a therapeutic relationship that fosters their ability to explore their own experiences in a self-directed manner.

3.4   Commonalities and differences across the theoretical perspectives

The three main psychotherapeutic paradigms reviewed above have commonalities but also significant differences with regards to the therapeutic relationship. One area of convergence is the extent to which therapists seek to cultivate a relationship that is similar to positive relationships in the wider world. The majority of therapeutic approaches (across all paradigms) are perhaps at one end of this continuum, seeking to cultivate a warm and supportive relationship.

A second dimension relates to the extent to which the quality of the relationship is important because it facilitates a change process (as in CBT, for instance) or because, in some way, the relationship itself is the change process (as in various psychodynamic and humanistic approaches). Interestingly, emotion-focused therapy is a humanistic psychotherapy that straddles both of these positions; the relationship is important because it is transformative in its own right and because it facilitates in-session experiential tasks (see Information box 13.1).

Another dimension is the extent to which the therapeutic relationship is viewed as a meeting between individuals of different statuses ('expert' and 'client'; 'doctor' and 'patient'; 'well' and 'unwell' person) or as a meeting between equals. This may be implicit or explicit within a given paradigm; for example, humanistic practitioners aspire to foster a relationship of equals. Irrespective of theoretical orientation, however, this understanding may manifest in how people dress, the title they are known by, and the setting in which therapy happens (e.g. counselling centre versus psychiatric hospital).

Information box 13.1: The therapeutic relationship as conceptualised within emotion-focused therapy

Emotion-focused therapy (Greenberg, 2015) is a neohumanistic, evidence-based, experiential psychotherapy in the tradition of the person-centred and Gestalt approaches. Within emotion-focused therapy, the therapeutic relationship is understood to be both transformative in and of itself, and facilitative of in-session experiential tasks. The therapist seeks to provide a relationship characterised by positive regard, empathy and congruence/ genuineness (the Rogerian core conditions). This relationship is considered to facilitate the client's inward exploration of their experience, and to help them access, tolerate and make sense of feelings they might otherwise become dysregulated by or seek to avoid.

In witnessing the client's pain and responding with compassion and validation, the therapist's presence is seen as constituting a corrective emotional experience. The therapist's empathy is also predominantly focused on the client's response (in-session emotional experience), which further facilitates productive emotional processing. The therapist draws on their therapeutic alliance with the client to guide them through in-session experiential tasks (e.g. **two-chair dialogue**), the purpose of which is to access, tolerate and ultimately transform core, chronically painful emotions.

Two-chair dialogue
A therapeutic technique in which the client is asked to move between two empty chairs that represent conflicting parts of their self (e.g. the 'criticising self' and the 'criticised self') and engage in an imaginative dialogue between them.

Conclusion

This chapter has introduced the concept of the therapeutic relationship, summarised some of the key research findings relating to the therapeutic relationship, and looked at various ways in which different forms of therapy conceptualise and use the relationship. Despite the multiplicity of ways of thinking about the therapeutic relationship, the chapter described how almost all schools of therapy see the therapeutic relationship as critical to successful therapeutic outcomes. This includes those approaches which do not conventionally emphasise the central role of the relationship. Its central role has been supported by decades of research, which has persuasively demonstrated that, irrespective of the type of treatment, the psychotherapy relationship makes substantial and consistent contributions to client outcomes. To quote Norcross and Lambert (2018, p. 313), 'the relationship works!'.

Further reading

- This book summarises key research evidence for the role of the therapeutic relationship:
Norcross, J.C., and Lambert, M.J. (eds.) (2019) *Psychotherapy relationships that work. Volume 1: evidence-based therapist contributions.* New York: Oxford University Press.

- This paper explores the impacts on the therapist when encountering and transforming the client's vulnerability in emotion-focused therapy:

  Timulak, L. (2014) 'Witnessing clients' emotional transformation: an emotion-focused therapist's experience of providing therapy', *Journal of Clinical Psychology*, 70(8), pp. 741–752.

- This book is an evidence-based guide to alliance building across a range of psychotherapeutic orientations:

  Muran, J.C. and Barber, J.P. (eds.) (2011) *The therapeutic alliance: an evidence-based guide to practice.* New York: Guilford Press.

References

Bachelor, A. (1995) 'Clients' perception of the therapeutic alliance: a qualitative analysis', *Journal of Counseling Psychology*, 42(3), pp. 323–337.

Bedi, R.P., Davis, M.D. and Williams, M. (2005) 'Critical incidents in the formation of the therapeutic alliance from the client's perspective', *Psychotherapy: Theory, Research, Practice, Training*, 42(3), pp. 311–323.

Blackburn, I.M., James, I.A., Milne, D.L., Baker, C., Standart, S., Garland, A., and Reichelt, F.K. (2001) 'The revised cognitive therapy scale (CTS-R): psychometric properties', *Behavioural and Cognitive Psychotherapy*, 29(4), pp. 431–446.

Bordin, E.S. (1979) 'The generalizability of the psychoanalytic concept of the working alliance', *Psychotherapy: Theory, Research and Practice*, 16(3), pp. 252–260.

Constantino, M.J., Vîslă, A., Coyne, A.E. and Boswell, J.F. (2018) 'A meta-analysis of the association between patients' early treatment outcome expectation and their posttreatment outcomes', *Psychotherapy*, 55(4), pp. 473–485.

Duff, C.T. and Bedi, R.P. (2010) 'Counsellor behaviours that predict therapeutic alliance: from the client's perspective', *Counselling Psychology Quarterly*, 23(1), pp. 91–110.

Elliott, R., Bohart, A.C., Watson, J.C. and Murphy, D. (2018) 'Therapist empathy and client outcome: an updated meta-analysis', *Psychotherapy*, 55(4), pp. 399–410.

Eubanks, C.F., Muran, J.C. and Safran, J.D. (2018) 'Alliance rupture repair: a meta-analysis', *Psychotherapy*, 55(4), pp. 508–519.

Farber, B.A., Suzuki, J.Y. and Lynch, D.A. (2018) 'Positive regard and psychotherapy outcome: a meta-analytic review', *Psychotherapy*, 55(4), pp. 411–423.

Flückiger, C., Del Re, A.C., Wampold, B.E. and Horvath, A.O. (2018) 'The alliance in adult psychotherapy: a meta-analytic synthesis', *Psychotherapy*, 55(4), pp. 316–340.

Gilbert, P. and Leahy, R.L. (2007) *The therapeutic relationship in the cognitive behavioral psychotherapies*. London: Routledge.

Greenberg, L.S. (2015) *Emotion-focused therapy: coaching clients to work through their feelings*. Washington, DC: American Psychological Association.

Hayes, J.A., Gelso, C.J., Goldberg, S. and Kivlighan, D.M. (2018) 'Countertransference management and effective psychotherapy: meta-analytic findings', *Psychotherapy*, 55(4), pp. 496–507.

Hill, C.E., Knox, S. and Pinto-Coelho, K.G. (2018) 'Therapist self-disclosure and immediacy: a qualitative meta-analysis', *Psychotherapy*, 55(4), pp. 445–460.

Horvath, A.O., Del Re, A.C., Flückiger, C. and Symonds, D. (2011) 'Alliance in individual psychotherapy', *Psychotherapy*, 48(1), pp. 9–16.

Horvath, A.O. and Greenberg, L. (1986) 'The development of the Working Alliance Inventory', in Greenberg, L.S. and Pinsof, W.M. (eds.) *The psychotherapeutic process: a research handbook*. New York: Guilford Press, pp. 529–556.

Kolden, G.G., Wang, C.C., Austin, S.B., Chang, Y. and Klein, M.H. (2018) 'Congruence/genuineness: a meta-analysis', *Psychotherapy*, 55(4), pp. 424–433.

Krupnick, J.L., Sotsky, S.M., Elkin, I., Simmens, S., Moyer, J., Watkins, J. and Pilkonis, P.A. (2006) 'The role of the therapeutic alliance in psychotherapy and pharmacotherapy outcome: findings in the National Institute of Mental Health Treatment of Depression Collaborative Research Program', *Focus*, 4(2), pp. 269–277.

Martin, D.J., Garske, J.P. and Davis, M.K. (2000) 'Relation of the therapeutic alliance with outcome and other variables: a meta-analytic review', *Journal of Consulting and Clinical Psychology*, 68(3), pp. 438–450.

Norcross, J.C. (2001) 'Purposes, processes and products of the task force on empirically supported therapy relationships', *Psychotherapy: Theory, Research, Practice, Training*, 38(4), pp. 345–356. doi:10.1037/0033-3204.38.4.345.

Norcross, J.C. (ed.) (2002) *Psychotherapy relationships that work: therapist contributions and responsiveness to patients*. New York: Oxford University Press.

Norcross, J.C. and Lambert, M.J. (2018) 'Psychotherapy relationships that work III', *Psychotherapy: Theory, Research and Practice*, 55(4), pp. 303–315.

Norcross, J.C. and Lambert, M.J. (eds.) (2019) *Psychotherapy relationships that work. Volume 1: evidence-based therapist contributions*. New York: Oxford University Press.

Norcross, J.C. (ed.) (2011) *Psychotherapy relationships that work: evidence-based responsiveness*. 2nd edn. New York: Oxford University Press.

Rogers, C.R. (1957) 'The necessary and sufficient conditions of therapeutic personality change', *Journal of Consulting Psychology*, 21(2), pp. 95–103.

Rogers, C.R. (1959) 'A theory of therapy, personality, and interpersonal relationships: as developed in the client-centered framework', in Koch, S. (ed.) *Psychology: a study of a science. Volume 3: formulations of the person and the social context*. New York: McGraw-Hill, pp. 184–256.

Rogers, C.R. (1961) *On becoming a person*. Boston: Houghton Mifflin Company.

Tryon, G.S., Birch, S.E. and Verkuilen, J. (2018) 'Meta-analyses of the relation of goal consensus and collaboration to psychotherapy outcome', *Psychotherapy*, 55(4), pp. 372–383.

Chapter 14
Beyond the individual

Andreas Vossler

Contents

Introduction

'Making connections' by Sumaira Ali

This chapter focuses on counselling approaches that reach beyond the individual – both in the way they understand mental health difficulties and in terms of the family and group settings they use for their practice. As Chapters 3 and 9 explained, early therapeutic traditions in the development of modern western 'talking cures' emphasised the individual, understanding mental health difficulties as mainly intrapersonal problems. However, it can be argued that this focus on 'individual' distress is limited and potentially less effective, as it fails to take account of relational causes – problems that develop beyond the individual, in relationships and interactions with other people (as argued in Chapter 7).

Recognising these limitations, the first 'systemic-oriented' therapists emerged in the 1950s (e.g. Virginia Satir; Satir, 1990) and started to invite family members to therapy sessions so they could work with family interactions. The different systemic approaches that later developed share the view that mental health difficulties are not developed within individuals, but rather emerge as a result of relationship patterns and dynamics, interactions and language between individuals in different contexts (Vetere and Dallos, 2003). The value of looking beyond the individual was also discovered by therapists who started to work with their clients in a group setting (partly due to a lack of sufficient resources for individual therapy). Group programmes use the power of group dynamics/processes and peer support to help improve client well-being. Individual group members are likely to gain a better understanding of themselves through the feedback they receive from other group members and the therapist (Yalom and Leszcz, 2005).

This chapter aims to:

- introduce the development of systemic thinking and the main theoretical assumptions of systemic approaches

- outline the basic principles and techniques used in systemic practice, which aim to address the interdependent nature of social interactions

- outline the key processes and factors in effective group work, including those related to the group (e.g. structural factors) and to the individual (e.g. individual characteristics)

- explore the ways in which group interventions are employed in different therapeutic traditions, including psychoanalysis and CBT.

1 Systemic approaches

Systemic approaches share the view that individual clients are 'relational beings' who can only be understood by exploring the different contextual settings (e.g. work, cultural/religious and wider society) and relationship systems (e.g. present family relationships and family of origin) in which they are embedded. This understanding moves the therapeutic focus away from the individual to the relational and social context in which clients live (Vossler, 2010). Figure 14.1 presents a simplified example of how the systemic perspective can reformulate individual problems as relational issues.

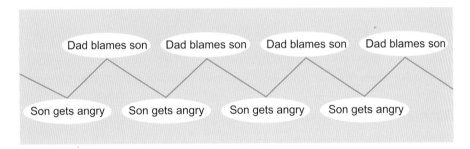

Figure 14.1 An example interaction pattern between a father and a teenage son

---

Activity 14.1: Recursive interaction patterns

Allow about 10 minutes

Does the interaction pattern in Figure 14.1 remind you of anything from your own experiences (as a member of a family/group)? Make some notes on how you think such a pattern may develop, and how it may be resolved.

Discussion

Figure 14.1 provides an illustration of a **recursive interaction pattern** (also called a repetitive dance in systemic therapy): the dad's blame initiates the son's angry reaction, which in turn triggers more of the dad's blame, and so on. Dad's behaviour can be seen as both cause and effect of the son's action, and vice versa. Each individual behaviour in this example can be better explained from a relational perspective, as it is maintained by the action of the other person.

You might have thought of a similar conflict situation in your own personal relationships where you felt stuck in a cycle, and where it was

Recursive interaction pattern
Reoccurring interaction sequences in which the behaviours and feelings of one person are triggered and maintained by the behaviours and feelings of another person, and vice versa.

difficult to remember afterwards who started the argument (perhaps you even felt it was irrelevant). Interaction patterns in families and groups are often more complex than in the example in Figure 14.1, as more family/group members are usually involved in these repetitive dances. Systemic approaches help clients to understand the bigger relational picture of their problems and change their own interactional contribution, which in turn can interrupt a problematic cycle, such as the one illustrated above (regardless of who started the conflict loop).

1.1 The development of systemic therapy

Systemic thinking in counselling and psychotherapy has developed in waves since the 1950s, with different approaches emerging throughout its development stages. Although systemic practice has 'moved away from several schools of thought to a unified practice' (Dallos and Draper, 2015, p. 169), systemic practitioners still use techniques and concepts from earlier development stages of systemic therapy in a pragmatic and eclectic manner (Pinquart, Oslejsek and Teubert, 2016). It is therefore useful to be aware of the main ideas developed in different systemic schools, and how they have shaped systemic thinking and practice today. The following overview illustrates how the evolution of systemic approaches has paralleled, and been influenced by, theoretical concepts that have occurred in mainstream psychology, and even sociology (Vetere and Dallos, 2003).

Double-bind message
An emotionally distressing message making two conflicting demands on different logical levels, neither of which can be ignored/escaped.

A famous, early example of a systemic concept is the classic double-bind theory (Bateson *et al.*, 1956; Bateson, 1972). Based on their research on communication in families, Gregory Bateson and colleagues hypothesised that growing up in families where **double-bind messages** prevail may lead to the onset of schizophrenia among young people. An example of such a paradoxical communication pattern, in this case for a little child, is hearing a parent saying they love them while, at the same time, being punished by that parent. While the concept was later criticised, mainly as it seems to put unwarranted blame for the onset of mental health difficulties on parents, its underlying assumption – that it is not the individuals who are 'ill' or 'disturbed' but rather the communication between them – is seen as groundbreaking in systemic thinking (Vossler, Squire and Bingham, 2017).

From normative to neutral perspectives on family functioning

Early systemic approaches were primarily focused on the structure and organisation of social systems (especially families), and the way they use information and feedback to self-regulate and adapt. A system was defined as a unified whole which consists of interrelated parts (Nichols and Everett, 1986). It was assumed that changes in one part of the system (e.g. a family member) would affect the whole system, and that the whole system would be different from the sum of its parts (Vossler, 2010). The individual problems of family members were considered to have a function in keeping the family system in balance (Fryszer and Schwing, 2014). Based on this systems analogy, two main systemic approaches developed:

- *Structural family therapy* (Minuchin, 1974): This approach is primarily concerned with family structures such as boundaries, hierarchies and coalitions. Therapists aim to identify structures that are considered to be dysfunctional (e.g. weak hierarchies, inappropriate alliances, restrictive rules, children in overly powerful positions) and help the client family to move to more functional structures and interaction patterns.

- *Strategic family therapy* (Haley, 1963): This is mainly focused on strategic interactional aspects in family functioning, assuming that the problematic behaviour displayed by one family member is maintained by the actions of other family members. Therapists often use directive and strategic interventions to disrupt problematic sequences (e.g. homework assignments prescribing a behaviour modification that can break a repetitive interaction pattern).

Both approaches propose rather normative positions on family functioning and offer clear ideas about what constitutes 'functional' and 'dysfunctional' (Fryszer and Schwing, 2014).

Later systemic approaches rejected these early normative ideas and took a more neutral and curious stance on family functioning and possible therapy outcomes. For example, the influential Milan family therapy team (Selvini-Palazzoli *et al.*, 1978; Cecchin, 1987) tried to instigate change by challenging existing communication patterns and underlying beliefs in client families. To do so, they developed working hypotheses for each family's presenting problems and employed creative intervention, such as 'positive connotations' (e.g. telling the family that their difficulties are logical and meaningful in the given context) and homework assignments (e.g. to 'prescribe' behaviour or symptoms in the family at certain times) (Boscolo *et al.*, 1987). However, in their clinical work, they developed the understanding that, due to the autonomous and self-determined nature of client systems, therapists are not able to control the effect of the interventions or predict their outcome.

From first- to second-order cybernetics

Cybernetics
The science of control and communication in systems (both machine and living).

Another major transition in systemic thinking and therapy was the shift from first-order to second-order **cybernetics** (Wiener, 1961). Influenced by predominant positivistic positions of the 1950s and 1960s, early systemic approaches assumed that it is possible for therapists to objectively observe and describe the family relationship dynamics and communication pattern. From this 'first-order' position (with a focus on observed systems), therapists were seen as 'experts' who could devise the 'right' interventions, based on their observations, that would lead to change in the family system (Vetere and Dallos, 2003). However, from the 1970s onwards systemic approaches acknowledged that observations cannot be objective but are filtered and shaped by the therapist's own standpoints, assumptions and prejudices (Maturana and Varela, 1992). From this 'second-order' perspective (with a focus on observing systems), therapists are inevitably part of the system they observe, and their perceptions and observations of the client family are influenced and co-created by interactions with the clients during therapy sessions (Fryszer and Schwing, 2014).

Constructivism
A philosophical perspective stressing the uniqueness of individual perceptions and subjective reality constructions.

This shift was – and indeed, systematic thinking still is – underpinned by ideas derived from **constructivism** (Dallos and Draper, 2015). From this perspective it is assumed that reality is never independent of the observer, meaning that each person lives in a 'personal biosphere' (Vetere and Dallos, 2003) with unique personal beliefs and views of the world. This implies for systemic practice that there is not just one 'truth' about a problem situation but a variety of possible views and stories that are all subjectively 'true' and in line with the individual context (e.g. the individual person's background, assumptions, expectations, etc.). Rather than an expert–client interaction (first-order cybernetics), systemic therapy is now seen as a collaborative exploration of the different meanings and beliefs in the family system. The therapist adopts a 'not-knowing' position to avoid imposing their 'expert' opinion (Amundson, Stewart and Valentine, 1993).

Since the 1990s, systemic thinking and approaches have started to pay increased attention to social and cultural influences and the role language plays in constructing and defining realities. This development was informed by social constructionist theories (McNamee and Gergen, 1992) that shifted the emphasis from individual reality construction (constructivism) to how beliefs and experiences of clients, and perceptions of therapists, are influenced and shaped by societal norms and discourses (i.e. they are socially constructed). The language used in social conversations (e.g. labels and terms such as 'neurotic' and 'mad') is seen as crucial to transporting social/cultural values and ideologies and defining social realities. Systemic approaches based on these postmodernist assumptions aim to collaboratively change the 'stories' clients tell themselves about their problems and their life (as in narrative therapy; White and Epston, 1990) and focus on solutions and competencies rather than deficits and problems (as in solution-focused therapy; de Shazer, 1985).

1.2   Basic principles and techniques in systemic practice

The fictional case of Malik and his family can help to illustrate some of the basic principles and techniques used in systemic counselling today.

Case illustration: Tensions between Malik and his family

Malik is a 15-year-old boy living with his British Pakistani parents and two younger siblings in Manchester. His father works long, unsocial hours as a taxi driver in the city. His mother stays at home to look after Malik and his two sisters. Over the last few months, Malik has started to hang around with a group of peers from his school in the evenings, often coming home late and with alcohol on his breath. His parents and family friends also suspect that members of this (predominantly white) peer group have been involved in shoplifting and have been fighting with another gang in the local park (Malik's role in this, if any, is unclear).

This situation has led to various arguments between Malik and his father about Malik's involvement with the peer group, and the time he is allowed to stay out in the evenings. After one of these arguments, Malik left the home without permission and stayed with one of his friends, returning home the next morning once his father had left for work. Malik's mother stays out of the arguments between her husband and son, although she is very concerned that the whole situation could escalate.

Malik's parents, and especially his father, are worried that if they allow Malik too much freedom and independence, he might become too westernised and will fail to meet their expectations or, even worse, become a criminal. They fear he might be looking for a girlfriend in his newfound peer group, which could clash with their plans to arrange a marriage for him. Malik, on the other hand, feels his father is especially rigid in his opinions and doesn't trust Malik to make his own decisions. He feels that, compared to the other boys in his class, he is kept on a very tight rein by his father, and that his parents don't really understand what he cares about.

If Malik and his family underwent systemic counselling, the counsellor would initially be likely to spend some time establishing a good connection with the client system (a process referred to as 'joining' in systemic counselling) and understanding how each family member perceives the difficulties. Led by a therapeutic stance of neutrality and curiosity, and informed by constructivist thinking, they would then start to explore the differing meanings and beliefs within the family (e.g. Malik's belief that his parents don't trust him; his parents' concerns about his future). They would be especially interested in the way the 'realities' in the client system are socially constructed – how they are shaped and influenced by cultural norms and discourses (e.g. what are Pakistani and Muslim ideas about what a good father or mother does, and about how much freedom and independence young boys should have?), and how these are expressed through the language used and stories told by different family members.

Circular causality
The idea that interactions in social systems are interdependent and circular (event A is both the cause and effect of event B).

The systemic counsellor would pay attention to the relational dynamics and recursive interaction patterns within the family (as introduced in Figure 14.1 and Activity 14.1). In doing so, they would draw on the central systemic concept of **circular causality** – the idea that interactions in social systems are interdependent and that causation is circular rather than linear (the behaviour of one person can be understood at the same time as the cause and effect of the behaviour of another person; Dallos and Draper, 2015). In counselling, Malik's father might explain that he is putting up a fight because Malik wants to leave the house too late in the evening, whereas Malik might say that his wish to 'escape' is a reaction to fights with his dad (about restricting his freedom). The inherent logic of Malik's and his father's perceptions is one of linear causality ('A is the cause of B'). However, from a systemic (circular) perspective, Malik's 'escapes' can be seen as both a response to his father's restricting interventions and as a trigger for them ('A is both the cause and effect of B').

This interaction is an example of a complementary escalation in systems, where one person's behaviour is maintained and reinforced by the actions of the other – 'the more one person does of one particular thing, the more another person does of another' (Fryszer and Schwing, 2014, p. 51). Another example could be between Malik's parents; for example, the more authoritarian the father acts towards Malik, the more permissive and indulgent his mother might treat him, and vice versa. By introducing a circular understanding, the systemic counsellor could help Malik's family to stop blaming personality traits for their problems (through thoughts such as 'My dad is rigid and stubborn' or 'Malik is disrespectful') and to discover alternative options they each have for stopping the recursive cycle (by reflecting on and changing their own interactional contribution; Jones and Asen, 2000). This would release them from being 'stuck' in a stress-causing interaction pattern.

Rather than focusing on deficits, the systemic counsellor would be interested in exploring strengths and resources within the family system and would search for constructive aspects, even in seemingly destructive behaviour. For example, they could use the **reframing** technique (described below) to introduce new meaning for negatively connotated actions. Based on observations and conversations in the counselling room, the systemic counsellor would develop preliminary hypotheses to guide their work with the family. They could choose from a range of creative methods to introduce alternative descriptions and perspectives and to facilitate change. Most systemic methods used to explore system relationships and interaction patterns (for assessment) can also be used to introduce new insights for the clients (as interventions). Two of these techniques are introduced in Table 14.1, below, accompanied by examples of how they could be utilised in the case of Malik and his family.

Reframing
The technique of changing the meaning of a problem situation or behaviour by creating an alternative explanation for the problem/behaviour from a different perspective.

Table 14.1 Reframing and circular questioning in systemic practice

Technique	Description	Example
Reframing	A technique of relabelling client ideas and descriptions by reframing them. The counsellor offers plausible alternative interpretations of the meaning or function of a situation or behaviour seen as problematic by clients (Watzlawick, Weakland and Fisch, 1974). Reframing can help to reduce polarisation of positions and blame in the client system by attaching a different (mostly positive) meaning to emotions or behaviours seen as problematic (Vossler, 2010). It facilitates change from a fixed/ unalterable meaning-frame of reference to an implicitly flexible frame that is open to change.	Malik's father's anger and the fights he has with Malik (when Malik leaves the house) could be relabelled as care and worry about his son. Malik's escapes could be reframed as an expression of anxiety about feeling rejected, or a desire to be trusted.
Circular questioning	An interview technique based on the systemic concept of circular causality. The counsellor invites clients to consider relational aspects and the 'problematic' situation/ behaviour context. The aim is to illuminate the interconnectedness of system members and introduce new information/ perspectives (Vossler, Squire and Bingham, 2017). Forms include comparison, ranking, future/hypothetical, and triadic questions (asking a third person about the meaning behind behaviours/feelings expressed by one person towards another).	'Who in your family first realises when Malik doesn't come home at night?' To Malik's father: 'How do you think your wife views Malik's desire to spend time with his new friends?' To Malik's mother: 'What do you think Malik has to do to make his father happy?' To Malik: 'What would happen between your mother and father if you came home with a girlfriend?'

2 Group therapy

The development of group therapy for mental health difficulties, at least in a more formal and organised sense, began in the UK during the Second World War and the post-war years (Fehr, 2019). While there had been earlier advances in group psychotherapy in the US (e.g. Pratt's groups for emotional problems that related to pulmonary tuberculosis; Burrow's early concept of group analysis; Hadden, 1955), the key pioneers of group therapy in the UK – S.H. Foulkes and Wilfred Bion – used group concepts and formats while working with soldiers returning from the war at Northfield Military Hospital. Their work was based on psychoanalytic ideas (discussed in Chapter 9) such as the recognition that, in groups, transference processes are 'focused on both the members and the analyst' (not just the analyst, as in individual therapy; Fehr, 2019, p. 14). It was also assumed that unconscious processes of group members could be acted out in the form of irrational processes in group sessions. Bion (1961) later focused his work on exploring the way groups function (e.g. emotional group states that may interfere with the purpose of a group; Bion, 1991), while Foulkes went on to develop group analytic psychotherapy (Foulkes, 1983[1948]). Both played an important role in establishing the first therapeutic communities in the UK.

Since the 1950s, various other important influences have shaped today's group therapy practices – influences that cannot all be covered in a single chapter. One such figure is Irvin D. Yalom, a US psychiatrist and group therapist who developed an interpersonal group therapy model based on his clinical experience and research literature review. His standard text, *The theory and practice of group psychotherapy* (Yalom and Leszcz, 2005), explores and describes group dynamics from initial formation to the end of the group's life, and the role and function of individual group members and group leaders within the group. Yalom also proposed a list of 12 therapeutic factors for positive change and success in group work (see Section 2.1).

The rest of this chapter will introduce central processes and factors that are generally relevant for most types of group therapy, and explore how group interventions are employed in different therapeutic traditions.

2.1   Key processes and factors in therapeutic group work

The 'life cycle' of a group has several stages. The account below offers one (anonymous) person's experience of the life of their therapeutic group. The account has been rewritten for this chapter, but it maintains the essence of the original source.

Client voices: Experiencing group therapy

I approached the initial group therapy session with trepidation. I soon found out I was not alone and that other members had their own anxieties about meeting new people, being judged, not being accepted or exposing themselves too much. Right up front the group needed to build dialogue and trust. That is an important part of the process, yet everyone, it seemed, was afraid to be the first person to reveal something deep because it would make them vulnerable. Two people discussed their negative feelings for one another, but beyond that we spoke in superficialities. Finally, someone began revealing some personal issues and that opened up the group to sharing and self-revelation.

As the group began to share more, we realised that knowing someone else had experienced the same emotion or situation connected us, and gave us a feeling of security. I began to experience a closeness, and a bond of understanding, with these people who had been strangers. There was one incident that showed me how I was shifting attitudes from past relationships on to someone in the group, in this case a group member who rarely revealed anything about himself. I came to recognise that my strong reaction in this situation was due to unresolved feelings for others in my life – including my father – who acted as detached as this person. The last step in our group was when we parted ways. Some were happy to get on with their lives while others were sad to leave this supportive community.

The group touched my life and helped me get a better understanding of my own issues and how they impacted my daily life, although some of the learnings only came later, when I processed what happened in the group. In particular, by being open and exposing myself to possible rejection, I was able to get over some of my fears. Finally, it was helpful having a supportive group of people who cared about me and were empathetic to what I was going through.

(Source: based on Fehr, 2019, pp. 25–29)

This account of group therapy identifies different stages in the life cycle of a group. The first stage of group formation is typically associated with feelings of anxiety and disorientation (especially in unstructured groups). In later stages, greater levels of trust and cohesiveness develop in the group, and members usually start to feel less vulnerable and begin to self-disclose more intimate material. With the help of the group therapist and other group members, they will then be able to access and show more of their 'true self' (Winnicott, 1965). The final stages can be emotive, as group members might feel both the loss of the supportive environment and a sense of achievement related to their progress (Fehr, 2019).

Yalom's 12 therapeutic factors are also relevant to this account. They are as follows:

- *Universality factor*: Group members recognise that other members share similar feelings, thoughts and problems.

- *Existential awareness*: Recognition of personal/universal isolation, freedom, mortality and responsibility for life decisions.

- *Instillation of hope*: Recognition that other members' success can be helpful, which provides optimism for one's own improvement.

- *Cohesiveness*: Feelings of trust, belonging and togetherness experienced by the group members.

- *Catharsis*: Release of strong feelings about past or present experiences.

- *Corrective recapitulation of the primary family experience*: Opportunity to re-enact critical family dynamics with group members in a corrective manner.

- *Self-understanding*: Insight into own psychological motivation, underlying behaviour and emotional reactions.

- *Interpersonal learning*: Insight and self-awareness of how an individual group member comes across to others (through feedback provided by others).

- *Development of socialising techniques*: Improved social skills through feedback and reality confrontation in the group.

- *Imitative behaviour*: Observing and imitating how others share personal feelings.

- *Altruism*: Group members feel more positive about themselves through helping others in the group.

- *Imparting information*: Education or advice provided by the therapist or group members.

Some of these therapeutic factors seem to have played a direct role in the client's experience of group therapy above (universality factor, cohesiveness, catharsis, corrective recapitulation of the primary family experience, self-understanding). While not explicitly mentioned in the account, it can be assumed that the client benefited from interpersonal learning and the development of socialising techniques. They might also have learnt through modelling their behaviour on others (imitative behaviour) and felt more positive about themselves when helping others in the group (altruism). Finally, they might have received imparting information from other group members or the group therapist about key factors surrounding the treatment, or any difficulties experienced (especially in psychoeducational groups, which provide information and advice for clients with mental health difficulties and/or their social support networks).

At least part of the benefits of group therapy seem related to specific therapeutic factors offered in this setting – such as positive peer modelling opportunities, reinforcement, and social support from other group members. These beneficial factors are also utilised by self-help group programmes that do not strictly constitute group therapy and are not run by a group therapist. A well-known and well-established example is the 12-step self-help group programmes, initially developed by Alcoholics Anonymous and now used more widely by self-help groups for substance abuse and dependency problems. The 12 steps are a set of principles for overcoming addiction. People who have a desire to stop their addiction (the only requirement for membership) meet in autonomous local groups to support each other and work through the steps.

The information box below provides on overview of the complex interplay of factors contributing to group therapy outcomes, which include small group processes that also occur in self-help group programmes.

> ## Information box 14.1: Research on therapy group processes and outcomes
>
> How do therapeutic groups promote change? Even more so than for individual therapy, finding research answers to this question is not easy, as group processes are characterised by a complex interplay of factors. Burlingame, MacKenzie and Strauss (2004) have identified the following independent forces that contribute to group therapy outcomes:
>
> - *Formal change theory*: The therapeutic interventions applied within the group based on theoretical models (e.g. CBT or psychoanalysis) and/or support, skills training and psychoeducation.
>
> - *Small group process*: Specific group processes/effects, such as group member interactions and cohesion.
>
> - *Client factors*: Individual factors such as personality characteristics, attachment style and the nature of a person's mental health difficulties.
>
> - *Group structural factors*: Characteristics of the therapeutic group, such as its size, the number/length of sessions and cultural factors.
>
> - *Group leader factors*: Individual factors such as their leadership style, but also factors such as their level of experience.
>
> Through a review of research (which covered more than 250 studies on the efficacy of group therapy for 12 'disorders'), Burlingame, Strauss and Joyce (2013) conclude that there is 'clear support for group treatment with good or excellent evidence for most disorders reviewed' (p. 664). They further suggest that, generally, group treatment is as effective as individual treatment (format equivalence) and superior in terms of cost-effectiveness. However, most of the reviewed studies employed randomised controlled trials to focus their investigation on group interventions based on a theoretical model (i.e. they applied a formal change theory), whereas specific group processes/effects and interaction effects between the factors listed above often remain neglected in these studies.

2.2 Psychoanalytic group therapy

Psychoanalytic group therapy has its roots in the early work of Foulkes and Bion (as described above) and applies psychoanalytic thinking to the social and interpersonal group situation. In group analysis, group members are seen as sharing group norms that reflect the norms of the wider community/society (the group is seen as a microcosm of society). It is assumed that what is said and done in the group situation is influenced by unconscious processes within the group; the 'group is regarded as a unit, capable of shared transferences, defences and phantasies' (Pearce and Haigh, 2017, p. 124). Confronted with the behaviour, attitudes and personalities of various other group members, individuals might discover similarities with their own self (known as a mirroring process; Pines, 1984). Group members might also react spontaneously when emotional issues that resonate with their own feelings and experiences are raised by others; for example, they might respond with **identification**, rejection or **projection** (known as a resonance process; Foulkes, 1991).

Psychoanalytic groups are usually run with minimal structure (there are very few instructions given by the therapist and there are no set topics). The focus of the group analytic work is on the here-and-now interactions between group members and on free-flowing group discussions (which is regarded as equivalent to free association in psychoanalysis; Foulkes, 1983[1948])). Through observation, introspection and reflection on what clients present, the therapist can make inferences and develop formulations. Their interpretations (see Chapter 9 for a reminder of the definition) focus on transference reactions, resistances and defences – of individuals or the group as a whole – and aim to make unconscious processes more conscious (Pines, 1983). The evolution of group analytic theory is closely linked to the development of democratic therapeutic community practice in the UK, with both sharing the same foundations as Foulkes' and Bion's groundbreaking work at Northfield Military Hospital (which is considered to be the first example of an intentional therapeutic community; Pearce and Haigh, 2017). Chapter 19 will introduce work in therapeutic communities.

Identification
The process of feeling or becoming like another person; of adopting a quality or attribute of that person.

Projection
One of the defence mechanisms conceptualised by Sigmund Freud. A person ascribes undesirable or threatening unconscious impulses to someone else (rather than admitting to or dealing with them).

2.3   Other developments and applications of group therapy

An important influence on the development of group therapy was the encounter group movement that evolved from the 'T-group' (or training group) tradition in the US (Adler and Goleman, 1975). It became popular in the 1960s and 1970s when Carl Rogers (1970) conducted encounter groups based on person-centred principles. In these self-structured and time-limited encounters, participants have the chance to gain new understandings of their own behaviour through interaction with others around 'here and now' issues. The focus of encounter groups is usually more on experiential learning (leading to the personal growth of participants) than on providing therapy (Lieberman, Miles and Yalom, 1973).

The provision of CBT in a group format was first proposed in the 1970s and is now firmly established in many western healthcare systems – partly because CBT groups seem more cost-effective than individual-focused CBT (Bieling, McCabe and Anthony, 2006). CBT group therapy programmes have been developed for a range of mental health difficulties, including specific anxiety disorders such as social phobia (Davis, 2012), obsessive-compulsive disorder (Raffin *et al.*, 2009) and panic disorder with agoraphobia (Galassi *et al.*, 2007). They have also been developed for depression (Okumura and Ichikura, 2014), psychosis (Lecomte, 2016) and other difficulties (e.g. insomnia; Koffel, Koffel and Gehrman, 2015). In recent years, group-focused, mindfulness-based cognitive therapy has become popular in various settings (e.g. in prisons). It offers a modified form of cognitive therapy – one that incorporates mindfulness practices such as meditation and breathing exercises (e.g. Shulman *et al.*, 2018).

All CBT group programmes use similar methods (e.g. psychoeducation, cognitive restructuring and graded exposure – see Chapter 10 for a reminder of the definition of the latter) and usually follow a preset manual. CBT group therapists typically play a more active role in guiding the group through each session. Recently, there has been more focus on the importance of group processes and structure, and how practitioners can manage these aspects of group practice more effectively to improve outcomes. Mental health service providers have recognised the benefits and often greater efficiency (Morrison, 2001) of therapeutic groups, which are now an indispensable and essential part of, for example, the UK's NHS services for mental health problems.

Pause for reflection

Imagine, as a practitioner, you want to invite a client to attend group therapy instead of individual therapy. What would you say to motivate them to choose this intervention?

Conclusion

This chapter has covered the evolution of systemic therapy and group therapy and the ways they have widened the traditional therapeutic focus on the individual. Systemic principles and techniques have been introduced that can help practitioners to look beyond the individual to understand clients and their problems within the various contextual layers in which they are embedded (from family relationships to wider society). The chapter has argued that clients can benefit from a range of universal processes specific to therapeutic group work, and from the specific therapeutic factors offered in this setting (e.g. positive peer modelling and peer support). Group interventions range from psychodynamic group therapy to therapeutic programmes offered to people with similar problems (e.g. mindfulness and psychoeducational groups) and self-help groups that follow a set of principles in supporting each other (e.g. Alcoholics Anonymous' 12-step programme). Research has provided evidence for the benefits of both therapeutic group work and systemic family therapy, although more attention needs to be given to the specific processes and factors at work in group and family settings.

Further reading

- This is a great introduction to systemic family therapy, providing a comprehensive overview of the development of core concepts and techniques of systemic approaches:

  Dallos, R. and Draper, R. (2015) *An introduction to systemic family therapy*. 4th edn. Maidenhead: Open University Press.

- This is the standard book in the field – the classic group psychotherapy text:

  Yalom, I.D. and Leszcz, M. (2005) *The theory and practice of group psychotherapy*. 5th edn. New York: Basic Books.

- This paper offers a systematic review of the evidence base for family therapy and systemic interventions:

  Carr, A. (2016) 'How and why do family and systemic therapies work?', *Australian and New Zealand Journal of Family Therapy*, 37, pp. 37–55.

References

Adler, N.E. and Goleman, D. (1975) 'Goal setting, T-group participation, and self-rated change: an experimental study', *The Journal of Applied Behavioral Science*, 11(2), pp. 197–208.

Amundson, J., Stewart, K. and Valentine, L. (1993) 'Temptations of power and certainty', *Journal of Marital and Family Therapy*, 19(2), pp. 111–123.

Bateson, G. (1972) 'Toward a theory of schizophrenia', in Bateson, G. (ed.) *Steps to an ecology of mind*. Chicago: University of Chicago Press, pp. 201–227.

Bateson, G., Jackson, D., Hayley, J. and Weakland, J. (1956) 'Towards a theory of schizophrenia', *Behavioural Science*, 1(4), pp. 173–198.

Bieling, P.J., McCabe, R.E. and Anthony, M.M. (2006) *Cognitive-behavioral therapy in groups*. New York: The Guildford Press.

Bion, W.R. (1961) *Experiences in groups*. London: Tavistock Publications/Routledge.

Bion, W.R. (1991) *Experiences in groups and other papers*. New York, NY: Tavistock Publications/Routledge.

Boscolo, L., Cecchin, G., Hoffman, L. and Penn, P. (1987) *Milan systemic family therapy*. New York: Basic Books.

Burlingame, G.M., MacKenzie, K.R. and Strauss, B. (2004) 'Small group treatment: evidence for effectiveness and mechanisms of change', in Lambert, M.J. (ed.) *'Bergin and Garfield's handbook of psychotherapy and behavior change. 5th edn*. Hoboken, NJ: Wiley, pp. 647–696.

Burlingame, G.M., Strauss, B. and Joyce, A.S. (2013) 'Change mechanisms and effectiveness of small group treatments', in Lambert, M.J. (ed.) *Bergin and Garfield's handbook of psychotherapy and behavior change. 6th edn*. Hoboken, NJ: Wiley, pp. 640–689.

Cecchin, G. (1987) 'Hypothesizing, circularity, and neutrality revisited: an invitation to curiosity', *Family Process*, 26(4), pp. 405–413.

Dallos, R. and Draper, R. (2015) *An introduction to family therapy: systematic theory and practice*. 4th edn. Maidenhead: Open University Press.

Davis, M.A. (2012) 'Literature review on counseling groups for social phobia', *Graduate Journal of Counseling Psychology*, 3(1), pp. 1–13.

de Shazer, S. (1985) *Keys to solution in brief therapy*. New York: W.W. Norton and Company.

Fehr, S. (2019) *Introduction to group therapy: a practical guide*. 3rd edn. Oxford and New York: Routledge.

Foulkes, S.H. (1983[1948]) *Introduction to group-analytic psychotherapy: studies in the social integration of individuals and groups*. London: Karnac Books.

Foulkes, S.H. (1991) *Selected papers: psychoanalysis and group analysis*. London: Routledge.

Fryszer, A. and Schwing, R. (2014) *Handbook of systemic psychotherapy*. Goettingen: Vandenhoeck & Rupprecht Gmbh & Co.

Galassi, F., Quercioli, S., Charismas, D., Niccolai, V. and Barciulli, E. (2007) 'Cognitive-behavioral group treatment for panic disorder with agoraphobia', *Journal of Clinical Psychology*, 63(4), pp. 409–416.

Hadden, S.B. (1955) 'Historic background of group psychotherapy', *International Journal of Group Psychotherapy*, 5(2), pp. 162–168.

Haley, J. (1963) *Strategies of psychotherapy*. New York: Grune and Stratton.

Jones, E. and Asen, E. (2000) *Systemic couple therapy and depression*. London: Karnac Books.

Koffel, E.A., Koffel, J.B. and Gehrman, P.R. (2015) 'A meta-analysis of group cognitive behavioral therapy for insomnia', *Sleep Medicine Reviews*, 19, pp. 6–16.

Lecomte, T. (2016) *Group CBT for psychosis: a guidebook for clinicians*. New York: Oxford University Press.

Lieberman, M.A., Miles, M.B. and Yalom, I.D. (1973) *Encounter groups: first facts*. New York: Basic Books.

Maturana, H. and Varela, F. (1992) *The tree of knowledge: the biological roots of human understanding*. Rev. edn. Boston, MA: Shambhala Publications.

McNamee, S. and Gergen, K. (eds.) (1992) *Therapy as social construction*. London: SAGE.

Minuchin, S. (1974) *Families and family therapy*. Cambridge, MA: Harvard University Press.

Morrison, N. (2001) 'Group cognitive therapy: treatment of choice or sub-optimal option?', *Behavioural and Cognitive Psychotherapy*, 29(3), pp. 311–332.

Nichols, W.C. and Everett, C.A. (1986) *Systemic family therapy: an integrative approach*. New York: Guilford Press.

Okumura, Y. and Ichikura, K. (2014) 'Efficacy and acceptability of group cognitive behavioral therapy for depression: a systematic review and meta-analysis', *Journal of Affective Disorders*, 164, pp. 155–164.

Pearce, S. and Haigh, R. (2017) *The theory and practice of democratic therapeutic community treatment*. London and Philadelphia: Jessica Kingsley Publishers.

Pines, M. (1983) 'The contribution of S.H. Foulkes to group therapy', in Pines, M. (ed.) *The evolution of group analysis*. London: Routledge and Kegan Paul, pp. 265–285.

Pines, M. (1984) 'Mirroring in group analysis as a developmental and therapeutic process', in Lear, T.E. (ed.) *Spheres of group analysis*. London: Group-Analytic Society Publications, pp. 118–136.

Pinquart, M., Oslejsek, B. and Teubert, D. (2016) 'Efficacy of systemic therapy on adults with mental disorders: a meta-analysis', *Psychotherapy Research*, 26(2), pp. 241–257.

Raffin, A.L., Fachel, J.M., Ferrao, Y.A., Pasquoto de Souza, F. and Cordioli, A. V. (2009) 'Predictors of response to group cognitive-behavioral therapy in the treatment of obsessive-compulsive disorder', *European Psychiatry*, 24(5), pp. 297–306.

Rogers, C. (1970) *Carl Rogers on encounter groups*. New York: Harper & Row.

Satir, V. (1990) *Peoplemaking*. London: Souvenir Press.

Selvini-Palazzoli, M., Boscolo, L., Cecchin, G. and Prata, G. (1978) *Paradox and counterparadox*. New York: Jason Aronson.

Shulman, B., Dueck, R., Ryan, D., Breau, G., Sadowski, I. and Misri, S. (2018) 'Feasibility of a mindfulness-based cognitive therapy group intervention as an adjunctive treatment for postpartum depression and anxiety', *Journal of Affective Disorders*, 235, pp. 61–67.

Vetere, A. and Dallos, R. (2003) *Working systemically with families: formulation, intervention and evaluation*. London: Karnac Books.

Vossler, A. (2010) 'Systemic approaches', in Barker, M., Vossler, A. and Langdridge, D. (eds.) *Understanding counselling and psychotherapy*. London: SAGE, pp. 191–210.

Vossler, A., Squire, B. and Bingham, C. (2017) 'Systemic approaches', in Vossler, A., Harvard, C., Pike, G., Barker, M. and Raabe, B. (eds.) *Mad or bad? A critical approach to counselling and forensic psychology*. London: SAGE, pp. 223–236.

Watzlawick, P., Weakland, J.H. and Fisch, R. (1974) *Change: principles of problem formulation and problem resolution*. New York and London: W.W. Norton and Company.

White, M. and Epston, D. (1990) *Narrative means to therapeutic ends*. New York: W.W. Norton and Company.

Wiener, N. (1961) *Cybernetics: or control and communication in the animal and the machine*. Cambridge, MA: MIT Press.

Winnicott, D.W. (1965) 'Ego distortion in terms of true and false self', in Winnicott, D.W. *The maturational processes and the facilitating environment: studies in the theory of emotional development*. London: The Hogarth Press and the Institute of Psycho-analysis.

Yalom, I.D. and Leszcz, M. (2005) *The theory and practice of group psychotherapy*. 5th edn. New York: Basic Books.

Chapter 15

Beyond face to face: technology-based counselling

Andreas Vossler

Contents

Introduction

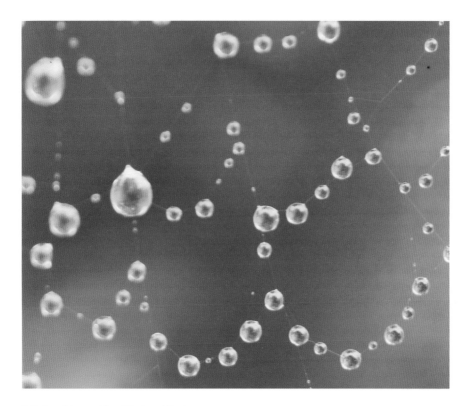

'Web of tears' by Elaine Carty

Chapter 14 described how systemic and group therapies have widened the traditional therapeutic focus beyond the individual client. In a similar way, technology-based counselling services are changing mental health and counselling practice by moving it beyond face-to-face settings. However, since practitioners started using technology to provide help for mental health problems, opinions about technology-supported services have been divided.

More progressive voices stress the advantages and potential of technology-based counselling, such as how relatively accessible it is (in terms of service access and cost) and the possibilities it offers for helping underserved populations (such as people with disabilities and/or in remote geographical areas; e.g. Clarke *et al.*, 2016). 'Traditionalist' clients and practitioners, on the other hand, seem generally sceptical about any move away from the conventional in-person therapy setting. Psychotherapy in a digital context might feel threatening to them (Balick, 2014), and they can be concerned about the safety and effectiveness of technology-based counselling. Where a person stands in this debate might also depend on their personal relationship with the digital world, and whether or not they grew up with digital technology and have a natural fluency in using it – that is, their level of digital literacy (Buckingham, 2013).

This chapter aims to:

- provide an overview of the different forms of technology-based services available for people who experience mental health difficulties

- discuss the potential and limitations of interventions that go beyond face-to-face counselling, including those related to accessibility and the expression of emotion

- explore the specific practical and ethical issues faced by practitioners and clients in providing and receiving technology-based services, which by their very nature involve at least a reduced human component.

1 Different forms of technology-based counselling

What different forms of **technology-based counselling** (or 'e-therapy') services have in common is that they deliver help by electronic means, and/or that practitioners and clients are not physically present in the same space. However, beyond this, the interventions differ significantly; for example, in terms of the technology employed for the service, and whether it provides counselling in the traditional sense (e.g. through a contracted, bounded relationship between the client and the therapist) or through computerised self-help information that can be therapeutic (Barak, Klein and Proudfoot, 2009). For a balanced evaluation of the potential advantages and limitations of technology-based counselling, it is therefore essential to first understand the differences between the available interventions and how they might be experienced by service users.

Technology-based help for mental health issues started more than 60 years ago, with telephone helplines. These are now very well established in the UK, offered by many services and charities who provide practical information and crisis support through generic telephone helplines (e.g. Samaritans and Childline) and/or thematic telephone hotlines for specific needs and problems (e.g. HIV/AIDS, substance addiction and sexual abuse; Vossler, 2010). Many practitioners working in private practice offer telephone counselling – in a more therapeutic sense – as a contracted, ongoing relationship between a counsellor and a client, conducted at specific prearranged times entirely over audio communication (public telephone networks or internet-based telephony; Rosenfield, 2003).

The use of e-therapy has rapidly increased with the advent and growth of the internet (Goss and Anthony, 2003). E-therapy services can generally be situated along a continuum, with those involving a strong human interaction component (e.g. telephone counselling) at one end, and standalone interventions involving no human interaction at the other end (e.g. many mental health apps). The rest of this section will briefly introduce the main forms of technology-based counselling along this continuum, from 'high human factor' (videoconference counselling) to 'high tech factor' (apps/chatbots) services (see Figure 15.1).

Technology-based counselling
Forms of help and support for mental health problems that are delivered by electronic means.

Figure 15.1 Continuum of technology-based counselling, with 'high human factor' services at one end and 'high tech factor' services at the other

1.1   Videoconference counselling

Counselling via videoconference was reportedly first trialled back in 1961 for group psychotherapy as a way to offer a 'two-way television' designed to extend mental health service provision to remote areas (Wittson, Affleck and Johnson, 1961). Technological advances and telecommunication applications that specialise in providing video chats (e.g. Skype; D'Arcy *et al.*, 2015) have since made videoconferencing much more widely available. With the concurrent use of both audio and video, videoconferencing counselling (sometimes referred to as 'telemedicine', 'telehealth', 'webcam counselling' and 'video-link therapy') comes comparatively close to the traditional face-to-face format. Research suggests that videoconference counselling can be an effective means of delivering treatment (Simpson, 2009) and has similar clinical outcomes to face-to-face psychotherapy (Backhaus *et al.*, 2012). The frequent practice of integrating video sessions with face-to-face sessions may suggest that videoconferencing is seen as complementary to face-to-face psychotherapy rather than as a substitute for it (Cipolletta, Frassoni and Faccio, 2018).

1.2   Text-based online counselling

Next on the client–practitioner contact continuum are text-based services that are delivered on personal computers, tablets or smartphones without an audio or video component. While 'online therapy' and 'online counselling' are sometimes used in a wider sense, the terms are usually employed to describe text-based services that are provided by a practitioner (rather than therapy programmes partly or entirely delivered by a computer program). Many providers offer both *synchronous* (real-time) services – such as live chats – and *asynchronous* (time-delayed) services – such as online discussion forums. Online counselling can also be delivered asynchronously via email exchanges between the counsellor and the client. Practitioners can combine the different forms of text-based online counselling (e.g. they might provide synchronous chat room counselling followed up by an asynchronous email exchange; Vossler, 2010).

Research literature on the therapeutic effects of expressive or reflective writing (Goss, 2013; Stuckey and Nobel, 2010; Pennebaker and Chung, 2007) suggests that just the act of writing about thoughts and feelings in text-based online counselling can be beneficial for clients. This research shows that expressive writing has the potential to alleviate stress and anxiety and improve well-being and understanding of oneself, which can be explained by **emotion regulation** processes (Koole, 2009; Gross, 2014). Writing about difficult experiences seems to help people to reflect on deep thoughts and feelings and to articulate interior processes (Rimé, 2009), thus facilitating one's ability to cope with challenging experiences (Gortner, Rude and Pennebaker, 2006). Online counselling can utilise these benefits of expressive writing (Wright, 2002); therapeutic email exchanges are 'perhaps [...] the inevitable future of therapeutic letters' (Moules, 2009, p. 109).

Emotion regulation
Refers to the processes by which a person influences the emotions they have, when they have them, and how they experience and express them.

Activity 15.1: Writing an email to yourself

Allow about 30 minutes

Think about a situation in the past when you felt angry or upset (or indeed, both). Spend around 15 minutes writing an email (or letter) about the situation (what happened, who was involved, etc.). Make sure you write everything in one sitting, and don't reflect too much about what you write. When you have finished, send the email/letter to your own email account/postal address. Let at least a day pass before you open and read through it. What feelings are evident from your email/letter, and were you unaware that you held any of those feelings before you wrote it?

Discussion

This activity might give you a sense of how expressive writing can increase self-awareness and help a person to explore their thoughts, perceptions and underlying feelings in a more focused and engaged manner. Aspects that you were previously unaware of might become clearer when expressed as part of a written story.

In the last two decades, text-based online counselling has significantly grown in popularity in the UK. Faced with overstretched NHS mental health services and long waiting lists, an increasing number of people are now opting for online counselling (Bennion *et al*, 2017; Ratcliff, 2017). Clients can choose from a vast range of services, from youth agencies, employee assistance providers and university counselling services to private counselling practitioners and commercial online therapy platforms. Some of these services are available for free. Commercial providers and private practitioners will charge, with sessions tending to be cheaper than face-to-face therapy (Ratcliff, 2017). Online counselling is also offered as part of the Improving Access to Psychological Therapies (IAPT) programme within the NHS. At the time of writing, Ieso Digital Health is commissioned by over 40 NHS Clinical Commissioning Groups (CCGs) to provide online cognitive behavioural therapy (CBT) for patients with a range of common mental health difficulties (e.g. anxiety, depression, post-traumatic stress disorder, phobias and social anxiety; Martinez and Farhan, 2019). These online CBT sessions follow the same format as traditional face-to-face CBT and are delivered by a fully qualified practitioner.

The case illustration below exemplifies how online counselling can be helpful for young people. The case is fictional but based on real service-users' experiences of online counselling services for young people in the UK.

Case illustration: Lu receives online counselling

Lu felt she was spiralling downwards but she had no one to talk to and began to think it would have been better if she'd never been born. She was afraid that her parents would never understand or accept her – Lu's parents are traditional Chinese, and when she was very young, they would talk about her getting married and having children. How could she tell them she liked girls as well as boys?

Then one day, Lu saw a poster on the wall of her school's library about a free online counselling service. After her parents went to bed, she looked up the website. Lu saw that she could sign up without giving her name, so that's what she did.

Through the service platform, Lu was able to find an online counsellor who she felt 'got' what she was going through – someone who wasn't judgemental, which made the sessions feel like a 'safe space.' Lu quickly began to trust her counsellor and, over the next two months, she was able to meet weekly with her on a one-to-one basis for 50-minute chat room sessions (though sometimes Lu felt the need to cut them short).

Lu was surprised by what she got from the experience:

'One unexpected thing was the discussion forum. Not only could I read about other kids going through the same thing that I was, but sometimes I could even help others by sharing my own story. I also got support from the forum moderator.

'Because it was anonymous, I felt freer to talk about my feelings at a time when I could barely admit them to myself. I still haven't gotten to the point where I feel I can talk to my parents, but I do now feel braver about looking for a face-to-face counsellor to help me with coming out about my sexuality in the future.'

Pause for reflection

What do you think are the service properties and contextual factors that were helpful for Lu? Do you think it made a significant difference that she could use the service anonymously?

1.3 Computerised therapy programmes

Computerised therapy programmes (also referred to as 'internet-based therapy programmes') are offered via computer programs and are delivered to devices such as personal computers, laptops, tablets and smartphones. As such, they are often delivered with reduced or even no human contact. The programmes are usually manual-based and highly structured. They are presented in a multimedia format through a range of applications and include animations, graphics, videos, interactive episodes, homework assignments and access to supplementary resources. The client's progress throughout therapy is monitored using self-assessment items and integrated symptom and distress ratings. Interaction with a therapist might be limited to weekly contact via phone or email, although there are also 'therapist-guided' programmes available, whereby a named therapist guides the client through the programme (Hedman, Botella and Berger, 2016).

By far the most common form of computerised psychotherapy is computerised cognitive behavioural therapy (CCBT). CBT seems particularly well suited to being provided in an internet-based format, as it is a reasonably structured and skills-based approach (with psychoeducational components) that can be translated into a therapy manual (see Chapter 10). CCBT typically draws on self-help principles and content, which is why it is sometimes also called 'internet-based self-help therapy'. Like self-help books and videos before them, computerised systems aim to embody and boost user features that are considered to be pivotal for positive counselling outcomes, such as engagement, self-efficacy and motivation (Vossler, 2010).

The National Institute for Health and Care Excellence (NICE) (2009) and the Scottish Intercollegiate Guidelines Network (SIGN) (2010) recommend self-help programmes based on the principles of CBT as an initial lower-intensity treatment for a range of mental health difficulties. CCBT programmes are also provided to clients in the NHS/IAPT context as well as in specialist CBT therapy clinics (Cavanagh and Millings, 2013). An example of such a programme is SilverCloud, an eight-week CCBT programme for people experiencing stress, anxiety and depression that can be completed at a time and pace set by the user (at the time of writing, it is a recommended course in the NHS Apps Library).

1.4 Mental health apps

The number of available computer/device apps for mental health has rapidly increased in recent years, along with the dramatic growth of smartphone and tablet usage in the UK (it is estimated that 4 out of 5 adults now have a smartphone; Martinez and Farhan, 2019). While most mental health apps seem to offer well-being support rather than clinical care (Anthes, 2016), healthcare providers increasingly rely on these digital tools to provide or supplement mainstream interventions, or as a first low-intensity step for help-seeking clients (as suggested in the NHS's Long Term Plan; NHS England, 2019); for example, as part of the IAPT programme.

The NHS Apps Library offers a selection of apps to help people manage and improve their mental health (Bennion *et al.*, 2017). These tools are approved and recommended based on a defined set of criteria, which includes data protection (NHS, 2019). An example of an app listed in the NHS Apps Library is Calm Harm, which is a digital tool developed to support people in resisting or managing the urge to self-harm. It is based on the principles of dialectical behaviour therapy, a therapeutic approach that is often used to treat people with mood difficulties. The most recently developed mental health apps also employ social networking, which can facilitate useful and dynamic interactions among users (Bennion *et al.*, 2017).

The latest development at the 'high tech' end of the interventions continuum is **conversational agents** using artificial intelligence (AI) to mimic therapeutic support. These so-called 'chatbots' are automated messaging software programs that converse with users through voice or text, with research pointing to their potential to mimic human conversations (Miner, Milstein and Hancock, 2017). An example of such a chatbot is 'Woebot', launched in 2017. Woebot is programmed with CBT principles to help people cope with feelings of depression and anxiety. At the time of writing, the therapeutic potential of fully automated conversational agents, such as Woebot, seems limited. They only seem to allow scripted interactions and struggle to respond adequately to nuanced concerns, which means that they are not a suitable replacement for human support (Browne, Arthur and Slozberg, 2018). Due to the failure of Woebot to respond appropriately to clues indicating child sexual abuse, the Children's Commissioner for England has categorised the app as currently not fit for purpose for use by young people (White, 2018).

Conversational agent
A software program developed to converse with humans by interpreting and responding to statements made in ordinary natural language.

In practice, of course, there are also services that draw on different types of technology-based counselling, such as the service introduced in Information box 15.1. E-therapies can also be paired with traditional forms of counselling (e.g. supplementing with online counselling). The different types of technology-based counselling look and work quite differently in practice, which means that practitioners and clients need to decide what works best for whom, and for which problems, in light of the advantages and disadvantages of each.

Information box 15.1: The Big White Wall

The Big White Wall (BWW) is a successful social enterprise set up in 2007 by British entrepreneur Jen Hyatt, in partnership with the Tavistock and Portman NHS foundation trust. It is an online well-being and mental health support portal that offers a range of services (including peer and professional support and creative self-expression) in one place.

BWW is a fast-growing service providing free support to the employees of a long list of companies and organisations, and to students of around 30 UK universities, which pay BWW a licence fee. In recent years, the service has also expanded to a range of different countries. Depending on the user's needs (and the contract their employer or university has with BWW), there are three service areas available:

- *An online community/support network*: The BWW baseline service is an online community that is accessible around the clock. Users can add or respond to comments posted on 'the wall' and forums (all contributions are completely anonymous). The website is monitored/moderated at all times by clinically trained support staff known as 'wall guides', who ensure the safety and anonymity of all members. Users can also use a range of art and writing therapies, psychoeducational materials, self-assessment tools, and discussion forums ('talkabouts').

- *Guided-support online courses*: In this area, users find a range of self-managed and clinically facilitated programmes for individuals and groups on topics such as managing anxiety, depression, negative thinking, quitting smoking, alcohol use and improved sleep. Users can self-refer to this structured, CBT-based content provided in an online group environment (and monitored 24 hours a day by counsellors).

- *Live therapy*: This area offers a range of one-to-one real-time therapies delivered via instant text messages, audio and/or videoconferences from BWW therapists (meeting times are agreed beforehand). Users can choose a therapist from a list of approved counsellors who provide NICE-approved treatments for anxiety, depression and other common mental health conditions. This area is only available via a GP referral.

Research into the impact of the BWW on users' mental health seems to lag behind the fast expansion of the service (at the time of writing, results of a randomised controlled trial on its efficacy are being analysed). However, evidence exists showing a generally positive effect of peer support in the area of online mental health communities (e.g. Park and Convey, 2017; Prescott, Hanley and Ujhelyi, 2017).

Pause for reflection

Imagine you are going to seek help for a mental health difficulty. Which type of technology-based counselling described in this section would you prefer to receive? Do you think there are any situations or problems that could be helped more effectively by these services than by traditional face-to-face counselling?

2   The properties and potential of technology-based counselling

The case illustration of Lu (Section 1.2) highlights a range of specific properties shared by the different forms of technology-based counselling, and the potential inherent in these kinds of services. The case example illustrates two important advantages of many technology-based counselling services: their high level of accessibility and the degree of flexibility offered to users (Clarke *et al.*, 2016; D'Arcy *et al.*, 2015). Lu joined the online counselling platform without having to overcome any barriers associated with traditional healthcare (e.g. waiting times and GP referrals). She was able to access the service when and from where it suited her, using her mobile phone. E-therapy can often be accessed anonymously (as in Lu's case) and delivered by non-commercial providers for free or at a low cost, which can make it an attractive alternative to face-to-face counselling (Rozbroj *et al.*, 2015). It can also provide a service option for clients in remote geographical areas and for those who cannot visit traditional services because of disability or the nature of their mental health difficulties (e.g. agoraphobia; Martinez and Farhan, 2019).

Anonymity and accessibility are also important factors for reaching out to people who are worried about the stigma associated with mental health difficulties, and to marginalised client groups who feel their needs are not appropriately met by traditional mental health services. For example, stigma and negative therapy experiences are often reported by lesbian, gay and bisexual people as barriers to accessing traditional services (Department of Health and Equality and Human Rights Group, 2009; Guasp and Taylor, 2015). Like Lu in the case illustration, children and young people can have concerns and fears about engaging in face-to-face counselling (Gibson and Cartwright, 2014), or might not have access to in-person support due to a lack of mental health services available for this age group (Ersahin and Hanley, 2017). For these often hard-to-reach and underserved user groups, technology-based counselling has the potential to provide a safe alternative that might include peer support (as in Lu's case) and tailor-made interventions to meet the specific needs of these clients (Lucassen *et al.*, 2015; Rozbroj *et al.*, 2015).

In the case illustration, Lu seems to have quickly developed a good and trusting relationship with her online counsellor. This is in line with research findings indicating that, while the employed technology can make it more difficult to develop a therapeutic relationship (e.g. due to the lack of nonverbal cues or the tone of voice in online counselling), it is still possible in this setting to establish and maintain an alliance sufficient to facilitate psychological change (Berger, 2016; Hanley, 2012). With words, acronyms and emoticons (pictorial representations of facial expressions used to convey emotions), therapists and clients can create mental representations of each other that help to build an alliance in text-based online counselling (Suler, 2010). For videoconference counselling, Simpson and Reid (2014) report clients commenting that 'the enhanced control and personal space that they feel in video therapy can enhance the therapeutic alliance' (p. 295). Bickmore, Gruber and Picard (2005) even suggest that users may be able to develop a form of therapeutic alliance with a conversational agent system if 'relational behaviours' are explicitly designed into the agent's computer interface.

Lu also seems to have experienced a greater degree of autonomy and control when messaging with her counsellor in the online environment (she 'felt freer to talk' and cut the sessions short when needed). Clients undergoing different forms of e-therapy typically report having increased control over counselling processes and interventions – for example, in mobile phone text counselling (Gibson and Cartwright, 2014) and videoconferencing (Drum and Littleton, 2014) – especially when delivered in an anonymous context. Clients often seem to have more control in this context over session timing and endings, and they become less concerned about how they are perceived by the counsellor (Gibson and Cartwright, 2014). They show fewer inhibitions in disclosing intimate information, which is often brought up at a much faster pace online (Fletcher-Tomenius and Vossler, 2009). This phenomenon has been described as the **online disinhibition effect** (Suler, 2004) and can be explained by anonymity and the lack of visual, auditory and contextual cues (e.g. information about social status or ethnic background). Such factors are especially relevant in text-based online counselling but also, to some degree, in telephone and videoconference counselling.

Online disinhibition effect
Refers to a lack of restraint when communicating online in comparison to communicating in person (can manifest in positive and negative ways).

2.1   Research evidence for technology-based counselling

Research evaluating text-based online counselling (as used by Lu in the case illustration above) generally tends to support the effectiveness of the intervention (D'Arcy *et al.*, 2015; Barak and Grohol, 2011). In their meta-analysis comparing face-to-face and online therapy (based on 14 studies involving 9764 clients), Barak *et al.* (2008) found no significant differences between therapy delivered face to face and the online interventions. There is also some qualitative evidence suggesting that online counselling might be experienced as more comfortable and less threatening than face-to-face counselling, which could be especially relevant for clients who experience social anxieties (D'Arcy *et al.*, 2015; Suler, 2010).

The evidence base for computerised therapy programmes has significantly expanded in recent years (Andersson, 2018), showing that these treatments often result in outcomes that are similar to those of conventional face-to-face psychotherapy (Berger, 2016; Carlbring *et al.*, (2018); Fenger *et al.*, 2016). However, the randomised controlled trials that are used to evaluate these programmes often don't capture service-users' and clients' experiences, which means it is questionable whether CCBT is equivalent to traditional therapy from a service-user perspective. Additionally, Cavanagh and Millings (2013) report that, in practice, dropout rates for self-help CCBT interventions are high (especially for unsupported low-contact CCBT).

Mental health apps are developed and changed at such a pace that it is difficult for researchers to evaluate the tools and their effectiveness in routine care (Bennion *et al.*, 2017). While there is some evidence to suggest that well-designed and empirically-based applications have the potential to improve outcomes for users, for many of these tools, evidence of their effectiveness is still lacking (Anthes, 2016; Martinez and Farhan, 2019).

The Methodology box below provides a brief overview of online research methods that are often used to evaluate the different forms of technology-based counselling.

Methodology: Online research methods

Online research methods (or internet-mediated research methods) are employed to collect data from, or about, people via the internet and its associated technologies. They can be used as part of both quantitative and qualitative research projects/designs and include different types of synchronous and asynchronous online methods, including:

- questionnaires/surveys supported by online survey software (e.g. Qualtrics or Survey Monkey)

- interviews via email or online instant messaging

- focus groups via group emails/mailing lists or discussion forums

- experiments

- clinical trials.

As with e-therapy, there are some advantages of online research methods compared to offline data collection. Online methods allow researchers to gather data from a large number of people in a fast and cost-effective manner, and can provide access to populations that might otherwise be difficult to reach (e.g. sexual minorities). Online research can also make it easier for participants to talk about sensitive topics (due to anonymity and the lack of physical proximity).

However, the depth of qualitative data collected online can be limited; it can be more difficult to follow up responses online than in person, and it might include more misrepresentations (e.g. participants lying about their age; Hewson, 2014). The collection of data on the internet also raises a range of practical and ethical issues which are different from, or not present in, offline research. These include concerns around online data security and confidentiality, and the blurred line between 'public' and 'private' in online spaces. Hewson (2016) and the British Psychological Society's *Ethics guidelines for internet-mediated research* (see the Further reading section) provide more information and guidance on these issues.

3   Challenges and limitations of technology-based counselling

The account below illustrates some of the limitations of technology-based counselling, some of the concerns around its growth and some of the ethical issues that are relevant in this context. This is a real account of videoconference counselling but the client's name has been changed.

Client voices: Ron's account of videoconference counselling

I had in-person therapy for anxieties and depression before, but when I moved abroad, I wanted to talk to someone in my own language, so tried therapy via Skype with a therapist back home.

It was a bit strange at the beginning, but the positive side to the online sessions was that it is much easier to fit into my schedule. After a few of the Skype sessions it felt more normal to have therapy 'at home'. However, when talking about difficult things, in the in-office sessions back home I would often cry, but something about the online experience almost makes it seem much more transactional – especially when asked to read your credit card number at the end of the Skype session.

I just think that the screens make the sessions less human, maybe? Perhaps because we spend so much time on the computer for work, so doing therapy through the same device creates a much more businesses-y feel to the interaction. Whereas for in-person sessions, often when you start to cry there is a tissue box that the therapist would normally pass to me, or that would be right nearby.

Is this to say that in-person sessions encourage us to push out more? Are they ultimately more healing? That I am not sure of – I am now looking for in-person therapy again.

Pause for reflection

Based on what you have read in this chapter about the different types of technology-based counselling, do you think Ron could have benefited from a different kind of e-therapy (or a mixed-technology service)? Or do you think he is rather in need of in-person counselling at this point?

It is notable how Ron describes his experience of videoconference counselling as different from in-person counselling (describing videoconferencing as 'much more transactional' and 'businesses-y', with a potential lack of presence and depth). His account resonates with sceptical voices in the field, who question whether technology-based services can provide therapy at all, or if they involve processes that are fundamentally different from, or inferior to, face-to-face therapy (Weinberg and Rolnick, 2019). Dependent on the specific form of e-therapy, the possibilities of expressing and sharing feelings and emotions can be relatively limited. The nuances of therapeutic dynamics – as we know them in face-to-face counselling – can be reduced by the lack of nonverbal communication and real-time encounters (in asynchronous forms), or completely removed by the lack of any human component (as in, for example, chatbot programs). The absence of contextual cues might also create uncertainties and anxieties on both sides, especially if clients and counsellors are not used to online work.

In his account, Ron explains that, influenced by the 'less human' Skype counselling session experience, he decided to go back to face-to-face counselling. This is consistent with the observation that dropout rates (or attrition rates) continue to be comparatively high for technology-based mental health interventions. For computerised treatments, it is reported that a substantial proportion of users drop out in the early treatment stages (Melville, Casey and Kavanagh, 2010). For programmes for depression, the completion rate can be as low as 50 per cent (Christensen *et al.*, 2004). Although these rates are comparable to mean rates of non-attendance in IAPT services (between 42 per cent and 48 per cent; Marshall *et al.*, 2016), it has been suggested that an increased 'human factor' could strengthen user engagement with these interventions. This can be done by building in real-time social-networking peer support or by providing scheduled text messaging feedback to programme users (Clarke *et al.*, 2016).

In a broader sense, there is also the question of the role and function of technology-based counselling in mental health service provision. Mental health service providers often employ e-therapies as initial lower-intensity treatments for mental health difficulties in a stepped-care model of service provision (NICE, 2011). However, Ron from the client account above might have had no real choice in the service he received; videoconferencing with a therapist in his home country may have been the only way for him to receive therapy in his own language. In a similar way, and due to the resource pressures in mental health practice and the lack of spaces available for in-person services, telephone or online support might be the only viable service in some geographical areas. This can be problematic, as technology-based counselling is potentially unsuitable for certain user groups (e.g. older adults who are unfamiliar with technology) or problem situations (e.g. crisis or unexpected complications/suicide risks). Additionally, technology-based counselling completely excludes population groups who lack internet access (often due to lower socioeconomic status; Deloitte, 2018). Also, being assigned to computerised therapies might give service users the feeling that their difficulties are not serious enough to warrant a 'more human' treatment.

Finally, the use of technology to deliver counselling via telephone or the internet has created a whole range of ethical issues and questions about professional boundaries that need to be considered carefully by both users and practitioners. As with all internet applications, there will always be insecurities about the identities of those involved, and around the sensitive material that is transmitted (Rochlen, Zack and Speyer, 2004). Practitioners providing online counselling need to minimise potential risks (e.g. by using encryption, encoded software and passwords) and ensure transparency around their service (e.g. around their availability and the times when clients can expect email replies from them). It is also important to have agreed arrangements in place for technology breakdowns and crisis situations (Vossler, 2010).

Conclusion

No matter how one feels about it, e-therapy is here to stay, and it is likely to grow further. Clients can choose from a broad range of technology-based services and tools with different features (e.g. synchronous or asynchronous services) and various degrees of human interaction. While all of them aim to provide help for mental health problems, only videoconferencing and online counselling provide counselling in the form of a contracted, bounded relationship between a client and a practitioner. Computerised therapy programmes and mental health apps are, in essence, simply self-help tools that can be utilised therapeutically. Some forms, such as computerised therapy programmes, have a fast-growing evidence base; however, evidence of effectiveness is lacking for many mental health apps that have mushroomed in number in recent years.

Clients seem to benefit from the increased availability and accessibility of online services and the greater degree of autonomy and control when using them. Technology-based counselling is relatively cost-effective and seems to correspond well with current policy drives in healthcare, such as increased patient choice and the efforts to reduce mental health stigma. However, this chapter has demonstrated that e-therapy will not work for everyone and in every situation, and that its advantages and disadvantages should be weighed up in order to assess its usefulness as a treatment option. When delivering these services, providers need to adhere to well-defined and targeted quality standards, rather than treat these interventions simply as cost-cutting opportunities to fill provision gaps.

Further reading

- This book on online therapy includes a section on therapy 'beyond face to face' and 'beyond the individual' (Section 3, 'Online group therapy', chapters 13–17):

  Weinberg, H. and Rolnick, A. (eds.) (2019) *Theory and practice of online therapy: internet-delivered interventions for individuals, groups, families, and organizations.* New York: Routledge.

- The following guidelines provide information on practical and ethical issues related to doing online research:

  British Psychological Society (2017) *Ethics guidelines for internet-mediated research.* Available at: https://www.bps.org.uk/news-and-policy/ethics-guidelines-internet-mediated-research-2017 (Accessed: 5 May 2020).

- Ethical and professional issues related to providing technology-based counselling are further discussed in the following resources:

  Anthony, K. and Goss, S. (2009) *Guidelines for online counselling and psychotherapy: including guidelines for online supervision.* 3rd edn. Lutterworth: British Association for Counselling and Psychotherapy.

  Yellowlees, P., Shore, J. and Roberts, L. (2010) 'Practice guidelines for videoconferencing-based telemental health – October 2009', *Telemedicine Journal and e-Health*, 16(10), pp. 1074–1089.

References

Andersson, G. (2018) 'Internet interventions: past, present and future', *Internet Interventions*, 12, pp. 181–188.

Anthes, E. (2016) 'Mental health: there's an app for that', *Nature*, 532(7597), pp. 20–23. Available at: https://www.nature.com/news/mental-health-there-s-an-app-for-that-1.19694 (Accessed: 6 September 2019).

Backhaus, A., Agha, Z., Maglione, M.L., Repp, A., Ross, B., Zuest, D., Rice-Thorp, N.M., Lohr, J. and Thorp, S.R. (2012) 'Videoconferencing psychotherapy: a systematic review', *Psychological Services*, 9(2), pp. 111–131.

Balick, A. (2014) 'How to think about psychotherapy in a digital context', in Weitz, P. (ed.) *Psychotherapy 2.0: where psychotherapy and technology meet.* London and New York: Routledge, pp. 23–40.

Barak, A. and Grohol, J.M. (2011) 'Current and future trends in internet-supported mental health interventions', *Journal of Technology in Human Services*, 29(3), pp. 155–196.

Barak, A., Hen, L., Boniel-Nissim, M. and Shapira, N. (2008) 'A comprehensive review and a meta-analysis of the effectiveness of internet-based psychotherapeutic interventions', *Journal of Technology in Human Services*, 26(2–4), pp. 109–160.

Barak, A., Klein, B. and Proudfoot, J.G. (2009) 'Defining internet-supported therapeutic interventions', *Annals of Behavioral Medicine*, 38(1), pp. 4–17.

Bennion, M.R., Hardy, G., Moore, R.K. and Millings, A. (2017) 'E-therapies in England for stress, anxiety or depression: what is being used in the NHS? A survey of mental health services', *BMJ Open*, 7(1), e014844.

Berger, T. (2016) 'The therapeutic alliance in internet interventions: a narrative review and suggestions for future research', *Psychotherapy Research*, 27(5), pp. 511–524.

Bickmore, T., Gruber, A. and Picard, R. (2005) 'Establishing the computer-patient working alliance in automated health behavior change interventions', *Patient Education Counselling*, 59(1), pp. 21–30.

Browne, D., Arthur, M. and Slozberg, M. (2018) *Do mental health chatbots work?*. Available at: https://www.healthline.com/health/mental-health/chatbots-reviews#1 (Accessed: 25 October 2019).

Buckingham, D. (2013) 'Making sense of the 'digital generation': growing up with digital media', *Self & Society*, 40(3), pp. 7–15.

Carlbring, P., Andersson, G., Cuijpers, P., Riper, H. and Hedman-Lagerlöf, E. (2018) 'Internet-based vs. face-to-face cognitive behaviour therapy for psychiatric and somatic disorders: an updated systematic review and meta-analysis', *Cognitive Behaviour Therapy*, 47(1), pp. 1–18.

Cavanagh, K. and Millings (2013) 'Increasing engagement with computerised cognitive behavioural therapies', *EAI Endorsed Transactions on Ambient Systems*, January–June, 1(2), e3.

Christensen, H., Griffiths, K.M., Korten, A.E., Brittliffe, K. and Groves, C.A. (2004) 'Comparison of changes in anxiety and depression symptoms of spontaneous users and trial participants of a cognitive behaviour therapy website', *Journal of Medical Internet Research*, 6(4), e46.

Cipolletta, S., Frassoni, E. and Faccio, E. (2018) 'Construing a therapeutic relationship online: an analysis of videoconference sessions', *Clinical Psychologist*, 22(2), pp. 220–229.

Clarke, J., Proudfoot, J., Whitton, A., Birch, M.R., Boyd, M., Parker, G., Manicavasagar, V., Hadzi-Pavlovic, D. and Fogarty, A. (2016) 'Therapeutic alliance with a fully automated mobile phone and web-based intervention: secondary analysis of a randomized controlled trial', *JMIR Mental Health*, 3 (1), e10.

D'Arcy, J., Reynolds, W., Stiles, W.B. and Hanley, T. (2015) 'The online calming effect: does the internet provide a more comfortable modality for conducting psychotherapy', in Riva, G., Wiederhold, B.K. and Cipresso, P. (eds.) *The psychology of social networking: identity and relationships in online communities*. Warsaw/Berlin: De Gruyter Open, pp. 17–28.

Deloitte (2018) *2018 Global health care outlook: the evolution of smart health care*. Available at: https://www2.deloitte.com/content/dam/Deloitte/global/ Documents/Life-Sciences-Health-Care/gx-lshc-hc-outlook-2018.pdf (Accessed: 5 May 2020).

Department of Health and Equality and Human Rights Group (2009) *Sexual orientation: a practical guide for the NHS*. United Kingdom: Department of Health.

Drum, K.B. and Littleton, H.L. (2014) 'Therapeutic boundaries in telepsychology: unique issues and best practice recommendations', *Professional Psychology, Research and Practice*, 45(5), pp. 309–315.

Ersahin, Z. and Hanley, T. (2017) 'Using text-based synchronous chat to offer therapeutic support to students: a systematic review of the research literature', *Health Education Journal*, 76(5), pp. 531–543.

Fenger, M., Lindschou, J., Gluud, C., Winkel, P., Jørgensen, L., Kruse-Blinkenberg, S. and Lau, M. (2016) 'Internet-based self-help therapy with FearFighter™ versus no intervention for anxiety disorders in adults: study protocol for a randomised controlled trial', *Trials*, 17(1), p. 525.

Fletcher-Tomenius, L. and Vossler, A. (2009) 'Trust in online therapeutic relationships: the therapist's experience', *Counselling Psychology Review*, 24(2), pp. 24–34.

Gibson, K. and Cartwright, C. (2014) 'Young people's experiences of mobile phone text counselling: balancing connection and control', *Children and Youth Services Review*, 43, pp. 96–104.

Gortner, E., Rude, S.S. and Pennebaker, J.W. (2006) 'Benefits of expressive writing in lowering rumination and depressive symptoms', *Behaviour Therapy*, 37(3), pp. 292–303.

Goss, S. and Anthony, K. (eds.) (2003) *Technology in counselling and psychotherapy: a practitioner's guide*. London and New York: Palgrave Macmillan.

Goss, S. (2013) 'Research review: therapeutic writing', *TILT Therapeutic Innovation in Light of Technology Magazine*, 3(4), pp. 10–12.

Gross, J.J. (2014) *Handbook of emotion regulation*. 2nd edn. New York, NY: Guilford Press.

Guasp. A. and Taylor J. (2015) *Experiences of healthcare: Stonewall health briefing*. United Kingdom: Stonewall Institute. Available at: http://www.stonewall.org.uk/documents/experiences_of_healthcare.pdf (Accessed: 5 May 2020).

Hanley, T. (2012) 'Understanding the online therapeutic alliance through the eyes of adolescent service users', *Counselling and Psychotherapy Research*, 12(1), pp. 35–43.

Hedman, E., Botella, C. and Berger, T. (2016) 'Internet-based cognitive behaviour therapy for social anxiety disorder', in Lindefors. N. and Andersson, G. (eds.) *Guided internet-based treatments in psychiatry*. Cham: Springer, pp. 53–78.

Hewson, C. (2014) 'Qualitative approaches in internet-mediated research: opportunities, issues, possibilities', in Leavy, P. (ed.) *The Oxford handbook of qualitative research methods*. Oxford Library of Psychology Series New York, NY: Oxford University Press, pp. 423–452.

Hewson, C. (2016) 'Ethics issues in digital methods research', in Snee, H., Hine, C., Morey, Y., Roberts, S. and Watson, H. (eds.) *Digital methods for social science: an interdisciplinary guide to research innovation*. Basingstoke: Palgrave Macmillan, pp. 206–221.

Koole, S.L. (2009) 'The psychology of emotion regulation: an integrative review', *Cognition and Emotion*, 23(1), pp. 4–41.

Lucassen, M.F.G., Merry, S.N., Hatcher, S. and Frampton, C.M.A. (2015) 'Rainbow SPARX: a novel approach to addressing depression in sexual minority youth', *Cognitive and Behavioural Practice*, 22(2), pp. 203–216.

Marshall, D., Quinn, C., Child, S., Shenton, D., Pooler, J., Forber, S. and Byng, R. (2016) 'What IAPT services can learn from those who do not attend', *Journal of Mental Health*, 25(5), pp. 410–415.

Martinez, C. and Farhan, I. (2019) *Making the right choices: using data-driven technology to transform mental healthcare*. London: Reform.

Melville, K.M., Casey, L.M. and Kavanagh, D.J. (2010) 'Dropout from internet-based treatment for psychological disorders', *British Journal of Clinical Psychology*, 49(4), pp. 455–471.

Miner, A.S., Milstein, A. and Hancock, J.T. (2017) 'Talking to machines about personal mental health problems', *Journal of the American Medical Association*, 318(13), pp. 1217–1218.

Moules, N.J. (2009) 'The past and future of therapeutic letters: family suffering and healing words', *Journal of Family Nursing*, 15(1), pp. 102–111.

National Institute for Health and Care Excellence (NICE) (2009) *Depression: management of depression in primary and secondary care*. London: National Institute for Health and Care Excellence. Available at: https://www.nice.org.uk/guidance/cg90/chapter/1-Guidance (Accessed: 15 March 2020).

National Institute for Health and Care Excellence (NICE) (2011) *Commissioning stepped care for people with common mental health disorders*. Available at: http://www.swscn.org.uk/wp/wp-content/uploads/2015/03/non-guidance-commissioning-stepped-care-for-people-with-common-mental-health-disorders-pdf.pdf (Accessed: 6 September 2019).

NHS England (2019) 'NHS long term plan', *NHS England*. Available at: https://www.england.nhs.uk/long-term-plan/ (Accessed: 3 April 2020).

NHS (2019) 'How we assess health apps and digital tools', *NHS Digital*. Available at: https://digital.nhs.uk/services/nhs-apps-library/guidance-for-health-app-developers-commissioners-and-assessors/how-we-assess-health-apps-and-digital-tools#how-the-assessment-works (Accessed: 6 September 2019).

Park, A. and Convey, M. (2017) 'Longitudinal changes in psychological states in online health community members: understanding the long-term effects of participating in an online depression community', *Journal of Medical Internet Research*, 19(3), e71.

Pennebaker, J.W. and Chung, C.K. (2007) 'Expressive writing, emotional upheavals, and health', in Friedman, H. and Silver, R. (eds.) *Handbook of health psychology*. Oxford: Oxford University Press, pp. 263–284.

Prescott, J., Hanley, T. and Ujhelyi, K. (2017) 'Peer communication in online mental health forums for young people: directional and nondirectional support', *JMIR Mental Health*, 4(3), e29.

Ratcliff, R. (2017) 'Thousands go online for therapy. But does it work?', *The Guardian*, 12 February. Available at: https://www.theguardian.com/society/2017/feb/12/online-therapy-thousands-but-does-it-work (Accessed: 6 September 2019).

Rimé, B. (2009) 'More on the social sharing of emotion: in defense of the individual, of culture, of private disclosure, and in rebuttal of an old couple of ghosts known as "cognition and emotion"', *Emotion Review*, 1(1), pp. 94–96.

Rochlen, A., Zack, J. and Speyer, C. (2004) 'Online therapy: review of relevant definitions, debates, and current empirical support', *Journal of Clinical Psychology*, 60(3), pp. 269–283.

Rosenfield, M. (2003) 'Telephone counselling and psychotherapy in practice', in Goss, S. and Anthony, K. (eds.) *Technology in counselling and psychotherapy: a practitioner's guide*. London and New York: Palgrave Macmillan, pp. 93–108.

Rozbroj, T., Lyons, A., Pitts, M., Mitchell, A. and Christensen, H. (2015) 'Improving self-help e-therapy for depression and anxiety among sexual minorities: an analysis of focus groups with lesbians and gay men', *Journal of Medical Internet Research*, 17(3), e66.

Scottish Intercollegiate Guidelines Network (SIGN) (2010) *Treating depression without using prescribed medication. Booklet for patients and carers*. Available at: https://www.sign.ac.uk/assets/pat114.pdf (Accessed: 15 March 2020).

Simpson, S.G. (2009) 'Psychotherapy via videoconferencing: a review', *British Journal of Guidance and Counselling*, 37(3), pp. 271–286.

Simpson, S.G. and Reid, C.L. (2014) 'Therapeutic alliance in videoconferencing psychotherapy: a review', *Australian Journal of Rural Health*, 22(6), pp. 280–299.

Stuckey, H.L. and Nobel, L. (2010) 'The connection between art, healing and public health: a review of the current literature', *American Journal of Public Health*, 100(2), pp. 254–263.

Suler, J. (2004) 'The online disinhibition effect', *Cyberpsychology & Behaviour*, 7(3), pp. 321–326.

Suler, J. (2010) 'The psychology of text relationships', in Kraus, R. Stricker, G. and Speyer, C. (eds.) *Online counseling: a handbook for mental health professionals*. 2nd edn. San Diego, CA: Elsevier, pp. 22–53.

Vossler, A. (2010) 'Context and setting', in Barker, M., Vossler, A. and Langdridge, D. (eds.) *Understanding counselling and psychotherapy*. London: SAGE, pp. 237–258.

Weinberg, H. and Rolnick, A. (eds.) (2019) *Theory and practice of online therapy: internet-delivered interventions for individuals, groups, families, and organizations*. New York: Routledge.

White, G. (2018) 'Child advice chatbots fail to spot sexual abuse', *BBC News*, 11 December. Available at: https://www.bbc.co.uk/news/technology-46507900 (Accessed: 22 November 2019).

Wittson, C.L., Affleck, D.C. and Johnson, V. (1961) 'Two-way television in group therapy', *Mental Hospitals*, 12(10), pp. 22–23.

Wright, J. (2002) 'Online counselling: learning from writing therapy', *British Journal of Guidance and Counselling*, 30(3), pp. 285–298.

Chapter 16

Context of practice: boundaries and ethics

Clare Symons

Contents

Introduction

'Is anybody there' by Ashley Muirhead

In everyday life, the term 'boundaries' refers to formal and informal limits related to how we interact with others. Some are enshrined in law, such as the legal alcohol limit for drivers, while others are stated in professional codes or organisational procedures. These boundaries can provide physical safety, while others – for instance, confidentiality relating to medical records – provide emotional and psychological safety, enabling us to be open with healthcare providers. Boundaries in counselling share similarities with these everyday boundaries and are a particularly significant aspect of therapeutic work.

A paradox at the heart of the literature relating to therapeutic boundaries is debate around the need for flexibility as opposed to firmness in applying and maintaining those boundaries. On the one hand, boundaries should provide reliability, security and safety, maintained sturdily in the face of challenges from the client or that arise in different settings. On the other hand, boundaries that are securely held may be experienced by some clients as rigid, cold and brutal and, in such cases, therapists are encouraged to respond with flexible boundaries, appropriate to the client's needs. The seemingly paradoxical requirements of boundary management – to be neither flimsy nor unbending – can cause difficulties in practice. A dynamic engagement with boundary issues is vital to strike a balance that is both ethical and appropriately responsive to clients' needs.

This chapter aims to:

- outline what boundaries and contracting are and why they are important in counselling

- discuss the impact of contextual factors on boundaries in counselling, specifically those surrounding the counselling itself, the client and the counsellor

- consider violations of ethical practice and any ethical dilemmas that might arise, along with the impact of these and frameworks for resolution.

1   Boundaries in counselling

In counselling, the term **boundaries** refers to the limits, parameters or 'dividing lines' in practice which provide safety, primarily to the client. This is important because, when starting therapy, the client arrives in a vulnerable state. By maintaining appropriate boundaries, therapists seek to ensure that therapy can be practised safely and effectively for the client. A boundary such as **confidentiality**, for instance, can make it possible for clients to talk about previously unspoken or intensely emotional issues involving difficult feelings such as shame, guilt or anger.

Therapeutic boundaries also offer safety for the counsellor; for example, agreeing limits around availability can help avoid burnout. While this helps to maintain the counsellor's emotional health, it also supports the needs and safety of the client: if the counsellor looks after their mental, physical and emotional health by, for example, appropriately limiting their workload, they are more likely to be able to sustain their work with clients.

In counselling, boundaries usually include the following aspects:

- *Confidentiality*: This includes confidentiality around both the content of sessions and the fact that a person is attending counselling. There are usually limits to confidentiality; for example, when working as part of a multidisciplinary team, where confidentiality is shared among professionals. Issues relating to client risk can also limit confidentiality.

- *Privacy of setting*: Sessions take place in an interruption- and distraction-free environment.

- *Regularity and consistency of sessions*: The time, frequency, duration and location of sessions are stable, discounting inevitable disruptions such as planned or unplanned breaks.

- *The therapy fee*: This includes regular payment arrangements and what happens regarding cancelled sessions.

- *Limited contact outside sessions*: Outside-session contact is limited, although not always avoided entirely, and therapists have different boundaries in this regard.

Boundaries
Agreed limits in counselling. These are essential to provide safety for both the client and the counsellor.

Confidentiality
The practice of keeping details and information about the client private/refraining from sharing it with others without the client's agreement.

- *Limited or total avoidance of therapists' personal disclosures*: This keeps the focus on the client and helps to maintain a professional relationship.

- *A professional client–therapist relationship*: The relationship must be highly professional, and never social or sexual.

- *Avoidance of dual relationships with clients*: For example, being both their counsellor and trainer, or counsellor and friend.

- *Physical touch limited or avoided altogether*: For example, the therapist may avoid hugging the client or holding their hand, which can help to maintain a professional relationship.

- *Consideration of the overall duration of therapy*: Ideally, this includes working towards a planned ending and ensuring that boundaries are maintained once therapy has ended.

Pause for reflection

Imagine that you are a client seeing a counsellor for the first time about something you have never disclosed before. Which of the boundaries listed above would be most important to you when starting counselling, and why?

1.1 The importance of boundaries

A client's trust in their therapist is a necessary element in counselling because the client is vulnerable and the counsellor therefore potentially holds considerable power. The privacy of counselling and the openness involved in relating painful or troubling issues and deep feelings result in an **asymmetric power dynamic**. Different theoretical orientations will conceptualise this power differently; for example, humanistic approaches seek to minimise it (as described in Chapter 13). However, many factors can skew this dynamic further. For example, research demonstrates that clients tend to defer to their therapists by remaining silent about negative reactions, withholding criticism of their counsellor, or appearing to agree when they actually disagree (Rennie, 1994). This increases the power invested in the therapist and magnifies the potential vulnerability of the client. Sensitively held and carefully managed boundaries can help to rebalance power in favour of the client and can support safer work.

Asymmetric power dynamic
Inequality of the balance of power inherent in the counselling relationship, usually in favour of the counsellor.

Holding effective and appropriate boundaries is an important aspect of working to professional standards (Bond, 2015) and is underpinned in codes of **ethics** associated with professional bodies, including the British Association for Counselling and Psychotherapy (BACP), the United Kingdom Council for Psychotherapy and the British Psychological Society. These codes provide guidance for various areas of ethical practice, including boundaries. For instance, BACP's *Ethical*

Ethics
Moral principles that underpin how counsellors work and rules of conduct that govern counsellors' practice and their professional conduct more generally.

framework for the counselling professions (BACP, 2018a) addresses the need to establish and maintain boundaries that are consistent with the aims of counselling and are beneficial to the client (paragraph 33), and includes guidance on working with confidentiality and privacy (paragraph 55), breaks and endings (paragraphs 38–42) and complex aspects such as having personal relationships with clients after counselling ends (paragraph 37). Note that sexual relationships or other exploitations of clients are prohibited (paragraphs 34–35).

1.2   The counselling contract

The word 'contract' is familiar from different contexts and circumstances – starting a new job, buying or renting a property, getting a mobile phone deal, and so on. Here, contracts are 'legally enforceable agreements, usually regulating the sale, lease or transfer of land, or the provision of goods, advice or services for an agreed price' (Mitchels and Bond, 2010, p. 45). In relation to counselling, the word 'contract' describes more than legal elements, referring instead to an agreement between client and therapist relating to different aspects of the work, including many of the boundaries discussed above. Sills (2006) discusses three areas of **contracting**:

Contracting
Process of negotiating a mutual agreement between counsellor and client about the terms and purpose of counselling.

- *Administrative*: Covers practical arrangements such as when and where sessions will take place, the number of sessions, and details about confidentiality and its limits.

- *Professional*: Addresses the purpose and focus of counselling, possibly the agreement of goals and what the counsellor and the client are setting out to achieve together.

- *Psychological*: Relates to client and counsellor expectations. Paradoxically, Sills states that this can include unspoken or even unconscious elements, and highlights it as an area requiring consideration for these very reasons.

How the contract is agreed is also important. Although the exact nature of the contract will vary depending on contextual issues (discussed in Section 2), clarity and negotiation are important (BACP, 2018b). Exploring the client's expectations and clarifying any misunderstandings before beginning work can be beneficial and can support the client in feeling empowered. However, research into formal complaints about therapists shows that a failure to agree contracts explicitly and clearly can lead to problems in therapy and can be harmful to clients (Khele, Symons and Wheeler, 2008; Symons *et al.*, 2011). Effective contract agreement aims for a collaborative process, working towards a shared understanding of how therapeutic work will proceed.

In summary, boundaries in counselling are comprised of various elements, which are important for providing a safe space for clients to undertake the emotional work of counselling, and because of the power the counsellor holds. Providing clear and safe boundaries is a cornerstone of ethical practice, supported by ethical codes. Counsellors need to offer clearly articulated boundaries and agree them with clients at the outset of counselling – a process known as contracting.

2   Contextual issues

There are many contextual issues that counsellors must consider in relation to boundaries. The counselling setting itself and personal aspects of the client and counsellor are all capable of affecting boundaries and the way they are experienced. This section considers these aspects in turn.

2.1   The counselling

Contextual issues in counselling shape boundaries and how the therapist and client work with them. Each issue has a different emphasis or significance, depending on the practitioner's theoretical approach. While the therapeutic use of physical touch (e.g. a hug) is acceptable in some humanistic therapies, it would be inadvisable or taboo in others (Tune, 2001). Similarly, therapist self-disclosure is not normally considered acceptable in psychodynamic practice, but some amount of sharing would be seen by person-centred counsellors as essential in certain circumstances (Mearns and Thorne, 1988).

Another important contextual issue is the mode of delivery of counselling. Privacy can usually be protected in face-to-face sessions by working in a suitable room, but for online or telephone counselling (which can be conducted anywhere), counsellors need to think carefully about the privacy and suitability of where they undertake their work (BACP, 2019a). However, they also need to recognise that they do not control the client's wider environment; it is therefore important for counsellors to discuss the suitability of where clients choose to receive online or telephone counselling, as well as responses to interruptions (as touched on in Chapter 15).

That said, protecting privacy when working face-to-face is not without its challenges. If working in a school, for example, using a multi-purpose room could prove to be far more challenging than working in a dedicated service space that has specific rooms for sessions and a private reception area. Specific settings are also likely to affect other boundaries and how clients and therapists work with them. For example, working in a GP surgery where the client is not directly charged a fee will have implications that are different from those related to working in a voluntary agency, where a sliding scale of fees is charged according to what a client can afford, as in the fictional client case illustration, below.

Case illustration: Harveer attends voluntary counselling

Harveer has been attending counselling at a voluntary agency for two months. He is a marketing executive for a regional newspaper and has been attending counselling to talk about work-related stress and its negative effects on his family relationships. He is married with two children under five, who are cared for full-time by his wife. In order to make counselling accessible to as many people as possible, the voluntary service Harveer attends operates a sliding scale of fees. At assessment, based on his income, Harveer agreed a fee for counselling that is well above the average fee paid at the centre, around double what most other clients pay. However, in today's session, Harveer expressed worry about the cost of sessions and is unsure whether he can afford to continue. It is the agency's policy that counsellors can negotiate fees with clients to support them in continuing counselling.

Activity 16.1: Harveer's experience

Allow about 10 minutes

Try to answer the following questions:

1   How do you imagine Harveer might feel discussing his financial situation?
2   What might the counsellor need to consider in relation to the agency when negotiating the fee?
3   What factors related to the counsellor might affect how they work with this issue?

Discussion

Exploring money-related issues in counselling can prove challenging for both the client and the counsellor. There is much for the counsellor to consider in relation to the client, the agency and themselves.

These considerations include:

- practical issues (e.g. changes in financial circumstances since assessment)

- Harveer's thoughts about what he can afford

- Harveer's feelings about sharing his inability to afford the agreed amount and what it would mean to him to pay a reduced fee. Exploration of this can both facilitate continued counselling and uncover difficult aspects, such as feelings of shame

- gendered or cultural issues relating to being the family 'breadwinner' or accepting 'charity'

- the possibility that Harveer wants to end counselling but does not feel able to say this openly, opting instead to make continuation impossible

- the counsellor's position in respect of the voluntary agency. They are acting as the representative of the agency, which relies on client donations/fees to keep services widely available. Although negotiation of fees is appropriate, it is important to recognise that Harveer is not the only client the centre supports

- the counsellor's feelings around/relationship with money and what it means to them to work without receiving financial reward, which will affect the fee negotiation. These feelings might differ if they were seeing Harveer in private practice, where the counsellor would directly receive the fee.

2.2   The client

The issues that clients bring to counselling can influence how boundaries are worked with, so careful consideration should be given to this. McLeod (2013, p. 422) writes about a way of understanding boundaries as 'an indicator of a place where contact and "meeting" might occur', suggesting a way of working that, as well as being ethical and safe, is also responsive enough to facilitate emotional closeness. This can be a difficult balance to achieve, and there is no set formula to follow; the counsellor will need to be alert to how the client responds to the boundaries and explore this with them, as in the following fictional case illustration.

Case illustration: Paulette's counselling assessment

Paulette attended an assessment session prior to starting counselling provided by a college counselling service. Paulette is in her early 20s, studies sociology and describes herself as of mixed-race heritage. She lives at home with her mum and two teenage siblings. She is coming to counselling because she finds it difficult to make friends with other students. When others start conversations with her, she feels shy, finds it hard to trust and does not open up.

During her assessment, Paulette mentioned that, aged 11, she was bullied at school by older children who called her racist names and also hit and kicked her. The bullying went on for several months before Paulette told her mother, who went into the school and spoke to the head teacher about what was happening. The bullying stopped but Paulette was not involved in any discussions about the process or about how the school would ensure her safety. In school she still saw the children who bullied her, which made her feel unsafe because she was anxious about the bullying starting again.

Activity 16.2: Paulette's case

Allow about 10 minutes

Try to answer the following questions:

1   How safe or unsafe do you imagine Paulette might feel attending counselling?
2   What do you think the counsellor might do to help Paulette feel safe?
3   What difficulties might arise during counselling?

Discussion

For clients who have experienced harm like this and whose trust has been damaged, the counsellor will need to carefully consider how the client will experience boundaries in counselling. Paulette may find it difficult to trust the counsellor and may struggle to open up, in the same way as she struggles with people at college. Careful and gentle use of boundaries may support Paulette in feeling safer and able to work with the counsellor on her concerns, though this could take considerable time.

However, Paulette's experience of the school's response to her situation also needs consideration. As she wasn't told about the measures put in place to protect her, Paulette continued to feel unsafe. In counselling, it is usual practice to openly and explicitly discuss boundaries with clients, and doing so might hold particular significance for Paulette, helping her feel safe and protected.

2.3 The counsellor

The counsellor will also have an impact on how boundaries are experienced by clients, perhaps particularly regarding counsellor self-disclosure (Farber, 2006). While self-disclosure often relates to what the counsellor actively says about themselves, like sharing an emotional response to convey empathy, counsellors also reveal something of themselves when not directly speaking about their lives or experiences. Jewellery or choice of clothing might indicate something of the counsellor's social class, religious beliefs or, in the case of a new engagement or wedding ring, might suggest a change of personal circumstances. Clients will also make assumptions about counsellors based on aspects of their physical appearance.

Such perceptions are important because they can affect how clients engage with counselling. Research suggests that a perceived difference in social class, particularly where the client perceives the counsellor to be from a higher-status social class, can lead to difficulties in the course of counselling (Balmforth, 2009). Other aspects of appearance can have an impact; in a recent study exploring young people's perceptions of an overweight counsellor, the counsellor's body weight was considered to negatively affect therapy and to undermine the counsellor's professional credibility (Moller and Tischner, 2019). Additionally, physical appearance is not static, and changes can be visible to clients, whether ordinary (e.g. having a cold) or more significant (e.g. pregnancy, hair loss or physical injury).

Diversity: Differences in the counselling room

Differences between counsellors and clients can amplify the asymmetric power dynamic, which can produce potentially unhelpful or harmful effects. Some areas of potential differences in identity are protected by law. The requirements set out in the *Equality Act 2010* mean that counsellors, as providers of services, must not discriminate based on nine protected characteristics, which include age, sex and gender, religion and belief, and disability. However, ethical requirements go further, with the BACP *Ethical framework for the counselling professions* (2018a, paragraph 23, p. 15) stating that 'we will take the law concerning equality, diversity and inclusion into careful consideration and strive for a higher standard than the legal minimum'. This is important because other differences between clients and counsellors, such as employment status, level of education, and life experiences, can also cause disadvantage.

Sexual orientation is one of the areas where difference or sameness between counsellors and clients can have a considerable impact on the therapy. When working with lesbian, gay or bisexual clients, for example, a counsellor might disclose their own sexual orientation as a way of facilitating discussion of how perceived shared or differing experiences might impact on the client's involvement in the counselling (Brauner, 2000). Research shows that this can be particularly helpful when the therapist and client share a minority sexual orientation (Mahalik, Van Ormer and Simi, 2000; Jeffrey and Austin, 2007). However, research with gay and lesbian therapists (Moore and Jenkins, 2012) suggests it can also prove to be problematic, as it can feel risky for therapists to disclose their sexual orientation to clients, perhaps in response to being asked directly. This can potentially leave a therapist feeling vulnerable and in need of protecting themselves from possible homophobic comments from their client.

Research also shows that some counsellors can experience dilemmas in seeking to reconcile religious beliefs with the requirements of ethical practice (Bowers, Minnichiello and Plummer, 2010). In one study, although most Christian counsellors believed they were able to respond ethically to gay and lesbian clients, a minority held judgmental views about what they perceived to be gay or lesbian behaviours (Evans, 2003). In the extreme, such views can lead to a form of unethical practice in relation to gender identity and sexual orientation that seeks to 'cure' them – so-called 'conversion' or 'reparative' therapy. To counter this, the *Memorandum of understanding on conversion therapy in the UK* (BACP, 2019b) is a joint document signed by 20 health, counselling and psychotherapy organisations seeking to eradicate this practice, stating clearly that it is 'unethical and potentially harmful' (paragraph 5). The memorandum goes on to say that 'ethical practice ... requires the practitioner to ... be free from any agenda that favours one gender identity or sexual orientation as preferable over other gender and sexual diversities' (paragraph 6).

In summary, a variety of contextual issues can make working with boundaries more complex than it might at first appear. The setting, mode of delivery and theoretical orientation of the counselling are all lenses through which working with and experiencing boundaries are affected. The client's presenting issues and aspects of their identity need to be carefully considered by the counsellor in relation to boundaries and their meaning, relevance and impact in practice. Aspects of the counsellor's identity also need to be considered, whether revealed to the client through appearance or active self-disclosure.

3   Boundaries, dilemmas and ethics in practice

Working with boundaries can enrich therapeutic work and help counsellors to understand their clients' difficulties. However, this is not always a straightforward process, and there are risks to consider in relation to how counsellors work with boundaries and what changes to boundaries mean to clients. This section looks at some of the challenges that working with boundaries presents to counsellors and clients, and how they can potentially be overcome.

3.1   Flexibility and firmness

Boundaries hold an inherent dilemma for counsellors: to provide sufficient safety to facilitate therapy *and* be appropriately responsive to the needs of individual clients. This tension is reflected in the wide range of views throughout the literature, relating to what might be considered appropriate flexibility and firmness of boundaries. McLeod (2013, p. 421) states that boundaries can be 'rigid or permeable' and notes that psychodynamic and humanistic theorists view working with this tension very differently. Langs (1999), for instance, is a psychoanalytic theorist who has argued extensively for the value of clear, consistent, and what many might consider to be strictly held boundaries, to provide the necessary safety and **containment** that enables clients to explore distressing issues. In contrast, Mearns and Thorne (2007) advocate a flexible and responsive approach to boundaries that fosters emotional contact between the client and the counsellor.

Containment
A condition in which clients feel able to safely experience difficult or overwhelming feelings due to reliably held boundaries.

Research supports the notion that some flexibility, such as phoning a sick client, is positively associated with clients' perceptions of the benefits of therapy (Jones, Botsko and Gorman, 2003). 'Service beyond normal expectation' was mentioned by around 40 per cent of clients in a study about critical incidents in the formation or strengthening of the therapeutic alliance (Bedi, Davis and Williams, 2005, p. 318). However, such evidence is not an argument for therapy without boundaries, or for therapists to unthinkingly change and modify how they and their clients work with boundaries. The counsellor's challenge is to reconcile the seemingly contradictory requirements for firmness and flexibility, safety and responsiveness, as is appropriate and in the client's interest.

3.2   Boundary violations

Although boundaries help to support ethical practice, there is considerable evidence that they can be misused or mismanaged in harmful ways, and that boundary violations are linked with poor outcomes and harm to clients (Halter, Brown and Stone, 2007). Poor management of boundaries (e.g. around confidentiality or lack of clarity around contracting) represents a large proportion of complaints (Khele, Symons and Wheeler, 2008; Symons *et al.*, 2011). Accounts from clients illustrate the considerable and enduring harm that such malpractice can have, as shown in the client examples below.

Client voices: Experiencing harm from boundary violations

Client accounts of harm in therapy fall into several broad themes and paint a powerful picture of the nature and degree of injury inflicted by abusive or incompetent practice. Descriptions of sexual abuse by therapists feature heavily:

> He immediately put his arms around and held me very tightly. … He released his arms and touched my nose with his finger, which seemed to me a rather romantic gesture and I began to feel very apprehensive at what he was going to do to me. He held me again, tighter this time, and said, "I

know what you need is to be taken to bed, but I'm afraid that is out of my jurisdiction".

(Richardson, 2008, p. 119)

Many accounts of sexual abuse in therapy describe a range of boundary crossings and violations taking place prior to the beginning of sexual contact, suggesting a process of manipulation or grooming. Often this can leave the client unsure about what is happening and whether it is wrong, in spite of their confusion and discomfort:

> During this time [my therapist] brought up the subject of sex. He spoke at length on the subject, in a kind of caressing and gentle tone. The atmosphere in the room seemed to me to be electric, and yet as always, I told myself that it was probably part of the therapy, and any other interpretation was probably just my imagination.

(Poppy, 2001, p. 2)

Harm in therapy is associated not only with sexual abuse by therapists, but also with other aspects of practice, including therapists behaving inconsistently, unpredictably and unreliably:

> During one of our first sessions I asked her if she ever hugged clients and she replied, "You only have to ask". I had a hug the next session but the following week she said she couldn't offer me any further hugs for the time being. For the rest of the time I was seeing her I kept trying to change her mind again.

(Field, 2008, p. 87)

Irrespective of the nature of the boundary violations, client accounts powerfully convey the harm caused by such behaviour:

> Overall, [my first experience of therapy] left me with a pervasive and lingering sense of fragmentation, distraction and anxiety. … The memory of the trauma to which the therapy led, however, remains, and, in particular the hurt it caused. Had I not left when I did, the subsequent feeling of being both mentally dislocated and emotionally skinned alive

> might have been less intense, but who can say what might have happened if I had stayed?
>
> (Sands, 2000, pp. 198–199)

While research shows that only a minority of therapists receive complaints, and even fewer commit sexual boundary violations (Norris, Gutheil and Strasburger, 2003), ethical practice requires counsellors to be vigilant – to explore and examine their work around boundaries throughout counselling (not only when contracting), reflecting in depth on changes, challenges and dilemmas that arise as part of usual practice.

As previously discussed, contextual issues can affect how boundaries are maintained, as can aspects relating to the client and the counsellor. With clients who have experienced sexual abuse in childhood, for example, research shows that the counsellor's concern to help the client feel safe can lead to changes in boundaries, such as personal self-disclosures or giving the client their personal telephone number (Harper and Steadman, 2003). It is also important to recognise the impact of real-world events on boundaries; perhaps if the client arrives late due to traffic, or misses a payment because their account is overdrawn. These events can disrupt counselling and highlight the limits of a client's power to change external circumstances. However, it is also helpful to consider possible patterns and how clients might become stuck in them; for example, the client is repeatedly very late or misses paying several times.

Paying attention to these boundary crossings can offer opportunities to understand the client's difficulties in greater depth (Martin *et al.*, 2011). Responding to/negotiating the client's lived experience of boundaries in counselling can be empowering for clients (Amis, 2017). Being able to voice their feelings in the face of obstacles or frustrations (e.g. difficulty arriving in time for their appointments or managing their money) might be the first opportunity the client has ever had to do so; it is therefore important for counsellors to take time to listen. Allowing the client to agree changes to boundaries might represent the first time the client has experienced responsiveness to their needs. This can generate a sense of being able to exert control, both in counselling and in the client's wider life.

A key aspect of working therapeutically with boundaries is to remain attentive to the pressures and dilemmas that arise in practice. The case illustration below highlights the importance of doing so.

Case illustration: Working with boundaries in Sarah's counselling session

Sarah has been attending counselling in relation to her feelings about her mother's death almost a year ago, and today is session four. She starts very tearfully. It was her daughter's eighth birthday this week and she found it difficult not having her mum around. As the session goes on, Sarah tells the counsellor more about the circumstances of her mum's death: she died of pancreatic cancer which was not diagnosed until it was very advanced. Sarah feels strongly that the health professionals involved, particularly the GP, should have acted earlier, when her mum started to complain of symptoms. She feels certain that, had they done so, her mum would still be alive today.

Sarah becomes angrier as she speaks, talking about how her mum was let down by health staff failing to be there when she needed them. She becomes furious and animated, barely drawing breath. It is difficult for the counsellor to say anything to Sarah as she is speaking so fast. It is almost the end of the session and the counsellor has to decide what to do next. The counsellor has another client booked in shortly after this session.

Activity 16.3: Sarah's case

Allow about 15 minutes

Try to answer the following questions:

1   How do you imagine the counsellor feels in this session, as Sarah becomes increasingly angry and distressed?

2   The counsellor might decide to stick to the usual, agreed session-time boundary, ending in the middle of Sarah's tangible anger and distress. What do you think are the potential pros and cons of doing this?

3   Alternatively, the counsellor might decide to allow the session to run over time, recognising that a flexible approach could be appropriate

today, since Sarah might not yet be in a fit state to leave. What might be the advantages and disadvantages of doing this?

Discussion

There is very limited time in the session to reflect, so the counsellor would have to make their decision under pressure. Finishing on time could prove to be a relief to Sarah, allowing her to leave overwhelming, 'out of control' feelings in the counselling room. In addition, by sticking to the agreed boundaries, the counsellor would demonstrate trustworthiness and consistency. Alternatively, Sarah may experience this as shocking and abrupt, or cold and heartless. Sarah might feel as though the counsellor is as unreliable and negligent as the health professionals in her mum's life. This can all be explored with Sarah in a future session, but rupturing the therapeutic alliance now could make that impossible.

Showing flexibility and allowing Sarah to continue until she feels calmer could convey that her anger is important and worthy of acknowledgement and space. It might allow her to return to work or her family in a calmer state of mind. Recognising her need for more time might give Sarah a different experience of a professional response and could deepen her trust in the counsellor, strengthening the therapeutic alliance. However, it could be difficult to know how much time Sarah might need. What if she becomes more distressed? While it might seem helpful, warm and responsive, moving the session boundary could leave Sarah feeling unsafe and uncontained, trapped with feelings that threaten to overwhelm her.

Options may not be as polarised as they appear here. If the counsellor decides on firmness, they might communicate in a warm and caring manner the need to stick to the finish time. Similarly, if they decide on flexibility, they may apply it in a way that offers containment and security. There may also be other alternatives, such as ending the session as scheduled but allowing Sarah some time on her own until she feels ready to leave.

3.3   Ethical decision making

Experiencing an ethical dilemma can feel urgent and can be anxiety-provoking and uncomfortable, which in turn can make finding a resolution more problematic (Symons and Wheeler, 2005). Ethical problem-solving models can support practitioners by providing a framework of areas for consideration when deciding on action. There are many models; some address specific types of ethical decision making when working interculturally (Luke, Goodrich and Gilbride, 2013), or relating to touch in counselling (Calmes, Piazza and Laux, 2013). Generic models, such as BACP's *Ethical decision making model* (BACP, 2018c), offer structured steps combined with questions to aid reflection at each stage.

Ethical decision-making models usually encourage counsellors to:

- consider the nature and detail of the dilemma (what is happening and how it has arisen), along with both the client's feelings and their own responses to the dilemma, since both have a bearing on what might need to happen next

- consult ethical codes, practice guidance and evidence from research in order to support their knowledge and thinking about what might constitute good practice and how to resolve the dilemma

- consult their supervisor and, if appropriate, seek legal guidance

- evaluate available options before deciding what to do and how best to do it, while acting in the best interests of the client.

Time pressures, such as those in Sarah's case, mean that it is not always possible to engage with a model before making a decision, but it is also valuable for counsellors to apply the model retrospectively to evaluate decisions they have made and to learn from them.

In summary, working with boundaries in practice and exploring how clients experience them can enrich therapeutic work. However, counsellors need to pay sufficient attention to how they are working with boundaries and how clients respond to any flexibility around them. In practice, boundary dilemmas are commonplace and can prove challenging for counsellors, as they require careful reflection and engagement. Employing a structured model for considering ethical dilemmas can be valuable, alongside personal reflection and good use of supervision.

Conclusion

Clearly contracted, explicitly agreed boundaries are essential for counsellors to provide effective therapy and to create a feeling of safety for clients when undertaking emotionally challenging work that addresses potentially painful and difficult issues. Although many aspects of working with boundaries can be easily understood, the realities in practice mean that appropriate action is not always easily determined. Contextual issues, such as the counselling setting or the client's specific presenting issue, can influence and shape how boundaries are agreed as well as how they will evolve and work in practice. Additionally, the nature of boundaries and their apparently contradictory requirements (firmness and flexibility, but not rigidity or looseness) can give rise to complex, challenging dilemmas for counsellors. Effective, ethical practice requires counsellors to engage with these dilemmas, to reflect on their meaning and to think carefully about how they respond.

Further reading

- The codes of ethics of different professional bodies can easily be accessed on their websites for more detail about ethical issues: UK Council for Psychotherapy (2019) *UKCP code of ethics and professional practice*. Available at: https://www.psychotherapy.org.uk/wp-content/uploads/2019/06/UKCP-Code-of-Ethics-and-Professional-Practice-2019.pdf.

  British Association for Counselling and Psychotherapy (2018) *Ethical framework for the counselling professions*. Available at: https://www.bacp.co.uk/events-and-resources/ethics-and-standards/ethical-framework-for-the-counselling-professions.

- The following book provides a good overview of some of the topics discussed in this chapter:

  Amis, K. (2017) *Boundaries, power and ethical responsibility in counselling and psychotherapy*. London: SAGE.

- The journal article below broadly discusses boundaries and is relatively accessible:

  Hermansson, G. (1997) 'Boundaries and boundary management in counselling: the never-ending story', *British Journal of Guidance and Counselling*, 25(2), pp. 133–146.

References

Amis, K. (2017) *Boundaries, power and ethical responsibility in counselling and psychotherapy*. London: SAGE.

British Association for Counselling and Psychotherapy (BACP) (2018a) *Ethical framework for the counselling professions*. Lutterworth: BACP.

British Association for Counselling and Psychotherapy (BACP) (2018b) *Good practice in action 055 fact sheet: making the contract in the counselling professions*. Lutterworth: BACP.

British Association for Counselling and Psychotherapy (BACP) (2018c) *Ethical decision making model*. Lutterworth: BACP.

British Association for Counselling and Psychotherapy (BACP) (2019a) *Good practice in action 047 fact sheet: working online in the counselling professions*. Lutterworth: BACP.

British Association for Counselling and Psychotherapy (BACP) (2019b) *Memorandum of understanding on conversion therapy in the UK, version 2, revision A*. Available at: https://www.bacp.co.uk/events-and-resources/ethics-and-standards/mou (Accessed: 18 November 2019).

Balmforth, J. (2009) '"The weight of class": clients' experiences of how perceived differences in social class between counsellor and client affect the therapeutic relationship', *British Journal of Guidance and Counselling*, 37(3), pp. 375–386.

Bedi, R.P., Davis, M.D. and Williams, M. (2005) 'Critical incidents in the formation of the therapeutic alliance from the client's perspective', *Psychotherapy: Theory, Research, Practice, Training*, 42(3), pp. 311–323.

Bond, T. (2015) *Standards and ethics for counselling in action*. 4th edn. London: SAGE.

Bowers, R., Minichiello, V. and Plummer, D. (2010) 'Religious attitudes, homophobia and professional counseling', *Journal of LGBT Issues in Counseling*, 4(2), pp. 70–91.

Brauner, R. (2000) 'Embracing difference: addressing race, culture and sexuality', in Neal, C. and Davies, D. (eds.) *Issues in therapy with lesbian, gay, bisexual and transgender clients*. Maidenhead: Open University Press, pp. 7–21.

Calmes, S.A., Piazza, N.J. and Laux, J.M. (2013) 'The use of touch in counseling: an ethical decision-making model', *Counseling and Values*, 58(1), pp. 59–68.

Equality Act 2010 c. 15. London: The Stationery Office. Available at: https://www.legislation.gov.uk/ukpga/2010/15/contents (Accessed: 18 November 2019).

Evans, M. (2003) 'Christian counsellors' views on working with gay and lesbian clients: integrating religious beliefs with counselling ethics', *Counselling and Psychotherapy Research*, 3(1), pp. 55–60.

Farber, B. (2006) *Self-disclosure in psychotherapy*. London: The Guilford Press.

Field, J. (2008) 'Chapter 4 – Jo Field', in Richardson, S., Cunningham, M. *et al. Broken boundaries: stories of betrayal in relationships of care*. London: Witness, pp. 85–112.

Halter, M., Brown, H. and Stone, J. (2007) *Sexual boundary violations by health professionals – an overview of the published empirical literature*. London: The Council for Healthcare Regulatory Excellence.

Harper, K. and Steadman, J. (2003) 'Therapeutic boundary issues in working with childhood sexual-abuse survivors', *American Journal of Psychotherapy*, 57 (1), pp. 64–79.

Jeffrey, A. and Austin, T. (2007) 'Perspectives and practices of clinician self-disclosure to clients: a pilot comparison study of two disciplines', *The American Journal of Family Therapy*, 35(2), pp. 95–108.

Jones, M.A., Botsko, M. and Gorman, B.S. (2003) 'Predictors of psychotherapeutic benefit of lesbian, gay and bisexual clients: the effects of sexual orientation matching and other factors', *Psychotherapy: Theory, Research, Practice, Training*, 40(4), pp. 289–301.

Khele, S., Symons, C. and Wheeler, S. (2008) 'An analysis of complaints to the British Association for Counselling and Psychotherapy, 1996–2006', *Counselling and Psychotherapy Research*, 8(2), pp. 124–132.

Langs, R. (1999) *Psychotherapy and science*. London: SAGE.

Luke, M., Goodrich, K.M. and Gilbride, D.D. (2013) 'Intercultural model of ethical decision making: addressing worldview dilemmas in school counseling', *Counseling and Values*, 58(2), pp. 177–194.

Mahalik, J.R., Van Ormer, E.A. and Simi, N.L. (2000) 'Ethical issues in using self-disclosure in feminist therapy', in Brabeck, M.M. (ed.) *Psychology of women book series. Practising feminist ethics in psychology*. Washington DC: American Psychological Association, pp. 189–201.

Martin, C., Godfrey, M., Meekums, B. and Madill, A. (2011) 'Managing boundaries under pressure: a qualitative study of therapists' experiences of sexual attraction in therapy', *Counselling and Psychotherapy Research*, 11(4), pp. 248–256.

McLeod, J. (2013) *An introduction to counselling*. 5th edn. Maidenhead: Open University Press.

Mearns, D and Thorne, B. (1988) *Person-centred counselling in action*. London: SAGE.

Mearns, D. and Thorne, B. (2007) *Person-centred counselling in action*. 3rd edn. London: SAGE.

Mitchels, B. and Bond, T. (2010) *Essential law for counsellors and psychotherapists*. London: SAGE.

Moller, N. and Tischner, I. (2019) 'Young people's perception of fat counsellors: "How can THAT help me?"', *Qualitative Research in Psychology*, 16(1), pp. 34–53.

Moore, J. and Jenkins, P. (2012) '"Coming out" in therapy? Perceived risks and benefits of self-disclosure of sexual orientation by gay and lesbian therapists to straight clients', *Counselling and Psychotherapy Research*, 12(4), pp. 308–315.

Norris, D.M., Gutheil, T.G. and Strasburger, L.H. (2003) 'This couldn't happen to me: boundary problems and sexual misconduct in the psychotherapy relationship', *Psychiatric Services*, 54(4), pp. 517–522.

Poppy (2001) 'The victim's tale', in Casemore, R. (ed.) *Surviving complaints against counsellors and psychotherapists: towards understanding and healing*. Ross-on-Wye: PCCS Books, pp. 1–8.

Rennie, D.L. (1994) 'Clients' deference in psychotherapy', *Journal of Counseling Psychology*, 41(4), pp. 427–437.

Richardson, S. (2008) 'Chapter 5 – Sarah Richardson', in Richardson, S., Cunningham, M. *et al. Broken boundaries: stories of betrayal in relationships of care*. London: Witness, pp. 113–122.

Sands, A. (2000) *Falling for therapy: psychotherapy from a client's point of view*. Basingstoke: Palgrave Macmillan.

Sills, C. (2006) 'Contract and contract making', in Sills, C. (ed.) *Contracts in counselling and psychotherapy*. London: SAGE, pp. 9–26.

Symons, C., Khele, S., Rogers, J., Turner, J. and Wheeler, S. (2011) 'Allegations of serious professional misconduct: an analysis of the British Association for Counselling and Psychotherapy's Article 4.6 cases, 1998–2007', *Counselling and Psychotherapy Research*, 11(4), pp. 257–265.

Symons, C. and Wheeler, S. (2005) 'Counsellor conflict in managing the frame: dilemmas and decisions', *Counselling and Psychotherapy Research*, 5(1), pp. 19–26.

Tune, D. (2001) 'Is touch a valid therapeutic intervention? Early returns from a qualitative study of therapists' views', *Counselling and Psychotherapy Research*, 1(3), pp. 167–171.

Part 5

Contemporary issues: mental health and society

Chapter 17

The politics of research and evidence

Rebecca Hutten

Contents

Introduction

'Before we understood' by Lu Szweda

This chapter critically explores some of the arguments that surround issues of effectiveness, efficacy and **evidence-based practice** (EBP) (see Chapter 10, Section 4, for a reminder of the definitions of efficacy and effectiveness). While it might appear that the motivation behind EBP is to scientifically assess the effectiveness of particular treatments and interventions, some have argued that its assumptions favour particular forms of evidence and outcome. The assumptions and principles of EBP stem from evidence-based medicine (EBM) (covered in Chapter 10, Section 1.1), which aims to show that any treatment offered works, the potential for harm is low and the treatment is cost-effective. The rationale for EBP therefore seems strong, as it claims to offer transparent information that can inform service audits and provide political accountability (e.g. by enabling reporting on the

Evidence-based practice
Refers to professional practice and service provision that are informed by evidence.

equitable distribution of services in relation to target population needs and acceptability of provision to service users) (Pilgrim, 2009).

EBP has driven policy and funding decisions related to the provision of mental health services; for example, the National Institute for Health and Care Excellence (NICE) guidelines for depression. Yet, EBP is about more than methodology and traditional forms of scientific evidence; ethics, philosophy and values also need to be considered, alongside an understanding of EBP's limitations. This chapter traces the development of methods and approaches in EBM, and their application in psychotherapy and counselling research. It explores how these have led to controversy over the value of common treatments for depression – in particular, antidepressant medication, the use of cognitive behavioural therapy (CBT) and the development of Improving Access to Psychological Therapies (IAPT) services. The chapter concludes with a look at some alternative paradigms and approaches.

This chapter aims to:

- provide an overview of EBP, particularly in reference to the NICE guidelines

- highlight the importance of adopting a critical approach to using evidence in debates around the effectiveness of therapeutic interventions in mental health

- explore the limitations of evidence and the challenges involved in translating research into practice, using the examples of antidepressant medication and IAPT services

- discuss the need to explore and build alternative models of evidence, such as case studies, practice-near research and coproduction.

1 The development of evidence-based mental health interventions

EBM has been strongly influenced by the work of Archie Cochrane, who published his review on effectiveness and efficiency in the health service in 1972 (Cochrane, 1972). He argued that randomised controlled trials (RCTs) were essential to determine whether a medication worked and whether it was better or worse than the usual treatment or other medication (Kelly, 2018). His work was developed by David Sackett and colleagues, who drew attention to the many risks of potential bias in non-experimental approaches. They advocated for the use of RCTs as the 'gold standard' for judging whether a treatment did more harm than good and emphasised that clinical decisions should be based on evidence that is systematic, reproducible and unbiased (Sackett *et al.*, 1996). They promoted the idea of having 'rules' to rank the apparent quality, or trustworthiness, of evidence. RCTs that appeared to promote transparency, objectivity, honesty and accuracy were to be prioritised. This approach was taken up and institutionalised in the UK and internationally via the Cochrane Collaboration, established in 1993, which aimed for the accumulation of evidence to achieve increasingly precise answers to clinical questions (Kelly, 2018).

1.1 The NICE guidelines

In 1999, NICE was established to conduct appraisals of new medications to determine their value for money for the NHS and end the 'postcode lottery' of healthcare (Kelly, 2018, p. 3). Soon after, NICE began developing clinical guidelines for the treatment of physical and mental health conditions. These attracted public attention because they exposed the existence of NHS rationing. The guidelines were built on the use of 'evidence hierarchies' – developed by EBM pioneers – which ranked study designs by their internal validity (how well conducted and structured they were according to the study's own terms and requirements). Evidence from meta-analyses and **systematic reviews** of RCTs are typically placed at the top of these hierarchies, while qualitative evidence from personal experience is typically placed at the bottom (Pilgrim, 2009). Between these two extremes of the hierarchy sit other designs also ranked according to their quality and risk of bias (see Figure 17.1).

Systematic review
A review that summarises the results of available healthcare studies, including analysis of the quality of the studies, and thus aims to provide evidence on the effectiveness of particular healthcare interventions.

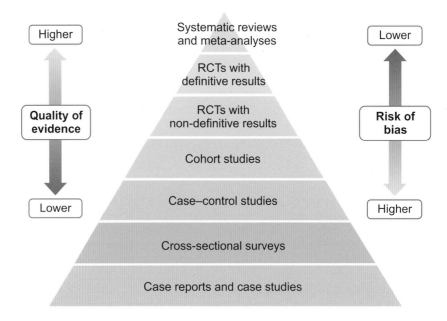

Figure 17.1 An example of an evidence hierarchy (Source: adapted from Petticrew and Roberts, 2003, Table 1)

Following the *Health and Social Care Act 2012*, NICE assumed responsibility for guidelines in social care. Its guideline review committees (predominantly comprised of experts and some lay representatives) played a central role in determining the outcome of reviews. Over time, in light of criticisms of the hierarchical approach, they adapted and extended their system of review; for example, they adopted the Grading of Recommendations, Assessment, Development and Evaluation (GRADE) scoring system to assess the risk of bias and the certainty of evidence (NICE, 2018). However, NICE has been consistently criticised for being too selective in its use of evidence, having a biased review methodology, and having a committee structure that lacks stakeholder representation and relies on recruitment processes that are insufficiently fair and open (e.g. McPherson *et al.*, 2018). In relation to mental health conditions such as depression, NICE's guidelines are said to ignore the impact that social and economic changes (e.g. cuts in service funding) have on service-users' experiences of depression and the delivery of treatment (McPherson *et al.*, 2018). The guidelines also seriously underutilise service-user experience research (McPherson and Beresford, 2019) and make little or no allowance for service-user choice or control, despite good qualitative evidence of their importance in user-led recovery (as will be explored in Section 3). In terms of its methodology, evidence related to long-term outcomes of treatments for depression (medication and/

or psychotherapy) has been excluded from NICE reviews due to the difficulty of reliably capturing these outcomes in RCTs (McPherson and Hengartner, 2019).

1.2 Criticisms of EBP

All this suggests that EBP is not as straightforward as it might at first seem. EBP risks being distorted by its reliance on certain kinds of evidence, which assume linear cause and effect relationships between interventions and their outcomes. The focus is on quantitative methods and experimental approaches derived from the positivist method (see Chapter 11, Section 4, for a reminder of the definition) which do not reflect the dynamic conditions and uncertainties of real life. It is not easy to ascertain what works for services or their users when both exist in wider, less predictable environments than that of a research study, and in a state of constant flux (Pilgrim, 2009). Measurement difficulties mean that benefits found to be statistically significant in research studies may actually be marginal in clinical practice (a small effect size over a large study population can disguise very unequal outcomes between subgroups and may suggest improvements that mean little to individuals) (Greenhalgh, Howick and Maskrey, 2014). Critics of EBP argue that an 'absence of evidence' for an intervention is too often taken as evidence for the absence of benefit, when in fact the methods used are insufficient to capture emergent, non-linear and multiplicative causal relationships typical of complex systems (Pilgrim, 2009; Greenhalgh and Papoutsi, 2018).

Crucially, the role of values in EBP tends to be overlooked. Decisions over resource allocation depend on moral and political imperatives, which evidence alone cannot justify. EBP appears to offer a rational way of translating research knowledge into practice, but the role of power and ideology is usually ignored (Head, 2010). It is often assumed that policies and practices follow and are shaped by evidence, rather than that they impact the available evidence (Greenhalgh and Russell, 2009; Saltelli and Giampietro, 2017). In EBM, there is an overwhelming focus on clinical- and cost-effectiveness at the expense of other factors that matter to service users, such as the appropriateness, accessibility and acceptability of care (Pilgrim, 2009). It is difficult to measure subjective dimensions of experience, and ethical considerations such as respect and dignity (for staff and service users) are at least as important as other forms of evidence

(Pilgrim, 2009). EBP works best where there is no dispute about the target for change; for example, where there is a clear and singular diagnosis. This is problematic in the field of mental health, where the notion of diagnosis is itself contested (Pilgrim, 2009; Allsopp *et al.*, 2019).

The chosen methods are open to manipulation by commercial, governmental and professional vested interests to promote certain outcomes (Greenhalgh, Howick and Maskrey, 2014). For example, many pharmaceutical companies fund repeated small efficacy trials until they can show a positive result (and ignore the negative findings), and neglect evaluation of effectiveness in real-world settings (i.e. in so-called pragmatic trials) which are costly and less likely to yield positive results (House, 2011; Kirsch, 2009). Evidence (and the research that underpins it) becomes weaponised in struggles between professional groups and institutions required to compete with each other for survival and control over resources (Muzio, Brock and Suddaby, 2013). Even where conflicts of interest are declared, researcher allegiance (belief in the superiority of a particular discipline or therapeutic modality) can influence how studies are conducted and used (Lieb *et al.*, 2016; Meichenbaum and Lilienfeld, 2018). Very few studies in medicine are led by service users (Greenhalgh *et al.*, 2015; Greenhalgh, 2019).

In clinical guideline committees (such as NICE), the volume of evidence can be unmanageable, making it difficult to effectively assess the evidence in the detail necessary to come to a judgement (Greenhalgh, Howick and Maskrey, 2014). Meta-analyses and systematic reviews, which are so often rated highly in evidence hierarchies, are only as good as the data on which the constituent studies are built (a concept sometimes described as GIGO, or 'garbage in, garbage out') (Horton, 2019; Sturmberg, 2019). Further, there is a tendency to implement guidelines inflexibly, using technology-driven prompts (e.g. in general practice), which results in management-driven rather than person-centred care (Greenhalgh, Howick and Maskrey, 2014).

2   The contested role of evidence in the case of antidepressants

Despite their widespread use for a range of conditions, and their inclusion in the NICE recommended treatment guidelines for depression (NICE, 2009, 2018), professional opinion over the evidence base for antidepressants remains divided. Large numbers of RCTs have been conducted which show antidepressants are more efficacious than placebo in adults with severe depression (Cipriani *et al.*, 2018). The effect sizes (a statistical measure of the size of the effect of a treatment), however, have been found to vary for different subtypes of depression, and to reduce to zero in mild depression (Cristea, 2015; Khan and Brown, 2015). This means that, although the studies are suggesting an overall reduction in the symptoms of depression, it is likely to be too small an effect to mean much to the individuals. Some antidepressants appear to work better than others, but all have side effects (Cipriani *et al.*, 2018).

Publication bias (the selective reporting of studies and the suppression of negative results) is known to lead to claims of exaggerated effects (Munkholm, Paludan-Müller and Boesen, 2019). Kirsch (2009), for example, estimated that as much as 40 per cent of research on antidepressant efficacy is suppressed and withheld from publication by the pharmaceutical industry. It has been suggested that other criteria used by NICE, such as certainty of evidence, risk of bias and indirectness of evidence, are also not sufficiently addressed, even in well-conducted meta-analytic reviews (Munkholm, Paludan-Müller and Boesen, 2019).

Some critics have drawn attention to the way that pharmaceutical companies encourage the narrative that antidepressants are correcting a specific chemical imbalance or underlying brain disorder, and how they use the rhetoric of EBM to support this. This narrative has been widely criticised as an oversimplification, reducing the complex aetiology of depression to a single biological 'disease' process (Pariante, 2018; Moncrieff, 2018; House, 2011). Critics view this theory as a product of pharmaceutical company marketing campaigns rather than as having any scientific basis (Moncrieff, 2018; House, 2011). Meanwhile, the reality of clinical trials is that they are based on more subjective measures than the robust assessments that might be expected in the natural sciences.

This subjectivity shows itself in the comparison of results between studies whose service users and investigators are unaware of which subjects are receiving the active treatment (the medication being tested) and which the control treatment (often a placebo), and studies where only the service users (not the investigators) are blind to this information. The latter type of study tends to yield more positive outcomes, suggesting that the expectations of the investigators are influencing the findings (Cristea, 2015). The impact of service-user expectation is well known through the **placebo effect**, but **nocebo effects** have also been demonstrated in this area (Benedetti, Frisaldi and Piedimonte, 2019). Clinical trials are also accused of ignoring real-world issues, such as the impact of withdrawal symptoms (Davies and Read, 2019; Horowitz and Taylor, 2019). It has been argued that long-term use of antidepressants can seriously undermine people's sense of self-efficacy and their ability to recover using their own resources, creating problems of chronicity and dependence on services (Moncrieff, 2018).

As highlighted in Chapter 4, it has been suggested that the proliferation of diagnostic categories and indicators in each revision of the *Diagnostic and statistical manual of mental disorders* has been exploited by pharmaceutical companies eager to develop new products (Cristea, 2015). Increasingly, trials are conducted on people who meet specific diagnostic criteria, when in practice many symptoms and indicators overlap (Allsopp *et al.*, 2019). NICE, for example, classifies conditions such as depression into distinct subcategories ('chronic', 'complex' and 'treatment resistant'), which precludes combining evidence across these groups and, it has been argued, leads to distorted treatment strategies for people who, in clinical practice, have much in common (McPherson *et al.*, 2018). It has also been argued that the separation of depression into different severity types (mild, moderate, severe, etc.) is based on the use of psychometric measurements which are actually dependent on subjective reports of people's mental states, and which therefore give a false sense of certainty regarding what treatment is appropriate for each type (McPherson *et al.*, 2018).

There are difficulties with the use of random samples, too. Older adults and those with multiple health conditions tend to be excluded from RCTs (Kelly, 2018). Randomisation ensures a balance between observables and unobservables but does not guarantee representativeness (Deaton and Cartwright, 2018). For example, trials rely on volunteers who are available and willing to participate at a

Placebo effect
The positive effect of a treatment that can be attributed to the expectation of the recipient.

Nocebo effect
The negative effect of a treatment that can be attributed to the negative expectation of the recipient.

specific time and place, which precludes many who are working, who care for others or who have disabilities (Deaton and Cartwright, 2018). This exacerbates the artificiality of the population studied and requires many assumptions to be met when translating findings from the trial context into a different setting. The target population is always more diverse in these respects (Deaton and Cartwright, 2018). This is known as the 'external validity' problem (as discussed in Chapter 4, Section 4).

In addition, any assessment of the treatment benefits will be influenced by how symptoms are measured, the timescales over which treatment and any discontinuation effects are monitored, and the role of concurrent treatments, such as psychotherapy (Batelaan *et al.*, 2017). Determining the particular treatment for an individual will require clinical judgement rather than the simple application of the results of a trial or meta-analysis. A range of factors appear to predict different experiences of antidepressants, including demographic factors, psychosocial factors, people's beliefs about depression and their relationship with their prescriber (Gibson, Cartwright and Read, 2016). The value (or lack of) of antidepressants thus needs to be understood in the context of this diversity of experience and the particular meaning that antidepressants take on in people's lives (Gibson, Cartwright and Read, 2016). It can be argued that medicalisation may be unhelpful in understanding and addressing people's 'difficulties of living' in an unfair and unequal world (House, 2011; this will be explored in Chapter 19).

3   Methodological issues in counselling and psychotherapy research

In addition to the use of RCTs in medicine, the appeal of EBP has led to their use in counselling and psychotherapy research. As with drug trials, RCTs attempt to establish demonstrable benefits within defined population groups for particular therapeutic approaches, compared with either a placebo or 'waiting list' control (where the progress of the treatment group is compared with a control group of people who remain on a waiting list for treatment), 'treatment as usual' (where the control group simply continues with its usual treatment, e.g. medication) or another therapy. Similarly to antidepressant research, the challenges involved in establishing unbiased results and translating these into routine clinical practice are considerable and possibly even insurmountable (Cape and Parry, 2010; Laska, Gurman and Wampold, 2014; Shedler, 2015). The interests of professional and regulatory bodies, as well as researchers' own allegiances, play a significant part in shaping what gets funded, the detailed design and implementation of trials, and how results are analysed and published. Tensions exist over the appropriateness of the RCT methodology for comparing 'specific' factors associated with modalities (e.g. CBT versus psychodynamic, or any modality compared or in combination with antidepressants), and for researching 'common' factors and processes inherent in all therapies (such as the therapeutic relationship) (Laska, Gurman and Wampold, 2014; Wampold, 2015). There is also considerable debate over the effect of the role of the therapist (some therapists get better results than others using the same treatments) in determining outcomes (Blow, 2017).

In psychotherapy trials, 'demonstrable benefits' are typically defined in the form of standardised outcome measures (see Chapter 11, Section 4, for a reminder of the definition). These are derived from population-level features and diagnostic indicators that can be highly subjective and do not capture the variability of individual experience, let alone the views of other stakeholders such as service users, relatives, therapists, employers, service providers and society at large (Cuijpers, 2019). Typically, standardised outcome measures are based on symptom reduction only and ignore important quality-of-life outcomes valued by service users (Connell, O'Cathain and Brazier, 2014). The focus on symptom reduction is appropriate for therapies such as CBT, which are primarily focused on such reduction, but is less so for those that are relational and meaning-oriented (see Information box 17.1). For example, personality and intrapsychic change is considered important in psychodynamic therapy, while self-actualisation would normally be a core outcome of person-centred therapy (Cuijpers, 2019). Quality of life, avoidance of negative outcomes, improved self-efficacy and empowerment have all been found to be important when the service-user's perspective is taken into account (Cuijpers, 2019; Ellison *et al.*, 2018).

Information box 17.1: The contested nature of recovery in the field of mental health

There is little consensus as to the meaning of recovery, although one definition is that it 'refers to the extent to which a person with mental health problems regains or attains a meaningful life, with or without their symptoms' (Pilgrim, 2009, p. 112). Three central 'versions' of recovery can be distinguished (Pilgrim, 2008, 2009):

- *The outcome of successful treatment from illness*: This perspective draws on biomedical psychiatry and implies that service users need to comply with medical treatment (primarily medication) to get better.

- *Rehabilitation from impairment*: This is based on the philosophy of social psychiatry and implies that service users need to engage in tailored packages of treatment, including social skills training, which enables them to avoid mental health services for as long as possible.

- *The outcome of successful survival from invalidation*: This perspective is associated with the rise of the service-user movement in mental health (explored in Chapter 2) and sees service contact (and associated diagnostic labelling) as part of the problem rather than the solution.

Each of these understandings of recovery has political implications. For example, rather than focusing on individuals' 'deficits', critics – including survivors – have argued for a refocusing of the concept to emphasise capabilities through the assessment of collective, socio-economic, community and family resources (Pilgrim, 2009).

As with drug trials, there are risks of overestimating the benefits of any mode of therapy when making comparisons between an intervention group and those who receive no treatment or who are on a waiting list (as this approach only shows that the therapy is better than doing nothing at all). For this reason, it is common within psychotherapy trials to compare a particular psychological therapy with 'treatment as usual' or a placebo. This could mean allocating people in the control group to standard GP care, or to some other intervention that has a similar structure and format to the therapy being tested but that is not delivered by a trained therapist. In theory, this provides a test of relative benefit, but it needs to be combined with other information, such as any costs associated with taking part, side effects and the implications of not pursuing alternative available treatments (Leichsenring, Steinert and Ioannidis, 2019). The characteristics of the two groups being compared also make a difference to how the results translate from a research setting into routine care. As already discussed, efficacy trials tend to exclude people who have disorders that are additional to the primary one targeted by the intervention, and yet, in clinical populations, such complications are commonplace and more difficult to treat successfully (Leichsenring, Steinert and Ioannidis, 2019).

Numerous other difficulties in psychotherapy and counselling research have been identified, including publication bias. The most common example is that studies showing the positive benefits of treatments are more likely to be published than those not showing benefits. Low rates of replication of significant findings between studies, insufficient descriptions of the interventions used (making comparisons difficult) and the lack of long-term treatment effect studies have also been identified (Leichsenring, Steinert and Ioannidis, 2019). A recent meta-analysis of outcome research on psychotherapy for adult depression (Cuijpers, 2017) found little difference between the six main therapy modalities after publication bias and trial quality had been taken into account. Most studies assessed service-user response to therapy at six months from randomisation, and very few assessed beyond twelve months. All therapies were found to be effective across a range of conditions, but they were less effective for people with chronic severity (e.g. dysthymia, or persistent mild depression). Service users also dropped out at a relatively high rate (one in five), and experiences of adverse effects from therapy were not systematically reported.

Several further difficulties are specific to psychotherapy trials. For example, most trial interventions are conducted by experienced therapists who adhere to a written treatment design (or protocol) for the purposes of research. This differs from real-world settings, where clinicians work and train in different ways and may develop their own adaptations. Selecting clinicians for trial purposes limits the applicability of the trial findings to routine practice, where repeated studies have shown that differences between clinicians (i.e. therapist effects) are a significant factor in determining outcomes (Blow, 2017; Owen *et al.*, 2015). Not all therapists are equal; some will outperform others, even when matched in terms of their training, years of experience and theoretical orientation (Leichsenring, Steinert and Ioannidis, 2019; de Felice *et al.*, 2019).

Activity 17.1: Evaluating therapy

Allow about 10 minutes

Having worked through Section 3, try to answer the following questions:

1   Which version of recovery (Information box 17.1) makes most sense to you?
2   What counselling outcomes are important to you?
3   How might this affect how you would evaluate the counselling or therapy in which you have participated (as either a clinician or a client/service user)?
4   How would you account for your own allegiances/values in making these decisions?

Discussion

It is likely that consideration of these questions will have made you think of quite specific issues in your own life. This emphasises how subjective these matters can be and how difficult it can be for research to take them into account and measure them.

4   Evidence-based service development: the case of IAPT

The development of the IAPT programme can be seen as an exemplar of EBP in action. Both in the programme's origins and the way local services have developed, the use of 'evidence' has been central to claims of cost-effectiveness, improving access to psychological therapies and recovery rates. The role of evidence, what it illuminates and what it obscures has, however, also led to controversy over IAPT's aims, service design, costs and outcomes.

In 2008, when IAPT started, the aim was 'to bridge the gap between research and practice' by training a large new workforce of psychological therapists in 'empirically supported treatments' (the US term for 'evidence-based') and 'deploying them in new services for the treatment of depression and anxiety disorders' (Clark, 2018, p. 159). The rationale thus had clear links with EBM. Funding was won on the back of two arguments put forward by the economist Richard Layard. The first centred on NICE's failure to meet its own recommendations for greater use of psychological therapies (CBT in particular) alongside medication as cost-effective treatments for depression (NICE, 2004). With long waiting times for any therapy and an almost total absence of CBT provision in many parts of the country, Layard successfully argued that the level of funding for mental health conditions lacked parity with that for physical health (LSE, 2006). Secondly, he linked this with an argument regarding the number of people falling out of work and claiming disability benefits for long periods due to mental ill health (Layard, 2005). Layard argued that IAPT would pay for itself by reducing the 'burden' to the government of anxiety and depression (mainly benefit payments and medical care) and increasing revenues from people returning to work (through taxation and increased productivity) (Clark, 2011). Thus, both the NICE guidelines and the economic argument regarding costs were vital in securing funding for IAPT. It is worth noting, however, the disease-centred terminology ('mental illness', 'disorder') and the value-laden metaphors (such as 'burden').

In terms of service design, the IAPT delivery model was based on stepped care principles, which specify that treatments should always commence with the least restrictive (in relation to the cost of the treatment and the burden on the service user) and should be 'self-correcting' (Clark, 2011). This latter point is addressed by systems of regular treatment review and the early detection of non-improvement. The IAPT model offered services from 'low intensity' interventions (such as guided self-help or computerised CBT) to more intensive treatments (such as 'high intensity' CBT) where needed (Clark, 2011). If and when the service user was ready, the treatment was 'stepped up' to the next level. These principles were driven by efficiency considerations, matching NICE-compliant therapies with people referred for particular indications of need, without the necessity for costly assessment (by highly trained and skilled clinicians) as in other mental health services. A key feature was the use of session-by-session outcome measures for every patient to aid progress monitoring, 'stepping up' or 'stepping down' decisions, and performance reporting for the services as a whole (Clark, 2011). The approach fitted with the rehabilitative model of recovery (see Information box 17.1). In addition, national training curricula were drawn up collaboratively with, and accredited by, the British Association for Behavioural and Cognitive Psychotherapists. Thus, the core features of EBP – targeting a specific population need, providing a system for performance management, ensuring cost-effectiveness and enabling political accountability – were all present. At the same time, the 'top-down' values and requirements of government and of the professional bodies became embedded.

Critics of the IAPT programme have argued that Layard's original argument was over-determined, treating all mental ill health and the associated costs as if they were caused by joblessness (Fraser, 2006; Pilgrim and McCranie, 2013). In IAPT, Layard is said to have successfully recruited the state as a 'psychological treatment product champion' (much as pharmaceutical companies are for antidepressants), to further its interests in 'turning its citizens from being benefit recipients into taxpayers' (Denman, 2007, p. 82). The development of condition-specific treatment protocols and manualised interventions in IAPT has not easily mapped on to the kinds of distress and disturbance seen in practice, nor given room for service-users' own and different expectations of treatment or recovery (Pilgrim, 2008, 2009; Lees, 2016; Loewenthal, 2017). Concerns have also been raised regarding the use of predefined cut-off points to establish 'caseness' (the extent to which someone is suitable for treatment) based on symptom-related measures only.

IAPT services are also criticised for being driven by targets for take-up, waiting times, measures of recovery (defined as moving below the cut-off point for caseness) and 'reliable improvement' (any reduction in caseness regardless of cut-offs) that might mean little to service users (NHS Digital, 2017). Formal treatment completion is possible after as few as two therapy sessions, and longer-term outcomes are not captured. In areas of greater socio-economic deprivation, referral rates have been notably higher while recovery rates have been lower (varying from 58.1 per cent for the least deprived area to 41 per cent for the most deprived area) (Moller *et al.*, 2019). In addition, outcomes have been worse for minority groups, including people of Muslim faith, people with special educational needs and gay, lesbian and bisexual people (Moller *et al.*, 2019). Small year-on-year increments in the proportion of the total population (with depression or anxiety) accessing IAPT, along with improvements in recovery rates, have thus masked important issues of unequal access and outcomes for major subgroups.

4.1   CBT as modality of choice

The current dominance of CBT has been closely linked with the rise of EBM. In the US and UK, CBT has been viewed as having the best evidence base, owing to the large number of trials that have been conducted, which consistently show improvements in outcomes based on symptomatic measures (Leichsenring and Steinart, 2017). However, repeated meta-analyses have shown CBT to be no more effective than other modalities (Cuijpers *et al.*, 2016; Wampold *et al.*, 2017). Most 'head-to-head' trials (comparing one therapeutic approach with another) focus on disorder-specific symptom measures rather than other important indicators of psychological functioning (as discussed in Section 3), and CBT treatments vary considerably in what is being offered to service users (Wampold *et al.*, 2017). When assessed for bias using the Cochrane criteria (as discussed in Section 1), only a small proportion of trials demonstrating the superiority of CBT have been found to be of high quality (Cuijpers *et al.*, 2016; Leichsenring and Steinart, 2017). Too often, CBT has demonstrated efficacy in only the weakest of comparisons, where outcomes are most likely to be influenced by nocebo effects (Leichsenring and Steinart, 2017). Similarly, high risks have been found from researcher allegiance and publication bias (Cuijpers *et al.*, 2016).

5   Alternative models to EBP

A number of alternative models to EBP exist, including case studies, practice-near research (which is focused on practice and usually carried out within the profession) and coproduced or lived experience studies (which were explored in Chapter 2). Single case study designs are generally qualitative in nature, but they may include some quantitative elements to document in detail any clinical cases that present significant challenges to established theory. These enable in-depth examinations of individual circumstances, contexts, meanings and the development of a therapeutic relationship over time. Case studies are carried out from the perspective of a specific discipline and reflect the modality of the clinician involved. An understanding of clinical phenomena may be developed by comparing different cases documented over time. The University of Essex in the UK has an institutional archive (the Single Case Archive), which is designed to facilitate this process.

Practice-near research might include clinical ethnography (e.g. Dominicé Dao *et al.*, 2018), in-depth process analysis of recorded therapy sessions (e.g. Swift, Tompkins and Parkin, 2017) and qualitative interviews with service users and/or clinicians (e.g. Donald and Carey, 2017). Findings from these studies may be analysed cumulatively, through qualitative meta-synthesis (e.g. Levitt, Pomerville and Surace, 2016). Within the paradigm of EBP, 'practice-based evidence' has also been promoted as a means of bridging the research–practice gap and reducing external validity problems (Barkham, Hardy and Mellor-Clark, 2010). This approach focuses on outcomes within routine service settings established using standardised measures, such as CORE (Clinical Outcomes in Routine Evaluation – refers to a portfolio of outcome measures developed since the mid-1990s, and now widely used in UK NHS psychological services) and administrative data already collected in services. It has been associated with the development of practice research networks (Lucock *et al.*, 2017), which facilitate comparisons between services and interventions over time (Holmqvist, Philips and Barkham, 2015).

As explored in Chapter 2, other research models exist that prioritise service-user perspectives, from patient and public involvement to fully service-user-led and coproduced research. These may include individual 'recovery narratives' (e.g. Woods, Hart and Spandler, 2019) or fully-fledged multi-method and interdisciplinary research programmes. Funding for programmes like this is rare, given the risk-averse EBP orientation of research funding bodies. Each of these has its own strengths, drawbacks and emancipatory potential (Oliver, Kothari and Mays, 2019; Rose and Kalathil, 2019).

Conclusion

This chapter has introduced the principles of EBP. On the surface, the practice appears to have significant merit, as it aims to determine the value of particular treatment approaches. However, it is also clear that serious questions have been raised regarding the reductive nature of the evidence used in EBP. The measures used are often subjective and limited in their scope (e.g. what gets measured and over what time period) and might exclude issues that are most valuable to the service user. In addition, there has been a lack of representation of diverse voices and, in particular, the almost total absence of a service-user perspective on the experiences of treatments and services.

Interventions are designed to minimise risk, maximise cost-effectiveness and ensure efficient service delivery to large numbers of people. But the question must be asked: whose interests are these criteria aimed at? It has been argued that the needs of the pharmaceutical industry and professional groups have shaped these practices, and that the proponents of antidepressants, and CBT in particular, have manipulated the rhetoric of these approaches to promote their own 'products' (House 2011; Wampold *et al.*, 2017). More generally, it has been suggested that EBP fits well with a public management agenda in mental health that focuses on the individual and their symptoms, rather than considering sources of distress that might be social in nature (Rizq, 2014a, 2014b; Simonet, 2015). This does not mean that EBP has no value; rather, it is important to critically consider what constitutes 'evidence', and also to draw on different disciplinary perspectives and alternative models.

Further reading

- An excellent and accessible account of problems with diagnosis in mental health can be found in the following book:
  Filer, N. (2019) *This book will change your mind about mental health: a journey into the heartland of psychiatry.* London: Faber & Faber.

- The following is an example of a user-led research study:

  Faulkner, A., Carr, S., Gould, D., Khisa, C., Hafford-Letchfield, T., Cohen, R., Megele, C. and Holley, J. (2019) '"Dignity and respect": an example of service user leadership and co-production in mental health research', *Health Expectations*, pp. 1–10. doi:10.1111/hex.12963.

- This book provides an overview of critical perspectives on clinical research and an outline of alternatives:

  Loewenthal, D. (ed.) (2015) *Critical psychotherapy, psychoanalysis and counselling: implications for practice.* Basingstoke: Palgrave Macmillan.

References

Allsopp, K., Read, J., Corcoran, J. and Kinderman, P. (2019) 'Heterogeneity in psychiatric diagnostic classification', *Psychiatry Research*, 279, pp. 15–22. doi:10.1016/j.psychres.2019.07.005.

Barkham, M., Hardy, G.E. and Mellor-Clark, J. (eds.) (2010) *Developing and delivering practice-based evidence: a guide for the psychological therapies.* Chichester, UK: John Wiley & Sons, Ltd. doi:10.1002/9780470687994.

Batelaan, N.M., Bosman, R.C., Muntingh, A., Scholten, W.D., Huijbregts, L.M. and van Balkom, A. (2017) 'Risk of relapse after antidepressant discontinuation in anxiety disorders, obsessive-compulsive disorder, and post-traumatic stress disorder: systematic review and meta-analysis of relapse prevention trials', *BMJ Clinical Research*, 358(j3927). doi:10.1136/bmj.j3927.

Benedetti, F., Frisaldi, E. and Piedimonte, A. (2019) 'The need to investigate nocebo effects in more detail', *World Psychiatry*, 18(2), pp. 227–228. doi:10.1002/wps.20627.

Blow, A.J. (2017) 'The therapist's role in effective therapy: three key priorities for research', *Administration and Policy in Mental Health and Mental Health Services Research*, 44(5), pp. 729–731. doi:10.1007/s10488-017-0804-3.

Cape, J. and Parry, G. (2010) 'Clinical practice guidelines development in evidence-based psychotherapy', in Barkham, M., Hardy, G.E. and Mellor-Clark, J. (eds.) *Developing and delivering practice-based evidence: a guide for the psychological therapies.* Chichester, UK: John Wiley & Sons, Ltd, pp. 171–190.

Cipriani, A. *et al.* (2018) 'Comparative efficacy and acceptability of 21 antidepressant drugs for the acute treatment of adults with major depressive disorder: a systematic review and network meta-analysis', *The Lancet*, 391 (10128), pp. 1357–1366. doi:10.1016/S0140-6736(17)32802-7.

Clark, D.M. (2011) 'Implementing NICE guidelines for the psychological treatment of depression and anxiety disorders: the IAPT experience', *International Review of Psychiatry*, 23(4), pp. 318–327. doi:10.3109/09540261.2011.606803.

Clark, D.M. (2018) 'Realizing the mass public benefit of evidence-based psychological therapies: the IAPT program', *Annual Review of Clinical Psychology*, 14(1), pp. 159–183. doi:10.1146/annurev-clinpsy-050817-084833.

Cochrane, A.L. (1972) *Effectiveness and efficiency: random reflections on health services.* London: Nuffield Provincial Hospitals Trust.

Connell, J., O'Cathain, A. and Brazier, J. (2014) 'Measuring quality of life in mental health: are we asking the right questions?', *Social Science & Medicine*, 120, pp. 12–20. doi:10.1016/j.socscimed.2014.08.026.

Cristea, I. (2015) 'Antidepressants vs placebo for depression: forget the gap', *The Mental Elf*. Available at: http://www.nationalelfservice.net/mental-health/

depression/antidepressants-vs-placebo-for-depression-forget-the-gap/ (Accessed: 16 November 2019).

Cuijpers, P., Cristea, I.A., Karyotaki, E., Reijnders, M. and Huibers, M.J.H. (2016) 'How effective are cognitive behavior therapies for major depression and anxiety disorders? A meta-analytic update of the evidence', *World Psychiatry*, 15(3), pp. 245–258. doi:10.1002/wps.20346.

Cuijpers, P. (2017) 'Four decades of outcome research on psychotherapies for adult depression: an overview of a series of meta-analyses', *Canadian Psychology/Psychologie canadienne*, 58(1), pp. 7–19. doi:10.1037/cap0000096.

Cuijpers, P. (2019) 'Targets and outcomes of psychotherapies for mental disorders: an overview', *World Psychiatry*, 18(3), pp. 276–285. doi:10.1002/wps.20661.

Davies, J. and Read, J. (2019) 'A systematic review into the incidence, severity and duration of antidepressant withdrawal effects: are guidelines evidence-based?', *Addictive Behaviors*, pp. 111–121. doi:10.1016/j.addbeh.2018.08.027.

de Felice, G., Giuliani, A., Halfon, S., Andreassi, S., Paoloni, G. and Orsucci, F.F. (2019) 'The misleading Dodo Bird verdict. How much of the outcome variance is explained by common and specific factors?', *New Ideas in Psychology*, 54, pp. 50–55. doi:10.1016/j.newideapsych.2019.01.006.

Deaton, A. and Cartwright, N. (2018) 'Reflections on randomized control trials', *Social Science & Medicine*, 210, pp. 86–90. doi:10.1016/j.socscimed.2018.04.046.

Denman, C. (2007) 'The organization and delivery of psychological treatments', *International Review of Psychiatry*, 19(1), pp. 81–92.

Dominicé Dao, M., Inglin, S., Vilpert, S. and Hudelson, P. (2018) 'The relevance of clinical ethnography: reflections on 10 years of a cultural consultation service', *BMC Health Services Research*, 18(1), p. 19. doi:10.1186/s12913-017-2823-x.

Donald, I.N. and Carey, T.A. (2017) 'Improving knowledge about the effectiveness of psychotherapy', *Psychotherapy and Politics International*, 15(3), p. e1424. doi:10.1002/ppi.1424.

Ellison, M.L., Belanger, L.K., Niles, B.L., Evans, L.C. and Bauer, M.S. (2018) 'Explication and definition of mental health recovery: a systematic review', *Administration and Policy in Mental Health*, 45(1), pp. 91–102. doi:10.1007/s10488-016-0767-9.

Fraser, M. (2006) 'Let's talk: a different take on improving access to psychological therapies', *The Journal of Mental Health Training, Education and Practice* , 1(2), p. 23–26. Available at: http://www.emeraldinsight.com/doi/abs/10.1108/17556228200600013 (Accessed: 13 July 2019).

Gibson, K., Cartwright, C. and Read, J. (2016) '"In my life antidepressants have been…": a qualitative analysis of users' diverse experiences with antidepressants', *BMC Psychiatry*, 16, 135. doi:10.1186/s12888-016-0844-3.

Greenhalgh, T., Snow, R., Ryan, S., Rees, S. and Salisbury, H. (2015) 'Six "biases" against patients and carers in evidence-based medicine', *BMC Medicine*, 13(1), 200. doi:10.1186/s12916-015-0437-x.

Greenhalgh, T. (2019) 'Towards an institute for patient-led research', *The BMJ Opinion*. Available at: https://blogs.bmj.com/bmj/2019/11/12/trisha-greenhalgh-towards-an-institute-for-patient-led-research/ (Accessed: 16 November 2019).

Greenhalgh, T., Howick, J. and Maskrey, N. (2014) 'Evidence based medicine: a movement in crisis?', *BMJ*, 348, pp. g3725–g3725. doi:10.1136/bmj.g3725.

Greenhalgh, T. and Papoutsi, C. (2018) 'Studying complexity in health services research: desperately seeking an overdue paradigm shift', *BMC Medicine*, 16, 95. doi:10.1186/s12916-018-1089-4.

Greenhalgh, T. and Russell, J. (2009) 'Evidence-based policymaking: a critique', *Perspectives in Biology and Medicine*, 52(2), pp. 304–318.

Head, B.W. (2010) 'Reconsidering evidence-based policy: key issues and challenges', *Policy and Society*, 29(2), pp. 77–94. doi:10.1016/j.polsoc.2010.03.001.

Holmqvist, R., Philips, B. and Barkham, M. (2015) 'Developing practice-based evidence: benefits, challenges, and tensions', *Psychotherapy Research*, 25(1), pp. 20–31. doi:10.1080/10503307.2013.861093.

Horowitz, M.A. and Taylor, D. (2019) 'Tapering of SSRI treatment to mitigate withdrawal symptoms', *The Lancet Psychiatry*, 6(6), pp. 538–546. doi:10.1016/S2215-0366(19)30032-X.

Horton, R. (2019) 'Offline: the gravy train of systematic reviews', *The Lancet*, 394(10211), 1790. doi:10.1016/S0140-6736(19)32766-7.

House, R. (2011) 'Welcome to the "Paradigm War": the case of antidepressant medication', *European Journal of Psychotherapy & Counselling*, 13(3), pp. 279–289. doi:10.1080/13642537.2011.596728.

Kelly, M.P. (2018) 'The need for a rationalist turn in evidence-based medicine', *Journal of Evaluation in Clinical Practice*, 24(5), pp. 1158–1165. doi:10.1111/jep.12974.

Khan, A. and Brown, W.A. (2015) 'Antidepressants versus placebo in major depression: an overview', *World Psychiatry*, 14(3), pp. 294–300.

Kirsch, I. (2009) *The emperor's new drugs: exploding the antidepressant myth.* London: The Bodley Head.

Laska, K., Gurman, A. and Wampold, B. (2014) 'Expanding the lens of evidence-based practice in psychotherapy: a common factors perspective', *Psychotherapy*, 51(4), pp. 467–481. Available at: http://psycnet.apa.org/journals/pst/51/4/467/ (Accessed: 22 May 2019).

Layard, R. (2005) *Mental health: Britain's biggest social problem?* Paper presented at the No.10 Strategy Unit Seminar on Mental Health on 20th

January 2005. London: LSE. Available at: http://eprints.lse.ac.uk/47428/ (Accessed: 13 May 2020).

Lees, J. (2016) *The future of psychological therapy: from managed care to transformational practice*. London and New York: Routledge.

Leichsenring, F. and Steinert, C. (2017) 'Is cognitive behavioral therapy the gold standard for psychotherapy? The need for plurality in treatment and research', *JAMA Opinion*, 318(14), pp. E1–E2. doi:10.1001/JAMA.2017.13737.

Leichsenring, F., Steinert, C. and Ioannidis, J.P.A. (2019) 'Toward a paradigm shift in treatment and research of mental disorders', *Psychological Medicine*, 49 (13), pp. 2111–2117. doi:10.1017/S0033291719002265.

Levitt, H.M., Pomerville, A. and Surace, F.I. (2016) 'A qualitative meta-analysis examining clients' experiences of psychotherapy: a new agenda.', *Psychological Bulletin*, 142(8), pp. 801–830. doi:10.1037/bul0000057.

Lieb, K., von der Osten-Sacken, J., Stoffers-Winterling, J., Reiss, N. and Barth, J. (2016) 'Conflicts of interest and spin in reviews of psychological therapies: a systematic review', *BMJ Open*, 6(4), pp. 1–8. doi:10.1136/bmjopen-2015-010606.

Loewenthal, D. (2017) 'Is the UK government's improving access to psychological therapies promoting individualism at the expense of the common good?', *European Journal of Psychotherapy & Counselling*, 19(2), pp. 117–123. doi:10.1080/13642537.2017.1313501.

London School of Economics and Political Science (LSE) (2006) *The depression report: a new deal for depression and anxiety disorders*. London: London School of Economics and Political Science. Available at: http://cep.lse.ac.uk/research/mentalhealth (Accessed: 20 May 2020).

Lucock, M., Barkham, M., Donohoe, G., Kellett, S., McMillan, D., Mullaney, S., Sainty, A., Saxon, D., Thwaites, R. and Delgadillo, J. (2017) 'The role of Practice Research Networks (PRN) in the development and implementation of evidence: the northern improving access to psychological therapies PRN case study', *Administration and Policy in Mental Health and Mental Health Services Research*, 44(6), pp. 919–931. doi:10.1007/s10488-017-0810-5.

McPherson, S., Rost, F., Town, J. and Abbass, A. (2018) 'Epistemological flaws in NICE review methodology and its impact on recommendations for psychodynamic psychotherapies for complex and persistent depression', *Psychoanalytic Psychotherapy*, 32(2), pp. 1–20. doi:10.1080/02668734.2018.1458331.

McPherson, S. and Beresford, P. (2019) 'Semantics of patient choice: how the UK national guideline for depression silences patients', *Disability & Society*, 34(3), pp. 491–497. doi:10.1080/09687599.2019.1589757.

McPherson, S. and Hengartner, M.P. (2019) 'Long-term outcomes of trials in the National Institute for Health and Care Excellence depression guideline', *BJPsych Open*, 5(5), e81. doi:10.1192/bjo.2019.65.

Meichenbaum, D. and Lilienfeld, S.O. (2018) 'How to spot hype in the field of psychotherapy: a 19-item checklist', *Professional Psychology: Research and Practice*, 49(1), pp. 22–30. doi:10.1037/pro0000172.

Moller, N.P., Ryan, G., Rollings, J. and Barkham, M. (2019) 'The 2018 UK NHS Digital annual report on the Improving Access to Psychological Therapies programme: a brief commentary', *BMC Psychiatry*, 19(1), 252. doi:10.1186/s12888-019-2235-z.

Moncrieff, J. (2018) 'Against the stream: antidepressants are not antidepressants – an alternative approach to drug action and implications for the use of antidepressants', *BJPsych Bulletin*, 42(1), pp. 42–44. doi:10.1192/bjb.2017.11.

Munkholm, K., Paludan-Müller, A.S. and Boesen, K. (2019) 'Considering the methodological limitations in the evidence base of antidepressants for depression: a reanalysis of a network meta-analysis', *BMJ Open*, 9(6), e024886. doi:10.1136/bmjopen-2018-024886.

Muzio, D., Brock, D.M. and Suddaby, R. (2013) 'Professions and institutional change: towards an institutionalist sociology of the professions', *Journal of Management Studies*, 50(5), pp. 699–721. doi:10.1111/joms.12030.

NHS Digital (2017) *Psychological Therapies: reports on the use of IAPT services, England, April 2017 Final, including reports on the integrated services pilot and quarter 4 2016/17*. Available at: https://digital.nhs.uk/catalogue/PUB30035 (Accessed: 26 July 2019).

National Institute for Health and Care Excellence (NICE) (2004) *Depression: management of depression in primary and secondary care: clinical guideline 23*. London: National Institute for Health and Care Excellence. Available at: https://www.nice.org.uk/guidance/cg23 (Accessed: 20 May 2020).

National Institute for Health and Care Excellence (NICE) (2009) *Depression in adults: recognition and management: NICE Clinical Guideline [CG90]*. Available at: nice.org.uk/guidance/cg90 (Accessed: 20 May 2020).

National Institute for Health and Care Excellence (NICE) (2018) *Developing NICE guidelines: the manual* (PMG20). 2014 edn. Manchester: National Institute for Health and Care Excellence. Available at: https://www.nice.org.uk/process/pmg20/resources/developing-nice-guidelines-the-manual-pdf-72286708700869 (Accessed: 20 May 2020).

Oliver, K., Kothari, A. and Mays, N. (2019) 'Coming to terms with the hidden costs of co-production', *Impact of Social Sciences blog*. Available at: https://blogs.lse.ac.uk/impactofsocialsciences/2019/06/19/coming-to-terms-with-the-hidden-costs-of-co-production/?utm_source=feedburner&utm_medium=em… 1/5 (Accessed: 26 June 2019).

Owen, J., Drinane, J.M., Idigo, K.C. and Valentine, J.C. (2015) 'Psychotherapist effects in meta-analyses: how accurate are treatment effects?', *Psychotherapy*, 52(3), pp. 321–328. doi:10.1037/pst0000014.

Pariante, C.M. (2018) 'A parallel universe where psychiatry is like the rest of medicine', *Epidemiology and Psychiatric Sciences*, 27(2), pp. 143–145. doi:10.1017/S2045796017000762.

Petticrew, M. and Roberts, H. (2003) 'Evidence, hierarchies, and typologies: horses for courses', *Journal of Epidemiology & Community Health*, 57(7), pp. 527–529. doi:10.1136/jech.57.7.527 [Table].

Pilgrim, D. (2008) '"Recovery" and current mental health policy', *Chronic Illness*, 4(4), pp. 295–304. doi:10.1177/1742395308097863.

Pilgrim, D. (2009) *Key concepts in mental health*. 2nd edn. London: SAGE.

Pilgrim, D. and McCranie, A. (2013) *Recovery and mental health: a critical sociological account*. Basingstoke: Palgrave Macmillan.

Rizq, R. (2014a) 'Perversion, neoliberalism and therapy: the audit culture in mental health services', *Psychoanalysis, Culture & Society*, 19(2), pp. 209–218. doi:10.1057/pcs.2014.15.

Rizq, R. (2014b) 'Perverting the course of therapy: the fetishisation of governance in public sector mental health services', *Psychoanalytic Psychotherapy*, 28(3), pp. 249–266. doi:10.1080/02668734.2014.933034.

Rose, D. and Kalathil, J. (2019) 'Power, privilege and knowledge: the untenable promise of co-production in mental "health"', *Frontiers in Sociology*, 4, p. 57. doi:10.3389/fsoc.2019.00057.

Sackett, D.L., Rosenberg, W.M., Gray, J.A.M., Haynes, R.B. and Richardson, W. S. (1996) 'Evidence based medicine: what it is and what it isn't', *BMJ*, 312 (7023), pp. 71–72. doi:10.1136/bmj.312.7023.71.

Saltelli, A. and Giampietro, M. (2017) 'What is wrong with evidence based policy, and how can it be improved?', *Futures*, 91, pp. 62–71. doi:10.1016/j.futures.2016.11.012.

Shedler, J. (2015) 'Where is the evidence for "evidence-based" therapy?', *The Journal of Psychological Therapies in Primary Care*, 4, pp. 47–59. doi:10.1016/j.psc.2018.02.001.

Simonet, D. (2015) 'The new public management theory in the British health care system', *Administration & Society*, 47(7), pp. 802–826. doi:10.1177/0095399713485001.

Sturmberg, J.P. (2019) 'Evidence-based medicine – not a panacea for the problems of a complex adaptive world', *Journal of Evaluation in Clinical Practice*,, 25(5), pp. 706–716. doi:10.1111/jep.13122.

Swift, J.K., Tompkins, K.A. and Parkin, S.R. (2017) 'Understanding the client's perspective of helpful and hindering events in psychotherapy sessions: a micro-process approach', *Journal of Clinical Psychology*, 73(11), pp. 1543–1555. doi:10.1002/jclp.22531.

Wampold, B.E. (2015) 'How important are the common factors in psychotherapy? An update', *World Psychiatry*, 14(3), pp. 270–277. doi:10.1002/wps.20238.

Wampold, B.E., Flückiger, C., Del Re, A.C., Yulish, N.E., Frost, N.D., Pace, B.T., Goldberg, S.B., Miller, S.D., Baardseth, T.P., Laska, K.M. and Hilsenroth, M.J. (2017) 'In pursuit of truth: a critical examination of meta-analyses of cognitive behavior therapy', *Psychotherapy Research*, 27(1), pp. 14–32. doi:10.1080/10503307.2016.1249433.

Woods, A., Hart, A. and Spandler, H. (2019) 'The recovery narrative: politics and possibilities of a genre', *Culture, Medicine, and Psychiatry*, pp. 1–27. doi:10.1007/s11013-019-09623-y.

Chapter 18

Mental health, criminal justice and the law

David W. Jones

Contents

Introduction

'There's no need to turn back spring' by Lu Szweda

This chapter introduces the relationship between issues of mental health, criminal justice and the law. As discussed in Chapter 1, questions of legal and criminal responsibility have played a part in shaping our systems and categories of mental health for a long time. In England, the circumstances in which someone might be confined due to 'insanity' has been subject to legislation since at least 1744, when local authorities were charged with accommodating those considered to be 'pauper lunatics' (see Chapter 1, Section 2.1, for a reminder of the definition). Debate about the ethics of the involuntary confinement and treatment of people viewed as suffering from mental health problems continues to this day. There have also been more dramatically enacted events surrounding the so-called insanity defence, with centuries of debate over how to establish that an individual's criminal offending might be excused on the grounds that they suffer from a mental disorder.

This chapter aims to:

- introduce some of the long-standing debates over the use of the insanity defence and questions of diminished responsibility for criminal acts

- introduce the grounds – stipulated by the Mental Health Act – for the detention and treatment of individuals against their will

- explore some of the questions raised by the problem of 'personality disorder' in the criminal justice system

- briefly introduce the profession of mental health work in the criminal justice system.

1 The insanity defence and diminished responsibility

As discussed in Chapter 1, there is a well-documented, long-held view that an individual's mental state will have important implications for the degree of guilt they might carry when found to have committed an offence (Reznek, 1997; Walker, 1968). For example, Matthew Hale, the seventeenth-century historically influential Chief Justice of England, declared that the presence of insanity could mean that an 'offender' should not be found guilty of an offence; but he also seemed to declare that such leniency should only apply to those who were 'totally deprived of the use of reason' and were 'in effect in the condition of brutes' (Hale, published posthumously, 1736, p. 31). This narrow definition was not new; it goes back to the thirteenth century at least (Bracton, c. 1250). Hale, however, went on to say that he was aware that more subtle forms of insanity were to be found that did not leave victims 'wholly destitute of the use of any reason', but they might be 'under a particular dementia in respect of some particular discourses, subjects', or perhaps 'partial in respect of degrees' (Hale, 1736, p. 31). Hale noted that such forms of 'partial insanity' did not excuse individuals for committing any serious offence, but that, in reality, it could be difficult to define the division between 'perfect' and 'partial' insanity, and that it should instead be down to 'judge and jury' to decide (Hale, 1736, p. 31).

Although Hale's position provided some grounds for considering more subtle forms of disorder (indeed, there is some evidence that courts became more sensitive to issues of insanity; Jones, 2016), it was only in the nineteenth century that forms of insanity with implications for criminal responsibility began to be theorised by the newly emerging profession of psychiatry. These developments were connected to the exploration of the mind that had led to the development of moral treatment (discussed in Chapter 1). The use of such diagnoses in the courts had some success in England. The ideas of partial insanity, moral insanity and monomania, used in the trial of Daniel M'Naghten (as outlined in Walker, 1968), led to one of the most controversial trials in legal history.

Figure 18.1 Daniel M'Naghten in Bethlem Royal Hospital, c. 1857–1859

The use of these concepts was not entirely new, but their apparent success in excusing M'Naghten's attempt on the life of the prime minister of the time and his killing of the prime minister's secretary led to a public furore (Jones, 2017). A group of experts – at the time establishing the profession of psychiatry – marshalled arguments that suggested they had detected a hidden form of insanity in M'Naghten. The idea was that, although M'Naghten had the capacity to reason (as evidenced by his ability to run the affairs of his life and to plan the attack), the hidden insanity nonetheless moved his thoughts to plan the assassination of the prime minister.

The negative reception to the verdict revolved around the anticipated threat to social order if potential villains were given free rein to commit even the most heinous of crimes. The subsequent House of Lords enquiry, which convened in response to this anxiety, emerged with the so-called 'M'Naghten rules', which narrowed the insanity defence in a manner that cast a long shadow across time and over systems of criminal justice across the globe. According to these 'rules', if a defendant could be shown to have 'known what they were doing' at the time of the offence, and 'knew that this was wrong', then they were guilty. This guilt was assumed regardless of whatever bizarre beliefs and drives might have motivated the defendant's behaviour. The more subtle forms of insanity that were being explored by the new profession were very deliberately ruled out of consideration. Had

M'Naghten himself been tried under these rules, he would surely have been found guilty. His declaration of intent to assassinate the prime minister, who he believed was persecuting him for his Scottish nationalist beliefs, would have dammed him.

The M'Naghten rules had a considerable impact on the criminal justice system, not only in Britain but across the world. Anything approaching a strict application of 'the rules' meant that the insanity defence could only be used in those cases where the defendant had lost their use of reasoning. This narrowing of the definition, combined with a binary choice between 'guilty' or 'not guilty', led to pressure for change. The first formal dent in the assumptions of the M'Naghten rules came through pressure to show leniency to women who had killed their own young children. It was clear that, over several centuries, courts had shown leniency to such women through using the insanity defence, but this leniency was not formalised until 1922, when the Infanticide Act was introduced to English law. This Act allowed special provision to be made for women who killed their newborn babies when 'they had not fully recovered from the effect of giving birth to such child, and by reason thereof the balance of her mind was then disturbed' (Ward, 1999, p. 163). If found guilty of infanticide, the charge was reduced from murder to **manslaughter**, thus avoiding the mandatory death sentence for murder. The Infanticide Act was updated in 1938, which extended this partial defence to up to 12 months following the birth. This law remains in place at the time of writing.

Activity 18.1: Perspectives on mental health and infanticide

Allow about 5 minutes

There is evidence of a long history of lenience being shown to women who killed their own children (Eigen, 1998). There has been some debate about why this happened. It can be suggested that this is a symptom of a male dominated society, which views women as less rational than men and more susceptible to the physiological and psychological impacts of events such as childbirth. From this perspective, it is a symptom of a society that is more likely to medicalise women and to be less tolerant of deviations from an idealised norm (Zedner, 1991).

Alternatively, do you think these observations are evidence of women being dealt with more considerately and leniently than men?

Manslaughter
For the charge of manslaughter, it is only necessary to prove that the defendant acted in such a dangerous, reckless or negligent way that their actions were likely to cause serious harm. This contrasts with murder, where the prosecution must show that the accused meant to do serious harm (even if they did not intend to kill).

Discussion

The second, alternative opinion has certainly been expressed. Ward (1999) argues that the infanticide provision was not about medicalisation; rather, it was brought about through pressure within the legal system. Courts were having to deal with relatively large numbers of desperate, poverty-stricken women who had killed their own babies. They evoked sympathy and courts were reluctant to sentence them to the otherwise inevitable death penalty. The use of medical evidence and terms was simply a convenience (Kramar and Watson, 2006).

A more general relaxation of the M'Naghten rules in England and Wales came about with the *Homicide Act 1957*, and its concept of diminished responsibility (largely imported from Scottish law; Walker, 1968). This introduced a compromise between 'guilty' and 'not guilty' verdicts in murder trials. Someone could be found not guilty of murder on the grounds of diminished responsibility, but instead guilty of manslaughter. This verdict meant that the capital punishment of execution or life imprisonment was no longer mandatory, and the court could recommend that the defendant be taken to a hospital rather than to prison (Walker, 1968). The *Homicide Act 1957* stated that, for a diminished responsibility defence to be accepted on grounds of mental abnormality, it must be established that:

> where a person kills or is party to the killing of another, he shall not be convicted of murder if he was suffering from such an abnormality of mind (whether arising from a condition of arrested or retarded development of mind or any inherent causes or induced by disease or injury) as substantially impaired his mental responsibility for his acts or omissions in doing or being a party to the killing.
>
> (Home Office, 1957, Part 1, Section 2 (1))

The fundamental and central points of the Act were maintained, despite some modification by the *Coroners and Justice Act 2009*.

The term 'abnormality of mind' was replaced by 'abnormality of mental functioning' and it was stipulated that such abnormality:

- arises from a recognised medical condition

- provides an explanation for the defendant's acts or omissions in being party to the killing

- substantially impairs the defendant's ability to either understand the nature of their conduct, form a rational judgment or exercise self-control.

(Coroners and Justice Act, 2009)

Consolidation of a legal framework for issues of mental health occurred through the publication of the *Mental Health Act 1959*, as discussed in Section 2. The Act was updated in 1983 but the majority of the legal definitions and provisions were carried forward.

2   The legal framework and the Mental Health Act

The *Mental Health Act 1959* (MHA) represented a landmark as it sought to transform the shape of mental health services by fully integrating them with the provisions of the newly formed National Health Service (NHS) in the UK. It also foregrounded the role of medical experts in identifying the presence of mental abnormality. The Act brought together various pieces of legislation concerning mental illness that can be rather crudely divided into two categories that concern:

- how the presence of a mental health problem might be used as evidence that someone needs to be confined and treated in order to protect their own, or others', safety

- how the presence of a mental health problem might be used to determine matters of criminal responsibility and sentencing in criminal trials.

As has already been discussed in this chapter (and in Chapter 1), there is a long history of these forms of legislation. This section will introduce the controversial power that the MHA gives to professionals over the liberty of those deemed to be suffering from mental health problems. First, it will look at the 1959 Act. This is because many of the provisions of this Act were transferred to the 1983 Act, which itself was subject to only minor amendments in 2007.

2.1   Powers of detention

Over several sections, the 1959 MHA set out the grounds on which a person might be detained (hence why the term 'sectioned' is often used in relation to detaining someone under a particular section of the Act).

The grounds for the application (for detention), as stated in the Act, are:

> (a) [that] he is suffering from mental disorder of a nature or degree which warrants the detention of the patient in a hospital under observation (with or without other medical treatment) for at least a limited period; and

(b) that he ought to be so detained in the interests of his own health or safety or with a view to the protection of other persons.

(Department of Health, 1959, Section 25)

The same wording was then used in the 1983 MHA (Department of Health, 1983) and retained in the amendments made by the *Mental Health Act 2007* (Department of Health, 2007). The 1959 and subsequent 1983 MHA defined 'mental disorder' as falling within one of the following categories:

- *Mental illness*: This was expected to include psychiatrically defined diagnoses, such as schizophrenia and depression.

- *Arrested or incomplete development of mind*: This included issues such as learning disabilities.

- *Psychopathic disorder*: Described as 'a persistent disorder or disability of mind … which results in abnormally aggressive or seriously irresponsible conduct … and requires or is susceptible to medical treatment' (Department of Health, 1959, Section 4).

- *Any other disorder or disability of mind*: This might include issues such as neurological difficulties.

It was controversy over the diagnosis of psychopathic disorder (to which this chapter will return in Section 4) that led to the removal of these separate categories in the 2007 amendment to the MHA. Instead, the very inclusive (and arguably rather circular) definition of mental disorder was introduced as 'any disorder or disability of the mind' (Department of Health, 2007, p. 1).

There are various sections of the MHA that detail how and why someone might be confined in hospital against their will. Section 135, for example, allows an **approved mental health professional** (AMHP) to seek a warrant that enables a police search for an individual viewed as suffering from a mental disorder, and the ability to take them to a **place of safety** for 24 hours so that an assessment can take place. In order to allow the warrant, a judicial officer called a Justice of the Peace (at the local magistrates' court) must assert that there are reasonable grounds for believing that the individual has a mental disorder and is being (or has been) ill-treated, neglected, kept under 'improper control' or is living alone, unable to care for themselves. A decision can then be made (usually within 24 hours) as to whether a full assessment should be carried out (which would

Approved mental health professional
Usually someone with a professionally recognised qualification in mental health work (who is not a medical doctor), such as a social worker, mental health nurse or clinical psychologist, who has a qualification to carry out the role.

Place of safety
A term used in connection with the Mental Health Act. It refers to a location to which someone deemed to be suffering from a mental disorder and who presents a danger to themselves or to others can be taken – usually a hospital or similar environment, but it can also be a police station.

require the use of Section 2 of the MHA) or whether there are grounds for a longer admission that would require a treatment section.

A Section 2 admission for observation and assessment should be signed by two doctors and an AMHP. It allows for an individual to be admitted to a hospital for further observation for up to 30 days. If, during this time, the individual is considered to be in need of treatment, then a Section 3 treatment order can be requested. This, again, needs to be supported by two qualified medical professionals and an AMHP. It also allows someone to be detained for up to six months, which is renewable and can be extended for 12-month periods. All those seeking to use these sections must maintain that the criteria outlined above have been met.

The use of the MHA to confine people against their will remains one of the most controversial aspects of the mental health system. Estimates suggest that over 50,000 people in England alone were so detained over a 12-month period (2018–19), and people identifying as black or black British were over four times more likely to be subject to detention (National Statistics, 2019). Many who are on the receiving end of these processes regard them as cruel and often traumatising in themselves – a view confirmed through a government-sponsored review of the MHA (Independent Review, 2018).

2.2 Controversies over the 2007 amendments to the Mental Health Act

As explained above, the fundamental provisions of the 1959 Act were carried in to the 1983 Act. Despite negotiation beginning in 1998, the UK government could only agree an amended Act in 2007 (Department of Health, 2007). Alongside the appearance of a very general definition of mental disorder, community treatment orders (which enable compulsory treatment for those living in the community) were also introduced, and the special role of approved social workers in the sectioning process was replaced by AMHPs.

These changes have not been without controversy. The former insistence on the involvement of social workers in sectioning had been viewed as a counterweight to a solely medical view of 'mental disorder', suggesting that any application to use the MHA must consider the *social* dimension. The broadening scope of the AMHP role implied that the social dimension might be downplayed (Rapaport, 2006). So far, however, it seems that the vast majority of these professionals actually come from social work (Carson, 2018). Community treatment orders are also viewed with some alarm by those concerned about a potential danger to civil liberties posed by affording professionals the ability to impose highly impactful medication on people who are not being monitored in hospital. These fears have not been allayed by evidence of the increasing use of community treatment orders (Trevithick *et al.*, 2018), and have been heightened when coupled with the rather circular definition of mental disorder used in the 2007 amendment. It was the UK government's insistence on ensuring that personality disorder was fully included in the Act that led to the proposal of a very general definition of mental disorder (Wright, 2002). Section 3 will look at this controversial category in a little more detail.

3   Mental disorder and the criminal justice system

Issues of mental health are very apparent in the prison system. Fazel and Danesh (2002) carried out a meta-analysis of 62 surveys from across the world that had attempted to measure the incidence of mental illness in prison populations. They found that serious mental disorders were widespread, but that the most common were personality disorders, with 65 per cent of male prisoners surveyed being so diagnosed. Rates of serious depression and psychosis were marginally higher than those found in the general population. Subsequent surveys have produced similar figures (e.g. Cramer, 2016), which clearly suggests that there is significant overlap between the concerns of the criminal justice system and established categories of mental disorder.

Underneath the diagnoses, there is of course real distress and unhappiness. For example, there is increasing evidence of the frequency of self-harm within prisons. Using data gathered over a five-year period between 2004 and 2009, Hawton et al. (2014) estimated that there were over 24,000 annual incidents of self-harm among the prison population in England and Wales (2018 incidents per 100 prisoners), while the Ministry of Justice (2018) provided evidence of increasing rates of suicide. The rates of self-harm were much higher among female inmates, although the incidents of more serious and potentially lethal self-harm were more common among male prisoners.

Pause for reflection

Do you think the high levels of mental health problems in prison systems can be understood in terms of the negative impact of incarceration itself, or can they be explained by the fact that many people with mental health difficulties are being caught up in the criminal justice system?

While there are many reasons to believe that experiences of prison will be detrimental to psychological health (indeed, there is an extensive literature on the psychological damage that prison can do; e.g. Edgemon and Clay-Warner, 2019), there is also evidence that prisons accommodate people whose histories and circumstances are characteristic of those who suffer from various mental health problems. As noted, analysis of the types of mental health difficulty found among prison populations suggests that the diagnoses within the 'personality disorder' category are the most common. Broadly speaking, the term 'personality disorder' refers to individuals whose relationships and emotional lives are marked by conflict, turbulence and distress. There is significant controversy about whether such problems are best understood as medical disorders (Pilgrim, 2001), but the diagnoses (particularly of antisocial personality disorder) are often associated with deprived and disrupted childhoods. Section 4 will discuss this issue in greater detail.

The association between other forms of mental disorder (such as schizophrenia) and crime is much less clear, despite the occasional incident that receives a lot of media attention, such as that of Nicola Edgington. In 2011, Edgington killed a stranger in a random attack, having previously killed her mother seven years earlier (*The Guardian*, 2013). Her long-standing diagnosis of schizophrenia was used to justify her (successful) defence against the charge of murder on the grounds of diminished responsibility, and a conviction for the lesser charge of manslaughter. However, while different interpretations have been made of the evidence (Pilgrim and Rogers, 2015), it can reasonably be suggested that people with such diagnoses are generally not significantly more likely than others to be involved in serious violence (Walsh, Buchanan and Fahy, 2002), at least when confounding factors such as drug abuse are taken into account (e.g. Müller-Isberner, 2017).

4 Criminal justice and personality disorder

Personality disorder diagnoses have roots in the early decades of the nineteenth century, when the emerging profession of psychiatry was concerned with developing expertise in the identification and treatment of forms of mental disorder that might lead to criminality. While the idea of specific psychological disorders had become unfashionable by the end of the nineteenth century, the notion was re-energised in the middle of the twentieth century, in the form of psychopathy or antisocial personality disorder.

It is likely that the influence of the Second World War was a key driver of this interest (Ramon, 1989). War had led both the UK and US governments to be persuaded of the importance of understanding the psychological health of their populations, and they had accordingly ploughed resources into the associated professions (Rose, 1989). The experience of battle trauma had convinced more people that the causes of mental distress were often rooted in environmental disruption and trauma rather than the faulty constitutions of particular individuals (Stone, 2004). Additionally, theories that associated criminality with genetic heritage became unfashionable in the shadow of the eugenically motivated Holocaust (Rembis, 2003). The wide reach of military recruitment meant that a diverse population was passing through the observational procedures of military psychiatrists who were employed to advise on how psychological assessment might be used to deploy human resources, and to provide effective treatments for the damage caused by battle trauma (Hoffman, 1992; Wanke, 1999). It was the close contact with a more diverse and 'typical' spread of the population that facilitated the 'discovery' of the extent of personality disorder (Coolidge and Segal, 1998) and experimentation with treatments that used group and community principles (Harrison, 2000), as discussed below.

Two publications – one on either side of the Atlantic – were to have notable but rather different influences. In the US, it was Hervey Cleckley's *The mask of sanity: an attempt to reinterpret the so-called psychopathic personality*, which was originally published in 1941. Cleckley's publication helped popularise the belief that some people cause harm by exhibiting cold-hearted, self-centred and ruthless behaviour (see Information box 18.1). There is some irony here, as

Cleckley himself disliked the term 'psychopathic' (hence the use of 'so-called' in the title). Nonetheless, Cleckley's ideas have been popularised through the work of a number of psychologists. Robert Hare (e.g. Hare, 1993), in particular, doggedly argued that psychopathy is a very specific condition. Notwithstanding these efforts, the term 'psychopathy' was largely superseded by the terms used in the *Diagnostic and statistical manual of mental disorders* (as discussed in Chapter 4), most notably those of the personality disorders (particularly antisocial personality disorder).

Information box 18.1: The clinical profile of 'the psychopath' according to Cleckley

- Superficial charm and good 'intelligence'
- Absence of delusions and other signs of irrational thinking
- Absence of 'nervousness' or psychoneurotic manifestations
- Unreliability
- Untruthfulness and insincerity
- Lack of remorse or shame
- Inadequately motivated antisocial behavior
- Poor judgment and failure to learn by experience
- Pathologic egocentricity and incapacity for love
- General poverty in major affective reactions
- Specific loss of insight
- Unresponsiveness in general interpersonal relations
- Fantastic and uninviting behavior with drink and sometimes without
- Suicide rarely carried out
- Sex life impersonal, trivial, and poorly integrated
- Failure to follow any life plan

(Cleckley, 1988, pp. 337–338)

In the UK, David Henderson's (1939) *Psychopathic states* had less reach but was taken seriously by the UK parliament, which categorised psychopathy as a specific disorder when it passed the 1959 MHA (Jones, 2016). While Cleckley remained largely silent on its aetiology (see Chapter 4, Section 3, for a reminder of the definition), Henderson portrayed psychopathy as a mental state that emerged from the dynamic between individuals and wider society. He took an optimistic view of the possibilities of treatments that centred on the social nature of the problem (group and community therapy treatments). This theorisation was reinforced by some of the wartime experiments with community and group treatments that took place in military psychiatry, and fitted well with moves to develop the welfare state and ensure that mental health services became a part of the new NHS (Harrison, 2000). Thus, the UK government took the view that psychopathy represented a significant social problem that could be tackled if the right treatments were made available, and the category of psychopathy was included in the 1959 MHA. Controversy and debate over its status within the psychiatric profession, however, meant that little was done to address 'the problem' for many decades (Walker and McCabe, 1973).

In the late 1990s, the perception of the potential danger posed by those with a personality disorder was propelled towards the top of the government agenda, and discussion remains prominent in the criminal justice system to this day. The catalyst was the conviction in 1997 of Michael Stone for the murder of Lin Russell and her daughter Megan, and the attempted murder of her daughter Josie (Jones, 2012). While the conviction for the brutal and apparently motiveless attack was controversial, it was Stone's psychiatric history that was to garner government attention. He had a diagnosis of antisocial personality disorder and had been hospitalised around 18 months prior to the attack. Stone was discharged – even though he was considered highly dangerous – on the grounds that his disorder was not considered treatable and he therefore had no place in hospital. Members of the government were outraged that psychiatry could take such an approach and proposed a series of initiatives that tried to push the NHS and the criminal justice system to take the issue of personality disorder seriously.

The 2003 policy directive, *Personality disorder: no longer a diagnosis of exclusion* (Department of Health, 2003), signalled the intent to see the NHS engage more with the problems associated with the disorder.

There have been a series of initiatives within the criminal justice system that aimed to provide specialist intervention with those considered to be highly dangerous. The initial Dangerous and Severe Personality Disorder projects (Home Office, 2005) shifted to the wider initiative, the Offender Personality Disorder Pathway Approach, a joint venture co-commissioned by NHS England and the National Offender Management Service (NOMS, 2015).This initiative aimed to support much larger numbers of offenders through an array of services (Benefield et al., 2015). Services were targeted at those who presented a high risk to others in relation to violence, sexual assault or criminal damage, and who were considered likely to be diagnosed with a severe personality disorder linked to their offending. While ostensibly the approach taken to understanding the development of personality disorder is broadly biopsychosocial, psychologists were given a key role: the plan for the management and treatment of the identified group was to be 'psychologically and socially informed and led by psychologically trained staff in [the National Offender Management Service] and the NHS' (NOMS, 2015, p. 3). Many services became available as part of the pathway and, by June 2016, there were over 36,000 people recruited on to it (Skett, Goode and Barton, 2017).

Focus on the psychological histories of such offenders may not be unwarranted. While there is debate about the validity of the specific diagnosis of antisocial personality disorder (or whatever particular label is used), there is also quite convincing evidence that the type of problems described by the diagnosis are associated with negative life events (Pagano et al., 2004) and, in particular, deprived childhoods (Bandelow et al., 2005). There is noteworthy congruence between longitudinal work that has followed individuals from childhood into adulthood. These studies suggest that difficult and disrupted childhoods are associated with later offending and the kind of mental health problems associated with personality disorders (particularly antisocial personality disorder but also narcissistic personality disorder and borderline personality disorder; e.g. Moffitt, 1993). While there has long been interest in the idea that problems such as psychopathy might be explained in terms of genetically driven neurological differences (e.g. Raine, 2013), such theories remain speculative, with little evidence to support them (Button et al., 2013; Viding, Larsson and Jones, 2008).

5   The contemporary professional context

Figure 18.2 Broadmoor Hospital opened in 1863 to accommodate 'criminal lunatics'

This chapter has made clear the extent of overlap between legal matters, issues of criminal justice, and mental health. It should be no surprise, therefore, to find that there are a number of areas of professional practice that have long reflected this overlap. When Bethlem Royal Hospital was rebuilt in 1815, it was designed to include blocks for male and female 'criminal lunatics' who were found not guilty on the grounds of insanity and then detained in accordance with the *Criminal Lunatics Act 1800* (Allderidge, 1974). The capacity was soon inadequate, so people in this category were sent to other asylums (Walker and McCabe, 1973).

This led to the construction of a special hospital at Broadmoor in 1863 (shown in Figure 18.2). Since then, Ashworth Hospital and Rampton Hospital have been built. In total, these three high-security hospitals provide around 700 beds. In addition, there are approximately 60 medium-security units that provide around 3500 places for those who are detained under the MHA and considered to pose a threat to the public, but may not necessarily be detained for criminal convictions. Further provision is made in a variety of low-security units (around 3700 beds) and psychiatric intensive care units for those deemed to be unmanageable on ordinary wards. Only those detained under the MHA can be kept on such a unit. Psychiatric intensive care units do not usually take referrals directly from the criminal justice system, but they might deal with people who have criminal histories. These wards will have high staff ratios and high levels of security and restrictions on patient freedom.

Most people who work with offender populations will say that problems related to mental health are a major feature of their work, but that this is not often fully recognised in terms of facility provision and funding. There are specialist training routes for both psychologists and psychiatrists who work with offenders. Indeed, as measured by the number of consultant posts (the more senior medical posts), forensic psychiatry (besides general psychiatry) is the third largest psychiatric speciality at the time of writing in 2020 (Royal College of Psychiatrists, 2019). There are also over 2000 people employed directly as forensic psychologists, and the majority of the 8000 clinical psychologists employed by the NHS work with forensic client groups (Health Careers, 2020). Additionally, there are many counsellors and psychotherapists who work in forensic settings; the Counselling in Prisons Network was set up in 2011 to pool resources and thinking among the many counsellors who work within the prison system.

There appears to be something of a contrast between the profile given to forensic matters within professional training and the numbers of people employed in the area. The topic tends to have low prominence in textbooks used for training in psychiatry and clinical psychology (e.g. Beinart, Kennedy and Llewelyn, 2009; Gelder *et al.*, 2012). Arguably, the profile of mental health work in the criminal justice system has been raised by the advent of the Offender Personality Disorder Pathway approach. At the same time, criminology's concern with mental disorders has tended, in the past 50 or so years, to be relegated as though it is a relatively minor topic of concern. The points raised in this chapter would suggest that this is an error.

Conclusion

This chapter has introduced the relationship between issues of criminal responsibility, mental health and the legal powers that can be used against those deemed to be suffering from mental health problems.

The following points have been made:

- Although the principle has been accepted for many centuries that those suffering from mental health problems might be excused punishment for their criminal behaviour, there are still unresolved debates about how to properly define the degree of disorder required to allow for any leniency.

- Arguably, the identification of a mental disorder is more likely to be used to curtail the liberty of individuals. The police and AMHPs have substantial powers under the MHA to detain people who have not necessarily committed any offence but who are thought to pose a risk to themselves or to others through their mental state.

- Surveys of prison populations suggest that mental health problems are rife among prison inmates, although by far the most common issues are those falling within the controversial category of personality disorder.

- The problem of personality disorder looms large in the criminal justice system. While its status as a medical disorder is controversial, it is associated with negative life events and experiences that seemingly give rise to negative mental health outcomes.

As discussed in Chapter 1, criminal responsibility has been an important topic in relation to the emergence of psychiatry and associated practices in the field of mental health. Of course, for some of the critics of psychiatry, this connection between matters of criminal justice and mental health is not surprising at all. It can be argued that the systems of both criminal justice and mental health are concerned with patrolling the borders between behaviour that is considered acceptable and that which needs to be confined or altered. In addition, the debates over the uncertain nature of these borders mean that major decisions over people's liberty are being made every day. This is despite the fact that the significance of this topic is not always well recognised.

Further reading

- This chapter provides a comprehensive summary of the relationship between questions of mental disorder and issues of criminal justice: Jones, D.W. (2020) 'Mental disorder: madness, personality disorder and criminal responsibility', in *Understanding criminal behaviour: psychosocial perspectives on criminality and violence*. 2nd edn. Abingdon: Routledge, pp. 32–65.

- This is a guide to the *Mental Health Act*:

  Maden, A. and Spencer-Lange, T. (2010) *Essential mental health law: a guide to the new Mental Health Act*. London: Hammersmith Press.

- This book provides the history of the way that mental disorder has been dealt with in the prison system, with a focus on the past 40 years:

  Seddon, T. (2007) *Punishment and madness: governing prisoners with mental health problems*. Cavendish: Routledge.

References

Allderidge, P.H. (1974) 'Criminal insanity: Bethlem to Broadmoor', *Proceedings of the Royal Society of Medicine*, 67(9), pp. 897–904.

Bandelow, B., Krause, J., Wedekind, D., Broocks, A., Hajak, G. and Ruther, E. (2005) 'Early traumatic life events, parental attitudes, family history, and birth risk factors in patients with borderline personality disorder and healthy controls', *Psychiatry Research*, 134(2), pp. 169–179.

Beinart, H., Kennedy, P. and Llewelyn, S. (2009) *Clinical psychology in practice*. Oxford: BPS Blackwell.

Benefield, N., Joseph, N., Skett, S., Bridgland, S., D'Cruz, L., Goode, I. and Turner, K. (2015) 'The Offender Personality Disorder Strategy jointly delivered by NOMS and NHS England', *Prison Service Journal*, 218, pp. 4–9.

Bracton, H. (c.1250) *De Legibus et Consuetudinibus Angliæ (On the Laws and Customs of England)*. Available at: http://bracton.law.harvard.edu/ (Accessed: 23 February 2020).

Button, K.S., Ioannidis, J.P., Mokrysz, C., Nosek, B. A., Flint, J., Robinson, E. S. and Munafò, M.R. (2013) 'Power failure: why small sample size undermines the reliability of neuroscience', *Nature Reviews. Neuroscience*, 14(5), pp. 365–376.

Carson, G. (2018) 'Approved mental health professional numbers continue decline', *Community Care*, 14 February. Available at: https://www.communitycare.co.uk/2018/02/14/approved-mental-health-professional-numbers-continue-decline-community-care-finds/ (Accessed: 1 September 2019).

Cleckley, H. (1988) *The mask of sanity: an attempt to re-interpret the so-called psychopathic personality*. 5th edn. Maryland Heights: Mosby Company.

Coolidge, F.L. and Segal, D.L. (1998) 'Evolution of personality disorder diagnosis in the Diagnostic and Statistical Manual of Mental Disorders', *Clinical Psychology Review*, 18(5), pp. 585–599.

Coroners and Justice Act 2009, c. 25. Available at: http://www.legislation.gov.uk/ukpga/2009/25/pdfs/ukpga_20090025_en.pdf (Accessed: 1 June 2020).

Cramer, V. (2016) *The prevalence of mental disorders among convicted inmates in Norwegian prisons*. Oslo: Oslo University Hospital.

Department of Health (2007) *Mental Health Act 2007* London: HMSO.

Department of Health (2003) *Personality disorder: no longer a diagnosis of exclusion*. London: Department of Health.

Department of Health (1983) *Mental Health Act 1983*. London: HMSO.

Department of Health (1959) *Mental Health Act 1959*. London: HMSO.

Edgemon, T.G. and Clay-Warner, J. (2019) 'Inmate mental health and the pains of imprisonment', *Society and Mental Health*, 9(1), pp. 33–50.

Eigen, J.P. (1998) 'Criminal lunacy in early modern England: did gender make a difference?', *International Journal of Law and Psychiatry*, 21(4), pp. 409–419.

Fazel, S. and Danesh, J. (2002) 'Serious mental disorder in 23,000 prisoners: a systematic review of 62 surveys', *The Lancet*, 359(9306), pp. 545–550.

Gelder, M., Andreasen, N., Lopez-Ibhor, J. and Geddes, J. (2012) *New Oxford textbook of psychiatry*. 2nd edn. Oxford: Oxford University Press.

Hale, M. (1736) *The history of the pleas of the crown*. London: Gyles.

Hare, R. (1993) *Without conscience: the disturbing world of the psychopaths among us*. New York: The Guilford Press.

Harrison, T. (2000) *Bion, Rickman, Foulkes and the Northfield experiments: advancing on a different front*. London: Jessica Kingsley.

Hawton, K., Linsell, L., Adeniji, T., Sariaslan, A. and Fazel, S. (2014) 'Self-harm in prisons in England and Wales: an epidemiological study of prevalence, risk factors, clustering, and subsequent suicide', *The Lancet*, 383 (9923), pp. 1147–1154.

Health Careers (2020) 'Clinical psychologist', *Health Education England* . Available at: https://www.healthcareers.nhs.uk/explore-roles/psychological-therapies/roles/clinical-psychologist (Accessed: 30 March 2020).

Henderson, D.K. (1939) *Psychopathic states*. London: Chapman and Hall.

Hoffman, L. (1992) 'American psychologists and wartime research on Germany, 1941–1945', *American Psychologist*, 47(2), pp. 264–273.

Home Office (1957) *The Homicide Act*. London: HMSO.

Home Office (2005) *Dangerous and Severe Personality Disorder (DSPD) programme – key points*. London: Home Office.

Independent Review (2018) *Modernising the Mental Health Act: increasing choice, reducing compulsion. Final report of the Independent Review of the Mental Health Act 1983*. Available at: https://www.gov.uk/government/publications/modernising-the-mental-health-act-final-report-from-the-independent-review (Accessed: 20 May 2020).

Jones, D.W. (2012) 'Psychosocial perspectives: men, madness and violence', in Hall, S. and Winlow, S. (eds.) *New directions in criminological theory*. Oxford: Routledge, pp. 183–198.

Jones, D.W. (2016) *Disordered personalities and crime: an analysis of the history of moral insanity*. Abingdon: Routledge.

Jones, D.W. (2017) 'Moral insanity and psychological disorder: the hybrid roots of psychiatry', *History of Psychiatry*, 28(3), pp. 263–279.

Kramar, J.K. and Watson, W.D. (2006) 'The insanities of reproduction: medico-legal knowledge and the development of infanticide law', *Social and Legal Studies*, 15(2), pp. 237–255.

Ministry of Justice (2018) *Safety in custody quarterly: update to June 2018*. London: Ministry of Justice.

Moffitt, T. (1993) 'Adolescence-limited and life-course-persistent antisocial behaviour: a developmental taxonomy', *Psychological Review*, 100(4), pp. 674–701.

Müller-Isberner, R. (2017) 'The use of scientific evidence about schizophrenia and violence in clinical services: a challenge that is not being met', *The Canadian Journal of Psychiatry*, 62(2), pp. 84–85.

National Offender Management Service (NOMS) (2015) *The Offender Personality Disorder Pathway Strategy 2015*. London: National Offender Management Service, NHS England.

National Statistics (2019) *Mental Health Act Statistics, Annual Figures 2018–19*. London: NHS Digital.

Pagano, M.E., Skodol, A.E., Stout, R.L., Shea, M. T., Yen, S., Grilo, C.M., Sanislow, C.A., Bender, D.S., McGlashan, T.H., Zanarini, M.C. and Gunderson, J.G. (2004) 'Stressful life events as predictors of functioning: findings from the Collaborative Longitudinal Personality Disorders Study', *Acta Psychiaticra Scandanavia*, 110(6), pp. 421–429.

Pilgrim, D. (2001) 'Disordered personalities and disordered concepts', *Journal of Mental Health*, 10(3), pp. 253–265.

Pilgrim, D. and Rogers, A. (2015) *A sociology of mental health*. London: SAGE.

Raine, A. (2013) *The anatomy of violence: the biological roots of crime*. New York: Allen Lane.

Ramon, S. (1989) 'Psychopathy: its professional and social context in Britain', in Miller, P and Rose, N. (eds.) *The power of psychiatry*. Cambridge: Polity, pp.214–239.

Rapaport, J. (2006) 'New roles in mental health: the creation of the approved mental health practitioner', *Journal of Integrated Care*, 14(5), pp. 37–46.

Rembis, M.A. (2003) *Breeding up the human herd: gender, power, and eugenics in Illinois 1890–1940*. Arizona: University of Arizona Press.

Reznek, L. (1997) *Evil or ill? Justifying the insanity defence*. London: Routledge.

Rose, N. (1989) *Governing the soul: the shaping of the private self*. London: Routledge.

Royal College of Psychiatrists (2019) *Pre-report summary of the 2019 census*. London: Royal College of Psychiatry.

Skett, S. Goode, I. and Barton, S. (2017) 'A joint NHS and NOMS Offender Personality Disorder Pathways Strategy: a perspective from 5 years of operation: OPD strategy', *Criminal Behaviour and Mental Health*, 27(3), pp. 214–221.

Stone, M. (2004) 'Shellshock and the psychologists', in Bynum, W.F., Porter, R. and Shepherd, M. (eds.) *The anatomy of madness: essays in the history of psychiatry*. London: Routledge, pp. 242–271.

The Guardian (2013) 'Freed killer found guilty of murdering stranger in knife attack', 7 February. Available at: https://www.theguardian.com/uk/2013/feb/07/nicola-edgington-guilty-murder-stranger (Accessed: 19 November 2019).

Trevithick, L., Carlile, J., Nodiyal, S. and Keown, P. (2018) 'Community treatment orders: an analysis of the first five years of use in England', *The British Journal of Psychiatry*, 212(3), pp. 175–179. doi:10.1192/bjp.2017.5.

Viding, E., Larsson, H. and Jones, A.P. (2008) 'Quantitative genetic studies of antisocial behaviour', *Philosophical Transactions of the Royal Society B: Biological Sciences*, 363(1503), pp. 2519–2527.

Walker, N. (1968) *Crime and insanity in England. Volume 1: the historical perspective*. Edinburgh: Edinburgh University Press.

Walker, N. and McCabe, S. (1973) *Crime and insanity in England. Volume 2: new solutions and new problems*. Edinburgh: Edinburgh University Press.

Walsh, E., Buchanan, A. and Fahy, T. (2002) 'Violence and schizophrenia: examining the evidence', *British Journal of Psychiatry*, 180(6), pp. 490–495.

Wanke, P. (1999) 'American military psychiatry and its role among ground forces in World War II', *The Journal of Military History*, 63(1), pp. 127–146.

Ward, T. (1999) 'The sad subject of infanticide: law medicine and child murder', *Social and Legal Studies*, 8(2), pp. 163–180.

Wright, K. (2002) *Reform of the Mental Health Act 1983: the draft Mental Health Bill*. London: House of Commons Library Research Paper 02/80.

Zedner, L. (1991) *Women, crime and custody in Victorian England*. Oxford: Clarendon Press.

Chapter 19

Individual or social problems?

David Kaposi

Contents

Introduction

'Intrusif' by Hannah Marling

Around the time of writing in 2020, an editorial in *The Guardian* lamented the fact that, in England, over 71 million prescriptions for antidepressants were written in 2018, representing a rise of 3 million in one year and a doubling over a single decade. The article reports that antidepressants are prescribed twice as frequently as antibiotics, and that 16 per cent of the English adult population is now being medicated for depression. It is no wonder that the editorial concludes that prescribed medication 'must not be the only therapy offered to depressed people, who can benefit from other forms of help – including the chance to think about what has made them unwell' (*The Guardian*, 2019). (Chapter 5 explored different approaches to treating depression.)

Indeed, according to the latest of a seven-yearly England-wide survey (McManus *et al.*, 2016), one in six people over 16 years of age experienced anxiety, depression or another so-called common mental health problem in the week before the survey. The results also revealed that 19.5 per cent of men and 33.7 per cent of women had been diagnosed by a professional at some point in their lives. In relation to less 'common' problems, while 'psychotic' disorders were found in just under 1 per cent of the population, 13.7 per cent of people aged over 16 screened positive for the diagnostic category of personality disorder. Meanwhile, a separate review of relevant studies between 2000 and 2018 reported that eating disorders have, on average, been found at a prevalence of 19.4 per cent (women) and 13.8 per cent (men) in the diverse international population surveyed (Galmiche *et al.*, 2019).

This unsettling list of statistics naturally prompts the question that concerned *The Guardian* in its editorial, and that has characterised the histories of psychiatry and psychology: With regard to severe mental distress, should we take a predominantly biologically concerned medical position, or a more psychological one? As you saw in Chapters 1, 4 and 8, this is a *fundamental* dilemma, as the various treatment approaches understand the very nature of mental distress in accordance with their own theoretical principles: either as an illness/abnormality, or as a meaningful (even though problematic) response.

The focus of this chapter is not on the differences between the main approaches to mental health; rather, it is on the *common ground* that can often be found between both positions in the 'medication versus talking' debate. Advocates of either position tend to approach distress in terms of the 'individual': the origin of distress is considered to be found in the individual and, as such, it is the individual that needs to be 'cured'. What is often left out of this argument is the possibility that, while distress is experienced by the individual, it may nonetheless derive from social circumstances. Thus, it can only be adequately addressed, therapeutically or otherwise, when these social circumstances are taken into account.

This chapter aims to:

- consider mental distress from a social (relational or societal-political) rather than an individual (biological or psychological) perspective

- explore possible 'micro' and 'macro' social origins of mental distress

- explore possible 'micro' and 'macro' social interventions for mental distress.

1   Social origins of mental distress

This section will explore how various clinicians and researchers have considered the 'social origins' of mental distress. First, it looks at how the immediate social context may impact on an individual's mental health. Then, it considers broader social and political questions.

1.1   Micro origins: life events and relationships

Similarly to issues around the 'talking cure', the debates regarding the (individual or social) origins of mental distress can be found within the work of Sigmund Freud. On the one hand, in 1897 Freud infamously revoked his earlier hypothesis attributing mental distress, or neurosis, to childhood sexual abuse (as explored in Chapter 9). From that point onwards, Freud categorically asserted that neurosis derives, not from traumatic social reality, but from early impulses and fantasies. Freud thus conceptualised mental distress as a problem of the individual (Freud, 2001[1925]). On the other hand, while maintaining his convictions regarding the primacy of the individual's inner life, Freud's later work also gradually recognised the importance of social relationships in constituting mental health. Thus, he paved the way for generations of clinicians who 're-found' the importance of **social trauma** (Freud, 2001[1923]; Greenberg and Mitchell, 1984).

Social trauma
Refers to the idea that, while trauma is experienced by individuals, it also derives from a social context. This idea contrasts with an individualised conception of trauma.

In the twentieth century, theoretical opinion and professional practice alternated between a focus on social and individual factors. Sometimes (more commonly in psychiatry and psychology), mental health was regarded solely in terms of the individual, and was taken to result from individual characteristics, such as an 'ingrained personality'. At other times (and perhaps more commonly in social policy or social care), the focus was on the circumstances of those individuals.

The 1970s saw an important intervention in this debate. A groundbreaking research programme, headed by sociologist George Brown and psychologist Tirril Harris, closely examined the circumstances in which depressive episodes occur (Brown and Harris, 1978). The researchers demonstrated that, as a general rule, the onset of depression occurs as a response to the threat of long-term harmful consequences following a major life event (e.g. job loss or a major illness in the family): around 90 per cent of adult women who fell depressed in the year leading up to the research had experienced an extreme, stressful life event in that period, while only 30 per cent of those who did not become depressed had experienced such an event. This finding, confirmed in subsequent studies (Brown and Harris, 1989; Brown, 2002), strongly suggested the primacy of social factors in the origins of mental distress. For Brown and Harris, when it came to depression, there was no going back to citing only pure personality factors, inner impulses or cognitive distortions stripped of their social contexts as causal factors.

The project moved on to explore the exact nature of these stressful events by examining the social context in which events triggering depressive episodes took place. The researchers identified the immediate trigger for the depressive episodes as experiences that only made sense with regards to those individuals; that is, the events had to be personally meaningful regarding the concerns, values, plans and social roles to which the individuals were highly committed (see the 'Role-based meaning' component in Figure 19.1). To lead to a depressive episode the events had to entail three types of affect: entrapment, humiliation and loss ('Specific meaning' in Figure 19.1). Ultimately, the perceived **helplessness** resulting from these affects (one of the 'Memory-linked emotional schemas' in Figure 19.1) appeared to be directly linked to the onset of depression (Brown, 2002).

Helplessness
An affective state where an individual feels they cannot make a difference to their situation. They lack power to enact positive change in their lives. This may be an effect of events leading to entrapment, humiliation or loss.

At the same time, Brown and Harris realised that, while such experiences clearly make people vulnerable to depression, they cannot solely account for its onset. Many people in the study who faced stressful events in areas of their lives – even those who experienced loss, entrapment or humiliation – did not get depressed. The researchers therefore took account of further context – what they termed 'core ties' – to determine what it was that made individuals vulnerable to such events and experiences. These **core ties** comprise key external, environmental ties such as the availability of close personal support, but also internal, psychological ties such as those that relate to the individual's feeling of self-worth or their potential.

Core tie
A relationship capable of fundamentally influencing a person's mental health. The relationship may be with an external other or with the individual's self.

The last element of the depression puzzle concerned the development of these core ties. Individuals vulnerable to the stresses of certain life events (which could trigger the experience of entrapment, humiliation or loss and lead to depressive episodes) tended to have a history of early familial loss or neglect, and often physical or sexual abuse. Psychologically, these experiences appeared to lead to the development of emotional schemas that may aggravate rather than mitigate the impact of the threatening events. Environmentally, the experiences appeared to promote relational choices and patterns that had the same adverse effect (see the 'Memory-linked emotional schemas' component in Figure 19.1).

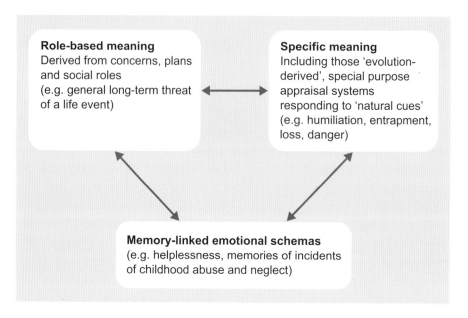

Figure 19.1 Brown and Harris' three types of meaning involved in event evaluation (Source: Brown, 2002, p. 262, Figure 2)

The fictional case illustration below offers an example of how these processes may play out. The case was originally offered by Brown and Harris and has been modified for the purposes of this chapter.

Case illustration: Nympha's experience of depression

Nympha's son, James, means everything to her. She needs to work long hours to sustain herself and her son, but she would look forward to the weekend so that they could do something together.

Nympha always knew James had problems in school, but it was still a shock when his head teacher called her in to tell her this directly. The teacher used strong words, which really threw Nympha. It's not that any of this was news – James' learning had never been at the forefront of his mind – but Nympha kept looking at other mothers close by and thinking: 'What are they going to think? I am a failure! I should have done better!'. When the teacher said that Nympha must do better, she felt herself turning red.

Nympha knows that if she mentions any of this at home, her husband, John, is just going to beat her and James then disappear to the pub. 'That's how he relates to us; through his belt', she thinks to herself. So she simply sits down, feeling low and unable to move.

(Source: adapted from Brown and Harris, 1978)

Activity 19.1: Event evaluation in Nympha's experience

Allow about 5 minutes

Having explored Figure 19.1 and the case illustration of Nympha, try to bring the two together. How can you make sense of Nympha's experience using Brown and Harris' ideas? What triggered her depressive episode?

Discussion

- *Roles and plans*: Nympha appears to be a committed mother and provider. The relationship with her son seems important to her, but also intense.

- *Specific meaning*: Nympha already knew about James' misbehaviour in school, so the information provided by the head teacher probably doesn't represent a 'loss' for Nympha (in the sense of lost time or opportunities for her son). Perhaps the head teacher used stronger words and depicted a starker situation than Nympha was familiar with, but the crucial factors triggering depression seem to lie elsewhere. Nympha experiences humiliation when focusing on the presence of other mothers (whom she regards as judgemental) and when she imagines a violent and neglectful response from her husband. She also experiences entrapment: she feels there is no way out of this situation.

- *Memory-linked emotional schemas*: We do not know whether Nympha's childhood was a nurturing one, or whether she currently has core ties to help her through this experience of humiliation and entrapment. However, she does indicate that the only response she will receive is a beating from her husband, which suggests that these core elements are missing.

Brown and Harris' decade-long research programme has clear relevance to mental distress. The development of this research eventually promoted not only an appreciation of social context but also a particular *understanding* of it, shifting from the traditional, straightforward emphasis on social events (in particular, traumatic abuse) to a broader understanding of past and present *relationships between people* (and **cumulative trauma**). In this sense, one cannot talk of a simple change in focus from the individual to the social, or to the role of external traumatic events, without reference to internal impulses.

This more contemporary idea of Freud's concept of social trauma did not forget the original conceptualisation of trauma as a one-off event. But, as this section has described, it was also expanded to cover the micro-dynamics of neglectful relationships, which may result in a traumatic childhood and a constantly re-traumatising present.

Cumulative trauma
A kind of trauma that derives not from a singular event but a sequence of relatively smaller incidents. These often occur with regularity in ongoing relationships, such as in the family, school, or peer relationships.

> ## Pause for reflection
>
> What do you think Freud, throughout the different periods of his work, would have thought of Brown and Harris' research?

1.2   Macro origins: poverty and inequality

If mental distress follows certain stressful events in life and involves problematic relationships, the question arises: What about the wider societal-political context surrounding those who experience mental distress? It may be that certain social contexts precipitate such detrimental events and relations, while others offer more protection from them.

The first point to note is the long-established association between mental distress and poverty (Marmot, 2010; Mechanic, 2000). Studies across both time and nations have contributed to this general finding (Delgadillo, Farnfield and North, 2018; Muntaner *et al.*, 2004; Lundt *et al.*, 2010; Silva, Loureiro and Cardoso, 2016). Indeed, an astonishing result from a 2007 national survey in England showed that men in the lowest income group were 35 times more likely than men in the highest income group to have depression (McManus *et al.*, 2009).

The exact nature of the link between poverty and depression is not entirely clear, however. It may seem apparent that the connection is lack of financial means: people living in poverty do not have the money to avoid the kind of stressors that have detrimental consequences for mental health, or to build the kind of social networks that can counteract these stressors. However, the evidence regarding this seemingly obvious explanation is mixed: the strength of the link between income and depression appears to considerably weaken when other factors are taken into consideration (Lundt *et al.*, 2010).

What is more, relatively recent research by epidemiologists Richard Wilkinson and Kate Pickett highlighted further considerations that appear to cast doubt on a purely 'materialistic' explanation for the association between poverty and mental distress. They observed that it is not simply the case that the poorest people are much more likely than the richest to succumb to diagnosable mental distress; rather, various forms of mental distress, just like many other social and health problems, have a so-called **social gradient** (Wilkinson and Pickett, 2018). This means that the differential likelihood does not hold only when comparing the extremes – *any* advance on the socio-economic ladder reduces the chances of mental distress.

Social gradient
Refers to the phenomenon where even small socio-economic differences entail corresponding differences in (mental) health and well-being.

Wilkinson and Picket also observed that there is considerable difference in the proportion of people with mental health issues between different countries that are (more or less) of equal wealth;

Figure 19.2 shows, for instance, that people in the UK were more than twice as likely to suffer with a mental disorder than those in Germany.

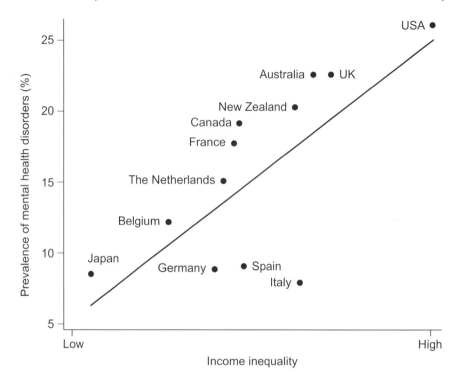

Figure 19.2 Correlation between income inequality and prevalence of mental illness (Source: Wilkinson and Pickett, 2010, p. 67)

Taking these two observations together, Wilkinson and Pickett suggest that, rather than purely material factors, it is the socio-economic *status* people have *relative to the status of others* in the same society that impacts mental health. Even if people are poor in absolute terms, a less hierarchical society may put less emphasis on their poverty status or may offer them better chances to get out of poverty. Additionally, even if a person is relatively rich, observing others belonging to a different, 'higher' class may make them more susceptible to mental distress. It is therefore *inequality* – the gap between the wealthy and the deprived – that may ultimately contribute to the adverse life events and the relationship contexts that make people vulnerable to depression.

Pickett and Wilkinson explain that 'mental health is profoundly influenced by the quality and sufficiency of social relationships and … both are harmed by inequality' (Pickett and Wilkinson, 2010, p. 427). As they see it, the more unequal the society, the more status matters and the more anxiety about status there consequently will be. It is this pervasive anxiety (which is not just a characteristic of people in poverty but of everyone in a society) that corrodes trust and cohesion in communities, or – to use Brown and Harris' phrase – corrodes core ties. Mental health problems are therefore seen as different responses to this fundamental anxiety about one's status in their community (Wilkinson and Pickett, 2018).

Not everyone is as sanguine about the inequality hypothesis for mental health as Wilkinson and Pickett. Some find the link spurious, or at least weaker than suggested (Mechanic, 2000). For the purposes of this chapter, though, it is important to note that, just as micro considerations confirm the importance of life events, these macro examinations of the political or economic determinants of mental health also highlight the importance of social bonds. While obviously broadening the focus from individual to social, these considerations do not neglect the individual; rather, they understand the individual in the context of their relationships with others, and with themselves.

2   Social interventions for mental distress

Section 1 outlined how social relationships (both external and internalised) may play a crucial role in the formation of mental distress. This section will follow on from this notion by exploring the question: How can mental distress be alleviated if it ultimately derives from a social/relational context?

2.1   Micro interventions: therapeutic approaches

While reading Part 3 of this book, you might have developed the idea that, both conceptually and practically, therapeutic approaches exclusively focus on individual clients in isolated rooms. There is some truth in this. As Section 1 of this chapter acknowledged, psychological approaches often tend to prioritise an individual's understanding of mental distress. However, as you saw in Chapter 14, some approaches expand the therapeutic space to include couples, families or groups. What also matters is that these approaches do not just advocate the practical addition of more 'bodies' in the room; rather, systemic or relational psychodynamic approaches involve more people, perspectives and experiences precisely because they see mental distress itself as originating in, and being sustained through, relationships (see Chapter 9 on relational psychodynamic psychotherapy).

Therapeutic community
A participative, group-based approach to often chronic or serious mental health problems.

Indeed, in Britain (as noted in Chapter 14), it was psychodynamic clinicians Wilfred Bion and S.H. Foulkes who created what became one of the most transformative non-individualistic practices: **therapeutic community** (Pearce and Haigh, 2017). Instead of controlling and managing people experiencing considerable distress, those in therapeutic communities were encouraged to live together and cooperate, decide on tasks, and manage conflicts around daily real-world routines such as cooking and cleaning. The rules for this shared therapeutic life were typically agreed democratically, and each member who decided to join the community was obliged to agree and adhere to these rules.

The idea behind therapeutic communities inspired many subsequent developments. One radical extension led to an alliance with the service-user movement (explored in Chapter 2) and emphasised the role of peer support in recovery. Here, mutual aid and support from those with similar experiences of mental distress replaced professional intervention. This normalised even extremely severe forms of mental distress, which were no longer pathologised. Thus, they were no longer construed as requiring ongoing external interference; rather, they were treated as meaningful, creative responses to traumatic life experiences.

Other extensions of therapeutic community emphasise different ideas. Since 1948 the Mulberry Bush School in Oxfordshire, UK, for instance, has been offering education and residential therapeutic care to 5–13 year-old children who, in their early years, had been severely traumatised and abused (Price *et al.*, 2018). The Mulberry Bush comprises residential homes, a school, clinical therapies and network teams on one self-contained site. It offers help and understanding to children trying to manage the unbearable (and often unconscious) feelings they have been left with. Among other behaviours, these children may exhibit extreme violence, inappropriate sexual behaviour and general destructive urges aimed at themselves and others.

The school's approach has been influenced by relational psychodynamic ideas, especially those of Donald Winnicott (introduced in Chapter 9). The starting point is the understanding of even the most violent or antisocial behaviours as a form of communication: it is the only recourse the self has to communicate extreme distress. The approach goes back to Winnicott's take on what he called 'antisocial tendency'. Winnicott proposed that acts such as stealing and arson can be understood as last-resort attempts to communicate feelings that cannot otherwise be expressed. According to Winnicott, these also express individuals' hope that someone will understand the acts and what they represent (Winnicott, 2007[1956]).

Delinquent behaviour, therefore, has to be understood in depth rather than merely tolerated or accepted. In the Mulberry Bush School, this is facilitated by reflective practice (which aims to make sense of such behaviour) and the provision of a continuous cohesive or 'holding' experience (where the child's overwhelming feelings can be 'held together' rather than violently expelled or 'poured out'; see Chapter 9, Section 3, for a reminder of the definition of holding). The school's approach to holding had been influenced (once again via Winnicott) by pre-Second World War community therapy initiatives at Hawkspur in Essex, UK, for 'maladjusted' young men. The basic idea of the Hawkspur camp was that those with similar experiences may learn from each other via sustained proximity and interactions. The camp closed down in 1939 but had a long influence within the clinical world.

Its ideas may be perceived in two of the present operations at the Mulberry Bush. One is the potential for those who share an experience to learn from each other in a group setting; schooling, for example, is integrated with therapeutic residential care. The other is the expansion of the therapeutic space beyond one-to-one encounters; the school is infused with the ethos of reflective thinking well beyond designated encounters with specialised 'therapists' (Price *et al*, 2018).

In offering an expanded therapeutic provision, the Mulberry Bush School's approach (deriving in part from the fact that it looks after children rather than adults), may seem different from largely autonomous, democratic therapeutic communities and exclusively peer-support-led initiatives. Yet all these endeavours very much have one thing in common: the idea that recovery happens through reflecting and living within a community space and through a person's relationships with others (peers and/or professionals).

2.2   Macro interventions: bridging the therapeutic with the political

Section 2.1 explored therapeutic interventions on a local, community level. This section will present broader social and political interventions. The section introduces a theoretical framework developed to promote attempts to identify the social determinants of mental health (discussed in Section 1) and to practically address mental distress with regard to these determinants (Section 2.1). In the context of the UK, this broad framework coalesced from diverse theoretical and practice-based endeavours in the late 1980s, and is known as **community psychology** (Orford, 2008).

Community psychology
An approach to mental health that emphasises the social origins of mental distress, the role of power and disempowerment, practical interventions, and the importance of the involvement of the individuals and the community concerned.

In line with the main thrust of this chapter, the first principle of community psychology is a focus on social context as constitutive of individual mental health and distress. While it is always individuals who embody and suffer such distress, from a community psychology position this is never an issue exclusive to individuals themselves; rather, the ultimate determinants are located at the micro and macro levels of social relationships. In this way, community psychology has a great deal in common with other theoretical efforts that emerged in the 1970s and 1980s to counter what was considered the individualistic bias of much of western psychiatry, psychotherapy/counselling and academic psychology (Gergen, 1999). Due to its focus on distress and practice, however, community psychology exhibits three further features which distinguish it from alternative approaches.

The first is an emphasis on power, or, more specifically, (dis) empowerment. From this perspective, generally stigmatised individual responses are seen as a 'normal reaction to an abnormal situation' (Martín-Baró, 1994, p. 111). Community psychologists encounter people in distress, which, by their own definition, means that they encounter oppressed, marginalised and impoverished populations who rarely have any real influence on the social factors that affect them. It is therefore crucial to understand how power operates in society, both on an interpersonal and an economic/political level.

The second distinguishing feature is a political orientation and focus on activism. Proponents of community psychology regard acts of understanding and analysis on their own as insufficient; something needs to be done to *alleviate* people's distress. As explained in the previous section, local interventions emphasise specific therapeutic approaches or peer-led recovery initiatives. Community psychology interventions also seek and advocate for policy change on a national political level. Ultimately, the aim may be to transform the social and political conditions that are considered to have a substantial effect on how people feel and think about themselves (see the Methodology box for further information).

Methodology: Community psychology and political intervention

Psychological research is often considered either from a theoretical or practical perspective. Community psychology, however, introduces a novel dimension to research: politics. For example, as the nationwide group Psychologists for Social Change (PSC) argues, 'without engaging at a macro level… psychologists will only be left to try and temper the outcomes of destructive social policy, inequality and oppression' (McGrath, Griffin and Mundy, 2016, p. 46). The group's emphasis is on direct engagement with political and even economic questions, involvement in social policy and, ultimately, on preventive transformation. As such, from its inception in 2014, PSC has persistently engaged with the psychological consequences of governmental 'austerity' policies.

PSC identified five 'austerity ailments' that the group believed to be direct consequences of governmental policy. These austerity ailments are affective states that have been proven to lead to mental distress and common mental health diagnoses. The argument, therefore, is that, regardless of the validity of the financial or economic arguments for political decisions, the devastating psychological states they can induce must also be taken into account. The group is therefore not content to address this distress only once individuals are experiencing it; PSC uses psychological research to intervene on a political level and to *prevent* such diagnosable distress from occurring in the first place.

Activity 19.2: Austerity ailments and their causes

Allow about 5 minutes

Below are listed the five austerity ailments that PSC has identified (as touched on in the Methodology box), followed by a list of government austerity measures. Which measure do you think would lead to which ailment?

Austerity ailments:

- Shame and humiliation

- Fear and distrust

- Instability and insecurity

- Isolation and loneliness

- Feeling trapped and powerless

Austerity measures/policies:

- Zero-hour contracts

- Complications for benefit claimants (e.g. in accessing benefits)

- Growth of food banks

- Funding cuts to domestic violence shelters

- Service cuts to older-adult care and social care

Discussion

The use of food banks may lead to feelings of shame and humiliation. Benefit claimants often encounter a hostile atmosphere, resulting in fear and distrust. Zero-hour contracts may result in instability and insecurity. Cuts to social care may lead to isolation and loneliness in those who rely on them and, similarly, cuts to domestic violence shelters may lead to feeling trapped and powerless (McGrath, Griffin and Mundy, 2016).

The third feature of community psychology is the importance it places on the active participation of those who suffer from mental distress in attempts to change the conditions that affect them. From a true community-psychology perspective, the socio-political change envisaged is to be implemented with those who are distressed, rather than on behalf of them.

A highly influential example in British community psychology is the social action psychotherapy model, originally devised by clinical psychologist Sue Holland (Holland, 1991, 1992). Starting in 1980, Holland's project ran for over a decade and involved a West London council housing estate. It worked with an extremely underprivileged population of multi-ethnic working-class women, who often had complicated and abusive past and present familial relationships, and whose situations were further aggravated by social and economic oppression. Given the women's vulnerability to mental health breakdown, Holland's model started with weekly one-to-one psychotherapy sessions to help them explore the meaning behind their symptoms and move 'from experiencing [themselves] as a machine/patient who has broken down, into a more knowing sense of [themselves] and [their] personal histories' (Holland, 1992, p. 71).

Beyond the usual functions, therapists provided continuity over time. Even after the formal sessions were over, the therapists remained available either for long-term and extended short-term work, or for one-off sessions arising out of emergency or a client's need for reassurance. Additionally, clients whose one-to-one sessions came to an end were encouraged to attend groups organised by ex-clients. In these groups, healing one's wounded self was complemented by sharing experiences of common suffering and collective strength.

Arguably, the most distinctive element of the social action psychotherapy model emerged from these groups. The groups acted not just to facilitate sharing and bonding, but also to raise participant awareness of structural and systemic conditions that limited their choices and stifled their needs. In the last phase of the model, the women began an active collaboration with Women's Action for Mental Health, a local support, advocacy and counselling service. Thus, they were now able to see social and political frameworks as having significantly contributed to their 'breakdown' (Holland, 1992). Their feelings of helplessness were replaced with a sense of understanding and agency.

The social action psychotherapy model showcases all crucial features of the community psychology framework. Not only does it aim to alleviate distress from socio-political conditions through face-to-face communal contact, it also seeks to intervene in these conditions. The model does not just seek intervention *for* a community, but *with* a community. In doing this, it acknowledges that mental health and political liberation may only happen along the journey 'from private symptom to public action' (Holland, 1991, p. 58). Expressing the ultimate message of community psychology, the social action psychotherapy model maintains that it is social and political action that may have the ultimate therapeutic effect.

Pause for reflection

What tensions may exist between community psychology's therapeutic and political principles? What if someone cannot or does not want to participate in their own empowerment?

Conclusion

This chapter has introduced perspectives on the possible social origins of mental distress. Accordingly, it has reviewed possible ways of approaching and treating mental distress when it is understood as a social problem. As discussed, some researchers and clinicians focus on micro causes (and their therapeutic treatment) related to the primacy of intimate relationships in the family or in peer groups. Others examine how these relationships are embedded or brought about by wider social and political constellations. What is seen as 'therapeutic' here concerns interventions in such broader affairs.

By way of conclusion, it must first be noted that the chapter may be read as a firm rebuttal of perspectives that understand mental health as an individual problem. The case for considering the social dimension of mental health is overwhelming. At the same time, it is important to note the transformation that this social dimension has undergone, as outlined throughout the chapter. What started with a straightforward opposition between the individual and the social – between internal emotions and external events – may now appear more complicated, as 'the social' came to mean the relationships in which people are involved. People experience both their individual characteristics and external events; experiences gain meaning – and thus ultimately affect our mental health – through our relationships. Whether in a room or a more expanded space, and whether with an individual client or through a peer-support community, it is how we relate to others and to ourselves that may alleviate mental distress.

Further reading

- This textbook offers a comprehensive introduction to theoretical, empirical and practical aspects of community psychology: Orford, J. (2008) *Community psychology: challenges, controversies and emerging consensus*. London: Wiley.

- This journal article provides a concise overview of Brown's empirical research programme into the social origins of depression:

  Brown, G. (2002) 'Social roles, context and evolution in the origins of depression', *Journal of Health and Social Behaviour*, 43(3), pp. 255–276.

References

Brown, G. (2002) 'Social roles, context and evolution in the origins of depression', *Journal of Health and Social Behavior*, 43(3), pp. 255–276.

Brown, G. and Harris, T. (1978) *Social origins of depression: a study of psychiatric disorder in women*. London: Tavistock Publications.

Brown, G. and Harris, T. (1989) *Life events and illness*. London: The Guilford Press.

Delgadillo, J., Farnfield, A. and North, A. (2018) 'Social inequalities in the demand, supply and utilisation of psychological treatment', *Counselling and Psychotherapy Research*, 18(2), pp. 114–121.

Freud, S. (2001[1923]) *The standard edition of the complete psychological works of Sigmund Freud. Volume 19: the ego and the id and other works*. London: Vintage, pp. 12–68.

Freud, S. (2001[1925]) *The standard edition of the complete psychological works of Sigmund Freud. Volume 20: an autobiographical study*. London: Vintage, pp. 7–74.

Galmiche, M., Déchelotte, P., Lambert, G. and Tavolacci, M.P. (2019) 'Prevalence of eating disorders over the 2000–2018 period: a systematic literature review', *The American Journal of Clinical Nutrition*, 109(5), pp. 1402–1413.

Gergen, K.J. (1999) *An invitation to social construction*. London: SAGE.

Greenberg, J. and Mitchell, S. (1984) *Object relations in psychoanalytic theory*. Cambridge, MA: Harvard University Press.

Holland, S. (1991) 'From private symptoms to public action', *Feminism & Psychology*, 1(1), pp. 58–62.

Holland, S. (1992) 'From social abuse to social action: a neighborhood psychotherapy and social action project for women', in Ussher, J. and Nicholson, P. (eds.) *Gender issues in clinical psychology*. London: Routledge, pp. 68–77.

Lundt, C., Breen, A., Flisher, A.J., Kakuma, R., Corrigall, J., Joska, J.A., Swartz, L. and Patel, V. (2010) 'Poverty and common mental disorders in low and middle income countries: a systematic review', *Social Science & Medicine*, 71(3), pp. 517–528.

Marmot, M. (2010) *Fair society, healthy lives*. London: The Marmot Review.

Martín-Baró, I. (1994) *Writings for a liberation psychology*. Cambridge, MA: Harvard University Press.

McGrath, L., Griffin, V. and Mundy, E. (2016) 'The psychological impact of austerity: a briefing paper', *Educational Psychology Research and Practice*, 2(2), pp. 46–57.

McManus, S., Bebbington, P., Jenkins, R. and Brugha, T. (eds.) (2016) *Mental health and wellbeing in England: Adult Psychiatric Morbidity Survey 2014*. Leeds: NHS Digital.

McManus, S., Meltzer, S., Brugha, T., Bebbington, P. and Jenkins, R. (eds.) (2009) *Adult psychiatric morbidity in England, 2007: results of a household survey*. Leeds: NHS Digital.

Mechanic, D. (2000) 'Rediscovering the social determinants of health', *Health Review*, 19(3), pp. 269–276.

Muntaner, C., Eaton, W.W., Miech, R. and O'Campo, P. (2004) 'Socioeconomic position and major mental disorders', *Epidemiologic Reviews*, 26(1), pp. 53–62.

Orford, J. (2008) *Community psychology: challenges, controversies and emerging consensus*. London: John Wiley & Sons.

Pearce, S. and Haigh, R. (2017) *The theory and practice of democratic therapeutic community treatment*. London: Jessica Kingsley.

Pickett, K. and Wilkinson, R. (2010) 'Inequality: an underacknowledged source of mental illness and distress', *The British Journal of Psychiatry*, 197(6), pp. 426–428.

Price, H., Jones, D., Herd, J. and Sampson, A. (2018) 'Between love and behaviour management: the psychodynamic reflective milieu at the Mulberry Bush School', *Journal of Social Work Practice*, 32(4), pp. 391–407.

Silva, M., Loureiro, A. and Cardoso, G. (2016) 'Social determinants of mental health: a review of the evidence', *The European Journal of Psychiatry*, 30(4), pp. 259–292.

The Guardian (2019) 'The Guardian view on antidepressant use: no cure-all', 31 March. Available at: https://www.theguardian.com/commentisfree/2019/mar/31/the-guardian-view-on-antidepressant-use-no-cure-all (Accessed: 15 October 2019).

Wilkinson, R. and Pickett, K. (2010) *The spirit level: why equality is better for everyone*. London: Penguin.

Wilkinson, R. and Pickett, K. (2018) *The inner level: how more equal societies reduce stress, restore sanity and improve everyone's wellbeing*. London: Allen Lane.

Winnicott, D. (2007[1956]) 'The antisocial tendency' in Winnicott, D. *Through paediatrics to psychoanalysis*. London: Karnac, pp. 306–315.

Chapter 20

Living in a therapeutic culture

Joanne Brown and Barry Richards

Contents

Introduction

'Happiness' by Nina Haywood

The aim of this chapter is ambitious. When you have studied it, you should be able to describe and analyse 'therapeutic culture', an important general feature of contemporary societies and one that underpins the growth of the counselling and psychotherapy professions. Therapeutic culture also deeply influences many other aspects of life. The development of this culture is widely recognised by researchers and social commentators; most people agree it is there but, as the chapter aims to show, major differences of opinion exist about how to evaluate it. This chapter invites you to explore the meanings ascribed to therapeutic culture by different people, and to consider how varied feelings regarding the values of therapeutic culture currently shape public attitudes towards the talking cures and mental health issues more generally.

A huge body of literature exists covering the global emergence of therapeutic culture. This chapter will offer an outline of the major forms that this culture takes, a summary of key issues in the debates surrounding it, and a particular model for understanding and evaluating it. The chapter will refer to some landmark examples from the literature, and it will illustrate how therapeutic principles now help to shape everyday life. However, there is much more to be said on this subject than can be covered in a single chapter. The further reading suggestions will give you a starting point for going beyond the overview provided here.

This chapter aims to:

- encourage critical thought about the relationship between counselling/psychotherapy and changes in wider culture and society

- introduce the concept of therapeutic culture as a way of capturing a major aspect of that relationship

- outline ongoing debates about the beneficial and/or detrimental nature of therapeutic culture

- argue for the potential benefits of a therapeutic culture combining emotion with reflection and compassion.

1 Defining therapeutic culture

Figure 20.1 Memorial flowers left for Princess Diana, following her death in 1997

Let's start with a broad definition of **therapeutic culture**, which will be refined later in the chapter. It is a cluster of values and practices concerned with mental health and psychological well-being. Therapeutic culture involves a wide public interest in and attention to emotions in everyday life (especially those involved in relationships), and an interest in individuals' psychological make-up and in how we come to be as we are (especially how the adult personality is shaped by early experience). Moreover, in therapeutic culture we see the influence of counselling and psychotherapy in mainstream culture (in memoirs, well-being rhetoric at work, on chat shows, in music and so on) and not just in the rising number of people who access psychological therapy. The term is used in different ways by different writers, while others use the term 'therapy culture' instead. This chapter adopts the term 'therapeutic' because the actual practices of therapy are only one part of this culture.

These features can be distinguished from, though are related to, some broad trends in contemporary culture. One is the so-called **psychologisation** of society, evident in the huge popularity of studying psychology, which for decades has been among the most popular choices of undergraduate courses, and in the very widespread use of

Therapeutic culture
A culture in which practices of psychotherapy and counselling are well-established, and in which there is in many social settings, and in popular culture, an attention to psychological well-being and emotional life generally, and to the influence on our states of mind of both our past histories and our present situations.

Psychologisation
Refers to the description or explanation of a behaviour in terms of psychological processes. It may refer to a way of understanding a particular phenomenon or, as used here, to describe a broad trend in wider culture.

psychological ideas and techniques in many different areas of life. Another is the growing interest in emotional life and particularly in the expression of emotion. One marker of this trend towards a more 'emotionalised' society was the global expression of grief in response to the death of Princess Diana (the Princess of Wales) in 1997 (e.g. Richards, 2007). Figure 20.1 shows many flowers left as a memorial to Diana, and her funeral procession was a global media mega-event. 'Therapeutic' concerns with trying to heal and with emotional life are a distinct phenomenon that can be seen as within or under the influence of these broader trends towards psychologisation and **emotionalisation**.

The sociologist Frank Furedi (2003) suggests that 'a culture becomes therapeutic when the form of thinking expands from informing the relationship between the individual and therapist to shaping public perceptions about a variety of issues' (p. 22). To add to this, we have suggested the following explanation:

> To refer to a culture as therapeutic is to suggest that the social scripts, lenses and vocabularies through which people understand themselves and their lives are strongly inflected by the interior-oriented language of 'the therapeutic' (with talk about feelings, attachments, self-esteem, anxiety, stress, well-being, security, trauma, loss, mourning, and so on).
>
> (Richards and Brown, 2011, p. 19)

This sort of language has its origins in psychoanalysis and other related branches of psychology which, from the early twentieth century, were developing ideas and asking questions about our emotional lives. However, as the century went on, there was a substantial incursion of therapeutic ideas, terms and practices into everyday popular culture. The sociologist Eva Illouz (2007, p. 100) says of what she calls the 'therapeutic emotional style' that, while it is based originally on 'a body of texts and theories produced ... by experts ... it is perhaps primarily also a body of knowledge diffused worldwide through a wide variety of culture industries', through all the media channels along which popular culture flows.

The rise of the psychological therapies and of therapeutic culture has occurred alongside key media developments: the appearance of television in the second half of the twentieth century, then of social

Emotionalisation
Refers to the trend towards increasing emotional expressivity in social behaviours, including those in everyday social life and those presented in the media. It is used here to refer to 'fake' or manipulated performances of emotion in addition to authentic and spontaneous expressions.

media in the present century. Our **mediatised culture**, in which the content and forms of media deeply shape our experience and understanding of the world, has helped drive the spread of therapeutic values. An increasing proportion of media content has foregrounded emotional life and offered ways of understanding and managing emotional experience. For example, on mainstream talk shows celebrities and public figures talk about, say, their struggles with depression or addiction. Therapeutic themes have come to be an important element in many genres of mass entertainment screen drama, not least in *The Sopranos* (Bainbridge, 2011).

Mediatised culture
Refers to the ways in which both traditional and social media have transcended commentary and reflection on what's happening in the world and have themselves become part of the substance and texture of the world.

Pause for reflection

Compare your life to that of your grandparents or other older relatives. Do you think that they spoke about their emotions and their intimate life in the same way that you and your contemporaries might? Did they have the same kind of cultural resources that you have (media, music, literature, film), or are times different now?

2   The emergence and evolution of therapeutic culture

It is important to note that life was not always like it is today. In the early days of television, for example, dominant fictional forms such as westerns and police dramas were typically very action-oriented. Neither the cowboys nor the detectives were portrayed as having inner lives of any sort, and they were certainly not the complex and troubled personalities of today's box-set characters. When did this inclusion of therapeutic culture first emerge in the post-industrial societies to which it is still most relevant? According to Illouz (2007, 2008) it emerged in the inter-war period of the twentieth century, on the basis of Freud's dramatic discoveries and their enthusiastic reception in the US and parts of Europe. Later, as a more welfare-oriented social order began to consolidate in the period after the Second World War, social scientists began to note the growing importance of what Paul Halmos (1958) called 'the faith of the counsellors', referring to the emergence of the counselling profession and of the values that drove it. By the mid-1960s, it was possible for the US scholar Philip Rieff (1966) to argue that a psychotherapeutic outlook – and psychoanalytic understanding in particular – had achieved great influence in western culture and was reshaping moral parameters.

Following Rieff, many writers have developed accounts of the complex therapeutic transformation of everyday life. In policy discourses, academia, popular culture and organisational cultures it has become increasingly normative to pay some attention to emotional lives, often drawing on concepts such as emotional intelligence and emotional literacy. A public health agenda has developed around the notion of psychological well-being, in some ways echoing the **mental hygiene movement** of the early twentieth century. There is an aspiration to understand and to mitigate the psychological disturbances to which so many people are subject; perhaps even to cure, or at least to manage, disturbance more effectively to reduce emotional suffering and enhance individual fulfilment and societal well-being.

In 1959, the sociologist C. Wright Mills said that the so-called **sociological imagination** was the 'intellectual common denominator of the times' (Wright Mills, 1959, p. 15). Wright Mills was referring to his observation that, in the post-Second World War period, an awareness of 'society' as an environment that shaped people (e.g. one's

Mental hygiene movement

An early twentieth-century movement that sought to raise awareness of the societal importance of mental health, and of the social and psychological factors that its proponents believed were crucial underpinnings of good mental health. It was an important influence on policies and public attitudes.

Sociological imagination

A shared imagination that enables us to understand the 'internal realities' of ourselves by looking at how our lives are shaped by larger social and historical forces.

class position) was widely shared among many beyond the social science community. Today it can be argued that a **therapeutic imagination**, expressed in **reflexive** talk about feelings and relational worlds, is the intellectual common denominator of the times, and its prevalence points to how therapeutic culture has become an essential feature of late modernity (Beck and Beck-Gernsheim, 1995; Berman, 1982; Giddens, 1991; Lasch, 1978). Illouz (2008, p. 5) goes so far as to say that the coming of 'the therapeutic' has influenced our identities at the deepest level. Of course, the therapeutic trend is not the only cultural shift that is happening, and is not without its critics (as will be discussed in Section 3), but it is a significant one.

The claim that we live in a therapeutic era is supported by much everyday experience, both from people's personal lives and wider culture, as suggested above. Having become an almost taken-for-granted feature of everyday life, this claim is not an easy thing to evaluate by the usual methods of social research. The only conventional survey of the UK population that has directly tried to assess the emergence of a therapeutic culture did find some evidence of it in the much more positive attitudes towards 'emotions talk' among younger people (Anderson, Brownlie and Given, 2009), but more research is needed to establish the history of its rise.

Therapeutic imagination
Refers to the idea that we understand our internal realities through reference to feelings and our relational worlds. Whereas therapeutic culture refers to our external environment, a therapeutic imagination describes how our ways of thinking have been changed by this wider culture.

Reflexivity
Refers to the process of considering or evaluating one's experience or one's self from different angles and with a readiness to question existing beliefs. Reflexivity challenges habitual, mechanical and impulsive thinking because it requires a person to dedicate time to questioning what they think they understand.

3   Critiques of therapeutic culture

Theorists differ in their opinions as to whether therapeutic culture is a positive or negative trend. Some welcome and some decry the rising influence of therapeutic outlooks on everyday life. Furedi (2003) and Rose (1989), for example, view the therapeutic with suspicion, seeing it as a means of managing subjectivity and behaviour in the same way that religious morals and codes might. For such hostile or sceptical observers, therapeutic culture amounts to obfuscating and sentimental 'psychobabble'. Additionally, whereas religions have tended to emphasise the individual's responsibility towards others, Furedi argues that a therapeutic interpretation of the roots of people's actions amounts to a denial of responsibility for what they do. If early experience is the source of who people are, then they cannot be blamed for their actions, however antisocial they might be. Furedi believes that the therapeutic ethos undermines both responsibility and self-reliance, since it requires a person to depend on the expertise of the therapeutic professional.

Ecclestone and Hayes (2008) also suggest that the therapeutic outlook encourages us all to feel that we are 'to a greater or lesser extent, emotionally fragile and vulnerable and, as a consequence we need particular forms of emotional support' (p. x). They claim that those who don't agree with this are accused of denying or repressing their true feelings. They also see a therapeutic mindset as likely to make us more passive and docile citizens, 'because a diminished and uncertain self can pose no questions and offer no challenge to anyone' (p. 104).

Among critics of therapeutic culture, it is important to distinguish between those who are hostile to therapy itself – particularly to psychoanalysis, which they see as the source of the ills that they describe – and those who are, sometimes strongly, sympathetic to it. The historian Christopher Lasch's influential *The culture of narcissism* (1978), which still provokes rich debate today, is often cited as a critique of the therapeutic age. Like Furedi, Lasch attacks the therapeutic regimes of the last century, in which the presumptuous and normative interventions of psychological (and other) professionals have undermined self-confidence at a fundamental level, particularly that of parents in rearing their children. However, the focus of his critique is not psychotherapy itself, but doctrinaire and intrusive uses of various psychological theories, especially to regulate the care of babies and children. Lasch actually sees psychoanalysis as a source of crucial insights, but which have been obscured or distorted by the development of the myriad therapies on offer in the consumer marketplace of the self.

Like Lasch, Illouz (2007, 2008) has a sympathetic view of psychoanalysis and a more complex view of therapeutic culture as a whole but, like Furedi, she is also critical of that culture in her final analysis. However, her critique is the opposite of Furedi's: she contends that the problem with the therapeutic outlook is that it blames people for their sufferings, by seeing them as stemming from the condition of their internal world rather than as resulting from inequalities and oppressions in the external world. Still, both these thinkers share the critique that therapeutic culture can obfuscate the socio-political causes of distress and de-emphasise the socio-historical forces affecting our lives, by individualising and de-politicising societal and political issues (as discussed in Chapter 19).

For those more in favour, therapeutic culture represents a growing emotional literacy and more empathic and supportive environments in education, work and other settings, which, overall, serve to increase a society's emotional resources and enhance collective mental health. One of the first sociologists to comment on the therapeutic trend, while not naming it as such, was Anthony Giddens (1991) who, along with others, examined the increasingly reflexive nature of contemporary societies. He argued that the growing attention people pay to their sense of personal identity leads them to reflect more on close personal relationships and to seek more self-determination in their emotional lives. This requires people to be more aware of their and others' emotional needs. The emphasis on the concern for others runs counter to the notion put forward by critics of therapeutic discourses – that is, that they necessarily contribute to the erosion of political and social engagement/concern.

Section 4 will look at the way in which therapeutic culture enables people to speak more openly about their mental health difficulties, thus challenging stigma and shame. While jibes about being 'touchy-feely' are common, there are now well-established beliefs in the importance of emotions and the value of owning and reflecting on them, and in the possibilities of exploring and containing them. Therapeutic ideas about the importance of recognising and responding to emotional distress and trauma can also be seen in the #MeToo social media movement against sexual harassment and sexual assault, and the increasing prevalence of successful convictions for perpetrators of child sexual abuse. An increased focus on the emotional effects and trauma of war and conflict, and changes in gender roles (e.g. the greater emotional expressivity now afforded men and the greater sharing of emotional labour between men and women in the tasks of parenting) further point to the expansion of the therapeutic.

Overall, therapeutic culture can be seen as either a positive development – a move towards a more compassionate culture – or as a means of sheltering narcissism and political passivity. We take the view that, although there is much more that is positive in the therapeutic than its critics would allow, one-sided generalisations should be avoided. Activity 20.1 encourages you to think about how to evaluate the move towards greater emotional expressivity and self-reflection in contemporary culture.

Activity 20.1: Evaluating therapeutic culture

Allow about 20 minutes

Consider what a therapeutic outlook or culture means to you. What do you think are the essential ingredients of a therapeutic imagination, and in what settings have you seen it in action? You could think about your personal experiences; for example, at school, in hospital, in work, in the media, online or in your friendship group or family. Alternatively, you could consider something you have observed, such as a chat show or reality TV show that foregrounded talk about feelings and relationships. Write down a few examples.

Now consider whether each experience was positive or negative. Did it contribute towards a move to a more compassionate society, or towards a culture of narcissism? If you considered an example from the media, what essential components do you think were required in order to say it had a therapeutic quality for its participants and audience?

You are now entering the debate about what a therapeutic culture is and how to evaluate it.

4   The three elements of therapeutic culture

We suggest that a fully therapeutic culture would consist of three components (Richards and Brown, 2002): it must combine the principles of emotional expression, reflective rationality, and compassion (which literally means 'to suffer with or together'). These are the constituents of therapy itself, but they are obviously also found in life in general. The therapeutic practices that emerged in the twentieth century combined them in particular ways, and in the therapeutic culture that developed alongside professional therapies, we see those combinations at work in different contexts outside of therapy.

These three elements can be thought of as loosely corresponding to the Freudian idea that there are three different parts or regions of the mind. These are the 'id' (the largely unconscious, impulsive and emotional part of the mind); the 'superego' (the source of our conscience and concern for others); and the 'ego' (the mediator between the conflicting demands of the id and the superego, and between the self and the constraining realities of the external world). The ego and the superego function at both conscious and unconscious levels.

It was Freud who invented the talking cure, whose terms have entered everyday language (the Freudian slip, narcissism, egotism, the Oedipus complex and so on), and whose work was foundational in the rise of the therapeutic.

According to psychoanalysis, all three areas of the mind need to be held in creative tension in order to live more therapeutically – that is, being hyper-rational and out of touch with feelings is problematic. For example, think of the classic character Dr. Spock from *Star Trek*, whose mind only allows for logic. Conversely, being emotionally dysregulated – lacking reason or perspective – is also problematic (think of so-called crimes of passion, where one's capacity for rationality is lost). So, we can see how important it is to have a developed capacity for emotion *and* rationality. Psychoanalysis asks us to be in touch with feeling, but also to develop a capacity to think through what we feel. Moreover, in psychoanalysis this dual capacity is 'object-related': it is applied to others as much as to the self.

This psychoanalytic model of the mind has been likened to Greek philosophy, in which the soul is seen as divided between a temperate horse, an insolent horse and a charioteer/rider (Bergmann, 1987). One could liken the rider to Freud's concept of the ego, which must try to allow for emotional spontaneity and needs to be expressed with awareness and concern for those around us. The rider is trying to harness the horse's power (passion, driven by the id) while also adhering to social rules of engagement (societal norms, driven by the superego). To continue with this metaphor, the rider knows that he or she is not the only one in the field struggling to contain power and impulsivity. The fact that we need to live, love and work with others, rather than simply soothe our own anxieties and satisfy our own needs, is part of life's 'reality principle' (Freud, 1958[1911]). This can be in tension with life's 'pleasure principle', where one might only concentrate on themselves. Psychoanalysis also contains an ethical dimension, because healthy development is tied to moving from more narcissistic states of mind to a concern for others. Narcissistic states of mind only allow room for one mind (Morgan, 2018).

It is important to note, however, that a therapeutic mindset does not necessarily indicate that someone has undertaken therapeutic training. Indeed, one might advise against trying to analyse people outside of the boundaries of the consulting room; Freud cautioned against such 'wild analysis'. Section 4.1 will discuss the case of chat shows and reality TV, where the psychological well-being of participants might be damaged by the structure of the show or their experience of disclosing details of their personal lives to the public.

4.1   Therapeutic culture or emotionalised culture?

In 2019, the UK talk show *The Jeremy Kyle Show* was cancelled after 16 years over concerns about those taking part. It invited participants to resolve personal and family issues on air, and one of its contestants died in 2019 after taking part in the show. It could be argued that the show only focused on one element of a therapeutic imagination (emotional excitation), and that it did not combine this with a capacity for reflective rationality or compassion. From the definition of 'therapeutic' suggested in this chapter, this TV programme cannot then qualify as such, despite drawing on psychological and emotional material. The hugely popular UK reality TV show *Love Island* (which became an international franchise) has been in the news for similar reasons. The show involves contestants entering a villa with the aim of coupling up/finding love. Viewers vote for their favourite couple, and the couple who receives the most votes wins a £50,000 prize.

Pause for reflection

Using the definition of a therapeutic culture provided in the chapter, do you think *Love Island* is therapeutic for its contestants and/or for its audience?

As discussed earlier, Princess Diana's death prompted an unprecedented outpouring of grief from the public, which led social theorists to debate the nature of this emotionalisation process in public life. The relevant question is whether public displays of emotion on chat shows, or en masse at sports events, concerts, political rallies, and so on, are therapeutic. Do they necessarily indicate a developed capacity for emotional expression *along with* reflective rationality *and* compassion? Or are these examples of id-governed emotionality – horses running wild?

4.2 Therapeutic culture or rationalised culture?

Dalal (2018) argues that cognitive behavioural therapy (CBT) can be very successful in helping people recover from certain forms of psychological suffering, but he bemoans the way in which 'CBT's ambitions expanded to colonise all forms of psychological suffering' (p. 6). He questions the philosophical premise and evidence base for CBT, but here, the question is whether the 'CBT tsunami' and Improving Access to Psychological Therapies (IAPT; discussed in Chapter 17) are indicative of a therapeutic culture as defined in this chapter. Dalal argues that the 'cognitivist revolution' (p. 51) which underlies CBT is based on a model of a mechanistic mind and what he calls hyper-rationalist thoughts. In this model, the mind is making logical errors which can be rationally challenged in order to produce new, more adaptive thoughts based on alternative evidence (as outlined in Chapter 10). Some might say that the power of feeling and emotion is then *underplayed* in this psychological model. Of course, as you read in Chapter 10, there is more nuance and detail to CBT, but this critique nonetheless argues that a hyper-rational model of the mind dominates psychological services in the UK's NHS.

You might want to reflect on whether the IAPT programme promotes a developed capacity for emotion, reflective rationality *and* compassion, or whether it is all logic riding what is imagined to be a 'compliant horse'.

4.3   Therapeutic culture or narcissistic culture?

This chapter has argued that a developed capacity for reflective rationality and emotion is not enough to constitute a therapeutic imagination; it needs to be linked to compassion. One could argue that a compassionate state of mind ('to suffer with or together') is opposed to a more narcissistic state of mind, especially in excessive forms of narcissism.

So, do we live in more compassionate times? Psychoanalysis deconstructs any fixed or impermeable division between sanity and insanity; that is, we all have minds that can unsettle and disturb us, and we find comfort and community in recognising this. Mental health service users have been at the forefront of challenging stigma about mental health difficulties, but Brown (2010) has also argued that it is democratising and important to read accounts from practitioners about their experience of mental suffering. For example, in Rippere and Williams' (1985) edited collection *Wounded healers*, one consultant psychiatrist wrote about his experience of depression and of being 'bitterly ashamed at not being a tower of strength and I feared detection more than anything. ...The psychiatric hospital is intolerant of weakness in its staff. Compassion is for patients; for "them" not "us"' (p. 15).

Without such accounts, the fantasy permeates that there is a world of stable 'adulthood' and emotional maturity, untouched by doubt, contradiction and frailty. A therapeutic culture is one which enables people to speak about this, thus challenging shame and stigma. Frank (1995) argues that stories of ill-health are a reminder of our common humanity. Frank is writing about the experience of physical ill-health (which has emotional consequences, of course). We might not want to use medicalised terms such as 'illness' for mental health difficulties, but testimonies such as those above are personal and simultaneously political, because they challenge any stigmatised notions about who might feel depressed or anxious.

Princess Diana was interviewed in 1995 on the UK's BBC One (BBC, 1997) and famously spoke about her marriage, self-harm and bulimia, thus challenging the stereotype of British royalty as being emotionally guarded. It was also well publicised that she had been in therapy with Susie Orbach, who is a psychoanalytic therapist. Prince Harry has more recently (e.g. Gordon, 2017) spoken about how he sought counselling in his late twenties in order to help him work through his repressed feelings about the death of his mother, Princess Diana. The charity Heads Together was set up by Prince William, Prince Harry and the Duchess of Cambridge to tackle stigma and promote service innovations – another illustration of a cultural context where there is much more acceptance of and concern about mental health difficulties.

All of these examples could be used to argue that we do indeed live in a more therapeutic culture imbued with compassion. However, since our analysis (Richards and Brown, 2002), socio-technological developments in communication and media have deeply influenced many aspects of everyday life, and have posed new questions about the rise of therapeutic culture. The global establishment of social networking sites, such as Facebook, Instagram and Twitter, has raised new questions about whether these sites aid compassion or narcissism. The hatred and contempt which seem to dominate some online spaces have sharpened debates about freedom of speech and may suggest that social media is antithetical to the therapeutic.

For example, Lemma (2017) asks how concerned we should be about a culture which encourages a constant scrutiny of the self. She argues that the use of technology can be defensive or developmental. When it is defensive, 'our smartphones are like amplifiers and broadcasters for our id' (Lemma, 2017, p. 72). She suggests that this is because the internet can function to dissolve the restraining superego of the individual when online, or to displace it by presenting itself as a seductive but perverse superego.

Lemma's case studies show the way in which new technologies bring possibilities for self-exploration and development but also carry risk. They illustrate how the internet is a potential place of play, but they also highlight what Wrottesley (2018) refers to as the darker side of digital technology for those whose sense of self is fragile. Although

Lemma looks at the therapeutic potential of the internet, she notes that aspects of contemporary culture such as 'immediate gratification, quick fixes, consumerism, normalised voyeurism and the idealisation of exposure [are] antithetical to some of the core tenets of the analytic enterprise' (Lemma, 2017, p. 138).

What do you think? Is digital technology anti-relational and encouraging of narcissism? Or does our digital culture promote a developed capacity for emotion, reflective rationality and compassion? The fictional case illustrations of Vicki and Johnny look at the therapeutic and narcissistic ways in which the internet can be used.

Case illustrations: Vicki and Johnny use the internet

Vicki is at college. Her friend, Sarah, reveals that she has borderline personality disorder – Sarah looked this up and believes she fits the criteria. Sarah also tells Vicki that their flatmate has obsessive-compulsive disorder. Vicki feels uneasy but does not want to appear to be unsympathetic. She goes online to look at what borderline personality disorder is and thinks that Sarah might be attention seeking, but she feels guilty for thinking this of her close friend. Vicki does not think that their flatmate has obsessive-compulsive disorder; rather, she is simply tidy. Vicki is irritated by this exaggerated language but dares not contradict Sarah, who is convinced she has borderline personality disorder and wants to be given special consideration at college.

Johnny is 36. He spends most of his spare time looking at pornography online. Johnny thinks that everyone should be able to be more sexually free, although he hides this from his partner who he thinks will disapprove. His partner wants a monogamous relationship, but Johnny cannot imagine only having sex with one person for the rest of his life. His best friend, Dave, thinks that Johnny is addicted to pornography and has advised him to go into therapy. Johnny resents the way in which Dave has pathologised his healthy sexual appetite and thinks that Dave is oppressed by cultural mores.

Activity 20.2: Vicki and Johnny – therapeutic or narcissistic?

Allow about 15 minutes

Consider the following questions:

1   Do the case illustrations remind you of any similar scenarios that you have encountered?

2   How might you use the concept of a therapeutic imagination to evaluate them, or to evaluate your own experience?

3   What questions might you need to ask Johnny or Vicki in order to consider whether these are examples of a narcissistic or a therapeutic use of technology?

The three elements of a therapeutic imagination – emotional expression, reflective rationality and compassion – can be used to think about how to explore the answer to these questions in relation to the case studies and everyday life. There are no right or wrong answers because many elements are involved which require careful thought, and which should be approached with curiosity rather than judgement.

Conclusion

This chapter has encouraged consideration of the relationship between counselling/psychotherapy and changes in wider culture and society. It has argued that the rise of psychotherapy and counselling is part of a wide and profound cultural shift, which has brought our inner lives more into public view and made the exploration and management of distressing states of mind something that is frequently addressed in popular culture as well as in professional settings.

The chapter outlined what the term 'therapeutic culture' is usually taken to mean. It also described how a number of social theorists see therapeutic culture as a major feature of global culture today, although it is most marked in western 'consumer societies'. Therapeutic culture includes *both* the proliferation of talking therapies and counselling, and the wide influence in many areas of life (education, popular culture, social policy, organisations, etc.) of ideas and principles derived from the therapeutic sphere. As you have seen, there are keen debates about the overall societal value of these ideas and principles, and the chapter has invited you to form your own views on these debates.

The precise and in-depth model of therapeutic culture presented here stresses the potential benefits in offering an integration of emotion, reflection and compassion. On this basis, the therapeutic can be distinguished from thoughtless emotionalism, mechanistic rationalism and antisocial narcissism.

The concept of therapeutic culture has fed directly into the three cross-cutting themes of this book:

- A therapeutic culture can enable people to speak about their mental health difficulties and recovery, thus challenging stigma. Service users in mental health have been at the forefront of challenging stigma in psychiatry, society and therapeutic discourses.

- A therapeutic imagination can be combined with sociological theory in order to provide powerful analyses of the tensions and conflicts associated with differences of culture, race, gender and sexuality.

- Therapeutic principles can guide the development of reflexive research methods able to capture the depth and complexity of lived experience and its roots in our emotional and conflicted selves.

Further reading

- This chapter links therapeutic culture to the educational setting, where the influence of therapeutic values is of great potential benefit but also carries some risks. It raises important ethical questions:

  Brown, J. (2018) 'Dilemmas of disclosure in mental health therapeutic education', in Wintrup, J., Biggs, H., Brannelly, T., Fenwick, A. and Inghamet, R. (eds.) *Ethics from the ground up*. London: Red Globe Press, pp. 32–44.

- Giddens argued that we are witnessing a new form of intimacy characterised by greater reflexivity and equality in relationships. His book is an example of the way in which sociology has focused on emotion as a source of knowledge about cultural change:

  Giddens, A. (1992) *The transformation of intimacy: love, sexuality and eroticism in modern societies*. Cambridge: Polity Press.

- This book looks at new technology and its impact on social relating. Lemma is particularly interested in the impact of digital media on the experience of embodiment and sexuality. She also discusses the way in which new media offer opportunities for the delivery of therapy:

  Lemma, A. (2017) *The digital age on the couch: psychoanalytic practice and new media*. London: Routledge.

References

Anderson, S., Brownlie, J. and Given, L. (2009) 'Therapy culture? Attitudes towards emotional support in Britain', in Park, A., Curtice, J., Thomson, K., Phillips, M. and Clery, E. (eds.) *British social attitudes: the 25th report*. London: SAGE, pp. 155–172.

Bainbridge, C. (2011) 'From "the Freud squad" to "the good Freud guide": a genealogy of media images of psychoanalysis and reflections on their role in the public imagination', in Bainbridge, C. and Yates, C. (eds.) *Free Associations: Therapy culture/culture as therapy: media and the inner world special edition*, 62, pp. 31–59. Available at: http://freeassociations.org.uk/FA_New/OJS/index.php/fa/issue/view/5 (Accessed: 24 April 2020).

BBC (1997) *The Panorama Interview*. Available at: https://www.bbc.co.uk/news/special/politics97/diana/panorama.html (Accessed: 3 April 2020).

Beck, U. and Beck-Gernsheim, E. (1995) *The normal chaos of love*. Cambridge: Polity.

Bergmann, M. (1987) *The anatomy of loving: the story of man's quest to know what love is*. New York: Columbia University Press.

Berman, M. (1982) *All that is solid melts into air*. Harmondsworth: Penguin.

Brown, J. (2010) 'Life begins at? Psychological reflections on mental health and maturity', in Burnett, J. (ed.) *Contemporary adulthood: calendars, cartographies, and constructions*. London: Routledge, pp. 120–130.

Dalal, F. (2018) *CBT: the cognitive behavioural tsunami*. London: Routledge.

Ecclestone, K. and Hayes, D. (2008) *The dangerous rise of therapeutic education*. Abingdon and New York: Routledge.

Frank, A.W. (1995) *The wounded storyteller: body, illness and ethics*. Chicago: University of Chicago Press.

Freud, S. (1958[1911]) *The standard edition of the complete psychological works of Sigmund Freud. Volume 12: formulation on the two principles of mental functioning*. London: Hogarth, pp. 218–226.

Furedi, F. (2003) *Therapy culture: cultivating vulnerability in an uncertain age*. London: Routledge.

Giddens, A. (1991) *Modernity and self-identity: self and society in the late modern age*. Cambridge: Polity.

Gordon, B. (2017) *Bryony Gordon Speaks to Prince Harry for Mad World Podcast* (2017 Archive). Available at: https://m.youtube.com/watch?v=xZzp84rtCbs, accessed 19.5.20 (Accessed: 22 May 2020).

Halmos, P. (1958) *The faith of the counsellors*. London: Constable.

Illouz, E. (2007) *Cold intimacies: the making of emotional capitalism*. Cambridge: Polity.

Illouz, E. (2008) *Saving the modern soul: therapy, emotions, and the culture of self-help*. Oakland, CA: University of California Press.

Lasch, C. (1978) *The culture of narcissism*. New York: W.W. Norton & Company.

Lemma, A. (2017) *The digital age on the couch: psychoanalytic practice and new media*. London: Routledge.

Morgan, M. (2018) *A couple state of mind*. Abingdon and New York: Routledge.

Richards, B. (2007) *Emotional governance: politics, media and terror*. Basingstoke: Palgrave Macmillan.

Richards, B. and Brown, J. (2002) 'The therapeutic culture hypothesis: a critical discussion', in Johansson, T. and Sernhede, O. (eds.) *Lifestyle, desire and politics: contemporary identities*. Gothenburg: Daedalos, pp. 97–114.

Richards, B. and Brown, J. (2011) 'Media as drivers of a therapeutic trend', *Free Associations: Psychoanalysis and Culture, Media, Group*, 62, pp. 18–30.

Rieff, P. (1966) *The triumph of the therapeutic: uses of faith after Freud*. Chicago: University of Chicago Press.

Rippere, V. and Williams, R. (eds.) (1985) *Wounded healers: mental health workers' experiences of depression*. Oxford: Wiley-Blackwell.

Rose, N. (1989) *Governing the soul: the shaping of the private self*. London: Free Association Books.

Wright Mills, C. (1959) *The sociological imagination*. Oxford: Oxford University Press.

Wrottesley, C. (2018) 'Response to "The disintermediation of desire: from 3D (esire) to 2D(esire)" by Alessandra Lemma', *Couple and Family Psychoanalysis*, 8(2), pp. 123–130.

Conclusion

Naomi Moller, Andreas Vossler, David W. Jones and David Kaposi

Contents

Conclusion to understanding mental health and counselling

This brief chapter concludes *Understanding mental health and counselling* with an invitation to contemplate the meaning of endings for you as well as to revisit the key aims and themes of the book and consider what you have taken away from it in terms of your own learning. Additionally, this chapter provides a list of resources for seeking support and advice for mental health difficulties.

Over the course of this book you have been introduced to the key debates in mental health and counselling, and the core approaches taken to working with mental health problems in counselling and psychotherapy. In the five parts of the book you have read about:

- the fundamental debates concerning the contested nature of mental 'illness' and the institutions that have developed to provide 'treatment'

- the issues that cause people to seek therapy

- the main approaches used in counselling and psychotherapy

- issues central to how counselling and psychotherapy are practised and mental health problems are treated in different practice settings

- social understandings of mental health and how social, political and economic forces inform contemporary practice.

The importance of endings

This concluding chapter is a good place to think about endings, both in counselling and psychotherapy and in terms of what they mean for you. Endings are important – and often challenging – in counselling as well as in life. The importance of endings in counselling is reflected in their mention in ethical guidelines for therapeutic practice. For example, the British Association for Counselling and Psychotherapy's *Ethical framework for the counselling professions* (item 39) requires that counsellors 'endeavour to inform clients well in advance of approaching endings and be sensitive to ... client's expectations and concerns when we [counsellors and clients] are approaching the end of our work together' (British Association for Counselling and Psychotherapy, 2018, p. 19).

On the one hand, endings provide an opportunity to review the work that has been done – both what has changed and what has not – to embed the core learning and to contemplate what comes next (Shaharabani, Shafran and Rafaeli, 2018). On the other, they can evoke strong feelings for both clients and counsellors (Knox *et al.*, 2011) because they echo all the other endings and losses we experience: deaths, relationship break-ups and those endings and losses owing to the relentless passage of time (Gelso and Woodhouse, 2002). For this reason, endings provide an important therapeutic opportunity to revisit past losses in life as well as ruptures in the therapeutic relationship, with a view to perhaps doing things differently this time. In the case of this book, having reached the end might bring a feeling of pride (got it done!) or a sense of relief (done at last!). Alternatively, there might be some sense of anxiety: Now the book is done, what next?

Pause for reflection

What does this ending (of the book) mean for you? What do endings (in general) mean for you? Do you brush them off or are they often painful? Why do you think that you respond to endings in the way that you do?

Aims and themes of the book

The aims of this book, as stated in the Introduction, were to explore critical perspectives and debates around both the theory and practice of mental health and counselling and to consider the ways in which decisions about how to respond to individuals experiencing mental health distress are influenced by the historical development and current manifestations of how mental health (human distress) is understood.

The core themes of the book were:

- the central importance of prioritising service-user and client voices, and of making sure that the experiences and understandings of those who are on the receiving end of mental health/counselling services are acknowledged, respected and honoured

- the understanding that individual and group differences matter, so that what is 'true' or 'works' for one group may not for another, and thus that it is always key to consider diversity and diverse experiences

- the importance of thinking critically about how knowledge in mental health and counselling is created, in particular through research, and recognising the strengths and limitations of different approaches to research in mental health and counselling.

Pause for reflection

Now that you have come to the end of this book, what do you think are the most important things that you have learnt? (New learning could be academic, personal or both.) Would you include any of the book themes? This book is an introduction to the area; do you have any thoughts about how to take your learning further? (Remember, in each chapter of this book there are suggestions for further reading; the reference lists also provide a useful resource for those who are curious about particular topics.)

We hope this book has helped to grow your understanding and curiosity about mental health and counselling, and honed your criticality. We also hope that this book will have helped you on your own journey – perhaps towards work in mental health/counselling or in terms of your own self-understanding.

Finally, below there is a list of resources and services for those who are struggling with mental health concerns. These are provided because mental health (of course) is something that all of us have and because as an editorial team we are very aware that mental health and counselling are for many people not just academic topics but personally meaningful. It is in this spirit and with the hope it may be useful that the list is offered.

– Naomi, Andreas, David and David

Sources of support and advice

Samaritans

www.samaritans.org

24/7 freephone helpline: 116 123

jo@samaritans.org (24 hours response time)

Samaritans provides 24/7 emotional support for anyone struggling to cope.

Side by Side

Access Side by Side through the national charity, Mind:

www.mind.org.uk

Side by Side is a friendly, supportive online community for people experiencing a mental health problem.

SHOUT

www.giveusashout.org

Text: 85258

SHOUT is a 24/7 free text line for mental health crisis and worries. It is useful if you need help fast but can't talk on the phone for whatever reason.

National Survivor User Network

https://www.nsun.org.uk/help-and-support

NSUN is a service-user-led network that campaigns to improve the lives of people who experience mental distress. Check out the link above for lots of suggestions of where to get help and support.

Hearing Voices Network

www.hearing-voices.org

HVN is an organisation that offers support and groups for people who hear voices, see visions or have other unusual perceptions.

Mind Infoline

0300 123 3393 (Monday to Friday 9 a.m. to 6 p.m. except bank holidays)

info@mind.org.uk

Text: 86463

An information and signposting service that gives details of local branches of Mind (the mental health charity), other local services and Mind's Legal advice line, as well as information about mental health problems and treatment options.

In addition to the resources and services listed above, there are also organisations that provide support for particular populations (e.g. LGBTQ+ people) or particular difficulties (e.g. domestic violence or eating disorders). More details and services can be found in the 'Information and support' section of Mind's website (http://www.mind.org.uk/information-support/).

Remember too that you can ask your GP for a referral to counselling if you think that this would be helpful for you. In some areas of the country you can also self-refer to counselling.

References

British Association for Counselling and Psychotherapy (2018) *Ethical framework for the counselling professions*. Available at: https://www.bacp.co.uk/events-and-resources/ethics-and-standards/ethical-framework-for-the-counselling-professions (Accessed: 28 April 2020).

Gelso, C.J. and Woodhouse, S.S. (2002) 'The termination of psychotherapy: what research tells us about the process of ending treatment', in Tryon, G.S. (ed.) *Counseling based on process research: applying what we know*. Boston, MA: Allyn & Bacon, pp. 344–369.

Knox, S., Adrians, N., Everson, E., Hess, S., Hill, C. and Crook-Lyon, R. (2011) 'Clients' perspectives on therapy termination', *Psychotherapy Research*, 21(2), pp. 154–167.

Shaharabani Saidon, H., Shafran, N. and Rafaeli, E. (2018) 'Teach them how to say goodbye: the CMRA model for treatment endings', *Journal of Psychotherapy Integration*, 28(3), p. 385.

Acknowledgements

Grateful acknowledgement is made to the following sources.

Introduction

Book Introduction image left: NASA; Book Introduction image right: Jaime Permuth/Getty.

Part 1

Chapter 1 Introduction image: Joanna Crane; Figure 1.1 left: The Picture Art Collection/Alamy; Figure 1.1 right: Science History Images/Alamy; Figure 1.2: Historic Images/Alamy stock photo; Chapter 2 Introduction image: Rosie Cook; Figure 2.1: Rudy Loewe; Figure 2.2: Rachel Rowan Olive; Chapter 3 Introduction image: Lu Szweda; Figure 3.1: Axis Images/Alamy; Figure 3.2: https://commons. wikimedia.org/wiki/File:Aaron_Beck_2016.jpg. This file is licensed under the Creative Commons Attribution-Share Alike Licence http:// creativecommons.org/licenses/by-sa/3.0/; Chapter 4 Introduction image: Nevova Zdravka; Figure 4.1: Freedman, R. *et al.* (2013) 'The initial field trials of DSM-5: new blooms and old thorns, *American Journal of Psychiatry*, 170(1), pp. 1–5.

Part 2

Chapter 5 Introduction image: Russell Hughes; Chapter 5 Introduction Byers quote: Reprinted from 'What it is like going through a deep, dark depression' by Allyson Byers, by permission of Healthline Media, Inc.; Figure 5.1: Taken from Meacham, F. and Bergstrom, C.T. (2016) 'Adaptive behavior can produce maladaptive anxiety due to individual differences in experience', *Evolution*, Medicine & Public Health, 2016 (1), pp. 270–285; Chapter 6 Introduction image: Abby Philips; Chapter 6 Section 1 Mind quote: © Mind. This information is published in full at mind.org.uk; Chapter 7 Introduction image: Eleana Pourgouri; Information box 7.1 image: Dimaberkut/Dreamstime.com; Figure 7.1: Stroebe, M.S. and Schut, H. (2001) 'Meaning making in the dual process model of coping with bereavement', in Neimeyer, R.A. (ed.) *Meaning reconstruction and the experience of loss*. Washington, DC: American Psychological Association, pp. 55–73; Chapter 7 Section 3.2

Speedy poem: Jane Speedy; Chapter 8 Introduction image: Alexander Church; Figure 8.1: Adapted from Padesky, C.A. and Mooney, K.A. (1990) 'Clinical tip: presenting the cognitive model to clients', *International Cognitive Therapy Newsletter*, 6, pp. 13–14; Chapter 8 Section 2.2 image: Wavebreak Media Ltd/123RF.

Part 3

Chapter 9 Introduction image: Jonathan New; Chapter 9 Section 1 image: Georges Diegues/Alamy Stock Photo; Chapter 9 Section 3 image: Nuvolanevicata/Alamy Stock Photo; Chapter 10 Introduction image: Victor Guerrero; Figure 10.1: adapted from Padesky, C.A. and Mooney, K.A. (1990) 'Clinical tip: presenting the cognitive model to clients', *International Cognitive Therapy Newsletter*, 6, pp. 13–14; Chapter 11 Introduction image: Coral Locke; Figure 11.1: Maslow, A. H. (1954) *Motivation and personality*. New York, NY: Harper & Row; Figure 11.2: Peter Hermes Furian/123RF; Chapter 12 Introduction image: Victor Guerrero; Chapter 12 Section 3 image: SDI Productions/ Getty.

Part 4

Chapter 13 Introduction image: Carly Merchant; Chapter 13 Section 2.2 image: Katarzyna Bialasiewicz/123RF; Chapter 13 Section 3 image: archnoi1/123RF; Chapter 14 Introduction image: Sumaira Ali; Chapter 14 Section 2.1 image: Ian Allenden/123RF; Chapter 15 Introduction image: Elaine Carty; Chapter 15 Section 3 image: Baona/ Getty; Chapter 16 Introduction image: Ashley Muirhead; Chapter 16 Section 1.1 image: Adzicnatasa/123RF; Chapter 16 Section 3.2 image: Pornpak Khunatorn/Getty.

Part 5

Chapter 17 Introduction image: Lu Szweda; Figure 17.1: adapted from Petticrew, M. and Roberts, H. (2003) 'Evidence, hierarchies, and typologies: horses for courses', *Journal of Epidemiology & Community Health*, 57(7), pp. 527–529. doi:10.1136/jech.57.7.527; Chapter 18 Introduction image: Lu Szweda; Figure 18.2: Paul Doyle/Alamy Stock Photo; Chapter 19 Introduction image: Hannah Marling; Figure 19.1: Taken from Brown, G. (2002) 'Social roles, context and evolution in the origins of depression', *Journal of Health and Social Behavior*, 43(3), pp. 255–276; Figure 19.2: Taken from Wilkinson, R. and Pickett, K. (2010) *The spirit level: why equality is better for everyone.* London: Penguin; Chapter 20 Introduction image: Nina Haywood; Figure 20.1: https://commons.wikimedia.org/wiki/File:Flowers_for_Princess_Diana%27s_Funeral.jpg. This file is licensed under the Creative Commons Attribution Licence, http://creativecommons.org/licenses/by/3.0/.

Every effort has been made to contact copyright holders. If any have been inadvertently overlooked, the publishers will be pleased to make the necessary arrangements at the first opportunity.

Index